WOMEN FIGHT BACK

The centuries-long struggle for liberation

LIBERATION MEDIA

SAN FRANCISCO

ISBN: 978-0-9910303-4-7
Library of Congress Control Number: 2016963468
Cover photo: Victor Quintero

Written by

Donna Goodman

Editor

Ben Becker

Staff

Meghann Adams, Sarah Carlson, Anne Gamboni, Paul Greenberg,
Lili Guerrero, Saul Kanowitz, Tina Landis, Mazda Majidi,
Keith Pavlik, Daniel Sankey, Maxson Taylor

Liberation Media

2969 Mission Street #201
San Francisco, CA 94110
(415) 821-6171
books@LiberationMedia.org
www.LiberationMedia.org

Women Fight Back

Preface

THE idea for this book grew out of a mix of indignation and optimism: indignation toward the right-wing backlash against the gains women have won over more than 150 years of struggle for equality; and optimism that women would once again rise up and fight back to preserve and extend those gains.

In recent years the right wing has waged an unrelenting war on women, ranging from legislative and judicial attacks on contraception, abortion and other components of health care to blatant expressions of misogyny, including trivialization of the crime of rape and of the ongoing epidemic of violence against women.

These forces also believe that women's political, social and economic inequality are a reflection of natural law and are here to stay — all this after a historic women's liberation movement that shook America to its foundations.

The Republican Far Right is counting on a public perception that we live in a post-feminist era, in which women have won all the rights they need and there is nothing left to fight for. Worse, they believe women's rights can be attacked with impunity. The right has not yet been confronted with a coordinated and militant women's movement but by scattered and localized acts of resistance, reflecting the weakened state of today's feminist movement. The women's movement has been losing ground, and working-class women in particular have seen their conditions deteriorate.

The presidential election campaign of 2016 was seen by millions as a game changer. The Democratic Party campaign of Hillary Clinton was historic — the first time in U.S. history that a woman was nominated for president by a major political party. But Clinton's center-right politics, despite a few campaign concessions during the primaries to the social democratic program of Bernie Sanders, are in sharp contradiction to what is required to build an independent, militant women's movement rooted in the experiences of working-class and oppressed women.

Clinton personifies the overall right-wing trajectory of the Democratic Party. While the Democratic Party adopts some of the language of the movement, and promotes certain feminist goals, its historical allegiance to austerity, militarism and subservience to Wall Street cannot further the cause of women's liberation.

Even under these conditions, women are playing an active and often leadership role in the growing movements against oppression and exploitation, both at the grassroots and on the national level: The Movement for Black Lives, the climate justice movement, the years of mass demonstrations against Washington's imperialist wars, the short-lived but inspiring Occupy movement. This growing exposure to street protests has been combined with widespread interest in left-wing and even socialist politics. A broad united women's liberation movement can be revived, in close connection with these monumental social movements.

Oppression does not flow from individual policies or politicians. This book will show that women are denied genuine equality by a political and economic system that is built on inequality, exploitation and militarism.

One important aspect of the ideological assault on feminism has been to obscure and distort the actual history of women's struggle. This book will offer an understanding of the movement's powerful history: the tradition-shattering fights of the 1800s, the militant struggles of the early 20th century and the mass uprisings for liberation of the 1960s and 70s.

By connecting the important progress made by the vibrant women's movements of the past with the urgent needs of the present, this book is intended to help inspire women and their allies to re-energize an independent, national militant women's movement that fights for the liberation of all oppressed people.

ABOUT THE AUTHOR

Donna Goodman is a long-time peace and justice activist in New York's Hudson Valley. She has helped organize campaigns and demonstrations on women's rights, defending the Cuban revolution, freedom for the Palestinian people, ending the death penalty and the prison industrial complex, the movement for environmental justice, and against capitalism's ingrained poverty and inequality. Over the years Donna has shared the organizing of two dozen antiwar bus trips to Washington, D.C., and New York City.

She is a member of United University Professions (UUP), the faculty union of the State University of New York, where she serves as an elected delegate and co-chair of the Women's Rights and Concerns Committee, and where she has been active in the union's campaigns for pay equity and paid family leave. Most recently she has been a regional organizer for Women Organized to Resist and Defend (WORD) which has sponsored demonstrations and public meetings for Women's Equality Day and International Women's Day in defense of women's rights. She is a member of the Party for Socialism and Liberation and co-editor of the Hudson Valley Activist Newsletter. □

Introduction

Women advance through struggle

THE last phase of sustained women's organizing and struggle in the United States was 50 years old in 2015, calculating from the very beginnings of the 1965-1975 uprisings for liberation, known as the Second Wave. The First Wave was the 1840-1920 successful fights for the right to vote and other freedoms. A Third Wave was articulated in the early 1990s and continues, representing more of a theoretical and cultural shift within feminism and less of a new era of mass action.

The situation for masses of women in the United States has improved in significant ways since the 1960s uprising and we shall detail the victories and changes in this book. However, a large proportion of women in the U.S. — low wage and poor women, African American, Asian, Latina, Native American women — share only partially or minutely in those improvements. In the cultural realm, new forms of sexism and misogyny are still pervasive, but the blatant sexism that was routine and considered acceptable is now considerably weaker.

Obviously the women's struggle for genuine equality and against male dominance still has a long way to go in America if all women are to be included and if all political economic and social rights are to be obtained. All women in our society are exposed to a high rate of male violence and rape, among other outrages that must be stopped.

It is now well into the 21st Century and more than 40 years since the end of mass feminist activism in the United States. Almost as soon as that period ended, an era of right-wing counterreaction began in which women's rights have been under fierce attack. Is it not time to rebuild an activist movement of women and their allies to protect against the erosion of our past gains and resume the mass struggle for complete equality for all women? In one of America's most pronounced periods of economic and class inequality, with rising movements of low-wage workers, and for LGBTQ liberation, immigrant rights and Black liberation, a new women's movement would have potentially powerful allies in the struggle for a whole new society.

There are many feminists in America today but little sustained motion towards uniting in action to oppose those who would push us back. This reluctance, of course, could change quickly as it did in the mid-1960s, but as this book is being written, the political, social and economic conditions are different in 2016.

Many gains have been won as a result of this past activism, but as feminist Barbara Epstein wrote in Monthly Review as far back as May 2001:

> The overall decline of the women's movement has much more to do with a loss of a sense of urgency within than with attacks from without. ... Feminist activism has not ceased [though it has declined considerably since Epstein wrote—Ed.], nor have the numbers of women engaged in feminist activity or discussion declined. Millions of U.S. women talk to each other about women's concerns, using the vocabulary of feminism. ... Feminism has become more an idea than a movement, and one that often lacks the visionary quality that it once had.

This book will trace the history of the women's struggle for equality and against male domination in the United States. From the beginning, women have only advanced when they organized and publicly and boldly demanded their rights. The same of course is true for all who suffer oppression and discrimination in this country and throughout the world.

To reaffirm the necessity of struggle may seem like an elementary point, but it is one that is often forgotten.

Only a fightback can change things in all these situations. Many feminists today have deep feelings of solidarity with all the oppressed as well as women. There are many discussion groups, articles and conversations in social media, and some women's liberationists are involved in various social justice movements. But today's movement is neither cohesive nor activist, nor so far effective in mounting serious challenges to the powerful forces undermining the quest for genuine women's equality in America.

Reviewing the lessons of previous waves of struggle, while studying the changed conditions of the present, are critical theoretical steps to rebuild a fighting women's movement today. That is the objective of this book.

U.S. WOMEN DENIED RIGHTS FROM THE BEGINNING

In the several decades following the establishment of the federal government of the United States of America in 1789, white women were provided with extremely few civil and legal rights, if any. Enslaved black women, of course had no rights at all. They were overworked, beaten and systematically raped by their male owners. Free Black women had extremely few fragile rights, and always faced the danger of being "illegally" enslaved.

Married white women were totally under the legal and social control of their husbands, as were their children. The wives could not vote, keep their own wages, make contracts or own property, among many other indignities. In return the husband was obliged to support his wife.

The small minority of unmarried white adult women was allowed to own property, sue in court and be sued, serve as guardians and write wills. A few states, on their own, eased sexist inheritance restrictions for such women. But without a family fortune few women could make it on their own.

In essence, extreme male supremacy was conjoined with white racial supremacy and imprinted on the early laws of the United States democracy where "all men were created equal" but only white men of property could vote or wield power. It took until 1850 for property restrictions to be dropped for "lesser" white men.

The notion that the "created equal" section of the Declaration of Independence was designed for all people (in the obsolete "mankind" sense) is ludicrous. The Declaration was written and approved by 56 white men of property, including 44 slave owners. All of them regarded women as inferior to men. Rich white men founded this country. They profited from slavery, displaced the original peoples, exploited the working class, subjugated women to subordinate status and expedited the inherent inequality of capitalism.

PAINTING: JOHN TRUMBULL

*The United States was founded on principles of slavery
and disenfranchisement for women.*

Today, rich white men remain in control — even though one
Black man has twice been elevated to the presidency — because their
wealth and power entitles them to membership in what is properly
called the ruling class, which largely controls the political system.
After all, the "bottom" 90 percent of U.S. families possesses 25
percent of the nation's wealth. The top 10 percent enjoy 75 percent of
the wealth. The top 3 percent alone grab 54 percent. The combined
net worth of the richest 400 Americans is $5.7 trillion. That is power.

The top 10 percent invests wisely, not only in stocks and bonds
but in politicians and elections. Whatever nominal democracy existed
before is being shattered, especially since the right-wing Supreme
Court's 2010 *Citizens United* decision virtually gave billionaires the
right to elect presidents, governors and representatives.

UNCLE SAM DID NOT HELP WOMEN

Women's rights have greatly expanded in these 226 years since
the founding of the republic. It must never be forgotten that every
new victory for women's rights has been initiated by and fought for
by women themselves (and a smaller number of allied men). It took
at least 80 years of struggle in the streets, meeting halls, and homes
to finally obtain the right to vote in 1920 against intense sexist opposition. Jim Crow laws in the South and less formal segregation in the

North greatly reduced the Black vote, including that of Black
until the mid-1960s reforms. In recent years, the right wing, fac
by the conservative Supreme Court, has eviscerated the voting la
make it more difficult to cast a ballot for Black and other poor peo
who largely vote Democratic.

Progressive reforms have never been a gift from the government in Washington to the women of the United States. Political
movements of women, small and large, were behind every advance.
Typically this took the form of pitched and intense battle against the
state. In those few moments when state institutions have conceded
the demands of the movement — such as the Supreme Court's 1973
Roe v. Wade ruling in the matter of abortion rights — this has been the
product of decades of demands and struggle. Without women fighting
to control their own bodies against the backward views of church,
state and conservative citizens, the issue of abortion rights would
never have even been taken up at the Supreme Court.

The Second Wave of the women's struggle took place largely
within the context of what is known as the Sixties[1], a spectacular
period of various mass uprisings in U.S. society that advanced the
struggle of African Americans, working people, women, the antiwar
movement, students, the political left, LGBTQ people, people with
disabilities and other constituencies who were subject to exploitation,
oppression or both.

LIFE BEFORE 1965

While people may generally understand that gender expectations and stereotypes have greatly changed since 1965, few understand how extraordinary and profound this transformation has been
for women in the home and society. Sonia Pressman Fuentes, a
lawyer who was one of the founders of the National Organization for
Women, said the following in a 2001 speech:

> What was our country like in 1965? Basically, men
> and women lived in two different worlds. By and large, a
> woman's place was in the home. Her role was to marry
> and raise a family. If she was bright, common wisdom
> had it that she was to conceal that brightness. She was
> to be attractive — but not too attractive. She was not to

s, although she could work for a few
as a secretary, saleswoman, school-
ator, social worker, librarian, or
. at the time the jobs were usually
.rvants, field workers and low paying
.rvice economy.—Ed.]

Hopefully, she would be a virgin when she married. When she had children, she was to raise them differently [boys, girls] so that they, too, would continue in the modes of behavior appropriate to their sex. If she divorced, which would reflect poorly on her, she might receive an award of alimony and child support — although it was unlikely that she would actually receive the monies for more than a few years. If she failed to marry, she was an old maid, relegated to the periphery of life.

Married women could work outside the home only if dire household finances required it. Under no circumstances were they to earn more money than their husbands.

Women were not to be opinionated or assertive. They were expected to show an interest in fashion, books, ballet, cooking, sewing, knitting, and volunteer activities. Political activities were acceptable as long as they were conducted behind the scenes. Of course, not all women wanted or were able to fit into this pattern, and there were always exceptions. But most women did what they were told because society exacted a high price from deviants.[2]

In part, Pressman presumes the middle-class white woman's experience to be typical here. But the basic oppressive rules that she outlines — applicable to woman of all classes — are entirely correct.

Reflecting the roiling political period of the 1960s, the feminist movements of the Second Wave uprising, which included liberals, radicals, social democrats, socialists, communists and anarchists, put forward hard-hitting demands and fought for them as activists in the

public arena. They belonged to a number of different org
that often disagreed with each other, but they were united oɪ
ing the male supremacist conditions that prevailed at the time -
succeeded in many endeavors.

A large section of women's liberationists believed that a rev
lution in the United States was both necessary and imminent, as wa
also true in the student, Black freedom, antiwar and left-wing movements. That coming revolution would not just change property and
class relations, but also fundamentally transform family and gender
relations, and the place of women in all aspects of society.

THE CLINTON CROSSROADS

The 2016 presidential election campaign brought feminism
into sharp focus for a public that often ignores it as a relevant political subject.

Utilizing institutional connections within the Democratic Party
machine and the corporate-owned media, Hillary Clinton defeated
Sen. Bernie Sanders in the Democratic primary and became the first
woman to run for the U.S. presidency for one of the two major parties.

Many people campaigned for Clinton simply because it is long
past time for a woman to be president. A huge portion of Clinton's
support was owed to the unpopularity of her right-wing Republican
opponent Donald Trump, who personified so many of the worst
trends in U.S. society: sexism, racism, anti-immigrant scapegoating
and the extreme narcissism of the billionaire class.

Ruling-class figures worked hard throughout the election season
to manipulate feminist politics to steer people towards Clinton. This
distortion of the women's struggle and Clinton's purported role in it
drew strong rebukes from radical women who are actually engaged
in the struggle.

This superficial presentation of feminist politics was not particularly persuasive either. It was not enough to inspire a large turnout
from the Democratic Party base in the general election, especially
working-class voters in crucial battleground states. It was not enough
to swing women voters from the Republican Party. It was not enough
to change Clinton's reputation as a status quo politician, and was
therefore insufficient to beat Trump, who ran demagogically as the
"change" candidate.

...sult shocked most people, the weaknesses
...nism were evident earlier. During the
Senator Bernie Sanders, polls leading
...onvention showed that Clinton's lead
...strongest among women aged 50 and older,
...ng for Clinton. But Sanders outpolled Clinton
...women voters, with 58 percent of those under age 50
...g him, and the disparity becoming even more pronounced
...ounger age groups.[3]

Many of these younger voters wanted a woman president as well but were dubious of Clinton's ruling-class politics. She is a symbol of the Democratic Party's center-right imperialist leadership. Sanders' progressive program spoke considerably more to the concrete needs of the country's working class — and most certainly to the youth.

Another factor is the resistance among many younger feminists to supporting a candidate based on gender alone. These voters insist on a more inclusive feminist politic that embraces a range of struggles for racial and economic justice.

After the Democratic Convention ended, most Sanders supporters were planning to vote for Clinton. An August 14, 2016 USA Today Rock the Vote poll showed that 71 percent of young voters aged 18-34 who had supported Sanders were planning to vote for Clinton. An August 7 ABC News Washington Post poll showed big support for Clinton among college educated white women and that 86 percent of all Bernie supporters had shifted to Clinton.

TODAY'S FEMINISM

Today's feminists are numerous, particularly younger women college students, working recent graduates, and academic faculty members. There are feminists in the labor movement and left organizations and they are active, which we will chronicle later. Aside from a few larger holdover liberal organizations, particularly the National Organization for Women (NOW), most feminists function individually or in small groups, as opposed to in mass organizations or any formal organizations at all. Social media, the Internet, a variety of feminist websites, and campus discussion groups are a prime means of communication and for expressing feminist views. The traffic on these

*Young women today are drawn
into a multitude of social movements.*

outlets is relatively heavy but they function more as "niches" — an important digital community, but not one that deeply penetrates the rest of society.

A number of today's younger feminists, who identify themselves as belonging to the Third Wave, have embraced a multi-issue agenda. This is not just a matter of being more inclusive to women of diverse backgrounds. Their feminism explicitly supports Black women, gay, lesbian, bisexual and transgender people and opposes all forms of oppression. However these political and theoretical shifts have not yet been linked to a new fighting independent women's movement that is a recognizable force within society and tied to a larger mass movement for revolutionary change.

This is not an indictment of the present generation of feminists — after all, the level of struggle among working-class and oppressed people has declined in comparison to the Sixties. Women's movements have never surged in isolation from other oppressed people and cannot be expected to now.

But there are organizational and theoretical aspects of today's feminist activism, which can obstruct the rise of a new militant women's movement if they are not stated clearly and then confronted.

Much of the movement, including many self-proclaimed radicals, have adopted core principles of post-modernism, an individualist and relativist point of view that acts as a barrier to mass organizing around certain principles and unifying theories. Writing in Monthly Review in 1995, Ellen Meiksins Wood declared:

> We are being told that we are living in a post-modern age, that the 'Enlightenment project' is dead, that all the old verities and ideologies have lost their relevance, that old principles of rationality no longer apply, and so on. ...

> Structure and causes have been replaced by fragments and contingencies. There is no such thing as a social system (e.g., the capitalist or socialist system) with its own systemic unity and 'laws of motion.' There are only many different kinds of power, oppression, identity and 'discourse.' Not only do we have to reject the old 'grand narratives,' like Enlightenment concepts of progress, we have to give up on any idea of intelligible historical process and causality, and with it, evidently, any idea of making history.

There need not be any contradiction between highlighting the varied experiences of different oppressed people, while also drawing a clear line between those who wield power and those who have an interest in overthrowing that power.

In the terminology often utilized by Sixties revolutionaries, there are "contradictions among the people" and then there are "contradictions between the people and the enemy." This distinction is lost by the post-modernists — who portray each individual as both friend and foe depending on where their identity positions them across a whole unordered spectrum of relationships and oppressions. They have done this in the name of giving voice to the marginalized, but in reality the left and socialist organizations have long supported the multi-issue struggle against oppression and exploitation throughout the last century in the United States. It has never been perfect, but the revolutionary left rapidly responded to and merged with the insurgent movement for women's rights in the late 1960s and the LGBTQ cause at various times since then. The left not only supports these struggles verbally or as friendly individuals, but shows solidarity in action, protesting at rallies, public meetings and in the streets against the common oppressor, which often turns out to be the policies of the U.S. government.

THE DECADES-LONG CONSERVATIVE BACKLASH

The accomplishments of Sixties activism sparked a conservative backlash seeking to destroy or modify many of the progressive advances that emerged from this period of enlightened social challenge. That backlash is continuing, as strongly as ever, because of right-wing control of the federal Congress, the Supreme Court and many state legislatures — a product of generous funding from the largely conservative 1 percent, and enthusiastic support from much of the religious right and the Tea Party-infused Republican Party in general. Their principal goal at the moment is to outlaw abortion, followed by chipping away at more women's rights.

Since the progressive victories of the Sixties, both "official" political parties, Republicans and Democrats, have gravitated further toward the right as the backlash intensified and conservatism proliferated in the United States.

The Republicans tossed their "moderate" faction onto the junk heap decades ago and shifted from a party of the right/center right to a party of the far right/right. In 2015, in addition to dominating Congress and the high court, the GOP had 31 governors and the Democrats 18 (Alaska has an independent governor). In terms of state legislatures, the Republicans controled 30 states, the Democrats only 11 (their lowest number in nearly 40 years), and eight state legislatures were split between both. (Nebraska is officially "nonpartisan" but controlled by conservatives.)

This has enabled the Republicans to launch a "war on women" throughout the country, during the last few years, that is primarily focused on, but not limited to, destroying abortion rights. The main victims are poor and Black women who lose abortion services more often than any other group because of difficulties getting transportation, money and time off from work.

Feminist columnist Katha Pollitt wrote in The Nation during the 2016 election campaign: "Nearly one in three women in the United States will have had at least one abortion by the time they reach menopause. ... [But] thanks to clandestine videos produced by the Center for Medical Progress, an anti-abortion outfit, Planned Parenthood is in its hour of need. Independent clinics all over the country are closing due to laws that purport to protect patient safety but are actually intended to put clinics out of business. Ostracism, death threats, bombings, and arson are driving providers out of the field and discouraging new ones from entering it. Restrictions intended to shame women and raise the cost of abortions are heaping up."[4]

The right-wing campaign has even expanded to deny access to birth control, allowing employers to deny their employees certain health options on account of their "religious beliefs."

Another issue of importance to women is economic discrimination — not just earning 78 cents to man's dollar but in other ways. This year, half the U.S. population survives on a low income or exists in poverty. The working class is staggering and the middle class is in deep trouble while the top 10 percent live like royalty and basically run the show.

According to the National Women's Law Center:

> Women make up 60 percent of the lower-paying workforce ($10.10 or less per hour), even after a slight decline over the past two decades. Almost 30 percent of the female workforce is low-wage, in contrast to less than 20 percent of the male workforce. Of these women, three-fourths are white. Yet the proportion of minority women is significantly higher than white women: 35.8 percent and 46.6 percent of African American and Latino women in contrast to 26.2 percent of white women. ...

> Among women in the low-wage workforce: Nearly half are women of color. Nearly four out of five have at least a high school degree. Half work full time. Close to

one-third are mothers — and 40 percent of them have
family incomes below $25,000. More than one-quarter are
age 50 and older.[5]

ORGANIZE AND UNITE TO ADVANCE OUR GOALS

The Democratic Party has demonstrated it is unwilling and
unable to hold back the right-wing threat or adequately defend the
rights of women, one of its most important constituencies. In the
1960s the Democrats, led by President Lyndon Johnson, passed some
of the most progressive legislation since the 1930s Great Depression.
That ended when the Democrats lost the 1968 election because of
their egregious sponsorship of the Vietnam War. Soon afterward they
began to change from a party of the center/center left to a party of
the center right, where it is today, though a "lesser evil" to the reactionary Republicans.

The Democratic leadership accomplished this switch by long
consigning congressional liberals to the sub-basement of power. No
legislation even distantly comparable to the Johnson period has been
enacted in 45 years. President Obama's signal achievement has been
the Affordable Care Act — originally a Republican project but dropped
when the GOP gravitated to the far right. The Democratic presidential
candidate will employ populist liberal rhetoric in each contest because
party voters demand a left opposition to the dangerous absurdities
dished out by the far right. But as with President Barack Obama in 2008
and 2012, nothing much could be expected from a Democratic victory.

On the national and state level as well, the right wing is fighting
against virtually all women's equality proposals and existing laws.
These include: equal pay for equal work; extending domestic violence
laws; the Freedom of Choice Act; stronger enforcement of sexual
harassment restrictions on the job and everywhere; the reasonable
accommodation of pregnant workers; safeguarding reproductive health
measures; health insurance contraceptive coverage; stronger laws
against human trafficking; strengthening military regulations regarding
sexual violence; birth control education and sex education curricula
that are not completely abstinence based; rights for LGTBQ people.

In addition, the GOP and a number of Democrats oppose more
support for family services that mainly benefit women, such as

increased support for single mothers with children; maternity leave with pay for all new moms; quality nationwide free pre-kindergarten; affordable and accessible childcare; and entirely new and more generous "welfare" measures to replace President Bill Clinton's cruel, punishing and failed 1996 program.

The Sixties showed that when women from different backgrounds and groups decide to "stand up, fight back," they can make history, despite problems, errors and factional differences.

Women and their allies are certainly staging a fightback in many of the states where the Republicans are raising havoc. But in the state-level fights women are outnumbered and lack the forces to stop the rabid rightist nationally coordinated attacks. We must all continue to stand with them.

A number of viable women's organizations either remain from the Sixties or were established more recently. They include NOW, which has hundreds of thousands of members, the Feminist Majority Foundation, Planned Parenthood, NARAL Pro-Choice America and the Coalition of Labor Union Women — all liberal groups. They do not constitute a broad movement, which needs many more numbers and a strong left wing. Some on the left completely oppose liberal feminism because of its compromises and limitations, but it has positive aspects that can be useful within the necessary organizational framework of "uniting all who can be united" to advance women's rights. Liberal groups can help provide strength should such a movement materialize.

Much of these women's organizations spend their time preparing or campaigning for elections. It only takes an hour to vote and it can be useful, but considerable united work and movement building is required to help revive the activist women's movement — a far more important endeavor given the lessons of history. ☐

THE PROBLEM IS SYSTEMIC

Chapter 1

The status of U.S. women — USA is *NOT* number one

It would be wrong to assume that the progressive changes won by women have eliminated oppression. To the contrary, despite considerable gains in rights and access over the last five decades, the status of U.S. women remains one of second-class citizenship, with economic, political and social inequality the norm, rather than the exception.

The United States lags considerably behind the social democracies of Western Europe, some of the emerging societies of Latin America, and a number of the formerly communist countries of Eastern Europe in terms of many categories of women's rights and progress — from economic equity to participation in government to support for families, and basic social status and rights.

Clearly it is political unwillingness and not the wealth of the nation that is the determining factor in providing benefits for its workers. The United States, the world's wealthiest country, has one of the highest wage gaps, below average participation of women in government and the very lowest level of family benefits for women workers.

This chapter will summarize U.S. women's place in society today in terms of changes in the family and the economy.

WOMEN IN THE FAMILY

To mark the changes to the nuclear family, one can simply look at the rates at which women now marry, have children, receive a higher education and participate in the workforce compared to the 1960s.

In 1960, 93 percent of women in their early 30s were married compared with 66 percent in the present era. Back then, only 30 percent of women in their 30s were employed, whereas now that figure is 71 percent.[1] Today families are also considerably smaller, with women having an average of 3.7 children in 1960 to 1.9 in 2011.

Changes in the structure of the family resulted in part from the progress gained by women in the women's liberation movement, which in turn spurred further changes in women's place in society. As more women joined the workforce, they gained economic independence, diminishing the dependence on a husband.

But that is only one side of this change. At the same time, shifts in the capitalist economy meant bosses moved aggressively to lower wages, export jobs and fight unions, making it less viable for a working man to support a family on his wage alone. As a result, the old model of the breadwinner father and homemaker mother no longer exists for the majority of families.

In 1960, 65 percent of children lived in a family in which the parents were married, the father worked and the mother stayed home. By 2012 only 22 percent lived in that kind of family — a stunning change. In 60 percent of two-parent households, both parents work outside the home.

More women are the chief or sole support of families, comprising 40 percent of families today as compared to 11 percent in 1960. In fact, more children now live in a household headed by a single mother than in one headed by a married couple with an employed father and homemaker mother.[2]

But because of women's lower position in the workplace, families headed by a single mother had a median income of only $23,000, compared to the national median of $57,100 of all families with children.[3]

Births to unmarried women have risen from 5 percent in 1960 to 41 percent in 2011. Breaking these figures down by race, 72 percent of births to Black women were to unmarried mothers, 53 percent of births to Latina women and 29 percent of births to white women.[4]

Conservative and some liberal economists falsely attribute poverty to these unmarried mothers. For one, they fail to take into account the overall declining significance of marriage, and the fact that "more than half of births that occur outside of marriage are to women who are cohabiting."[5]

While being unmarried may indeed be associated with higher levels of economic vulnerability for one's family, the question is why should it? In at least 17 European countries, the rate of births to unmarried women is higher than in the United States, and yet 16 of those countries rank above the United States in terms of children's average wellbeing — child poverty, nutrition, clothing, access to quality education, and so on.

The solution is not to push marriage as the answer — but to remove all the penalties and barriers that determine one's access to the limited social safety net based on cohabitation and marriage status.

WOMEN IN THE ECONOMY

The growing inequality that characterizes today's capitalist crisis and wage stagnation in America has hit women very hard, with little progress on pay equity and family benefits. Most women workers are clustered in low-paying jobs.

Women's status in the U.S. economy includes their unpaid as well as paid work. On average, women spend 41 minutes per day caring for household members and 126 minutes per day on housework. Men do triple the amount of childcare and double the amount of housework they did in 1965, but they still do on average an hour less per day than women.[6] If this unpaid work were given a dollar value and counted in the U.S. Gross Domestic Product, it would raise the GDP by 26 percent.[7]

In 2010, after the 2008-09 recession, women workers were nearly half the U.S. labor force. Almost 70 percent of working women are white, 13 percent Black, 13 percent Latina and 5 percent Asian. More women are working part time during the recovery than before the recession, and 20 percent of them are working part time because they cannot find full-time work. Only 11 percent of women workers belonged to unions in 2010, compared to 13 percent of men.[8]

It is noteworthy that so many of those in today's feminist movement are basically uncritical of capitalism, the socio-economic system that is responsible for so much hardship for women and their families. The system itself is based on inequality, exploitation and oppression, and has been built with racism, sexism, slavery, colonialism, imperialism and war on a massive scale. It is a worldwide system and in 2016, with an estimated global population of 7.3 billion, the richest 1 percent own more than 50 percent of the world's wealth, according to the anti-poverty charity Oxfam. The next top 19 percent possesses 44.5 percent. of the wealth. The final 80 percent of the world population survives on 5.5 percent of the wealth.

THE WAGE GAP

Women still suffer from a significant wage gap compared to men. Women's wages were about 60 percent of men's for much of the 20th century. They began to rise after the mass movements of the 1970s, but the wage gap plateaued around 2005 and has been stagnant, despite ups and downs in the economy, since then.[9]

In the 35 countries surveyed by the Organization for Economic Cooperation and Development (OECD), using 2014 figures, the gap between men's and women's wages ranges from a high of 36.6 percent in South Korea to a low of 5.62 percent in New Zealand. The OECD average wage gap is 15.46 percent. The United States wage gap of 17.9 percent is the twelfth highest, between Australia at 18 percent and the United Kingdom at 17.48 percent. Japan's wage gap is third highest, at 26.59 percent.

The Scandinavian social democracies of Sweden, Norway and Denmark have wage gaps of 15.13 percent, 7.01 percent and 7.8 percent respectively. Chile and Mexico, the only Latin American countries covered in the study, have wage gaps of 16 percent and 15.43 percent respectively.

It must be understood in discussing wage differentials that averages can be deceiving. Many working-class men and women earn far less than the average, which is boosted by hugely high earners and stock dividends claimed by a relatively small minority, usually well-off men. There are millions of men who make the same poverty wages as women.

Nationally, on average, women earn 78 cents for each male dollar. This means that a woman earning $22,000 a year loses not only the current year's wages, but over her 40-year work life she will be deprived of $332,000 in wages. Over a lifetime this translates also to lost pensions, Social Security payments and other benefits based on income. The wage gap for white women is 77 percent; for African American women it is 64 percent; for Latinas it is 56 percent, and for Asian women it is 79 percent. These gaps occur at all educational levels.[10] Where the wage gap has narrowed since the recession, in many cases the cause has been the lowering of male wages, not the raising of women's wages.[11]

The wage gap varies by state. Women earn 80 cents or more to the typical male dollar in New York, California, Florida and several

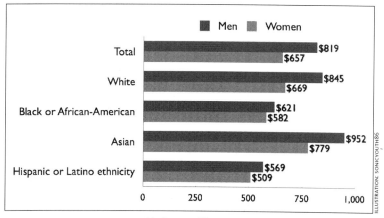

Median weekly earnings of full-time U.S. wage and salary workers, by sex, race and ethnicity, 2009

states in the southwest, New England and the upper Midwest. The largest gap occurs in West Virginia, Wyoming, Louisiana and Utah, where women's earnings are less than 70 cents to the male dollar. With few exceptions, the state wage gaps for African American and Latina women are greater than those of white women. Asian women fare better in a handful of states — Illinois, Tennessee, Montana — where their wages as a percentage of white male wages are higher than those of white women.[12]

Occupational segregation is also a factor in unequal pay. Women make up nearly two-thirds of the 3.3 million workers who make the federal minimum wage of $7.25 or are tipped workers making less than the minimum wage.[13] Of the 21 million additional workers making below $10.10/hour, 55 percent are women.

Not only do such wages make it impossible to support a family, but many of these workers are given arbitrary and inconsistent schedules, ruling out the ability to plan a workweek and tend to other responsibilities.

To make matters worse, these workers are rejected for supplemental public assistance and told they can get second jobs.

Among the lowest paid workers are domestic workers, 95 percent of whom are women. According to Ai-Jen Poo, executive director of the National Domestic Workers Alliance: "All work is gendered. And the economy that we have assigns different levels of value based off of that." She notes that the tasks that domestic workers perform — the cleaning, cooking, caring — are devalued by society, largely because it is women who do it. Doing low-paid work in isolation, in a private home, also leaves the worker more vulnerable to violence.[14]

Some 3.5 million workers are home care aides, 90 percent of whom are women. They take care of the sick, disabled and elderly in their homes. One third are Black, 16 percent are Latino and 25 percent were born outside the United States. Most earn less than $11 an hour and 25 percent live in poverty. Workplace injuries are common, but only 25 percent of home health aides have insurance for themselves.[15]

The Service Employees International Union (SEIU) has been the primary union behind organizing drives for low-wage retail workers, as well as home health care aides and restaurant workers — all highly profitable industries for the owners.[16]

Despite women's rise in educational achievement, surpassing men's in many areas, men far outnumber them in high-wage occupations. In 2014, women with advanced degrees earned 27 percent less than men with the same education; and men with bachelor's degrees earned more than women with advanced degrees. Discriminatory practices hold women back in the STEM fields (science, technology, engineering and mathematics). Women make up 36 percent of workers in some of the highest earning occupations in the country, such as physicians and surgeons. Yet they make 28 percent less than their male counterparts. Even in the occupations where they are over-represented, such as registered nurses, they still make 12 percent less than their male counterparts.[17]

Much media attention is paid to women breaking through the glass ceiling — attaining the highest tiers of corporate executive jobs once denied them. This sounds like a solid feminist goal, but, to quote journalist Laurie Penny, "While we all worry about the glass ceiling, there are millions of women standing in the basement — and the basement is flooding."[18]

Federal laws against pay discrimination date back to at least 1963. The Equal Pay Act of 1963 prohibits wage disparity based on sex for the same job in the same establishment. Title VII of the 1964 Civil Rights Act prohibits workplace discrimination based on race, sex and other categories and has been amended through the years to

Despite women's gains and accomplishments in education, men with the same education still make more.

cover LGBTQ and other workers and to include sexual harassment as a prohibited workplace discrimination.[19]

These were important reforms, providing new avenues of struggle, but they have done very little to uproot the basic inequality and bigotry around which the capitalist labor market is constructed. As we will discuss in later chapters, only a socialist planned economy would be able to truly root out these inequalities.

WOMEN AND THE PUBLIC SECTOR

The public sector, because of its connection to government, has historically been more susceptible to popular struggles and pressures from below as compared to the private sector. As a result, there are now better employment opportunities in the public sector for women and African American workers, where they represent a greater share of the workforce as compared to the private sector.

While government jobs pay less than the upper echelons of the private sector, these jobs have long been a reliable road to a living income, or what is sometimes described as the "middle class." (In reality, only those who own property or small businesses are technically middle class, and many public sector employees are just a better paid strata of the working class.) These jobs are more likely to be unionized, have a better record of adhering to standards of non-discrimination, provide better benefits and pensions, and traditionally have offered greater job security.

With the recession of 2008-09, state and local governments slashed their budgets, causing public sector jobs to disappear at an alarming rate. These job losses have disproportionately affected women and African Americans. A staggering 70 percent of the job losses were suffered by women. Even as the private sector began to recover from the recession, state and local governments experienced their worst job decline on record in 2011.[20]

Along with jobs, publicly funded programs — parks, sports, tutoring, and recreation — have been cut, multiplying the effects of job losses on families and communities, especially Black communities.[21]

Budget shortfalls in local and state governments are presented to the public as the fault of greedy, lazy workers, big government and corrupt unions. Instead they represent political choices that were made at the highest levels of government and have serious repercussions for the working-class women and African Americans who are suffering the most serious impacts of the cutbacks. In the years since the recession, governors and legislators in states such as Wisconsin, Ohio, Indiana and Michigan have limited or eliminated bargaining rights for public workers. They could not have been unaware that

The chart below shows how women, particularly African American women, were hardest hit in the 2008-2009 recession.

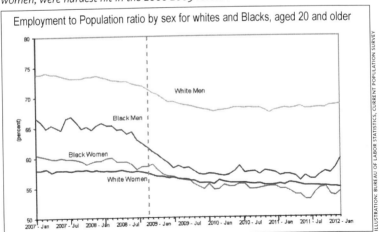

women, who made up 48.3 percent of the overall workforce, comprised almost 60 percent of state and local government workers and thus suffered 60 percent of the job losses. Or that African American workers, who accounted for 10.9 percent of total jobs and 10.3 percent of private sector jobs, held 12.8 percent of government jobs.

As these jobs with their union benefits are cut, these workers and their families lose the equity they have built up in the middle class since the post-World War II era. And, thanks to the gutting of welfare, they no longer have a safety net.

Raising taxes on the rich and cutting war spending would have cured the state and local government deficits in an instant. Instead, state governments, supported by corporate media, are using the deficits as an opportunity to slash collective bargaining rights, privatize and hollow out the public sphere, while claiming to increase efficiency and save taxpayer money.

Government workers are fighting the budget cuts, layoffs and privatization efforts. The Chicago and Seattle teachers strikes of 2012 and 2015; the nationwide rallies, caravans and boycotts staged by postal workers against post office closings and privatization; the demonstrations to save public hospitals; the teacher-parent-community solidarity around saving public schools from the encroachment of corporate business — these are examples of the kind of unity among women, workers and communities that must grow even stronger as part of a new mass movement. (For more on the teachers' strikes, see Chapter 10.)

MATERNITY AND FAMILY LEAVE

Even as women make up 47 percent of the workforce, the U.S. government, alone among the advanced capitalist states of the world, does not offer federally mandated and funded maternity leave, family leave, child care or any family benefits for U.S. workers. (Later in this chapter we offer a fuller comparison of U.S. benefits with those of other countries.) With the need for women's income rising, driven by changes in the family, declining male wages and other factors, the lack of family benefits has had a negative effect on women's ability to hold down full-time jobs, adding to the discrimination working mothers already face in the workplace. The struggle over benefits illustrates the connections between feminism and workers' rights.

Using 2013 figures, the OECD average of paid leave across the industrialized world — parental and other family leave — is 47.9 weeks. The Slovak Republic grants the longest paid maternity leave at 164 weeks. Other former communist countries are also among the highest: Poland, Czech Republic and Hungary grant more than two years paid leave; Russian Federation and Estonia grant more than a year and a half; Slovenia grants one year. The Scandinavian countries of Sweden, Denmark and Norway grant 60, 50, and 35 weeks respectively. Even struggling capitalist economies like Italy, Spain, and Greece guarantee 46, 16 and 17 weeks paid leave respectively. The United States is at zero.[22] [See Appendix 19 for a comprehensive list.]

The Family and Medical Leave Act (FMLA), signed into law by then-President Clinton in 1993, allows certain workers 12 weeks of job-protected unpaid leave for childbirth, adoption, or to care for a family member. Those who cannot afford the unpaid leave are out of luck.

In 2016 New York joined New Jersey, California and Rhode Island in passing a paid family leave law. These benefits are paid for by wage deductions from workers. The New York law will begin offering benefits in 2018, culminating in 12 weeks of partially paid leave in 2021. Unions are also negotiating for paid leave in their contracts. These benefits, along with accommodations for pregnant and breast-feeding women, flexible schedules, child care subsidies or workplace-located day care are being agitated for state by state, union by union and workplace by workplace. Coalitions of women's groups, labor unions and federations, religious and legal advocacy groups lobby continuously for these rights, primarily utilizing an insider strategy of building strong relationships with Democratic Party lawmakers.[23]

Generous paid maternity leave would go a long way to obviating the need for some of these special accommodations at work. Currently only 11 percent of private-sector workers and 17 percent of public-sector workers receive paid family leave from their jobs.

In the 2013 New York City mayoral race, City Council speaker and mayoral candidate Christine Quinn refused to allow a bill for paid sick leave to come up for a vote. She lost the election, and lost the votes of influential feminists, who, in an act of solidarity with the labor movement, asserted that electing the first female mayor did

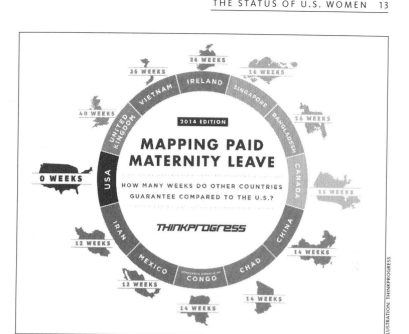

not compensate for neglecting the plight of women workers, who, as the primary caregivers in their families and the majority of low-wage workers without benefits, deserved paid sick leave.[24]

A 2014 New York Times article on the "motherhood penalty" noted that "one of the worst career moves a woman can make is to have children." For fathers, the effect is the opposite: men who are fathers are paid more than childless men or mothers. Women in the lowest paying jobs pay the highest penalties for having children, but this discrimination against mothers persists throughout the workforce — except at the very, very top.[25]

San Francisco teacher Nathalie Hrizi talks about her own union-negotiated maternity leave, which is only partially paid and must be supplemented by loans and private insurance. Still, that is more than the 25 percent of U.S. women who go back to work less than two weeks after giving birth. "Two weeks is nothing," says Hrizi. "Two weeks is barely walking well and you still don't know what day it is. Given the sleep deprivation, to have two weeks and go back to work can be a pretty dangerous situation." She noted that 7 percent of women took no time off.[26]

The magazine In These Times published a study of the real lives of women and the consequences of having insufficient or no paid family leave. These women struggle to time their births to make maximum use of vacation and sick time. They fight with employers and insurance companies when emergencies — premature births, disability and illness in newborns, maternal depression — force them to use up their allotted sick time before being really ready to return to work. This is in addition to the challenges of simply coping with the stresses of having a low income, job insecurity, the lack of affordable child care and caregiving. The article cites research that calls paid leave a "matter of life and death," with infant and child mortality dropping dramatically with increases in paid leave.

According to the article: "Paid parental leave frees mothers and fathers from choosing between their careers and time with their infants. For women, still most often the primary caregivers of young children, it results in higher employment rates, which in turn translates to lower poverty rates among mothers and their children." Not surprisingly women at the top of the pay scale and those with the highest levels of education were most likely to have longer leaves.[27]

The failure of the state and federal government to mandate and fund family leave has left most women to fend for themselves. The lucky ones who belong to unions can pressure their unions to fight for this benefit, although in this era, in which capital is on the offensive and labor is on the defensive, many companies have the power to simply brush off such demands.

INFANT AND MATERNAL MORTALITY

In matters of infant and maternal mortality, the United States has a level of technological production to practically eliminate it. Yet the most technologically developed country in the world denies adequate health care to millions because it has been organized principally on a for-profit basis. As such, the conditions facing the poorest communities in the United States rival those of the most underdeveloped countries in the world.

The United States has 50 percent more newborn deaths than all other industrialized countries combined. The U.S. infant mortality rate is more than double the rate of Finland, Japan, Portugal, Sweden, the Czech Republic and Norway. But there are wide differences among U.S. states. Mississippi, for example has an infant mortality rate of 9.6 per thousand, comparable to Botswana and Bahrain. The greatest differences in U.S. infant mortality rates are between rich and poor, with babies born to poor families suffering more than double the rate of mortality of babies born to wealthy families.[28]

In comparison to major world capitals, Washington D.C. has the highest rate of infant mortality — 7.9 per thousand — of the world's 24 wealthiest capitals. In contrast, Stockholm and Oslo have rates of 2 per thousand or below.[29]

Babies born to teenage mothers in the United States suffer among the highest rates of infant mortality. This is not a biological problem, but a product of the country's reactionary laws and sexist culture. Right-wing attacks on birth control, sex education and sexual health services have left millions of women without options and an understanding of their bodies. The state and religious institutions have so stigmatized teenage pregnancies that many young women are isolated from their families, communities, schools and health care providers at their greatest time of need, forcing them to confront the challenge of pregnancy alone. Disproportionately unemployed and low-income, their prenatal health suffers, and no strong prenatal care system exists in the country to help them. The result is that very young women are often left unprepared to deliver healthy infants.

The chart below shows how poorly the United States rates in infant mortality among industrialized nations.

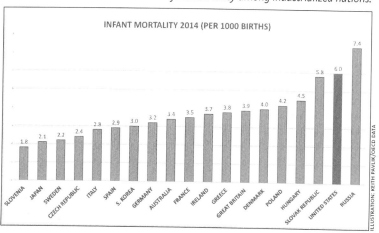

INFANT MORTALITY 2014 (PER 1000 BIRTHS)

ILLUSTRATION: KEITH PAVLIK/OECD DATA

Maternal mortality is also a national shame. The United States is one of only eight countries that has seen its maternal mortality rate increase in the years between 2003 and 2013. Its maternal mortality rate of 18.5 deaths for every 100,000 live births is more than double that of Saudi Arabia and China, and more than triple that of the U.K. Germany's maternal mortality rate fell from 18 per 100,000 in 1990 to 6.5 per 100,000 in 2013.

According to a 2011 Amnesty International report, while the amount spent on health care in the United States is the highest in the world, the cost of hospitalizations "related to pregnancy and child-birth are the highest hospitalization costs of any area of medicine." Yet women in the United States have a greater lifetime risk of dying of pregnancy-related complications than women in 49 other countries — "five times greater than in Greece, four times greater than in Germany, and three times greater than in Spain. More than two women die every day in the USA from pregnancy-related causes....

"African-American women are at especially high risk; they are nearly four times more likely to die of pregnancy-related complications than white women. Even for white women in the USA, however, the maternal mortality ratios are higher than for women in 24 other industrialized countries. These rates and disparities have not improved in more than 20 years. Maternal mortality ratios have actually increased from a low of 6.6 deaths per 100,000 live births in 1987 to 13.3 deaths per 100,000 live births in 2006.

"Despite the 34 percent decrease in global maternal mortality between 1990 and 2008, with 147 countries experiencing a decline in maternal death rates, the U.S. was among just 23 countries to see an increase in maternal mortality." Among other countries with these increases were war-torn Afghanistan and South Sudan, and economically distressed Greece.

U.S. women of low income are twice as likely to suffer maternal death as compared to high-income women. While the U.S. government has set a goal of 4.3 deaths per 100,000 live births, this has not been achieved for any racial group. For Black women the rate of maternal mortality is eight times greater than this goal, and for Native women it is four times greater. [30]

To take one hard-hit U.S. city, Detroit, the maternal mortality rate is triple the national average, and the infant mortality rate is worse than Bulgaria, Sri Lanka, Malaysia and Russia. The collapse of the economy and the loss of jobs and public services have left residents coping on their own, with the rise in infant and maternal mortality one of the consequences. Forty percent of Detroit residents live below the poverty line, and 83 percent are African American.[31]

CHILD CARE

Of the 34 countries surveyed by the OECD, the United States comes in 24th in access to preschool for three-year-olds and 26th in access for four-year-olds. Japan, the U.K. and Mexico enroll nearly 100 percent of their four-year-olds, while the United States enrolls barely 50 percent. Similar gaps exist for three-year-olds.

The United States also comes in near the bottom in terms of government funding for preschool education and child care. Most government funding for child care comes from the separate states. Head Start, the federally funded preschool program, enrolls only a small percentage of children who need the services. There is not a stated U.S. government goal, backed by a financial commitment, with respect to early childhood education or child care.[32]

As discussed in subsequent chapters, a bipartisan bill for universal child care passed Congress in 1971, at the height of the women's movement. The bill had a budget that was five times the current Head Start budget. President Richard Nixon vetoed it on the anti-communist basis that it would "commit the vast moral authority of the National Government to the side of communal approaches to child rearing over against the family-centered approach."

HOW THE SAFETY NET WAS SHREDDED

Then-President Clinton's 1996 welfare reform, "ending welfare as we know it," had a profoundly negative effect on poor women, robbing them of an already inadequate government program.

Aid to Families with Dependent Children (AFDC) was replaced with a temporary aid program to poor families with a five-year limit, regardless of the family's circumstance. It included an outrageous requirement for recipients to work at below minimum wage to receive their welfare check, with little provision for child care. Adding insult to injury, the new program was called the "Personal Responsibility and Work Opportunity Act," which not only further impoverished already

I'M WITH HER

The Democratic Clinton administration gutted welfare, long a dream of Republican presidents.

poor women but also shamed those who were unmarried. Few federal dollars were saved — welfare at the time comprised just over 1 percent of the federal budget — but the new legislation served the purpose of stigmatizing single mothers and poor women, who were disproportionately Black and Latina.

No one could deny that this assault on welfare was a women's issue, but by this time the feminist groups were scattered and fragmented, and largely isolated from poor and working-class communities. In a 2001 interview, Barbara Smith, author of Home Girls and a founder of the Combahee River Collective, asserted that "if we had had a strong and visible [B]lack feminist movement, I don't think we would have seen the debacle we saw over welfare."[33]

It was a Democratic administration that enthusiastically shredded what remained of the welfare safety net. In fact, since the early 1970s the "lesser evil" Democrats have not passed any legislation that has substantially improved the lot of the working class, lower middle class and the poor.

WOMEN IN GOVERNMENT

The anti-women and reactionary laws passed over the last several decades are reflected in the composition of government itself. While all capitalist governments are fundamentally exploitative and oppressive, many countries have seen the number of women representatives shoot upwards. In the United States, the change has been pitifully small.

As of 2015, the United States was 75th in the world in the percentage of women holding seats in the lower or single house of parliament. Only 19 percent of Congressional seats are held by women.

The countries that top the list are Rwanda at 64 percent, Bolivia at 53 percent and Cuba at 49 percent.[34]

POVERTY

The rise in income inequality, the growth of poverty and food insecurity, the lack of maternity leave for most American women workers, and inadequate access to prenatal and other health care is most pronounced today because the entire economic "recovery" from the Great Recession as of 2015 has gone into the pockets of the top 1 percent.

Poor women not only lack adequate access to health care, including prenatal care, because of income, but they also face bureaucratic hurdles in receiving the care they are entitled to from Medicaid.

The upshot of discriminatory wages, the absence of benefits, unemployment and the lack of a safety net is that millions of women are poor. Using 2014 data, the National Women's Law Center found that more than 14 percent of women, or 18 million, live in poverty. Of these, more than 8 million live in extreme poverty, which means below 50 percent of the federal poverty level. Put another way, nearly 60 percent of adults living in poverty are women.

Around 25 percent of Black, Native American and Latino women counted among the poor. Single mothers experienced even higher rates of poverty: 56.9 percent among Native Americans, 46 percent for Blacks and Hispanics, and 32 percent for whites. Women with disabilities experienced a poverty rate of nearly 32 percent, and elderly women living alone nearly 20 percent.[35]

LGBTQ workers suffer disproportionately from poverty. Lesbian couples are more likely than heterosexual couples to be poor, and LGBTQ single parents have greater rates of poverty, per capita, than straight single parents. And 15 percent of transgender people have a household income under $10,000 per year — four times the rate of the population as a whole.[36]

In addition to poverty, there are many other indicators of women's oppression in society, such as reproductive rights, exposure to violence, police brutality and prisons, and racial discrimination, which will be covered in subsequent chapters.

To review: Despite women's gains in equality within the family, responsibility for childcare resides largely with women. And even though most women work outside the home, childcare is viewed as a family responsibility, not a societal one. In other words, the gender division of labor in the home and in the labor market remains a decisive and deeply entrenched social reality in the day-to-day production and reproduction of capitalism. Women's oppression is built into the very fabric of capitalist society.

In the United States, the social safety net was especially thin even prior to the decades-long assault on services and benefits that disproportionately supported women. That austerity, combined with the absence of paid family leave, guaranteed child care and health care, has maintained an enormous burden of family and domestic labor mostly on women.

VIOLENCE AGAINST WOMEN

The indicators described above tell only a partial story. To get to the real lives of women, and their relative equality or subordination in society, it is important to see all the factors that enable them to live independent lives: not only workforce participation and equity, family benefits, affordable housing, and formal legal equality, but also absolute freedom from male violence, in the home, on the street and from the state.

While comparisons between countries show differences in economic, political and social rights of women, the issue of violence is global and remains at high levels across countries. Reviewing 2013 statistics, the U.N. estimates that 35 percent of women worldwide have experienced physical and/or sexual violence from an intimate partner or non-partner. Statistics for U.S. women fall within that range. Some national violence studies show that up to 70 percent of women have experienced physical and/or sexual violence in their lifetime from an intimate partner.[37]

According to a 2005 study by the World Health Organization, factors related to this violence include "the degree of economic inequality between men and women, levels of female mobility and autonomy, attitudes towards gender roles and violence against women, the extent to which extended family, neighbours, and friends intervene in domestic violence incidents, levels of male-male aggression and crime, and some measure of social capital."[38]

Similarly, a 2015 OECD report asserts that social norms and attitudes have at least as much to do with reducing domestic violence as laws and law enforcement. "Where there is a high social acceptance of domestic violence [including among women!], its prevalence is more than double the average of countries where there is little acceptance. The link continues to be significant even when taking into account the existence and quality of domestic violence laws and country income level, signaling that laws alone will not reduce violence against women."[39]

Thirty-five percent of women worldwide have experienced physical and/or sexual violence from an intimate partner or non-partner.

More than 125 countries have specific laws that penalize domestic violence. Yet 603 million women live in countries where it is not even considered a crime.[40]

The great majority of cases of serious violence are never reported to police. In the European Union it is estimated that only 13 to 14 percent of cases are reported, and that of all women killed in 2012, almost half were killed by intimate partners or family members.[41] ☐

Chapter 2
The origin of women's oppression

It took many millions of years for our ancestral Homo sapiens to become an identifiable species among the Great Apes (hominids) and many millions more before anatomically modern human beings evolved some 200,000 years ago. But it was only about 12,000 years ago, during the last ice age at the close of the Paleolithic Era, when climatic conditions warmed up sufficiently for humans to begin developing agriculture and the complex societies that exist today.

This means that for approximately 188,000 years, human beings generally lived in small groups as nomadic hunter-gatherers. This period is sometimes considered "pre-history" — because it was before written records.

But much history of human progress, such as tools and technological skills, the discovery and use of herbal medicines, and the structure of social and family life, has been discerned through the discovery of human artifacts, archeology and the fossil record, the examination of contemporary societies at earlier stages of development, and various scientific studies.

Science has not yet agreed on when our ancestors developed human behavior such as conversational language and multifaceted thought processes. Some believe it was at the time they became anatomically modern; others maintain it was about 50,000 years of development later. This still leaves well over 100,000 years of hunter-gatherer existence when these ancients looked, thought and behaved like modern people.

The question for feminists who demand equality and the end of male supremacy is obvious: Were women throughout human history always subordinate to men? Are men biologically constructed to lead and women to follow? Is this "human nature," as many suggest? Is this the "will of God" that women are inferior in almost all ways to men, as the great religions proclaim? Is it the way it always was and thus must be, as conservatives and traditionalists insist?

Marxism rejects all these pretexts. In the mid-1840s, Karl Marx and his collaborator Friedrich Engels posited that human beings are products of the natural world and are molded by human history, not fundamentally by biology, human nature or religion. They argued that women and men in pre-history existed for many thousands of years in a basic state of equality and shared responsibilities in extended families, many of which were matrilineal, i.e. where descent was through the female line. This did not mean females dominated males but that the structure was primarily egalitarian. A basic sexual division of labor was built into the mode of production. Men did the hunting and women did the gathering since women reproduced the species and cared for young children, closer to home.

These family and work arrangements produced various cultural conceptions of "gender" across societies — defining the roles and expectations of males and females tailored to the needs of their communities. In other words, there was a basic gender division of labor tied to a given society's social relations of production and reproduction. But the gender binary was not hierarchical, and bore little resemblance to the bourgeois norms of idealized masculinity and femininity. In some cases, these societies also had androgynous and/or "two-spirit" gender categories, often carrying special spiritual responsibilities in the community.

ENGELS ON THE HISTORY OF WOMEN'S OPPRESSION

When Marx was 26 in 1844 he began to oppose the existing bourgeois nuclear family structure as oppressive. He wrote of the Prussian law that "the sanctity of marriage is supposed to be enforced both upon men and women," but that in reality "the wife is regarded as the private property of her husband, [and] only the wife can be punished for adultery."[1]

How did this emerge? After Marx died, it was left to Engels to gather their notes from over the decades and secure new material to write a definitive analysis of the origins of women's oppression. He wrote his famous "The Origin of the Family, Private Property, and the State" in less than three months in 1884, not least because of the paucity of available research at that period.

He maintained that the transformation to male domination and the origin of the oppression of women occurred as the ice age ended and nomadic hunter gathers were able to develop agricultural societies in today's Middle East and other regions of the world. In the process Engels explained how crop surpluses, trading goods for products far and near, the establishment of animal herds ultimately led to male dominance over the female in a nuclear family. It

A young Friedrich Engels

also led to slavery to assist with the crops and cattle. As the title of the book mentioned, the oppressive family structure coincided with the development of private property, which forms the basis of class society. The roles of the state as a political form and the monogamous family as a social form protected the new property relationship by ensuring property inheritance from father to son.

Engels wrote, "The first class antagonism which appears in history coincides with the development of the antagonism between man and woman in monogamous marriage, and the first class oppression with that of the female sex by the male."

Engels wrote that monogamy "was a great historical advance, but at the same time it inaugurated, along with slavery and private wealth, that epoch, lasting until today, in which every advance is likewise a relative retrogression, in which the well being and development of the one group are attained by the misery and repression of the other. It is the cellular form of civilized society, in which we can already study the nature of the antagonisms and contradictions which develop fully in the latter."

These changes in gender, family and sexual relations occurred over thousands of years, in different forms and patterns, and across thousands of different communities without written records. It is impossible to provide a one-size-fits-all step-by-step narrative of the overthrow of mother-right and the replacement of various forms of group living with monogamous marriage.

As Australian Pat Brewer wrote in 1992:

> The origin of women's oppression is intertwined with the transition from pre-class to class society. The exact process by which this complex transition took place is a continuing subject of research and discussion even among those who subscribe to a historical materialist view. However, the fundamental lines along which women's oppression emerged are clear. The change in women's status developed along with the growing productivity of human labor based on agriculture. ...

> In these specific socio-economic conditions, as the exploitation of human beings became profitable for a privileged few, women, because of their biological role in production (i.e., the social production to maintain the existing generation and their production of the next generation), became valuable property. Like slaves and cattle, they were a source of wealth. They alone could produce new human beings whose labor power could be exploited. Thus the purchase of women by men, along with all rights to their future offspring, arose as one of the economic and social institutions of the new order based on private property. Women's primary social role was increasingly defined as domestic servant and child-bearer. ...

> The destruction of the egalitarian and communal traditions and structures of primitive communism was essential for the rise of an exploiting class and its accelerated private accumulation of wealth. This was the origin of the family institution. In fact, the word family itself, which is still used in the Latin-based languages of today, comes from the original Latin *famulus,* which means household slave, and *familia,* the totality of slaves belonging to one man.

The oppression of women was institutionalized through the family system. Women ceased to have an independent place in social production. Their productive role was determined by the family to which they belonged, by the man to whom they were subordinate. This economic dependence determined the second-class social status of women, on which the cohesiveness and continuity of the family has always depended. If women could simply take their children and leave, without suffering any social or economic hardship, the family would not have survived through the millennia."[2]

Engels was extremely discerning to associate women's oppression with the development of class society, the agricultural revolution, the end of communal tradition, and the establishment of monogamy with the male dominant over the female. But it must be understood that research into pre-history was in its very beginning stages when Engels wrote his extraordinary thesis largely on the most modern information he could rely on — the 1877 edition of U.S. historian Louis H. Morgan's "Ancient Society." Morgan included his firsthand investigations of the Iroquois Confederacy and broad knowledge of ancient societies — but much more knowledge has become available in subsequent decades.

Later research corrected some of Engels' assumptions. For instance, there are anthropological debates about how nomadic and fully "hunter-gatherer" early band societies were and the extent to which they utilized "base camps" and sedentary living. There are likewise debates about whether early band societies lived in conditions of generalized scarcity, or whether the availability of big-game hunting, at least for a period, made agriculture unnecessary.

In the PSL Publication "Revolution Manifesto," the chapter "Living and Cooperating Without a State" by Karina Garcia reviews some of this more recent anthropological research on the diverse living arrangements, social and sexual relations and family forms that existed in the communal stage. Garcia concludes that "In the broad outlines, the basic Marxist argument, that societies without classes existed, and that they were mostly matrilineal with equality for women, is a matter of fact not debate."

The Iroquois longhouse was a communal household.

Indeed, Engels' main arguments about pre-historic male-female equality until the development of agriculture, the egalitarian nature of pre-history's extended families, the origin of the class system that sustains male domination, among other insights, remain key contributions to the understanding of the oppression of women.

The cultural anthropologist Eleanor Burke Leacock (a feminist and Marxist who died in 1987) wrote books and articles based on her research and field work that supported a number of Engels' important assumptions and carried his work further. Her most important work in this regard is Myths of Male Dominance, first written in 1982 and reprinted 2009. In it she notes: "It might seem that Engels' discussion of family arrangements that have long ceased to exist in their pristine forms is somewhat esoteric and of little relevance today. However, it is crucial to the organizations of women for their liberation to understand that it is the monogamous family as an economic unit at the heart of class society that is basic to their subjugation."

Here it should be noted that the author is not talking about personal choices related to monogamy and the organization of one's family. Rather, Leacock is identifying the nuclear family as a core "economic unit" of class society — in which many women remain dependent on men's income and property, and in which household labor and child-rearing remains assigned to women. This would contrast with a monogamous family arrangement in which men and women are economically independent, and society guarantees a high-quality standard of living to all people, adults and children, and household and child-rearing labor is socialized.

The conclusion to this chapter, excerpted from an unpublished manuscript by Marxist political activist and feminist Jane Cutter, follows:

WOMEN WERE NOT ALWAYS OPPRESSED THROUGH HISTORY

Women's oppression is widespread, affecting women of all nationalities and of all classes. Poor and working-class women, lesbians, transgender women and women of color face additional and intertwined forms of oppression and exploitation. We may have been told, by religious leaders or via images in popular culture, that the patriarchal division between the sexes, the oppression of women, is an eternal factor in human society. In one way or another, we are all taught that the idea of women's inferior position in society and men's superior position is just a fact of life.

Even some feminists argue that the oppression of women derives from innate male characteristics of aggression and violence. However, anthropological and archeological research indicates that women have not always been oppressed. Anthropological research on traditional matrilineal hunting and gathering societies in the 19th century laid the basis for Engels' groundbreaking work.

In the 20th century, archaeological research by such researchers as Marija Gimbutas continues to provide evidence to suggest that there were widespread matrilineal societies across the world in Europe and elsewhere during the prehistoric epoch. Anthropological research also continues to be conducted on contemporary matrilineal societies found in the developing world. These studies also suggest that the oppression of women by men is not a human universal.

For the bulk of human existence, people lived together communally. This was an essential way of life for early humans, because, due to their low level of technology and production, their survival depended on sharing resources such as food and housing.

Archaeological research has uncovered many artifacts not only in Europe, but in other parts of the world as well, which depict female goddesses. Yet the monotheistic religions that developed later all portray a male God. What changed? Marxists believe that "being determines consciousness"— in other words, that ideologies reflect the values of those in power in a society. In a society in which gods were female, we can infer that women were held in great esteem.

We call these traditional (or primary) communist societies. "Home" in this context was not an isolated or isolating place. Instead, it is where the whole group or tribe congregated. That family structure changed and evolved over time. However, it is clear that the family line was traced through the mother's side of the family, that is, these were matrilineal societies. This may have been due to a lack of knowledge, or concern, about issues of paternity.

There is evidence to suggest that some societies viewed all people of a certain generation as parents, and also children of the next generation as the collective children of those parents. (Engels). In other words, children belonged to the entire tribe or group, not to the individual biological mother and father of each child. These kinds of values and beliefs are another reason why we call these societies "communist."

That the division of labor was based on the facts of reproduction should not be construed to imply that women were oppressed as women. Women were held in high esteem, as those who could bring forth life from their bodies, and thus in early spiritual forms were associated with "the creator." Anthropological evidence of more contemporary traditional societies shows women elders playing an important role in decision-making for the entire society, and being treated with respect. Women in these societies would be able to separate and end a relationship, and begin new ones, without penalty or stigma.

By the time of the development of animal breeding after the onset of the agricultural era, it is clear that people had figured out the basic facts of reproduction. It is in this era that forms of private property emerged. So it seems that a man, who had control of valuable resources, may have become interested in making sure that "his" children, his sons, would be able to control these resources after he had died. In a matrilineal society, where the family line is traced through the mother's side, in the event of divorce or separation, the children would go with the mother. In the event of death, inheritance would pass through the female line; a man's property would go to his sister's children.

And so occurred what Engels called the "world historic defeat of the female sex." Inheritance and family identity began to be traced through the male line. Restrictions began to be imposed on female sexuality, to ensure that the children were "legitimate," i.e., the children of her husband.

No such restrictions were placed on male sexuality. Men in many early class societies were allowed to have more than one wife, or to have concubines and mistresses, and could walk away from children conceived outside of marriage. Prostitution emerged historically in tandem with monogamous, patriarchal marriage, to cater to men's sexual desires outside of marriage. (Contrary to the popular saying, farming is truly the "world's oldest profession.")

In this patriarchal family form, a woman and her children were legally the property of the husband/father of the family.

From this emergence of patriarchal class society we can trace the development of many aspects of women's oppression that we see to this day. If a woman is the property of her husband, and her primary purpose is to provide him with heirs, then what rights does she have to control access to her body? Does she have the right to refuse sex with her husband? Does she have the right to avoid becoming pregnant or to terminate a pregnancy if she does not want children? If a woman is like a slave in relation to her husband, what protection does she have from physical abuse from her husband or other men in the family?

It is important to understand the origin of women's oppression, not as a lesson in history, but because by understanding that the oppression has not always existed, we can understand that it does not have to exist forever, either. If we understand that the oppression of women arose with the emergence of class society, we also understand that by ultimately eliminating class society as we know it and building socialism, we can end women's oppression.

This does not mean that women should put off struggling against women's oppression under capitalism. Working-class women need to struggle side by side with the members of our class on every issue, and try to unite with the most active and leading elements of those struggles. The struggles around reproductive rights and access, sexual violence, discrimination, sexism, and cutbacks to social services are integral to the struggle for women's liberation and the development of women's mass leadership is a key to any revolutionary movement today.[3] ☐

Chapter 3
Women in three socialist revolutions

T HE people of the United States have been taught nonstop for almost 100 years that the socialist revolutions in Russia (1917), China (1949) and Cuba (1959) constituted a danger to the world. Every U.S. president has demonized each country and its leadership. As such it is understandable that most people here possess little factual knowledge about the extraordinary advances for women that quickly followed each revolution. This chapter will briefly examine this history.

While many advances have been achieved through hard struggle by and for women in the more progressive or social-democratic capitalist countries, what distinguishes socialist women's movements from those in capitalist countries is the idea that complete women's liberation cannot be won independent of the liberation for all people and the total transformation of society.

Socialist revolutions in Russia, China and Cuba saw immediate gains for women in employment opportunities, income, worker protections, health care, reproductive rights, education, child care, personal freedoms and protections from violence.

THE UNION OF SOVIET SOCIALIST REPUBLICS

The U.S. ruling class made opposition to revolutionary socialism and communism a cornerstone of its political outlook ever since the successful Russian Revolution led by the Bolshevik Party in November 1917 that deposed Czar Nicholas II, the wealthy aristocracy and rich landholders. This was not out of any special loyalty to the czar or any principle to oppose changes of government. What was different in Russia was that it proved that those at the bottom of society, namely the working class, could seize power from the rich, and then hold that power. The Russian Revolution provided a living example of what had previously just been theory; it provided a universal lesson for oppressed people everywhere that there was hope in revolution.

The Russian revolutionary state, led by Vladimir I. Lenin, immediately began to fulfill its promise of "Bread, Peace and Land" for the workers and peasants of this huge, largely poor and backward agricultural society, where only a few major cities had experienced industrialization.

One of the first acts of the new government was to withdraw from World War I to demonstrate opposition to pitting worker against worker, angering the United States and other allied belligerents. In 1918, pro-Czarist counterrevolutionary forces (called the White Army, as opposed to the revolutionary Red Army), launched a bitter civil war to return Russia to aristocratic control. The United States and 13 other countries invaded Russia with troops and war materials on the side of the counterrevolutionaries. It took two years of fighting until it was clear they were unable to turn the Red tide, not least because as interlopers and supporters of the hated old ruling classes, they enjoyed very little support from the masses of Russian people. The revolutionaries' initial seizure of power was essentially quick and bloodless, but the civil war took millions of lives before the masses of Russia finally defeated the counterrevolution and consolidated their victory.

Before the revolution, women's work for the majority of Russians was hard household and farm labor. In the home, women had no rights and were at the mercy of their men. Violence against women was rampant. As World War I approached and Russia began to industrialize, women started to work in industry, making up a third of the country's relatively small industrial labor force. With no family benefits, women factory workers suffered a two-thirds rate of infant mortality. Women joined the Bolshevik party in large numbers, and the party called for pay equity, maternity leave, childcare at factories, and an end to wife-beating (which had been legal at the time) — and peace.[1]

After the revolution, the early years of the Soviet Union saw dramatic gains in the lives of women, both on paper and in practice. These gains were rooted in the participation of Russian working women in the Bolshevik Party and the connection between the working class and women's struggles. In fact, it was an International Women's Day march of women textile workers in Petrograd, in opposition to World War I, high prices and the oppression of women workers that led to the massive strike movement that overthrew the Czar in the first stage of the Russian Revolution in February 1917.[2]

Bolshevik women

Soviet women gained full legal and political equality immediately after the revolution, including the right to vote. Some of the more isolating and burdensome chores that constituted "women's work" began to be socialized, with the establishment of communal kitchens and dining halls, laundries and day care centers. Abortion was legalized, free and on demand. In the workplace, women became eligible for the same jobs as men, in the civil service, industry, the party and the armed forces. Women workers had paid maternity leave. Homosexuality was decriminalized. The right to divorce was equalized and the concept of "illegitimacy" was abolished. Universal education was mandated and began to wipe out rampant illiteracy.[3]

All this happened immediately after the revolution. This was an astonishing pace of change for the legal, social and economic rights of women — and undoubtedly unparalleled in any capitalist country, where the state makes winning the most elementary reforms a bitter struggle.

The main obstacle facing the central Soviet government in this period was that the country did not have an adequate system of administration or the technological means — given the paltry state of even basic communications — to immediately bring all these changes to every city, town and village. In these initial years, the revolutionary government's main role with respect to women's oppression was to wipe out old reactionary laws, and create new ones on the basis of equality. This created a new legal framework for women on the ground, acting individually or in special women's organizations, to fight and make the new laws a reality.

Alexandra Kollontai, a revolutionary communist and feminist, Commissar of Social Welfare and first woman to serve as a Soviet diplomat, staunchly backed the extensive changes in the status of women and was a leader of these special women's organizations. Kollontai's avant-garde views of sex and marriage were largely side-

Alexandra Kollontai

lined by men and women in her party, particularly what was called "free love." By this, she meant sexual and romantic relationship freed from bourgeois possessiveness and property. Her view of women is expressed in this quote: "I always believed that the time inevitably must come when woman will be judged by the same moral standards applied to man. For it is not her specific feminine virtue that gives her a place of honor in human society, but the worth of the useful mission accomplished by her, the worth of her personality as human being, as citizen, as thinker, as fighter."

Some of the gains for women were reversed in the 1930s under Stalin, when nearly all social, cultural and political trends were subordinated to the tasks of rebuilding national unity and strength, war preparations and production more generally. Women were again taught "their place" in the nuclear family. Homosexuality was re-criminalized and abortion was restricted. Marriage and divorce laws became more conservative, and the concept of illegitimacy was restored. From a socialist point of view, this path to build national unity — on the basis of alliance with the most conservative sectors of Russian society, rather than on a revolutionary basis — is not justifiable.[4]

Soviet women still enjoyed universal literacy and education, equal political rights, high employment and socialized medicine. Then in World War II, the Soviet Union shocked the world with its deployment of 800,000 women in combat roles, from front-line infantry units to fighter pilots. More generally, the women of the Soviet Union sacrificed tremendously to defend their country and defeat the Nazi menace — a task that ultimately took 27 million Soviet lives.

Some of the women's rights that had been lost in the 1930s were again restored during the 1950s.[5] At the same time, women continued to be burdened by the double shift, insufficient social services and male supremacist attitudes.[6] Without the material basis to completely reorganize the production and reproduction of society — namely to socialize all household labor, childrearing and the living arrangements that had been the basis of the "nuclear family" — gendered work, and the assumptions that came with that, could not simply be abolished.

The demise of socialism and triumph of capitalism in 1991 caused extreme hardship for the great majority of the population. Economic exploitation returned with a vengeance. Living standards and life expectancies plummeted in ways that had previously only been associated with natural disasters. For women, this took the form of lower wages, the elimination of social benefits and, for the first time in decades, unemployment. Prostitution exploded and Russian women became prime targets for international sex traffickers.

Washington supported and guided the new capitalist leaders in Moscow, who privatized and looted what had previously been socially owned property, selling virtually the entire economic inventory of the country — industries, buildings, natural resources, etc. — at ridiculously cheap prices to a new and rising class of "free market" billionaire oligarchs. The new ruling class also resuscitated the political and ideological leadership of the old Russian Orthodox Church, which in the main is highly conservative, preaching downright feudal and patriarchal values.

While women's labor force participation is 57 percent (as of 2013), there has been a 30 percent increase in the number of people living in poverty, with most of the poor comprising families with children, the unemployed, the elderly, the disabled and women.[7] The restoration of the Russian Orthodox Church, the activities of which had been significantly restricted for most of the Soviet Union's existence because of its role in organizing counterrevolutionary activities, also negatively impacted the rights of women. Towards the end of the Soviet Union, the country's leadership allowed the broadcast of Orthodox services on state television and today the Church hierarchy is again a core pillar of state legitimacy, promoting the subordination of women in the home and society, as well as anti-LGBTQ bigotry.

Women in the Russian Federation now suffer from "pervasive domestic violence," which is being fought by a growing women's movement and various organizations. At the government level, an international committee of the U.N. Convention on the Elimination of All Forms of Discrimination Against Women (CEDAW), of which Russia is a signatory, has criticized Russia for its failure to address domestic violence as a violation of women's — and not just children's

— rights. Russia is expected to respond with information about new policies and practices.[8]

Since revolutionary leader Lenin (1870-1924) has been demonized by the United States continuously since the revolution it will be of interest to many feminists reading this book to learn that he was strongly supportive of women's liberation. He pushed hard for all the reforms that were implemented until he died at age 54 from a series of strokes and the effects of an assassination attempt in 1918. It is difficult to think of any other national leader in history — let alone that time — that so used their power and influence to consistently champion women's rights.

Here is a selection of just four excerpts from his writings on women:

1918: "The experience of all liberation movements has shown that the success of a revolution depends on how much the women take part in it."

1919: "We in Russia no longer have the base, mean and infamous denial of rights to women or inequality of the sexes, that disgusting survival of feudalism and medievalism which is being renovated by the avaricious bourgeoisie ... in every other country in the world without exception."

1921: "You cannot draw the masses into politics without drawing in the women as well. For under capitalism the female half of the human race is doubly oppressed. The working woman and the peasant woman are oppressed by capital, but over and above that, even in the most democratic of the bourgeois republics, they remain, firstly, deprived of some rights because the law does not give them equality with men; and secondly — and this is the main thing — they remain in 'household bondage,' they continue to be 'household slaves,' for they are overburdened with the drudgery of the most squalid, backbreaking and stultifying toil in the kitchen and the family household. ..."

Again, in 1921: "Women workers take an ever increasing part in the administration of public enterprises and in the administration of the state. By engaging in the work of administration women will learn quickly and they will catch up with the men. Therefore, elect more women workers, both Communist and non-Party, to the Soviet (i.e., governing council). If she is only an honest woman worker who is capable of managing work sensibly and conscientiously, it makes no difference if she is not a member of the Party — elect her to the Moscow Soviet. Let there be more women workers in the Moscow Soviet! Let the Moscow proletariat show that it is prepared to do and is doing everything for the fight to victory, for the fight against the old inequality, against the old bourgeois humiliation of women! The proletariat cannot achieve complete freedom, unless it achieves complete freedom for women."

THE PEOPLE'S REPUBLIC OF CHINA

Chinese women suffered thousands of years of subordination to men, in the home, in society and in the state before the Communist Party, led by Mao Zedong, overthrew the old government in 1949 after more than 20 years of revolutionary struggle.

Abiding by the Confucian precepts of filial piety, women were expected to be obedient to men, as citizens obeyed the ruler and the young obeyed the elderly. The principles of women's subordination were expressed in the practices of female infanticide, wife beating, the sale and purchase of women, and foot binding.

Beginning in imperial circles in the 10th century, foot binding became prevalent throughout China. Girls as young as five years old would have their toes bent under and bound with cloth until they were permanently deformed and small as a symbol of supposed feminine beauty. The deformity prevented women from walking any distance and was one of the means by which they were kept close to home and dependent on men. While formally outlawed early in the 20th century, the practice did not disappear until the communist revolution.[9]

Women took part in rebellions and liberation movements beginning in the 1850s, fighting for free marriage, the right to education, and to end foot binding. Even after the establishment of the republic in the early 1900s, when the last monarchical dynasty dissolved, women were still fighting many of the same patriarchal norms and exclusions. But with the founding of the Communist Party of China, the struggles for revolution and for women's liberation were closely joined.[10]

The People's Republic of China declared its commitment to the equality of women from the very beginning, as reflected in Mao's famous words: "Women hold up half the sky." The PRC's basic law sought to "abolish the feudal system which holds women in bondage.

Young revolutionary women in China

Women shall enjoy equal rights with men in political, economic, cultural, educational and social life. Freedom of marriage for men and women shall be put into effect."

In 1955 Mao declared: "In order to build a great socialist society, it is of the utmost importance to arouse the broad masses of women to join in productive activity. Men and women must receive equal pay for equal work in production. Genuine equality between the sexes can only be realized in the process of the socialist transformation of society as a whole."

Arranged and child marriages were abolished. Divorce was liberalized and as a consequence the divorce rate skyrocketed — as it did 30 years later in the United States. Polygamy and the use of concubines were outlawed. Women were also recruited to join the labor force. Collective nurseries and dining halls were created to accommodate working women. The pace of China's process of women's liberation slowed down by the end of the 1950s. As economic development rose and fell, women's role in the economy changed, from high labor force participation when the economy could absorb higher numbers of new wage workers, to more restrictions in periods of downturn.

During the Cultural Revolution — the period of 1966 to 1976 when Mao and other leaders of the CPC called for the masses to rebel against reactionaries, purveyors of bourgeois ideas and all forms of oppression still operating in society, women's labor force participation and educational levels skyrocketed. They were, in fact, higher than any period before or since. But with the end and defeat of the Cultural Revolution, much of that progress was reversed. China has not completed the task of achieving equal status in society between women and men.

The mass of Chinese people were poor peasants when the communists marched into Beijing. Due to poverty, a large number of Chinese women had little alternative but to turn to prostitution. It has been estimated that in 1949 some 50,000 women worked in Shanghai's brothels alone. The communists banned prostitution, launching a successful campaign of re-education and job training for these women. Prostitution was resumed on a smaller scale in the late 1970s after the death of Mao, the purge of the left wing of the Communist Party and the decision to develop a largely capitalist economic system. The re-imposition of capitalist competition, and the elimination of the social safety net, inherently compels the creation of a permanently anxious working class, and the least secure section of that class inevitably will turn to whatever activity can guarantee their survival.

Since the Communist Party began to construct a largely capitalist economic system called "socialism with Chinese characteristics" in the 1980s, women have experienced pay gaps with men, both within industries and between industries that predominately employ men and women. Women's labor force participation is at 64 percent, but their status overall has reflected in large part the declining importance given to women's issues by the Party and the government. Male dominance has strengthened, as has women's traditional family role.[11]

The largest women's organization in China remains the All-China Women's Federation. Established in 1949 as a government organization, it began as a federation of regional women's organizations that was charged with building socialism along with improving the status of women in every locale. It became a mass organization within the CPC and later declared itself an NGO, which connects with women's movements internationally while also maintaining strong ties to the Party. Its work focuses on education, employment, and influencing government policy on women's equality and rights.[12]

'Women hold up half the sky.'

The erosion of women's rights has not proceeded without a struggle. For example, street actions in Beijing in 2015 have landed five Chinese feminists in jail for protesting such things as sexual harassment on public transportation, the dearth of public toilets for women and the scourge of domestic violence. While charged with disrupting public stability, they claimed that China has not lived up to the promises of the Chinese Revolution for women's equality. The women were released on bail after 37 days.[13]

THE REPUBLIC OF CUBA

Cuba, a small underdeveloped agricultural island in the shadow of the Yankee colossus 90 miles north, had been under military and then political control by the U.S. since 1899. This ended abruptly on New Year's Day 1959 when the revolutionary movement led by Fidel Castro ousted U.S. puppet dictator Fulgencio Batista. Within a year Uncle Sam began to impose draconian sanctions that expanded into a strict blockade, which is still in effect at the time of this writing. The U.S. government likewise launched an intense effort to subvert and overthrow the revolutionary government, using a multitude of tactics.

The condition and rights of women improved with the end of direct U.S. domination despite the hardships of the economic and trade blockade.

Cuba set the goal of full emancipation of women from the very beginning of its revolution. Calling the struggle for women's equality the "revolution within the revolution," Cuba has understood that women's liberation could not be achieved overnight but must be part of an ongoing process of education, legislation and the engagement of the country's women. Despite over a half century of imperialist trade blockade, constant political interference by the United States, and the economic hardships caused by the dissolution of the Soviet Union, Cuba has continued to move in the direction of increased rights, benefits and equality for women.

Women had to overcome decades of oppression, illiteracy and a complete lack of economic opportunity that existed before the revolution. Those who were employed outside the home worked mostly as domestic servants and agricultural laborers. Many worked as prostitutes. Others did home work, such as sewing or making cigars. The Cuban economy was not yet developed enough to provide sufficient jobs for this new workforce, so the state first focused on educating women so they would be employable in the future, when the economy could support them, and organizing them to teach others. In fact, young women and girls played leading roles in the revolution's literacy brigades, traveling through the countryside to teach rural residents how to read and write and helping to create one of the most literate societies in the world.

The Cuban Constitution explicitly grants women equal economic, political, cultural, social and familial rights with men and prohibits discrimination based on race, skin color, sex, national origin, religious belief or any other form of discrimination. These rights are further supported by provisions in various laws, including the groundbreaking Family Code of 1975, which requires men to participate equally in domestic labor, guarantees equal rights to women and men in marriage and divorce, equal parental rights, and equal property and social rights for women in the home. Revisions in the Penal Code, legislated in 1979 and 1984, provided additional penalties for violations of sexual equality.

Cuban soldiers march during a military parade in Havana's Revolution Square, 2011.

PHOTO: PRENSA LATINA

A young Espín with Raul Castro

Cuba was the first country to sign, and the second to ratify, the United Nations's 1979 Convention on the Elimination of all Forms of Discrimination against Women (CEDAW) in 1980-81. The United States has never ratified it. The National Action Plan was instituted in 1997 to implement the terms of the 4th U.N. Conference on Women in Beijing.

The Cuban women's movement has been important in furthering women's gains. Women took part in the revolution, including in leadership roles, from the beginning.

The Federation of Cuban Women (FMC) is the national agency responsible for the advancement of women. It was founded in 1960 by Vilma Espín, a leader of the revolution. The FMC is a non-governmental organization with close ties to the government.

The FMC has been integral in shaping the Family Code and fighting for its implementation.

According to Espín: "We had to change women's mentality — accustomed as they were to playing a secondary role in society. Our women had endured years of discrimination. We had to show her own possibilities, her ability to do all kinds of work. We had to make her feel the urgent needs of our revolution in the construction of a new life. We had to change both woman's image of herself and society's image of women."

An important early initiative to assist some of the most oppressed and exploited women in Cuba was the creation of schools for domestic servants. The first one opened in Havana in April 1961; eventually some 30,000 women were enrolled at hundreds of schools all over the country. Students studied the revolution: agrarian reform, rent reform and urban reform as well as vocational skills to prepare them for other work. By 1968 the schools were no longer needed and were closed.[14]

To help eliminate stereotypes, the FMC conducts trainings for public speakers and writers, and sets up counseling centers for women and families. Curriculum, textbooks and communications are constantly being revised to eliminate sexist, patriarchal or discriminatory language and values. Parenting (if not yet equal housework) is increasingly shared by fathers and mothers, and the new generation is growing up to expect these values. The federation has also established a program of sensitizing judges, lawyers, the police, and even law students to women's experiences and perspectives. They oversee the judiciary to ensure that women's complaints are answered at every stage of a suit or investigation.

Today, women in Cuba comprise 44 percent of the labor force. They are 66.4 percent of all technicians, mid-level professionals and higher-degree professionals. They make up 72 percent of all education workers, 67 percent of health workers, including 72 percent of doctors, and 43 percent of all science workers. These figures represent a remarkable achievement, all the more significant being accomplished by a poor nation under imperialist blockade.[15]

While much progress has been made in the area of pay equity, there is still work to be done to increase women's access to the very top levels of professions and government in which men predominate and to continue to change male attitudes toward shared housework and child raising, so that women are freed from the double day.[16]

Political participation, and that of women, is especially high in Cuba. The government's policy on the advancement of women, along with the work carried out by the FMC, has led to significant progress in women's participation in government. As of 2013 women comprise 48.9 percent of the National Assembly, ranking Cuba's legislature third in the world in women's participation.[17] About half the judges, including in the People's Supreme Court, are women.

Infant and maternal mortality and reproductive rights are a priority. Cuba's 2014 infant mortality rate — deaths under one year old — is 4.7 per thousand live births, on a par with Canada and the lowest in Latin America.[18] This figure is one-and-one-half points better than the U.S. in the aggregate, and lower than the District of Columbia's rate of 7.9 per thousand live births and Detroit's 13.3 per thousand.

Abortion is free, as is all health care, and available on demand. About 77 percent of sexually active women use contraception.

Infant daycare centers are a government-mandated benefit, as are paid maternity and paternity leave.[19]

Crimes of violence against women, especially rape and sexual assault, are severely punished in Cuba. In official circles, violence against women had previously been seen as something that was taken care of as part of the revolution. However, after the U.N.'s 4th World Conference on Women in Beijing in 1995, the FMC began traveling the country to find out if there was hidden violence and to set up mechanisms for reporting and for community intervention.

The traditional imbalance in workload in the home for men and women was cited by many as the most common form of (in effect) injustice affecting women within the family, not physical violence.

They also found that in view of the strong social cohesion and close communication networks between families and neighborhoods, cases of violence against women could not be hidden, and when it became known community intervention would be likely.

Mariela Castro, daughter of Vilma Espín and President Raul Castro, and leader of the National Center for Sex Education (CENESEX), addressed this issue in a 2008 interview:

Mariela Castro Espín speaking at the Day Against Homophobia and Transphobia in Matanzas, Cuba, 2016

Women everywhere, in all patriarchal societies, are the victims of violence. I call it the pathology of power, since it's about exerting power unevenly. ... We have severe laws against domestic violence and very harsh sentences, mainly for cases of sexually abused children. ... The FMC is launching more and more information and education campaigns to increase public awareness, especially among women, who are the main victims. But men are also victims of their upbringing and the way manhood is portrayed all over the world, which makes them very vulnerable and likely to become victimizers. So we have a lot of work to do, because what we're doing is not enough. ... It's more common among older people and decreasing among the younger ones. ... We have made great progress, but not enough to be able to at least make a few changes.[20]

Because gender-based violence cannot be eradicated by legal means alone, the country, led by CENESEX and the FMC, has launched education programs for men and boys as well as women and girls; arts and media campaigns to change the way women are represented in public images and tourist advertising; and programs to increase opportunities for women. These efforts were lauded by the United Nations Secretary General Ban Ki-moon in a 2014 speech in Havana.[21]

LGBTQ rights are advancing in Cuba, reversing a long history of macho and heterosexist culture. Sexual relations between same-sex consenting adults 16 and over have been legal in Cuba since 1979, although same-sex marriage has yet to be legalized. Havana now has an open and vibrant gay cultural scene. Educational campaigns on LGBTQ issues are currently implemented by CENESEX, and Cuba now provides citizens with gender affirmation surgery (called "gender change surgery" in Cuba) for free.

The years 2014-15 saw two significant occurrences in the direction of more rights for the LGBTQ community: Mariela Castro voted in the National Assembly against a new labor law that banned discrimination based on sexual orientation because it did not also ban discrimination based on gender identity. And on May 9, 2015, 1,000 LGBT Cubans, led by Mariela, marched in Havana in the eighth annual March against Homophobia and Transphobia, where 20 couples exchanged symbolic vows.

By law, women have pay equity with men in the labor force. Even in the 1990s, during the Special Period in Time of Peace, a period of extreme economic hardship as a result of the loss of Cuba's primary trading partner after the collapse of the Soviet Union, great efforts were made to keep gender equality during this economic crisis. The government had long outlawed prostitution and all but eradicated the practice by 1990, defining it a manifestation of colonialism and oppression. But prostitution returned to Cuba during the period of extreme economic calamity for the whole nation, in which they lost 85 percent of their foreign trade. It took almost a decade for the country to recover.

Before the Revolution, Cuba was a center of "sex tourism" for wealthy U.S. elites, but after the revolution the practice was largely eliminated with comprehensive educational, social and employment programs for Cuba's poor communities. During the Special Period, a dual economy arose from the combination of the extreme economic hardship and the acceptance of U.S. dollars from tourists. This further contributed to the return of prostitution, mainly in Havana. Pimping remains a criminal offense and there are no brothels or red light districts.

Cuba is a relatively poor country but has held firmly to its core socialist and humanitarian values even under the extreme conditions caused by the U.S. blockade and continual subversion, and the elimination of most of Cuba's socialist allies.

SUMMARY

The socialist revolutions described in this chapter set the foundation for profound political, economic and social gains for women, even if they were not accomplished overnight. The collapse of the international socialist movement and the restoration of capitalism in some of the formerly socialist countries has set back the struggle for women's equality all over the planet.

The 21st century socialist movement must of course include the eradication of women's inequality right up front. For example, the Program of the Party for Socialism and Liberation (PSL), which describes what a socialist government of poor and working people would set out to do, stipulates that "sexism and other forms of male chauvinism and oppression of women will be eliminated as an immediate task, recognizing that this goal will not be achieved automatically or by decree. It will be prohibited to advocate any form of sexism or male chauvinism."

The Program goes on to call for a guarantee of "the right of women workers to receive the same pay, benefits and treatment as their male counterparts," the absolute right to contraception, abortion services, high-quality pre- and post-natal health care and child care; and an end to all forms of discrimination against anyone on the basis of their sexual orientation or gender expression. ☐

HISTORY OF THE WOMEN'S STRUGGLE IN THE U.S.

Chapter 4
A new movement is born: the 1800s

GROWING WOMEN'S CONSCIOUSNESS

The organized struggle for women's rights began in the early 1800s and continued to grow and develop throughout the century, paving the way for the movements and victories that followed in the 1900s.

At the turn of the 1800s, on the cusp of the industrial revolution, the American economy was primarily agricultural, with mostly free labor in the North and slave labor in the South. The westward expansion saw battles over the extension of slavery, but for white women, restrictions on their public and private lives were somewhat more relaxed in the West than in the more settled East. In this preindustrial society most women were only minimally educated. Women were not even permitted to engage in public speaking or lecture to audiences of men and women — the first being Frances Wright in 1828 — and only a few dared to write books. Whatever consciousness women had of their inequality, in society or at home, was likely kept private or shared discreetly with trusted friends.

Literacy in the United States of 1800 approached 100 percent for free white males. Free white women's literacy lagged behind but caught up by mid-century. While elite women had access to literature, drama and languages, most women's reading consisted of the bible and practical manuals that instructed them in their domestic tasks.

For enslaved Africans, men and women, learning to read was often illegal and severely punished. Even free Blacks in the North and West, especially girls, were commonly denied education.

An intellectual turning point in women's consciousness of their position in society was the publication of British feminist Mary Wollstonecraft's 1792 book "A Vindication of the Rights of Woman,"

51

which articulated women's dissatisfaction with their station in life. Wollstonecraft looked at the exclusion of women from both the American and French revolutions. She understood that this exclusion was embedded in social and religious tradition, that the "rights of man" were bought with the subjugation of women and that it could be exposed and fought. She called for social equality between men and women in certain areas and believed that this could be achieved in part by expanding the educational opportunities for women.[1]

The book, and Wollstonecraft's personal life, scandalized late eighteenth century British society but deeply influenced American

and British feminists for decades to come. This new consciousness ran as a thread through the struggles that women took part in for the abolition of slavery, suffrage and other causes in the larger feminist movement.

In 1831 Maria Stewart, a free-born African American woman, became the first American-born woman of any color to lecture in public to audiences of mixed genders and races. She spoke on abolition, equal rights, educational opportunities, and racial pride and unity. She advocated Black self-determination and independence from whites. Public denunciation finally forced her to give up public speaking, and she went on to a career as an educator, opening two schools for free African American children in Washington, D.C.[2]

Maria Stewart

Also in the 1830s, Sarah and Angelina Grimke, daughters of a slaveholding family in South Carolina, became prominent abolitionists in the North. Firsthand knowledge of slavery gave great power to their speeches and brought out large numbers of abolitionists to hear them. They were also among the first women to speak in public before mixed audiences of men and women and were severely denounced for this by church leaders. Pushing back against Christian justifications for keeping women subordinate to

Sarah and Angelina Grimke

men, they became symbols of the deep connection between the fight against slavery and for women's rights.

Another influential writer was the American transcendentalist Margaret Fuller, whose "Woman in the 19th Century," published in 1845, was the first significant book to take the side of women's rights since Wollstonecraft's half a century earlier. In the book Fuller issued several important critiques of the role of women in society. She connected the servitude of women with that of slaves and believed, as was common among abolitionists, that this was a sin that held down the soul of the oppressor as well. She blasted the stifled lives of little girls and marriage as an institution in which women give up all rights and literally belonged to their husbands.[3]

These ideas were on the minds of mid-century reformers who sought to bring the American promise of equality to those who were denied. The causes of abolition, women's rights and later suffrage were deeply intertwined. Conventions, public speeches, publications and petitions were the tactics of the movements' mainstream.

THE BATTLE FOR ABOLITION

The anti-slavery movement began to gain strength after the Nat Turner rebellion; a slave uprising that took place in Virginia in 1831. Women were prominent in the movement as educators, writers, speakers and participants in the Underground Railroad (the hidden escape routes and safe houses for slaves to flee north and to Canada). Among white women, both factory workers and middle-class housewives gave their support to the cause. The movement was especially infused with sections of evangelical Protestants and Quakers.

Among the leading female abolitionists were Prudence Crandall, a young white Quaker teacher in Connecticut, who taught Black girls despite boycotts, fire bombings and finally her arrest; Lucretia Mott, also a Quaker, who dared to speak out at the American Anti-Slavery Society convention (which excluded women's membership until 1839), and made her home a stop on the Underground Railroad; the Grimke sisters; Frances Harper, a free Black woman from Maryland who was an activist in the abolition, temperance and suffrage movements, helped slaves escape North, and was a founder of the National Association of Colored Women; and Sojourner Truth, a former slave who became a prominent speaker

Harriet Tubman

on abolition, women's suffrage, prison reform and other causes.

Harriet Tubman personified the spirit of struggle and unity that is needed to liberate oppressed people. An escaped slave herself, she repeatedly slipped back into slave territory to conduct successful rescue missions to free friends and family members. She helped John Brown recruit fighters for his raid on Harpers Ferry.[4] She provided intelligence for the Union army, and planned and led a Civil War military raid, the only woman in American history to do so, resulting in the freeing of 750 slaves. In later life she became a committed suffragist. More than 100 years later, a collective of Black lesbian feminists would name itself for the Combahee River, where Tubman led her charge.[5]

Women nearly always occupied subordinate positions within abolitionist organizations until 1832, when they began to form their own associations. The first such group was created by free Black women in Salem, Mass. Women's meetings and public events were frequently met with mob violence.

According to contemporary Black activist Angela Davis, white women who worked in the abolitionist movement, "learned important lessons about their own subjugation." The movement also gave middle-class women the opportunity to achieve important work outside the role of wife and mother. In addition, "they were resisting an oppression which bore a certain resemblance to their own. Furthermore, they learned how to challenge male supremacy within the anti-slavery movement. They discovered that sexism, which seemed unalterable inside their marriages, could be questioned and fought in the arena of political struggle. Yes, white women would be called upon to defend fiercely their rights *as women* in order to fight for the emancipation of Black people."[6]

BEGINNINGS OF THE SUFFRAGE MOVEMENT

In 1848 the first convention for women's rights in U.S. history was held in Seneca Falls, N.Y. The convention was called by Elizabeth Cady Stanton and Lucretia Mott, along with other women who were involved in the abolitionist and temperance movements. Stanton and Mott, active abolitionists, had attended the World Anti-Slavery Convention in London in 1840, where women were excluded from the main hall. Their exclusion inspired them to organize for women's rights when they returned to the United States.

The Seneca Falls Convention produced the Declaration of Sentiments and Resolutions on the Rights of Women, written by Stanton and, paraphrasing the Declaration of Independence, declared that "all men and women are created equal."

The document was revolutionary for its time, calling for women's equality before god and the law; an end to double standards of social behavior; the right to public speech and assembly; the right of married women to their own property and wages (rather than belonging to their husbands); and, for the first time, the right of women to vote. In other words, the right to vote was one part of a larger transformation of social relations and the position of women in society.[7]

The suffrage resolution was controversial and the only one that was not passed unanimously. The outspoken support of Frederick Douglass, former slave and now an abolition leader and editor of the anti-slavery newspaper North Star, was decisive in getting the resolution passed. Among his many statements in support of women was this one: "Right is of no sex and truth is of no color. Women should be elevated to an equal position with man in every relation of life."

The Seneca Falls Convention launched a multi-issue women's rights movement, which began to focus increasingly on suffrage. National conventions were held annually from 1850 until the Civil War (1861-65), during which ending slavery became reformers' primary cause.

It was at a regional convention in Ohio, in 1851, that former slave Sojourner Truth gave her famous "Ain't I a Woman" speech. In answer to the previous speaker, a clergyman who ridiculed women for their weakness and declared they were unfit for the vote, Truth brought the house down:

I have ploughed and planted and gathered into barns, and no man could head me — and ain't I a woman? I could work as much and eat as much — when I could get it — and bear the lash as well! And ain't I a woman? I have born thirteen children, and seen most of 'em sold into slavery, and when I cried out with my mother's grief, none but Jesus heard me — and ain't I a woman?[8]

These conventions were attended by Northern white women and some free Black women, as well as some men. Southern white women did not by and large take part in these movements either for abolition or women's equality.

Among the key players in this growing suffrage movement, three leaders in particular stand out:

- Elizabeth Cady Stanton was an abolitionist who began to work for women's equality after being excluded from the London conference and also because of her own experience of the drudgery and isolation of domestic life and the restrictions it placed on women who wanted to participate in public life. She became a prominent theorist of the suffrage movement and, with Susan B. Anthony, formed a formidable leadership team. A lifelong critic of organized religion, Stanton spent her last years searching for a religion that pronounced men and women equals, and at age 80 published a Women's Bible. In Stanton's view, "The Bible and the Church have been the greatest stumbling blocks in the way of women's emancipation."[9]

- Susan B. Anthony was a Quaker from an abolitionist family near Rochester, N.Y. She was an innovative organizer, who, in 1854, was the first woman to conduct a statewide petition campaign to the New York State legislature. Organizing women from every county, she petitioned for three reforms: control by women of their own earnings, women's custody of children in case of divorce and women's right to vote. Legislators typically responded with laughter, a not uncommon male response to women's demands for equality for years to come, but within four years New York women had secured the right to own property, keep their own wages and sue in court.[10] In 1868 Anthony, along with Stanton, launched a weekly newspaper called The Revolution, which briefly became the voice of the National Women's Suffrage Association. Anthony, who remained single all her life, had this to say about marriage: "I never felt I could give up my life of freedom to become a man's housekeeper. When I was young, if a girl married poor she became a housekeeper and a drudge. If she married wealthy, she became a pet and a doll."[11]

* Lucy Stone was one of the first women in America to earn a college degree (from Oberlin in 1847) and one of the first to earn her living as a lecturer. She was a prominent speaker on abolition and women's rights and played a major role in raising public acceptance of women speaking in public. She was also one of the very first married women to refuse to take her husband's name. Stone was a proponent of the state-by-state strategy for gaining woman suffrage and was the founder and editor of the Woman's Journal, a weekly that supported rights for women. As an elderly woman she declared in 1893, "I think, with never-ending gratitude, that the young women of today do not and can never know at what price their right to free speech and to speak at all in public has been earned." [12]

MAJOR SPLIT OVER MALE-ONLY VOTE AMENDMENT

After the Civil War, the causes of Black freedom and woman suffrage were briefly joined in an organization called American Equal Rights Association (AERA), which sought to establish equal rights, including suffrage for all, irrespective of sex or race.

However splits soon emerged over whose rights would be granted first, Black men or women, and whose would take priority. There were those of course who saw no need to choose: why not give equal citizenship rights, and the franchise, to both? As Eleanor Flexner wrote in her extremely important history, "Century of Struggle," "Those who held out for linking the two issues of Negro and woman suffrage believed in all sincerity that they would help, not harm, each other."[13]

In 1866 the proposed 14th Amendment, which endowed citizenship rights regardless of race and called for equal protection under the law, inserted the word "male" into the Constitution for the first time in Section 2 dealing with reducing the representation of states that restricted the right to vote to its "male inhabitants." By implication the Amendment called into question the citizenship of women. Fearing that woman suffrage would now face an even steeper uphill battle, leaders fought unsuccessfully to have the word removed.

The rift deepened with the proposal and passage of the 15th Amendment, which said suffrage was not to be denied on account of "race, color or previous condition of servitude." It did not mention sex or gender.

The American Equal Rights Association split into two organizations over whether to support or oppose the Fifteenth Amendment.

Stanton, Anthony, Lucretia Mott and others opposed the 15th Amendment, forming the National Women's Suffrage Association (NWSA) in 1869.

The NWSA expressed anger at the perceived betrayal by abolitionists and Republicans who did not fight for women's suffrage, or had shelved it for a later date on the grounds that this was "the Negro's hour" and combining the two issues would doom the Fifteenth Amendment's passage. They feared that if reformers held out for both Black and woman suffrage, they would get neither.

Those women who felt betrayed by the Radical Republicans and the 15th Amendment believed that they had earned the support of the abolitionists. Women's groups had supported the Union army, Black emancipation and Reconstruction. But they were also a minority voice in this debate and women's suffrage did not yet have a critical mass of support.

At this critical moment of national struggle, Stanton and NWSA leaders, almost all of whom had previously been abolitionists, resorted to vile and racist arguments against Black male suffrage. They also used condescending language about male immigrants, as undeserving of the vote compared to educated white women. To slow and obstruct the Fifteenth Amendment, many top NWSA leaders entered into an alliance with the most hated white supremacist figures of the Democratic Party.

They began to use the same talking points about defending virtuous white women from "degraded" Black men, and some Southern Democrats began to champion woman's suffrage to offset the Black vote. This was the height of opportunism, and surely the lowest moment of the nineteenth century women's rights movement.

On the other side of the debate stood Lucy Stone, Frances Harper, Julia Ward Howe and others who founded the American Women's Suffrage Association (AWSA). They supported the passage of the 15th Amendment in its finished form as a critical step to consolidate the victory of abolition, build Black political power in the South and prevent the slavocracy from returning to power. This group initially believed that the divide and conquer tactics of the ruling class could be overcome and that a new amendment could get through that championed universal suffrage, regardless of race or sex.

Frederick Douglass also broke with Stanton and Anthony over the position of NWSA on the Black male vote. A staunch advocate of woman suffrage, he supported the 15th Amendment and asked women to wait: "When women, because they are women, are dragged from their homes and hung upon lamp-posts; when their children are torn from their arms and their brains dashed to the pavement; when they are objects of insult and outrage at every turn; when they are in danger of having their homes burnt down over their heads; when their children are not allowed to enter schools; then they will have an urgency to obtain the ballot. ...[I]t is true of the [B]lack woman, but not because she is a woman, but because she is [B]lack."[14]

For Black women, sometimes this moment is framed as a choice between their race and their sex. This is not the best framing of the question. The entire historical conjuncture was defined by the struggle against slavery and how the South, and the country, would be reconstructed after the Civil War. Would the formerly enslaved people be subjugated by their former masters in new form or would there be a political revolution to overturn the old power? The passage of the Fifteenth Amendment affirmed, at least for a time, the defeat of the slave masters and helped trigger a mass upsurge in participatory democracy in the South. The defeat or delay of this Amendment would have, by contrast, ratified Klan terror and counterrevolution. For most Black women at this historical moment, there was no question where they stood.[15]

This is not to say there was complete unity. Sojourner Truth, for instance, was more critical of the Fifteenth Amendment, worrying that reformers would subsequently forget the struggle of women. Nonetheless, she spoke, "I am glad to see that men are getting their rights, but I want women to get theirs, and while the water

Sojourner Truth

is stirring, I will step into the pool." Truth attempted to register and vote in the 1872 election, an act for which hundreds of women (including Anthony and Stanton) were arrested or fined.

Other political and tactical differences emerged between the two wings of the movement. The NWSA became the wing of the suffrage movement that included working-class, largely white, women and also promoted the right to divorce and reproductive freedom. Having opposed the ratification of the 15th Amendment, the NWSA advocated for a Sixteenth Amendment that would dictate universal suffrage for Black and white, without gender qualification. Later on, the NWSA would go on to organize pickets, hunger strikes and more militant actions.

The AWSA is considered by many analysts to be more conservative because of its singular focus on women's voting rights, to the exclusion of other women's issues, and on building a network of women's groups to carry out state-by-state lobbying with sympathetic male politicians. The AWSA included men, while the NWSA was all-women. However, the tactical differences on federal vs. state strategy, or the AWSA's single-issue orientation are unsubstantial compared to the fact that at a critical moment, one group of white feminists stood on principle for racial equality and another sided with white supremacists.

The two organizations merged two decades later in 1890 to become the National American Woman Suffrage Association (NAWSA), which pursued suffrage on both the state and federal levels. Ultimately the goal of the suffrage movement was universal suffrage as a constitutional right everywhere in the United States

Despite this new unity, the divisions over racism and class politics remained. In 1893 NAWSA passed a resolution that, without actually calling for a literacy requirement for voting, did emphasize the greater degree of literacy among women than among men, among white women than Black men and among U.S.-born women than immigrant men. Discussions within NAWSA of literacy and property qualifications continued into the new century.[16] NAWSA was also officially silent on lynching in the 1890s. All of this has been rightly understood as thinly veiled, coded appeals to the Jim Crow politicians who controlled the South and a substantial federal voting bloc.

The 19th Amendment, known as the Susan B. Anthony Amendment, was introduced in 1878. The Amendment states: "The right of citizens of the United States to vote shall not be denied or abridged by the United States or by any State on account of sex. Congress shall have power to enforce this article by appropriate legislation." It was not ratified until 1920.

The splits in the suffrage movement that began after the Civil War continued to be a thread in the women's movement until suffrage was won and beyond.

A trend of opportunism was particularly strong among the movement's middle- and upper-class white leadership. This is not unique to the women's movement, but has been a challenge to every reform movement under capitalism. At various political junctures, when the movement begins to achieve a critical mass, one section of the ruling class inevitably presents itself as a potential ally to achieve the reform in exchange for the movement adopting some reactionary program that comes at the expense of other communities and struggles.

The U.S. political order, organized around white supremacy and the needs of capital, at various times offered a hand to the women's movement on those terms, and at many moments the women's movement adapted itself in order to retain a relationship with power.

Later manifestations of the women's movement, with a revolutionary and working class orientation, would be able to exploit contradictions among the elite without compromising the politics of liberation.

On account of these contradictions within the women's movement, as well as the changing socio-economic environment, at the turn of the twentieth century, the ideological lines began to shift, now divided along class lines and also in terms of tactics.

WORKING WOMEN AND THE EARLY LABOR MOVEMENT

The nineteenth century saw women's entry into the paid labor force in large numbers. In 1800 very few jobs were open to women.

This despite the fact that more and more people were moving to cities from the farm and many single or widowed women had no wage earning man to support them. The non-agricultural jobs open to women in 1800 were limited to teachers, nurses and domestic servants.

Rural white women worked on farms, on their own or as paid laborers. They also sold food and crafts produced at home in the local marketplace. After the Civil War African American women worked largely as share croppers and in domestic service, in the North as well as the South. Increasing numbers went into the factories only decades later during World War I.[17]

As industrialization increased in the North, women went into the textile, garment, cigar and printing factories. By 1850 women constituted 24 percent of the manufacturing labor force, and their numbers rose in the next decade from 225,000 to 323,000.[18] Other women were employed as nurses, domestic servants and as teachers, whose wages were lower than those of factory workers.

The 1880s and 1890s saw major industrial growth. By 1890 women were 17 percent of the total labor force. Four million women were employed in 1890: one million were household servants, and nearly 700,000 were working in the manufacture and cleaning of clothing and textiles. Cheap labor was plentiful and in high demand, with immigrants and women filling the lowest paying jobs. Where women were employed in the same occupations as men, their wages were less than half of men's. The wages of African American and immigrant women were even lower than those of white American women.[19]

The national labor movement began to build in the 1880s.[20] The first union of working women had been created in the 1830s in the textile mills of Lowell, Mass. According to an AFL-CIO historical account, "For the young women from around New England who made the mills run, they were a living hell." After a wage cut in 1834, the millworkers went on strike, organizing several mills, rallying, and conducting a petition campaign. The bosses won, and would again in 1836. The "mill girls," as they were called, organized chapters of workers throughout Massachusetts and New Hampshire, and campaigned successfully, even without the vote, against an anti-worker state representative. Finally in 1847 New Hampshire became the first state to legislate the 10-hour day.

PHOTO: LEWIS WICKES HINE

Addie Card, reportedly 10- or 12-years-old, at the North Pormal Cotton Mill in Vermont. She started working during school vacation in 1910 and 'decided to stay.'

Although the law was not enforceable, this struggle marked the beginning of working women's organized fightback in the United States. One of the workers was quoted as saying of her sister workers, "They have at last learnt the lesson which a bitter experience teaches, not to those who style themselves their 'natural protectors' are they to look for the needful help, but to the strong and resolute of their own sex." [21] The working women often lived communally in boarding houses where they could share grievances and strategize for action.

In addition to trade unions, Working Women's Associations, one of which was organized by Susan B. Anthony,[22] welcomed all women who worked for a living, and Protective Associations helped working women with legal aid and other social welfare problems. Another organization was the National Labor Union, a loose association of unions founded in 1866 by William Sylvis, a radical president of the Iron molders Union, who was supportive of working women's rights and equality.[23]

Anthony and Stanton helped organize the Women's Typographical Union, Local #1 in 1869. In Anthony's words: "I think the girl who is able to earn her own living and pay her own way should be as happy as anybody on Earth. The sense of independence and security is very sweet."[24]

Although the women's local supported the male workers and initially had the support of the male leaders of the national union, in time they found the male membership unsupportive of women's needs and demands. The women's local ceased to exist in 1878. Thereafter women could join men's locals in this and other industries, and depended on the good will of their union brothers to take seriously the special problems of working women. This good will was only sporadically in evidence in union after union.[25]

The first unions to admit women as members alongside men were the cigar makers in 1867 and printers in 1869.[26]

The Daughters of St. Crispin (named after a shoemaker) formed in 1869 by shoe stitchers in Lynn, Mass. It was the first national union of women, and called for equal pay for equal work. The depression of the 1870s caused the demise of this and other unions, and the labor movement suffered a decline until the 1880s.[27]

Technology, even at a low level, affected the nature of work, and when it was not under the control of workers, it threatened their

Workers at a cotton mill in Indianapolis, Ind., 1908

PHOTO: LEWIS WICKES HINE

jobs. From 1863-1869, members of the Collar Laundry Union in Troy, N.Y., grew in numbers and power. They conducted successful strikes, won higher wages, set up a system of cooperative laundries and even shared their own resources with striking iron workers. Then in 1869, paper collars came onto the market, the women's jobs were lost and their union was dissolved.

African American working women in the South organized around domestic work. One of their most prominent labor actions was the formation of the Atlanta Washing Society.[28]

In the 1880s, 98 percent of Atlanta's Black working women were household workers, many of whom began working as young as 10-years-old, with more working as laundresses than in any other type of domestic work. Atlanta had more laundresses than male laborers.[29]

In 1881, 20 laundresses formed a trade organization, the Washing Society. They went on strike seeking higher pay, respect and autonomy over their work. They canvassed door-to-door to build their numbers, and included white laundresses in "an extraordinary sign of interracial solidarity for the time." They grew from 20 to 3,000 strikers in just three weeks. Despite arrests and fines, the women won some of their demands, including the right to control their industry. They also set an example for other domestic workers who began agitating, organizing and striking.[30]

It should not be lost on today's activists that despite more than 135 years of struggle since then — and even some victories — domestic workers, many of whom are immigrants, are continuing to fight for these same rights to this day. (See Chapter 10.)

Labor organizing grew across industries. The Knights of Labor, a formerly secret fraternal organization, began organizing men and women workers in 1881, calling for the 8-hour day and an end to child and convict labor. By 1886, 113 women's assemblies were formed within the order nationwide. Shoe stitchers and collar workers joined up, along with knitters, pencil makers, cabinet makers, housekeepers, farmers and many other occupations.[31]

The best known woman labor agitator of this period was Mary Harris (Mother) Jones, who worked for a time with the Knights of Labor before making her name as an organizer with the United Mine Workers, where she brought miners into the union, organized brigades of women to keep scabs away from the mines, pulled together

PHOTO: PIERCE AND JONES

Mary Harris 'Mother' Jones with children and adults beginning their
'Children's Crusade' walk from Philadelphia to Oyster Bay, New York,
to publicize the conditions of children working in textile mills, 1903.

marches by women in support of their striking family members, and led marches of child workers to the homes of wealthy capitalists and politicians. Mother Jones, a member of the Socialist Party, was not a supporter of women's suffrage, believing that the vote did not help male workers gain their rights, and that voting made one complicit with the class that was oppressing workers. "You don't need a vote to raise hell," she said.[32]

During the depression years of the 1890s women continued to organize both independent unions and locals of the American Federation of Labor (AFL) which consisted mostly of craft unions with well-paid workers. Although the AFL hired a woman organizer for a brief term in 1892, the federation was not interested in its early years in women workers, who were mostly low-paid and unskilled.

The women of the suffrage movement also paid attention to labor struggles, with varying politics. For example, Anthony and Stanton's paper The Revolution reported on the progress of women in the workplace and called for an end to wage discrimination, for equal pay for equal work and for a federal suffrage amendment. The paper's motto was "Men, their rights and nothing more; women, their rights and nothing less."[33]

Anthony's single minded focus on suffrage and sexism got in the way of her ability to recruit working-class women to the cause. Her solidarity did not always extend to all workers; as part of breaking down gender barriers to certain workplaces, she was not against women workers replacing male strikers as scabs.[34]

Women's unions lacked the resources to survive during hard times. It was not until the turn of the century that they would attract support from the middle-class women who were supporting the suffrage movement.[35]

The movement of working women had its contradictions. The workers themselves did not necessarily see themselves as feminists or fighters for women's liberation and equality. There were those, even in the leadership of women workers, who believed women's place was in the home, and that working for wages was to be done only in case of economic necessity. At the same time, women had few illusions about the ability of marriage to solve their economic problems.[36]

WOMEN'S INVOLVEMENT IN OTHER SOCIAL ISSUES

By the mid-1800s, thanks to women's activism, laws were passed in most states that allowed married women to hold property. Women's educational prospects improved at this time as well, with more women gaining entry to higher education and the professions. Women conducted campaigns using petitions, speeches, pamphlets, and the beginnings of lobbying legislatures for women's rights legislation.[37] Education was a notable area of Black-white solidarity, where Black and white women joined together in literacy campaigns in the post-war South and established classes for Black women and children.[38]

The movement for reproductive freedom began to gain traction in the late 1800s, out of necessity. Birth control and abortion had been legal in the United States until a Victorian-era social purity movement, under the guise of attacking vice and prostitution, organized against contraception, leading to the 1873 "Comstock Act," which prohibited distribution of birth control and information about it, including through the mail.

Historically, knowledge of contraception and abortion had rested with midwives, in a tradition that goes back to ancient times in China, Africa and the Middle East. The influence of conservative Christianity turned this knowledge into acts of sin. Under slavery, African American women had used birth control, and even infanticide as a form of resistance.[39]

Along with criminalizing birth control came the takeover of women's health care, including all decisions about their reproductive lives, by backward politicians and the male-dominated medical profession. It would take a militant women's movement to get it back.

THE WOMEN'S CLUB MOVEMENT

At mid-century, and especially after the Civil War, women's clubs grew among middle class white women. Technological advances freed them from some of the burdens of housework — although in some cases it simply raised expectations for what a women was supposed to be able to do in a day's work — and the influx of unskilled immigrant women provided a source of labor for this domestic work. With time, money and increasing access to education, these women turned to clubs for their own self-improvement, as well as a way of taking on the social concerns of the day. Some clubs, such as Sorosis, were formed in response to women's exclusion from professional organizations.

Beginning in the 1890s, social reformers such as Jane Addams founded settlement houses in Chicago, New York and other cities, to help ease the lives of poor immigrant families. The settlements provided services related to child welfare, education, community health and recreation. Jane Addams and others were also active in the suffrage and pacifist movements. Other middle- and upper- class women who directed and volunteered in these settlement programs cannot be said to represent the feminist movement of the time, but they did demonstrate women's increasing role in public life and in the social movements of the day.

Women's clubs spread throughout the nation, leading to the formation of the General Federation of Women's Clubs (GFWC) in 1890, with state federations following soon after. Membership reached over 20,000 in just two years and peaked at 850,000 in the 1950s. In the South, the clubs helped push women whose former lives had been

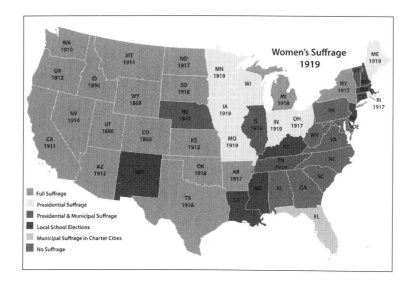

Women's Suffrage 1919

- Full Suffrage
- Presidential Suffrage
- Presidential & Municipal Suffrage
- Local School Elections
- Municipal Suffrage in Charter Cities
- No Suffrage

narrowly defined by the slavocracy into the larger world, with broader perspectives and new experiences.[40]

The clubs were not activist organizations *per se* nor did they provide revolutionary, working-class or feminist ideology to their members. However, the clubs shook up social relations. Membership in them gave women experience in leadership, travel and organization, an education in social problems, and exposure to new people, ideas and activities. Many who later became activists in the women's movement got their start in the clubs.

Some clubs were multi-issue, while others focused on one area of interest. Sorosis members were concerned with issues ranging from infant mortality to women's access to higher education. The New England Women's Club, co-founded by Julia Ward Howe, provided a social outlet for educated women. The YWCA focused its attention on young women in the work force who were away from home for the first time.

The biggest and most influential club movement was centered on temperance — to reduce the consumption of alcohol. Those who organized for temperance were only partly standing on moral grounds. Excessive drinking was a plague to many families, with the head of the household drinking up the family's earnings and beating his wife and children. Because married women were considered appendages of their husbands, with no rights of their own, they had no legal recourse against violations at the hands of their men. Hence the movement for temperance, and ultimately prohibition, was strong.

In the 1870s, the Women's Christian Temperance Union became a formidable multi-issue organization under the leadership of Frances Willard and the largest women's organization in the country. Willard's motto, "Do Everything," brought women into all areas of social reform: kindergartens, prisons, public health, prostitution, the eight-hour day — and suffrage. This helped bring legitimacy to the suffrage issue to women who had held back from political activism. Lucretia Mott, Lucy Stone and other important suffrage leaders got their political start not only in the abolition movement but also in the temperance movement. Not surprisingly, as the suffrage movement grew, among its most ardent opponents were the liquor interests.[41]

While not a women's organization, the Grange — an advocacy organization for farmers — had the most advanced position on equality for women of any large national organization. In addition to helping farmers to recover from the Civil War, they developed social and educational programs.

BLACK WOMEN AND THE CLUB MOVEMENT

These organizations were almost entirely white, reflecting the continued segregation of the races not only in the postwar South but also in the North. The General Federation of Women's Clubs itself was all white until after World War I.[42] Flexner notes that the exclusion of Black women from white women's clubs "continued to arise each time Negro women attempted to take their place beside white women for the achievement of their common aims."[43]

Free Black women's clubs had long existed in both the North and South. Some secret societies had existed even under slavery. Before the Civil War, Black women organized around abolition, in some cases working with white women, as well as charitable work and literary societies.

After the Civil War these clubs, which were led by middle-class women, included workers, tenant farmers and poor women in their membership. Toward the end of the century, in response to mass lynchings, the increasing sexual abuse of Black women and Black women's exclusion from the GFWC, Black women's clubs grew in number. They concerned themselves with community improvement, race pride, the fight for equal accommodation on railroads, and integration in community and national organizations. They organized services for the poor and for Black soldiers. The clubs also provided strong leadership in the fight against lynching.[44]

In 1896, a federation was formed called the National Association of Colored Women's Clubs, which played a major role in the struggle for Black women's suffrage, fighting against the racism within the suffrage movement, and fighting against lynching and Jim Crow laws. The National Association built on the leadership and examples of Ida B. Wells and Josephine St. Pierre Ruffin.

Wells, born into a family of ex-slaves, was a pioneering journalist whose groundbreaking exposés of lynching brought her international fame, placed lynching on the agenda of progressives and anti-racists in the United States and Great Britain, and earned her the ire — and violence — of the white establishment.

According to Angela Davis, "In her protracted crusade against lynching, Ida B. Wells had become an expert at agitation-confrontation tactics."[45] In one of her many exhortations against lynching, Wells wrote: "Our country's national crime is lynching. It is not the creature of an hour, the sudden outburst of uncontrolled fury, or the unspeakable brutality of an insane mob."[46]

Ruffin, an educated and affluent suffragist, editor and clubwoman, had been denied entry to a GFWC convention. Addressing the white women who would exclude Black women from their clubs, she spoke at the First National Conference of Colored Women: "Our woman's movement is [a] woman's movement in that it is led and directed by women for the good of women and men, for the benefit of *all* humanity, which is more than any one branch or section of it. We... ask the active interest of our men, and too, we are not drawing the color line; we are women, American women, as intensely interested in all that pertains to us as such as all other American women; we

Ida B. Wells

are. ...willing to join any others in the same work and cordially invit-
ing and welcoming any others to join in."[47] Ruffin would go on to be
a founder of the NAACP as well.

Mary Church Terrell served as the association's first president.
Terrell, who came from a family of former slaves, was one of the first
Black women to graduate from college and became a famous writer
and speaker on Black equality, women's suffrage and workers' rights.[48]

Looking over the course of the nineteenth century, one sees
that the whole spectrum of women's identity and women's rights
burst into public view as new forms of struggle and thought took
hold. Women's movements and organizers interacted with the issues
of slavery, racism, suffrage and labor, generating new ideas about the
social good and new forms of activism to accomplish them.

The questions that interested, united and also divided women
in the nineteenth century continued as concerns of the women's
movement up to the present time: How does the liberation of women
relate to the struggle against racism and the emancipation of the
working class? To what extent are men allies or enemies of the
women's struggles for autonomy and equality, and to what extent do
women need male allies? Where is the balance between individual
and collective struggles and victories? These questions would come
up again and again, as alliances and rivalries shifted, the women's
movement grew, and clear ideological trends began to take shape. ☐

Chapter 5
Suffrage and social justice: 1900-1940

THE early years of the 20th century saw political struggle in all areas of American life. The explosive growth of industrial monopoly capitalism of the late 19th century structured all the major changes of the era — urbanization, proletarianization, extreme inequality and instability, record immigration and the dawn of U.S. imperialism stretching overseas. All of society looked out at a world that appeared to be in perpetual flux and crisis, rapidly transforming how people lived, worked and interacted.

For women, the upending of tradition and new modes of social organization created new forms of exploitation and oppression, as well as openings for struggle and independence. From 1900 to the beginning of World War II, women fought for equality in all political and social arenas, playing a prominent role in the increasingly militant labor movement, the anti-World War I peace movement, changes in family relations and control over fertility, and the development of the socialist and communist movements in the United States.

THE STRUGGLE FOR SUFFRAGE

As of 1900, only four states, Wyoming, Utah, Idaho and Colorado, had legalized women's suffrage. From 1896 to 1910 no new states were won, and nationally the movement was in a rut. Susan B. Anthony's death in 1906 created a leadership vacuum at the national level, and movement activities languished in repetitive meetings and petitions.

During this time, the British suffrage movement under the leadership of Emmeline Pankhurst, began to engage in militant direct action that provoked violent police repression and imprisonment. Incarcerated suffragists demanded to be treated as political prisoners. Several went on well-publicized hunger strikes and suffered brutal forced feedings.

At one rally, Pankhurst noted: "Window-breaking, when English men do it, is regarded as honest expression of political opinion. Window-breaking, when English women do it, is treated as a crime."

Inspired by the British movement, Harriot Blatch, a journalist and daughter of Elizabeth Cady Stanton, founded the Equality League of Self-Supporting Women in 1907 in New York City. The League held mass meetings and outdoor parades and developed detailed membership files based on political districts in order to conduct targeted lobbying of politicians. Blatch wrote, "We all believed that suffrage propaganda must be made dramatic, that suffrage workers must be politically minded."[1]

The League brought working women and labor unions into the cause. Blatch and her allies "saw the need of drawing industrial women into the suffrage campaign and recognized that these women needed to be brought in contact, not with women of leisure, but with business and professional women who were also out in the world earning their living." At an Albany hearing on women's suffrage, the League invited working women to speak. Said one: "We working women are often told that we should stay at home and then everything would be all right. But we can't stay at home. We have to get out and work. ... Bosses think, and women come to think themselves, that they don't count for so much as men."[2] In 1910 the League came to be called the Women's Political Union.

Another suffrage leader who was inspired by the British movement was Carrie Chapman Catt, who in 1909 pulled together a coalition of New York suffrage groups into the Women Suffrage Party, which brought out large numbers of suffragists to put pressure on Tammany Hall, the New York City and state Democratic machine.

There were both victories and problems at the state level. Activists in Eastern states emulated the League's tactics and received support from the Suffrage Party. They held parades, trolley tours and car caravans of small towns, and descended upon state legislatures to demand the vote. On the West Coast, suffragists revived their state-by-state efforts and won the vote in Washington in 1910 and California in 1911, in a close vote that was decided by rural precincts and small towns.

However the South was almost solidly opposed, as were the manufacturing states of the Northeast. Election fraud stole the vote in Michigan. In Wisconsin and Ohio the liquor interests defeated suffrage, and in Illinois the governor refused to hold a vote.

Another problem with winning the vote at the state or local level was that newly enfranchised women became beholden to political parties, which could then omit suffrage from their parties' national platforms.

As of 1914, while suffrage was gradually won in some individual states, the federal suffrage amendment, which was introduced in Congress in 1878, had not been debated in the Senate since 1887 and had never reached the House floor.

It was Alice Paul who breathed new life into the movement for a constitutional suffrage amendment. Paul herself was a veteran of the British suffrage movement, where she spent time in prison and was subjected to forced-feeding while on a hunger strike. Returning to the United States in 1910, Paul teamed up with Lucy Burns, another militant suffragist who had worked with the British movement, and began efforts to pass a constitutional amendment.

In 1913, Paul and Burns organized, on behalf of NAWSA, the first successful national march down Pennsylvania Avenue in the District of Columbia, drawing some 8,000 women.[3] The march was planned for the day before Woodrow Wilson's inauguration to ensure maximum crowds on the streets.

Alice Paul sewing a suffrage flag

However hostile spectators rushed and attacked the marchers, causing a near riot that eventually cost the police chief his job. Newspapers reported on the fearless suffragists marching on through chaos. One report described a line of women students who "locked arms and formed a crowd-breaking vanguard." The story went on: "The parade itself, in spite of the delays, was a great success. Passing through two walls of antagonistic humanity, the marchers, for the most part, kept their tempers. They suffered insult, and closed their ears to jibes and jeers. Few faltered, though some of the older women were forced to drop out from time to time."[4]

Suffragist parade, 1917

The march not only suffered attacks from outside but also dissension from within. Although NAWSA had welcomed all women to the march, organizers tried to segregate it, in order not to upset Southern participants, having Black women march at the rear, after the men's contingent. Protests erupted among participants, and Black and white women ultimately marched together with their state contingents. Ida B. Wells was among those who refused to give in to segregation and marched with the Chicago delegation.[5]

Racist division had remained a critical weakness within the suffrage movement since the passage of the Fifteenth Amendment. The NAWSA convention of 1903 in New Orleans heard explicit proposals for property and educational qualifications for suffrage in order to maintain white supremacy.[6] The National Association of Colored Women's Clubs, which had its own suffrage department, was excluded from the NAWSA, and even as late as 1919, the application of the Black Northeastern Federation of Clubs for membership in NAWSA was rejected.

Despite their exclusion, many Black women remained committed to the cause of suffrage. Among the most prominent were Ida B. Wells, Mary Church Terrell and Mary McLeod Bethune.[7] [See Appendix 5 for biographies of Wells, Terrell and Bethune.]

Even after women's suffrage was achieved at the federal level, most clubs remained segregated, reflecting Jim Crow and the racial divisions that existed throughout society.

Separately, white and African American women built strong organizations that survived to support the women's movement that emerged decades later. Women's organizations also existed among Asian immigrant groups, and Latinas and Native American women organized within their own communities.[8]

Combatting the terror of lynching brought Black and white women's clubs together, under the leadership of Black women. Public crusades against lynching began with the exposes written by Ida B. Wells beginning in 1895 and were taken up by Black women's clubs. It became a national issue only with the formation in 1910 of the NAACP, which publicized facts and lobbied for legislation.[9] A new study published by the Equal Justice Initiative in February 2015 documents 4,000 lynchings of men, women and children between 1877 and 1950 — at least 700 more than were previously documented.[10]

The Association of Southern Women for the Prevention of Lynching, which was formed in 1930 by white women, worked to change public opinion in the South, especially the justification that lynchings were done to defend the honor of white women. They created a pledge to "create a new public opinion," which received 40,000 signatures, and also acted locally to stop lynchings. They stopped short of supporting an anti-lynching bill before Congress, however.[11] No federal anti-lynching law was ever passed.

The question of racism, both within the movement and outside of it, and the question of how to organize women of different backgrounds, emerged again as a primary question 50 years later during the Second Wave of feminism, in which there were integrated groups, majority white groups with Black caucuses, and separate white and Black groups. All were part of the surge of activism toward justice for women, but these considerable differences in strategies, tactics, and even goals — which were inevitable given the vast differences in women's lived experiences and class positions — gave the women's movement a broad and decentralized character.

THE COMPLEX ROAD TO THE 19TH AMENDMENT

Rallies, petitions and marches continued in 1914 and 1915, when the suffrage amendment was finally voted on in both houses of Congress. It was defeated.

Catt and Paul continued to fight for the amendment but differed strongly on tactics, on support for Wilson's 1916 re-election campaign and on support for World War I. Here again, the pull of opportunism became a central feature in the movement. Catt's forces joined the war effort in order to raise their political standing with those who would ultimately vote on suffrage. They built a centralized national organization that prepared states to secure ratification of the amendment once it was approved by Congress.

The women's movement was not the only one to split under the pressure — and perceived opportunities — of the war. The same process took place in the labor movement, with the AFL leadership supporting the war mobilization against the Industrial Workers of the World. In the socialist movement, the more radical forces around Eugene Debs bitterly opposed the war, while the reformists and social-imperialists supported it. Within the Black struggle, W.E.B. DuBois urged Black Americans to "close ranks," support the war, and prove their patriotism to win allies in the struggle against Jim Crow. DuBois would ultimately repudiate his earlier position, accepting the anti-war stance of his critics within the Black community.

In the women's movement, Paul's forces held the Democratic Party responsible for Woodrow Wilson's failure to endorse woman suffrage. She argued: "We women of America tell you that America is not a democracy. Twenty million women are denied the right to vote.

"They campaigned against Democratic candidates for Congress — even those who were pro-suffrage — and opposed Wilson's reelection in 1916."[12] Forming the National Woman's Party (NWP) in 1917, they held pro-suffrage silent vigils and picket lines outside the White House, for the first time in history, and publicly opposed the war, which the United States had entered in April of that year. Their anti-war stance provoked hostility, violence and arrests.

According to Flexner, "Too much emphasis has been put... on the merits of the picketing — its aid or harm in winning votes for women — and too little on the fact that the pickets were actually among the earliest victims in this country of the abrogation of civil liberties in wartime." The arrests, which began in June 1917, were confined to the demonstrators, who were never charged with disturbing the peace. No one who physically attacked the demonstrators was arrested. The women were imprisoned under terrible conditions. Like their British sisters, the suffragists protested the illegality and brutality of their arrests with hunger strikes, and the authorities responded with forced feeding.[13] They narrowly escaped being charged under the Espionage and Sedition Acts — probably because they filled their banners with noble-sounding quotes from President Wilson.

Despite the NWP's cruel treatment, rival suffragist groups never came to their aid, and publicly disavowed their tactics instead of condemning the arrests. Much of the public, however, was outraged at the injustice, and the women were finally released in November, with all charges dropped four months later.

The war brought women in large numbers into the workplace and public life and also gave the suffrage movement a propaganda point. With women taking on social and workplace responsibility during the war that was being fought for democracy, how could this democracy exclude women?[14]

In addition to suffrage activists, there were other political forces in favor of the woman's vote. The Socialist Party, founded in 1901 and with union leader Eugene V. Debs as its standard bearer, favored women's suffrage from the beginning and included women as candidates and in party leadership positions.

Miss Doris Stevens, the youngest member of the national executive committee of the National Woman's Party, was arrested and sentenced to 60 days in 1917.

The middle-class "Progressive" movement (which was politically diverse, and took both right-wing and left-wing forms) influenced people's thinking on many social issues and brought more women into political activity. Theodore Roosevelt's Progressive Party included women's suffrage in its 1912 party platform, helping to bring the suffrage issue out of the states and into the national political arena.

Each major party, Democratic and Republican, was split on suffrage and neither included the issue on its national platform. International developments, however, had just begun to exert influence on the U.S. situation: Soviet women were granted suffrage and many other rights immediately after Russia's communist-led revolution in

Women working in weapons manufacturing plant in World War I, Cambridge, Mass.

1917. British women won theirs in 1918. This proved an embarrass-ment to many in the U.S. ruling class who portrayed the country as a beacon of democracy.

The forces arrayed against suffrage were not only an expression of anti-woman sentiment on the part of sexist men. The well-oiled political machines of both parties, fueled by corruption and kickbacks saw the women's vote as a destabilizing factor that could threaten their privileges and operations.

One industry that had much to lose was the large alcohol busi-ness, which was a target of the women-led temperance movement. Other industries that strongly opposed woman suffrage were the rail-roads, oil interests and manufacturing, where bosses and investors feared being forced to pay women a fair wage and prevented from exploiting child labor. Many prominent upper-class women were also in the opposition, on behalf of their family and class interests.

The South was solidly anti-suffrage, arguing for state's rights — a reactionary anti-federalist slogan that sought to hold back this push for a centrally mandated advance in civil rights, which would disrupt the Jim Crow system of white supremacy.

In order to gain favor with potential Southern allies, some members of national suffrage groups engaged in a "Southern strategy." Their proposal was to allow the vote for educated women only — a clear attempt to appeal to white supremacy, as Black women were almost entirely denied access to educational institutions. They periodically tried to exclude Black suffragists from participation in conventions and marches, as in the 1913 march in Washington, D.C. There was also a current of suffragist leaders who tried to exclude poor immigrants from the franchise.[15]

Ten years after it was submitted, Congress finally voted in favor of a woman suffrage amendment in January 1918, one day after President Wilson himself at last declared his support. Four Congressmen dragged themselves out of sick beds to vote for suffrage. After being ratified by 36 states, the 19th Amendment was certified on August 26, 1920, 53 years after the first state suffrage referendum in 1867. The amendment reads, "The right of citizens of the United States to vote shall not be denied or abridged by the United States or by any State on account of sex." Susan B. Anthony wrote the original words.

For Black women in the South, the 19th Amendment was — like the 14th and 15th Amendments —largely a dead letter. Since the onset of Jim Crow laws in the 1880s, literacy and other tests, as well as poll taxes and "grandfather clauses," obstructed and largely eliminated Black voting in large sections of the South. Where these racist laws were not sufficient, Ku Klux Klan violence and stonewalling by election officials kept a great many Black people from voting. It took until the Black-led civil rights movement created the conditions for passage of the federal Voting Rights Act of 1965 that many of these roadblocks to voting were torn down. Even today with voter identification impediments, voting rights are being challenged by the right wing, with support from the conservative Supreme Court.[16]

While the vote did not bring an end to gender discrimination, any more than it erased racial and class inequality, it was a major step in the direction towards equality under the law. It was attained through struggle, not given out of the charitable feelings of the elite. In fact, the women of this first wave of feminism were scorned, ridiculed, and subjected to repression. Their tenacity, bravery and ingenuity set a high standard for the generations that followed.

Obtaining female suffrage was the culmination of the First Wave of the woman's fight for equality in the United States. It took more than 40 years for the Second Wave to get started, but that did not mean that feminism and fighters for women's rights simply disappeared.

WOMEN AND WORK

After passage of the 19th Amendment, women continued to challenge sexism in family and social life, and in popular culture. Women activists were also a political force in several ground-breaking social movements. Until the mass uprisings of the 1960s and 1970s, no single women's issue gained the same public prominence as suffrage, but women were in motion nonetheless.

Labor historian Dorothy Sue Cobble expressed the importance of women's activism after the First Wave:

> All too often chroniclers of women's reform define feminist activism narrowly and assume that all-female organizations dedicated only to sex equality are the prime bearers of the feminist impulse. From this perspective the 50 years following women's suffrage in 1920 appear as a retreat for women's rights, with a dwindling band of white middle-class feminists making minimal headway in a society largely dismissive of women's issues. Expanding the definition of feminism and of women's movements to include working-class and minority feminists rewrites this standard story.

> Instead of decline, we see a robust and diverse of group of feminists in mixed-sex organizations making considerable progress. Feminism and feminist activism did not diminish in the decades after suffrage: rather, from the 1930s to the 1960s, the struggle for the rights of low-income women and women of color surged forward as the labor and civil rights movements gained ground.[17]

Labor feminists wanted equality with men and also special treatment based on the particular needs of women. "Theirs was a vision of equality," Cobble wrote, "that claimed justice on the basis of their humanity, not on the basis of their sameness with men. Where the male standard, or what labor feminists called the 'masculine pattern' did not fit their needs, they rejected it."[18]

The fight for suffrage was also important to the struggle for a living wage and economic independence for women: without political influence, women were destined to continue to suffer economic inequality.[19] Working women's struggles focused above all on the appalling working conditions and low pay endured by women.

The labor requirements of a growing industrial economy, as well as innovations in technology, opened up the workplace for new workers. The desperate need of poor women, including many immigrants, for an income, and families' need for wives' and mothers' wages, drove more and more women into paid employment. In the decade between 1890 and 1900, the number of women in the workforce increased by nearly 33 percent, to 5.3 million. The next 10 years saw another increase to 7.4 million.[20] With this influx of women workers came new needs and demands — for fair working conditions, wages equal to those of men, representation by unions, and recognition of and help with women's "double day" — the full-time unpaid job women did at home after the shift of paid work.

In 1900 the largest cohort of women workers, nearly two million, were clustered in domestic work or service occupations. Some 700,000 worked in agriculture, and about half that number as teachers. More than a million women worked in factories, most of them in garment and textile trades. Women also began to be hired as office workers.

The period between the turn of the century and World War I saw the growth of labor unions comprised mostly of women, with the garment trades producing some of the first of these unions. Sweatshop conditions abounded in this industry, with filthy shops, windows nailed shut, long hours, low pay, deafening noise and harassment on the part of bosses. Locals of the International Ladies Garment Workers Union were born in 1900.[21] Other industries that had significant female union membership included tobacco, shoe making and book binding.[22]

International Women's Day, which is celebrated worldwide each March 8, was also established during this period. Initiated by the American Socialist Party, Women's Day was founded in 1909 to commemorate important strikes by women workers and to serve as a day of solidarity for working women. In calling for political, economic and social rights for women workers, the event lent a clear working-class aspect to the suffrage movement. In 1910 the Second International Conference of Socialist Women in Copenhagen, led by German communist Clara Zetkin, adopted Women's Day as an international holiday.[23] IWD also became a vehicle to protest against World War I. In fact, it was an IWD demonstration led by women workers in St. Petersburg in 1917 that sparked Russia's February Revolution in 1917, and paved the way for the Bolshevik Revolution eight months later.

In an environment when most traditional U.S. unions pushed for higher wages for men as the typical heads of household, many AFL leaders feared that women earners would drive down men's wages, and for the most part excluded women members — even while supporting women's suffrage and some other social reforms that feminists championed. Women workers clearly needed advocates of their own. The Women's Trade Union League (WTUL) served that purpose. Composed of working-class, middle-class and some wealthy women, it was formed in 1903 to help women workers organize into unions and secure better working conditions, to support their efforts financially, and to help them obtain legal advice and publicity for their struggles.

The cross-class women's solidarity at work in the WTUL would show up periodically in the life of the women's movements. Excluded from leadership positions and often membership in traditional labor unions and in the AFL, working women gained leadership experience and took on important responsibilities in the WTUL. WTUL's national program called for the eight-hour day, a fair wage and the elimination of night work. Yet the League received only lukewarm support from the AFL, which balked at the WTUL's primary goal of organizing more women into unions.

The WTUL strongly encouraged working women to fight for suffrage and encouraged the creation of Wage Earners' Suffrage Leagues. One of the League's founders, Leonora O'Reilly, who was a member of the Socialist Party as well as a suffragist, was a champion of working women's right to vote and a fierce critic of what Angela Davis describes as the "cult of motherhood" — the dominant notion that the one calling and purpose of women was to bear and raise children. O'Reilly pushed her working-class sisters to fight for the vote

Women garment workers from the Puritan Underwear Company (ILGWU) participating in the 1916 May Day parade, New York City

and to use the ballot to remove the politicians who were in league with big business.[24]

A public meeting on suffrage at Cooper Union in New York City in 1912 featured a talk by labor organizer Rose Schneiderman, who was also a Socialist Party member and a leader of the WTUL. In answer to a U.S. Senator's charge that women would lose their femininity if they achieved the vote, she said:

> We have women working in the foundries, stripped to the waist, if you please, because of the heat. Yet the senator says nothing about these women losing their charm. They have got to retain their charm and delicacy, and work in the foundries.
>
> Of course you know the reason they are employed in foundries is that they are cheaper and work longer hours

than men. Women in the laundries, for instance, stand for 13 or 14 hours in the terrible steam and heat with their hands in hot starch. Surely these women won't lose any more of their beauty and charm by putting a ballot in a ballot box once a year than they are likely to lose standing in foundries or laundries all year round. There is no harder contest than the contest for bread, let me tell you that.[25]

The AFL excluded unskilled workers, and that included most women and Black workers. On the other hand, the anarcho-syndicalist International Workers of the World (IWW), also called the Wobblies, welcomed women workers, skilled and unskilled workers, and placed no restrictions on race, gender or nationality. Founded in 1905, they rejected the cross-class collaboration of the WTUL as bourgeois. They also rejected independent feminist movements, including the movement for suffrage, declaring that the revolutionary overthrow of capitalism was the order of the day, and the coming reorganization of society would resolve issues of women's inequality.[26]

At the IWW's founding, Lucy Parsons gave a speech in which she said: "We, the women of this country, have no ballot even if we wished to use it, and the only way that we can be represented is to take a man to represent us. You men have made such a mess of it in representing us that we have not much confidence in asking you! We are the slaves of slaves. We are exploited more ruthlessly than men. Whenever wages are to be reduced the capitalist class use women to reduce them, and if there is anything that you men should do in the future it is to organize the women." In previous writings, Parsons had advocated women master the science of explosives for labor battles. Her husband Albert Parsons was among those who had been unjustly executed in Chicago's 1886 Haymarket Affair.

Lucy Parsons

WOMEN ON STRIKE

Strikes took place throughout the 20th century's first decade, but the most prominent ones were organized in 1909-

1910 by shirtwaist workers in New York and Philadelphia. A speech at a Cooper Union rally by a teenaged worker named Clara Lemlich was decisive in turning a meeting of speeches into a plea for a general strike, which came to be called "The Uprising of 20,000." It was the first general strike of its kind and the first large strike of women workers.[27] Strikers were arrested, fined and sentenced to labor camps. One judge, in sentencing a woman striker, pronounced: "You are striking against God and Nature, whose law is that man shall earn his bread by the sweat of his brow. You are on strike against God!"[28]

The WTUL supplied major support to the garment workers in their 1910 strike and helped bring working-class women into the suffrage movement.[29] The workers, mostly very young immigrants, also had support from the Socialist Party and held out on strike for 13 weeks. Ultimately individual shops made separate settlements with strikers, and overall, the strikers gained little. But they proved to the public, and to the labor movement, that women could be organized.

Also in 1910, 45,000 garment workers — women and men — conducted a women-led strike in Chicago, winning recognition of the principle of arbitration, collective bargaining and an employees' grievance committee, as well as a new local of the United Garment Workers union. Here also the WTUL provided material support and solidarity.[30]

On March 25, 1911, the terrible Triangle Shirtwaist Fire took place in New York City, killing 146 workers, again mostly very young immigrant women, who had been locked in and had no means of escape. The shop owners had yielded nothing after the uprising of the 20,000 and had maintained the same dangerous conditions in their sweatshop. They were tried after the fire but were acquitted of any crime and fined a mere $20. [See Appendix 6 for Rose Schneiderman's memorial speech to the WTUL on the Triangle fire.]

That same year the IWW-led textile strike, known as the Bread and Roses strike, took place in Lawrence, Mass. Elizabeth Gurley Flynn, the lead organizer at age 22, made special appeals to women workers as important activists and not auxiliaries, and women's participation and leadership were high throughout. Flynn was no stranger to struggle, having been expelled from high school five years earlier for her revolutionary speeches.

Schneiderman also addressed the strikers with her famous "Bread and Roses" speech: "What the woman who

*The children of Lawrence during the 1912
IWW-led 'Bread and Roses' strike*

labors wants is the right to live, not simply exist — the right to life
as the rich woman has the right to life, and the sun and music and
art. You have nothing that the humblest worker has not a right to
have also. The worker must have bread, but she must have roses,
too. Help, you women of privilege, give her the ballot to fight with."

The strike was successful, gaining significant pay raises for
workers and inspiring Joe Hill's famous song "Rebel Girl" in honor
of Flynn.[31] [See Appendex 8 for lyrics.] Two decades later Flynn
joined the Communist Party and became its chairwoman in 1961 at
71 years old.

The strike victory could not be sustained in the period that followed, however, and conditions for workers deteriorated, along with
the IWW's strength in Massachusetts.[32]

Reflecting back on the strike 50 years later, Flynn wrote: "What
precipitated the big strike in 1912, which is one of the great historical
struggles in our country, was a political act on the part of the State. The
hours of labor were reduced to 54 hours. You can imagine what they
were before. That was only for women and children, but it affected
something like 75% of the workers in the mills. On the first pay after
the law went into effect, the employers cut the wages proportionately to
the cut in hours and the wages were on the average of $7 and $8 a week
at that time, and the highest pay to loom fixers and more highly skilled

were getting possibly, $15 and $20. It was a margin between mere subsistence and starvation and so there was a spontaneous strike."[33]

At the government level, states were newly engaged in legislating minimum wage and maximum hours laws. Minimum wages for women were hotly contested; if women earned a high wage, they might not be interested in performing their unpaid household duties. At the same time, laws mandating health and safety protections and maximum hours for women were popular. The Triangle fire and the mass struggles of women workers had so shocked and gripped the nation that it created the political momentum for many reform efforts and regulations at the state level.

During World War I, government attention again turned to women workers for pragmatic reasons. With women employed in large numbers in dangerous jobs formerly held exclusively by men, in the areas of munitions, transportation, blast furnaces and the like, new government agencies were set up to provide some protections for women workers — and thereby keep up the war mobilization and morale on the homefront.[34]

After the war, the AFL and women's groups hoped that the labor protections and regulations from the war period could be consolidated. In 1920 the federal government, responding to pressure from the WTUL, women's groups and some labor unions, created the Women's Bureau as part of the Department of Labor, with the mandate to set policies, conduct investigations and promote fair working conditions for women.[35] But in general, all the temporary gains in wages and working conditions were wiped out, as the war regulations expired, bosses went on a major offensive to crush labor unions, and the government launched the Red Scare repression against radicals.

Immigrant workers were branded as communists, as part of corporate America's reactionary response to the Bolshevik Revolution. Organized labor suffered major defeats, the largest being a failed strike of 350,000 workers against U.S. Steel.

Women's unions also suffered defeats. For example a 1924 garment industry strike was roundly defeated, after which many textile jobs were relocated to the South, where there was less union activity and wages were lower.

Where white working women suffered economic exploitation, Black women suffered the additional oppression of discrimination.

When they were given jobs in the textile mills, they were sweeping and cleaning jobs that paid less than machine operators. Only during strikes were Black women hired, as scabs, in the higher paying, more skilled jobs.

In the 1920s, 49 percent of the American people still lived in rural communities. With the end of World War I, agricultural prices fell, and with the new mechanization of farming, the demand for agricultural labor also fell. As more and more women migrated to the cities of the North from the farms of the South, the racial discrimination remained, not only on the part of the bosses but also on the part of the immigrant white workers.[36]

After the stock market crash of 1929, fueled by capitalist overproduction and rampant speculation, the country entered a period of profound economic crisis that would last until 1940. Shantytowns grew up around major cities. Millions of farmers and agricultural workers fled their land. The official unemployment rate reached 25 percent.

It would take years before the class struggle started to rebound in a big way. In 1934, three citywide general strikes took place in Toledo, San Francisco and Minneapolis. Another big surge in women's

---

The sit-down movement at the height of the Great Depression spread into 'women's work' as well.

PHOTO: WORLD-TELEGRAM

labor activism took place in this context in the 1930s, when retail workers, led by labor organizer Myra Wolfgang, held sit-down strikes at Woolworth stores. Beginning in Detroit and expanding throughout the country, retail worker strikes won raises, better schedules, union recognition and job security.

Not all labor activists were unionists themselves. Working-class women in large numbers also joined labor auxiliaries. These women were wives, widows and friends of male unionists, who used their purchasing power as consumers to support union struggles and help to end child labor, sweatshops and unfair employment practices. They conducted boycotts and educational and union label campaigns, and organized picket lines and soup kitchens during strikes. In 1935 the auxiliaries affiliated with the AFL formed the American Federation of Women's Auxiliaries of Labor (AFWAL).[37]

During the Depression, women's very right to hold jobs was threatened. Business, government and even some labor leaders sought to solve the problem of high unemployment by restricting the right of married women to work for wages.

With the founding of the more leftist Congress of Industrial Organizations (CIO) in 1935, some of the union movement's barriers against women and workers of color began to erode. In part this was a practical matter, as organizing increased into new sectors of the workforce where the AFL's traditional exclusions would have been impossible. But also it reflected the militancy and ideological contributions of the country's rapidly growing communist movement, which revived the old IWW spirit of organizing all sectors of the working class. It would take several years for the CIO to turn to fighting for the certain specific needs of women workers.

In the meantime, women fought for their rights, as women and as workers, and at times were met with police brutality, prison, and even opposition within the more conservative sector of the union movement, and fought again, setting an example for later women's struggles. Battles were won and lost, and the women's movement pushed forward.

WOMEN IN THE PEACE MOVEMENT

Economic and political rights were not the only causes that invigorated women's struggles in the early 20th century. Women were a prominent presence in the peace and anti-war movements. Even Mother's Day has its roots in religious pacifist feminism — its founder Anna Jarvis was quickly horrified by its commercialization, however, and even arrested for disrupting a Mother's Day fundraiser.

The U.S. peace movement that developed around World War I was left wing and/or pacifist. Opponents of the war included the Socialist Party and the left wing of the labor movement, including the IWW. They argued that the war meant workers fighting workers on behalf of their capitalist ruling classes. Socialist leader Eugene Debs was charged with a 10-count sedition indictment by the government because of a June 1918 speech opposing the draft. He was sentenced to 10 years but released after three. In 1920, while in prison during the presidential election, he received nearly a million write-in votes for the top office.

The American Union Against Militarism (AUAM) counted many women among its activists and leaders. In 1915, a coalition of suffragists and peace activists that included Carrie Chapman Catt and Jane Addams formed the Women's Peace Party (WPP), which sent a delegation to the Women's International Committee for Permanent Peace in The Hague and which tried, unsuccessfully, to get President Wilson's support for peace proposals among the belligerent nations. After the U.S. entered the war in 1917, the coalition split — as did so many other organizations. The suffragists associated with Catt supported the war effort, in part to show their patriotism and gain the support of those who would vote on woman suffrage.

As in many other wars, pacifists such as Jane Addams were attacked as unpatriotic traitors. Addams, who became a leader in the social work and settlement house movement, went on to win the Nobel Peace Prize in 1931.

Rep. Jeanette Rankin (R-Montana), a pacifist who in 1916 became the first woman elected to the U.S. Congress, voted against U.S. entry into World War I. As a result she was not re-elected until 1940. A year later she cast the only vote against U.S. entry into World War II. Again she served just one term. In 1972, a 91-year-old Rankin considered a third House campaign to oppose the Vietnam War, but she died in 1973 at age 92.

After the war, the AUAM developed into the American Civil Liberties Union, and the Women's International Committee for Permanent Peace became the Women's International League for Peace and Freedom (WILPF), both of which remain active today.[38] Both also became targets of reactionary forces who accused the peace movement of supporting anti-patriotic Bolshevism. WILPF was the target of investigations throughout the 1920s.[39]

Women's anti-World War I activism created an important precedent for their participation in the much larger and more significant anti-war movement of the 1960s and '70s, as well as the post-9/11 movement of the early 2000s.

CONTRACEPTION: LEGALIZATION AND AVAILABILITY

Birth control and family planning continued to be areas of struggle during this period. As the 1900s began, women started to have more control over their fertility, including by delaying marriage. During World War I, as condoms became acceptable as a barrier to venereal disease, enforcement of anti-birth control legislation relaxed, and birth control clinics were allowed to operate under physician supervision. Spacing out births began to be seen as a legitimate health issue for women, and more and more doctors began to support contraception.

Margaret Sanger, a former nurse, became a leader of the birth control movement, opening the first birth control clinic in the United States in Brooklyn in 1916. Authorities closed it down in 10 days and arrested Sanger. Court decisions allowed her to open a new clinic in Manhattan seven years later. At this time, federal "anti-obscenity" laws prohibited dissemination of information about contraception, and postal authorities suppressed the distribution of Sanger's "The Woman Rebel" paper — as they did other radical newspapers.

Margaret Sanger

Sanger herself was a member of the Socialist Party and a friend of Emma Goldman, Eugene Debs, Elizabeth Gurley Flynn and other left activists, and helped to organize strike support and legal defense for the IWW. After many arrests and a period of exile, Sanger went on to found the American Birth Control League, which became part of the Planned Parenthood Federation in 1942.

In the 1920s Sanger had moved away from leftist politics and, influenced by neo-Malthusian theories, became involved in eugenics, which called for limiting the birth rate of people considered "unfit" based on IQ and disabilities. According to Loretta Ross, Sanger's involvement was opportunistic, in order to win over the public and medical establishment to support birth control, which was widely associated with the feminist and fringe concepts of "free love."[40] Others in the progressive and left movements saw her entanglement with eugenics as promoting an inherently racist form of population control.[41]

Indeed, across the Western world eugenics revealed the ugliest side of the middle- and upper-class "progressive" impulse to subject all of human and social development to the "scientific" expertise of middle-class technocrats. Applying this controlling, technocratic spirit to the reproductive lives of working-class women, and women of color, produced horrible sterilization campaigns and made real the fantasies of white supremacists.

According to a report from the leading Black feminist organization SisterSong, many of the quotes that are attributed to Sanger on birth control in the Black community have been invented or taken out of context. "There is no evidence that Sanger, or the Federation, intended to coerce Black women into using birth control" or supported racially-based involuntary sterilization, the report states. Anti-abortion groups have in fact invested considerable resources to spread the false idea that Sanger and Planned Parenthood were part of a conspiracy to commit genocide in the Black community.

In her birth control advocacy, Sanger collaborated with prominent figures in the Black political establishment, including W.E.B. DuBois and Mary McLeod Bethune.

In truth, Black women always had to fight for both access to birth control and an end to involuntary sterilization. The Colored Women's Club Movement denounced rampant sterilization of Black women and supported the establishment of family planning clinics in Black communities. Ministers and churches facilitated this, as well as the NAACP, National Urban League and leading Black newspapers. In the years from 1915 to 1920 Black infant mortality dropped 43 percent, from 181 per 1,000 live births to 102.[42]

Opposition to birth control came from the Catholic Church, white conservatives (who did not want birth control for white women), and also Black nationalist leaders such as Marcus Garvey, who believed the Black population should increase as a defense against racial and national oppression. Right-wing eugenics supporters advocated for birth control for people of color for racist, white supremacist reasons in contradiction

Image from a 1929 Birth Control Review

to feminist reasons for birth control. Ross wrote, "The elite sought to improve their control of society through the control of breeding."[43]

In 1938, a federal judge lifted the ban on birth control, but for a number of years most states continued to ban contraception. Amazingly, it was not until 1965 that the Supreme Court ruled it was illegal for states to deny contraception to married couples.

THE FIGHT AGAINST RAPE AND VIOLENCE

Women during this period also elevated the struggle against rape, violence and sexual harassment. Women have been victimized by rape and other forms of sexual violence throughout the history of class society, as an instrument of power and oppression. Society's response has varied over time and has depended in part on the race and class of both victim and perpetrator.

In the early 1900s, those who left violent spouses were largely treated sympathetically. Divorce laws, for example, took into account women's need to leave a violent spouse. This changed in the post-World War I era. After the war, some forms of gender violence were in fact decriminalized. Family courts and social workers became influenced by psychoanalysis and Freudian notions of female submissiveness and popularized the notion that women should be blamed for their own victimization. This was seen as a response to women's new independence and the growing feminist movement.[44] Working women also faced sexual harassment and threats from predatory bosses.

As more women went out alone in public, they faced an epidemic of street harassment. Women increasingly struck back, both physically and by agitating for protections such as the hiring of female police officers.[45] The harassment of Black women by white men was especially pronounced, and Black women were frequently targets of rape.

The rape of Black women by white men was embedded in U.S. history, dating from slavery and extending well into the 20th century. It terrorized women and also terrorized the entire Black community.[46]

Nonetheless, allegations of rape of white women by Black men were the primary pretext for lynching Black men in the South.

A commentary on feminist scholar Estelle Freedman's book "Redefining Rape: Sexual Violence in the Era of Suffrage and Segregation," notes, "The long-dominant view of rape in America envisioned a brutal attack on a chaste white woman by a male stranger, usually an African American." But in fact, "between the 1870s and the 1930s, at the height of racial segregation and lynching, and amid the campaign for woman suffrage, women's rights supporters and African American activists tried to ... gain legal protection from coercive sexual relations, assaults by white men on [B]lack women, street harassment, and the sexual abuse of children."[47]

Looking back, one is struck by the stunning backwardness of U.S. laws and popular conceptions of sexual violence.

The notion of acquaintance or marital rape was not even accepted. Nonconsensual sex that did not produce visible physical harm was not considered rape nor could sexual contact be considered rape if the woman was not previously "chaste." Given the legal impunity for and cultural acceptance of sexual violence, one can only imagine what this meant for women.

Women pushed back against male violence and threats, and their responses were scattered and small at first. Individual women would come to the defense of other women. Women's self-defense classes were held in parks in Chicago from 1906 to 1908. Journalists published articles about rape and harassment in the white and Black press.[48]

The fight for suffrage was also connected to the fight against sexual violence. The struggle for suffrage was in essence a fight for citizenship. Activists believed that only with political rights could women make changes in how they were treated and have access to the legal system for relief.

It would take decades for the resistance of women and their allies against rape and sexual violence to grow into the powerful fightback movement of the Second Wave and beyond. The term "domestic violence" did not even exist until the feminist movement

Self-defense, circa 1906

brought it into the mainstream in the 1970s — before then, it was so normalized that it did not even register as an important social issue.

Other issues in women's rights activism during this time included reform of marriage, divorce and child custody laws. At the turn of the 20th century, state laws were actually making it harder for women to divorce, even in cases of abuse.

Women fought the legal double standard in cases of adultery, with its harsh punishments for women, such as the loss of her property, and no penalty for men. Women also fought for reforms in laws governing property ownership, including laws that granted ownership of women's earnings to their husbands. These rights were won state by state, more easily in the frontier states of the West, as was true for suffrage.[49] In part this was because of the severe gender imbalance in the demographics of western states, which had attracted so many single men as settlers, farmers and laborers. The less consolidated political structures of the West also made them somewhat more responsive to movements from below.

EQUAL RIGHTS AMENDMENT

Once the suffrage amendment was passed, Alice Paul and other leaders of the National Woman's Party began to organize for passage of the ERA, which was first introduced in Congress in 1923. The proposed amendment stated, "Equality of rights under the law shall not be denied or abridged by the United States or by any State on account of sex."

Prominent forces in the feminist movement took positions for and against the amendment. They fell into two basic groups: "equal rights feminists" and "social justice activists." Equal rights feminists, who were among the staunchest supporters of the ERA, believed that once suffrage was won, women should seek to operate as equals with men in the political sphere and that women needed no special additional protections. For example, a 1923 Supreme Court decision that overturned a local minimum wage law for women in Washington D.C. was applauded by the National Woman's Party.

Social justice feminists fought for special benefits and protections for women, based on their particular needs, such as maternity leave, certain safety regulations, as well as benefits that would equalize the status of working women of color with white women if not with men. These feminists tried to get language incorporated into the ERA that would address these inequalities but to no avail.[50] The fight over the ERA continued for nearly 60 years, when it was finally defeated — and in 2014-15 it was reintroduced with far less fanfare. (See Chapter 8 for later developments on the ERA.)

The division between equal rights and social justice feminists continued into the Second Wave and beyond, reflecting core ideological camps. The "equal rights" section rests fundamentally on liberal theory — that women's equality will be won once all discriminatory barriers in society are knocked down, and they are able to freely make individual decisions and choices to govern their lives. It fundamentally aims for an equality of rights within bourgeois democracy. That is legal formal equality rather than genuine social and economic equality based on remedying or overturning the built-in inequality of the capitalist system.

Equal rights feminists stood somewhat apart from the larger struggles for racial and economic justice, treating women's equality as a separate struggle. Social justice feminists, by contrast, were involved with the major movements of the day, civil rights and labor, in addition to women's rights.[51] □

Chapter 6
War and postwar America: 1940-1960

MANY of the contributing factors for the feminist uprising of 1965 to 1975 derived from World War II and the extraordinary economic, social, political, cultural and family transformations that took place from 1940 to 1960.

It was also a period of a brief loosening and then strong reassertion of patriarchal dominance, of severe political witch-hunts and anticommunism, a return to conservatism after Roosevelt's New Deal, rampant racism and the emergence of a new generation of a Black fightback. The period also was characterized by new forms of sexual repression, targeting women and those with non-mainstream sexual orientations, gender expressions and identities. (The term LGBTQ is of more modern usage and did not exist then.) It also saw the intense beginning of the Cold War, the Korean War, and a real fear among the population of nuclear war.

But whereas the United States staggered out of the Great Depression into World War II, it bolted out of the war into a period of major economic growth, the rapid development of industry and finance, the freeing of pent up consumer demand dating back to the 1930s, a housing boom, a thriving automobile industry, and the growth of corporate conglomerates, consumerism and a ruling class that increasingly promoted social conformity as an integral part of patriotic unity.

The United States was the only substantial economic and political power standing in 1945. Much of Europe and Asia was destroyed and destitute. In Washington's view, it was the moment at last for the United States to assume unilateral command of the capitalist world order for the first time. There was immediate work to be done reorganizing, rebuilding and leading the world economically, politically and militarily, and reconstructing the United States into a prosperous patriotic society prepared to crush the "communist menace" for good.

The crippled Soviet Union stood alone in 1945. No country came near its total of 27 million military and civilian deaths and the destruction of most of its industrial base at the hands of Nazi Germany. The U.S. military lost 405,339 troops in battle and the U.S. homeland was not touched by war. Washington called Moscow "our great Soviet ally" during the war, but had no intention of helping the USSR dig out of the rubble, and there was no other socialist country to help. Amazingly, through great toil and sacrifice the USSR was back on its feet in a few years.

The status of women improved in the United States during the war years of 1941 through 1945, but deteriorated for the next 15 years until the 1960s. The political and social forces of the postwar period were formidable in demanding that women adhere to their traditional subordinate role in the family and society.

The U.S. government's main postwar domestic objective was to build an enduring white middle class, with millions of new homes in the suburbs, where the male head of household would drive his new car to work. This was facilitated by the GI Bill, which provided veterans with low-cost mortgages, free tuition and living expenses to attend university, high school or vocational education, and low-interest loans to start a business. This was a de facto form of white male affirmative action, although it never took this name and therefore is scarcely remembered as such.

The decades-long Black migration north away from Jim Crow violence and formal segregation was concentrated in the cities, as it remains today. The condition of Black Americans experienced little improvement in the 1940s and early '50s until the mid-decade beginnings of the civil rights movement and some court decisions weakened certain aspects of segregation and oppression.

Just before World War II about 20 percent of white women were in the workforce. Most of these workers were single and virtually all of them were in low-paying "women's" jobs. The wartime national emergency not only offered better jobs but allowed most women a freedom to leave home and enter the workforce that many never experienced before — not that all would or could take advantage of the moment.

The U.S. government, needing women for war work, brought millions into factories and government jobs, using the image of Rosie the Riveter as a symbol of women's ability to succeed at what heretofore was termed "man's work," and they did the job exceedingly well. They also joined women's military forces and directly helped to win the war against German and Japanese fascist imperialism.

Do the job *HE* left behind

Propaganda poster from World War II by the U.S. government

Here is how the situation looked when the United States entered World War II, according to the paper Mobilization of Women: American Home Front in World War II:

> Most Americans still held an old-fashioned notion of women's place in society; that is, they believed that a woman's proper role was in the home, working as a housewife. Husbands were expected to make the money on which a family lived; they controlled the household finances and held ultimate authority in the home. ... Most women entered the workforce upon completion of their schooling and worked until they got married, while men entered the workforce and stayed. World War II disrupted these patterns, thrusting men and women into new roles and activities related to the war. ... At the same time, industry was mobilizing to produce massive amounts of war materials. Approximately eighteen million additional workers would need to be hired to meet production goals.

Millions of women answered the call. Many were welcomed into a world of work that had been off limits to them before the war in various defense-related industries and other trades traditionally occupied by men only. Women were barred from such jobs earlier for alleged lack of ability and because such a high level of employment was reserved for the male breadwinner, not for his wife (who should stay home) or sister.

Factory jobs were rare for women until the war, when necessity swiftly exposed the widespread falsehood that women were unfit for such work. Hundreds of thousands of women worked six days a week for years building warships, bombs, landing craft, airships, tanks, artillery pieces and smaller arms. Two years after war was declared nearly 500,000 women worked in aircraft factories.

This is where Rosie the Riveter did her work, more as a highly successful recruiting poster than an individual worker. There she was, in blue coveralls, and a red bandana, showing her muscles as she rolled up her sleeves to help win the war. Rosie was everything an average woman was not supposed to be according the rules that kept women in their secondary place. But the U.S. government well knew that the rules had to be relaxed until the war ended.

Another huge employer was the federal government bureaucracy, which needed to fill many more jobs than ever before — work hitherto done by men. Up to a million women were hired to work at federal office jobs in Washington, D.C. Just about everyone called them "Government Girls," as they did themselves.

According to U.S. History in Context:

> By 1941, 40% to 50% of [B]lack American women were in the workforce as maids and cooks, both poorly paid jobs. At first, most employers in the war industries tried to avoid hiring [B]lack women. However, [B]lacks began to hold protest demonstrations in front of defense plants that employed whites only. To avert a huge protest march set for Washington, D.C., President Roosevelt issued Executive Order 8802 in June 1941. The order banned discrimination in the war industries. If companies failed to hire [B]lacks, or if managers tolerated white workers who refused to work with [B]lacks, they would lose their profitable defense orders.

> Thousands of [B]lack women migrated to the Great Lakes region and to both coasts in search of war industry work. Many moved from jobs that paid $2.50 a week to employment paying $40 a week. Many [B]lack women hired in the war industries were given the worst, most dangerous jobs. ..."[1] [Editor: At war's end they were the first fired.]

Workers at the Douglas Aircraft factory, Los Angeles

In addition to factory work and other home-front jobs, over 350,000 women joined the Armed Services, including the military nurse corps, serving at home and abroad. In May 1942, Congress instituted the Women's Auxiliary Army Corps, later upgraded to the Women's Army Corps, which had full military status. Its members, known as WACs, worked in more than 200 non-combatant jobs stateside and in every theater of the war. By 1945, there were more than 150,000 WACs and 6,000 female officers. In the Navy, 100,000 Women Accepted for Volunteer Emergency Service (WAVES) held the same status as naval reservists and provided support stateside. The Coast Guard Women's Reserves (10,000) and Marine Corps Women's Reserves (23,000) followed suit.

"More than 59,000 American nurses served in the Army Nurse Corps during World War II," according to Military History. Some 14,000 women joined the Navy Nurse Corps. "Nurses worked closer to the front lines than they ever had before. ... Nurses served under fire in field hospitals and evacuation hospitals, on hospital trains and hospital ships, and as flight nurses on medical transport planes." The skill and dedication of these nurses contributed to the extremely low post-injury mortality rate among American military forces in every theater of the war.[2]

According to Florida State University's Institute on World War II:

> Blacks in the 1940s, especially in the South, faced Jim Crow laws that treated German POWs (many of whom were confined in the U.S.) better than American citizens of color," "The military reflected this segregation as it limited [B]lack enlistees to less than 10%, or approximately 1.1 million, of troop force. To add insult to injury, most African American units were commanded by white officers.

> The role of [B]lack women in World War II is one that has been consistently undervalued. More than 6,500 [B]lack women volunteered in the Women's Army Corps. Of vital importance was the 6888th Central Postal Battalion. Major Charity Adams commanded the only all-[B]lack WAC unit to serve overseas. They were responsible for keeping mail flowing to the more than seven million servicemen and women in Europe. Fewer numbers of African American women were accepted in the other service branches, and their participation was limited. For example, the 512 [B]lack women in the Army Nurse Corps were confined to nursing either black troops or German prisoners of war.[3]

The number of women workers grew during World War II to just over 35 percent of the civilian work force. The U.S. population at the time was 152 million, less than half today's figure. Married women working outside the home increased from 13.9 percent to 22.5 percent during the war. Female union membership jumped from 800,000 before the war to 3 million at the end. Both the AFL and the CIO (not yet merged) campaigned for equal pay and seniority rights for women workers. Many CIO unions, such as the United Auto Workers, paid close attention to the views of women members.

Women succeeded exceptionally well in their civilian war-related and military jobs, and were proud of themselves and of their work to defeat fascist imperialism.

In various public opinion polls at this time up to 85 percent of women indicated they wanted to keep their jobs after the war. After all, they were much more independent, and earning considerably more money than ever before, though male workers still earned more for the same work, as they do now.

But then things changed drastically.

At war's end, Washington executed a 180-degree turn and insisted women's place was back in the traditional home doing housework, childcare and catering to the male "breadwinner." To emphasize its point the government closed down nearly all its free daycare centers for the children of women workers. In large part workplace discrimination against women was re-imposed in the postwar job market.

There is no doubt that jobs and seniority belonged to millions of returning GIs, over 16 million of whom were mobilized for war, including 12 million who left jobs to defend the country. That was fair and was promised upon entering to the military.

But millions of women lost jobs in factories, government offices and the military. The Encyclopedia of American Social History notes that in factories "women workers were fired at a far higher rate than their male counterparts. In the aircraft industry, for example, where women constituted 39 percent of the wartime work force, they made up 89 percent of those laid off with the coming of peace."

In 1945, 37 percent of women were employed. Five years later it was 32 percent in a peacetime economy that was surging forward. Many found traditional low-wage women's jobs but only a relative few were hired to the "men's jobs" and equivalent occupations for which they had proved their qualifications.

In the labor movement, many unions supported the restoration of the traditional male breadwinner; only the communist-led CIO unions made special efforts to protect the jobs and workplace gains of their women members and Black members.

Washington, by contrast, projected a message that women must return to marriage, children and housework. The social history encyclopedia points out:

> Most certainly women were put under an immense
> pressure to return to their traditional role as mothers
> and housewives, completely dedicated to their children

and dependent on their husbands. Some women felt the government was going too far when it started to promote the idea that women should be happy washing dishes, preparing meals, cleaning the house and being the 'ideal' woman. ...

Against the threat of a change in the feminine role, the official efforts were to make women take back their places as housewives but essentially to make them obey the wills of their husbands, who had already sacrificed so much in the war.

From Washington's point of view, restoring these traditional patriarchal relationships in the home was a major factor in building a new and more conservative white middle class.

If you were a teenage young woman in the 1950s you may have learned from reading the Home Economics High School Text Book to "Have dinner ready, prepare yourself, prepare the children, minimize all noise, be happy to see him, listen to him, make the evening his."

The most appalling, sexist images were normalized in 1950s corporate advertising.

When you returned home, reports American Memory of the 1950s, "Television, radio, and magazines bombarded [women] with the assurance that the kitchen was their realm and that loving food preparation for their families was the way to fulfillment."

According to U.S. History in Context:

After 15 years of crisis and upheaval at home and abroad, Americans of the 1945-1960 era, particularly the young middle-class couples moving to the suburbs, placed a high premium on material well-being, social stability, and family cohesion. ...

All this had important implications for middle-class women and the prevailing view of their appropriate role. The culture extolled domesticity and what one women's magazine called 'togetherness.' 'Rosie the Riveter'... gave way to maternal images of 'the happy housewife.' In Woman: The Lost Sex (1947), two Freudian scholars... blamed most of modern society's problems on women who had left the domestic sphere to compete with men. Dr. Benjamin Spock's best-selling "Baby and Child Care," first published in 1946, similarly assumed that women's primary, if not only, role should be as homemaker and mother. Television shows deified the American family, amiably presided over by hardworking dad and apron-clad mom. Advertisers cultivated the image of housewives as the ultimate consumers, endlessly preoccupied with deciding among different brands of detergents or vacuum cleaners.

How did women respond to cultural pressures intent on confining them to a narrow, restricted social role? On the one hand, feminist activism was nearly nonexistent. ... At the same time, other evidence suggests that many women did not placidly adapt to the niche society built for them. Despite the pressures aimed at confining women to the domestic sphere, the ranks of working women grew steadily after ebbing in the late 1940s. ... Even more significantly, the percentage of married women working outside the home doubled from 1940 to 1960. And the number of working women with children under age seventeen rose from 40 million in 1950 to 58 million in 1960. In a revealing poll of 1962, only *10% of the women surveyed wanted their daughters to have the same kind of life they had led.* [author's italics]

But in the 1950s women's discontents remained largely unarticulated and did not find collective or ideological expression ... until the political and cultural climate shifted in the early 1960s.[4]

Clearly, the conditions of the 1940s to the 1960s were a direct cause of the next decade's feminist rebellion. There was no lasting women's movement to fight back throughout the 1940s and 1950s. The only serious effort to reinforce women's rights and feminism began in 1946 when women in the Communist Party organized the progressive Congress of American Women (CAW). It lasted four years before collapsing under the weight of the anti-communist witch hunt.

The strong feminist views within the CAW were mainly the product of several years of sharp struggle by women within the Communist Party to put forward in theory and practice a recognition of the role of male supremacy (including in the working class), the oppression of women, and of the existence of sexism within the party, according to "Red Feminism," the extraordinary 2001 book by Kate Weigand.

In its 1946 position paper introducing the new organization, the CAW declared in its last paragraph:

> Until the day when the American woman is free to develop her mind and abilities to their fullest extent, without discrimination because of her sex, is free to work without neglecting her children, to live with her husband on an equal level, with adequate provision made for the care of that home without injury to her health; until she takes her full responsibilities as citizen and individual, supporting herself if necessary and her family where she has a family, at a decent wage, paid equally with men for the work she does; until she is freed from the terror of war, and lives in a world of peaceful friendship between nations, in a society without prejudice against Negro, Jew, national groups or women — her long struggle for emancipation must continue."

The CAW was racially integrated with members of various ethnicities and classes that were supporters of peace and justice and believed in fighting for women's rights. Functioning like a broad coalition of women activists from liberal to far left, CAW formed chapters in about 20 cities. Although there were claims of membership of over 100,000 or more, the organization was smaller. It became smaller still in 1949 when House Un-American Activities Committee charged that CAW was a propaganda arm for "Soviet political warfare" — a clear sign of the repression to come.

Membership was down to 3,000 when CAW disbanded itself in 1950 after communist leaders began being prosecuted and jailed for their stated belief in revolution, not for any particular criminal actions. (In 1957 the Supreme Court ruled defendants could only be prosecuted for their actions, but by then the party had been severely wounded and its membership largely driven underground or out of politics.)

Many of the hard fought feminist perspectives of the Congress of American Women ultimately entered into the women's movement of the Sixties when members or ex-members of the CP and CAW took part.

Claudia Jones, communist activist

An important history of the early feminist movement (from the beginning to 1920) was published by Harvard University Press in 1959 titled "Century of Struggle: The Woman's Rights Movement in the United States," (expanded edition 1975; enlarged edition 1996). It was influential on the feminist movement in the Sixties and remains indispensable to this day. The author, Eleanor Flexner, was a member of the circle of Communist Party women who fought for an advanced political perspective on women within the Party. Others associated with the communist movement and CAW, including writer Gerda Lerner, poet Eve Merriam, and writer/artist Betty Millard influenced the Sixties movement as well.

Party members and ex-members usually concealed their affiliation to avoid the red hunters and protect the women's movement from being labeled a communist front. It is known that FBI agents secretly penetrated just about all feminist groups in search of communists, as they did to virtually all the other movements during the 1960s.

Big change was in the works by 1959 but few saw it coming. Ten years later, feminist notable Gloria Steinem wrote an article in New York Magazine that captured how much had changed "Once upon a time — say, 10 or even five years ago — a Liberated Woman was somebody who had sex before marriage and a job afterward. Once upon the same time, a Liberated Zone was any foreign place lucky enough to have an American army in it. Both ideas seem antiquated now, and for pretty much the same reason: Liberation isn't exposure to the American values of Mom-and-apple-pie anymore (not even if Mom is allowed to work in an office and vote once in a while); it's the escape from them." □

Chapter 7
Feminism and the mass movements: 1960-1990

THE decade of the 1960s saw rebellions and uprisings that lasted until the mid-1970s and resulted in the overthrow of formal segregation, the rise of a formidable antiwar movement, the lasting impact of the women's liberation movement and the end of many stultifying conservative cultural conventions. The decades of right-wing and neoliberal reaction, that began in the latter part of the 1970s, reversed many but certainly not all of these progressive advances.

Black students from A&T State University in Greensboro, North Carolina kicked off the Sixties with a sit-in at Woolworths on Feb. 1, 1960, which galvanized the nation. The protests spread to Chattanooga, Nashville and other cities. The pace picked up the next year with the first Freedom Rides to protest segregation in Southern interstate transportation started by the Congress of Racial Equality (CORE). The Black and white nonviolent riders were confronted with horrific ferocity and racist hatred at virtually every stop.

Black movements led by Rev. Martin Luther King Jr., Malcolm X, the Black Panthers, Black working-class union militants and others struggled for freedom and equality throughout the decade, registering major gains in nearly every arena.

As the civil rights and Black freedom struggle continued, one after another aggrieved or radical constituency raised its own oppositional banners to change the status quo in the U.S. — Vietnam war opposition; the student movement and the New Left; the broad counterculture that swept away many stultifying cultural conventions; socialist and communist groups, which all got stronger, including the relatively new Maoist movement; the LGBTQ movement; rank-and-file labor militancy; the Chicano, Puerto Rican, Native and Asian movements; and of course the rambunctious movement for women's equality that sought the overthrow of male domination. All of these trends grew amid mass street confrontations, direct actions and a broader spirit of resistance, intersecting with one another from the mid-'60s and remaining an extremely powerful force for the next decade.

Women's activists Bella Abzug and Dagmar Wilson founded Women Strike for Peace in 1961, in opposition to nuclear proliferation. The group's first major action on Nov. 1 that year consisted of protests against nuclear weapons in 60 cities by some 50,000 primarily middle-class women. This action and other marches, pickets and sit-ins took place to pressure the United States and Soviet Union to sign the nuclear non-proliferation treaty. During the Vietnam War they initiated anti-draft counseling programs.

The mass movements reinforced each other. Some activists moved from one issue to another, and those who were once on the sidelines joined in. A number of leading women gained experience in the early years of the civil rights struggle and brought that knowledge to the women's uprising. The existence of several movements at once enhanced all of them, and each tended to support the other. In a way, while different groups and coalitions focused on different issues, in human terms the movements were all interwoven and participants considered themselves part of "The Movement." All opposed the U.S. war in Vietnam, making that movement the most powerful peace undertaking in U.S. history. Women constituted at least half the many millions who opposed the Vietnam War.

By the time this extraordinary era dissipated in the mid-'70s — around the time the Vietnamese people were finally victorious in the decades of long war against Japanese, then French, then American imperialism —all these movements had created a unique radical environment in America that brought about a number of important political and social advances.

THE WOMEN'S MOVEMENT

The publication of Betty Friedan's bestselling 1963 book "The Feminine Mystique" helped spur the Second Wave by illuminating women's largely concealed dissatisfaction with the drudgery and isolation of full time housework, child care, shopping, etc., in largely male dominant households where a woman was an unpaid housewife. Although the book has been criticized because of its concentration on the white middle class, it played a major role in spreading feminist consciousness and opening the eyes of millions of housewives to a virtually unidentified frustration, the "Problem That Has No Name." Friedan wrote:

> Each suburban wife struggles with it alone. As she made the beds, shopped for groceries, matched slipcover material, ate peanut butter sandwiches with her children, chauffeured Cub Scouts and Brownies, lay beside her husband at night — she was afraid to ask even of herself the silent question — 'Is this all?'[1]

Writing in Huffington Post 50 years after its publication, Professor Peter Dreier declared that the book "forever change[d] Americans' attitudes about women's role in society."

In common with many leftists who came through the hysterical anticommunism of the 1950s Freidan tended to conceal her left-wing ideological influences. She was a former labor journalist for one of the best left-wing unions — the United Electrical Workers (UE) — an organization that was ejected from the CIO in the late 1940s because of government and right-wing union opposition to leftist and "red" unions and union members. She denied ever being a member of the Communist Party though it is clear she sympathized with strong left-wing goals.

It is important to note that most working women in those years wanted more time at home with their children and saw the lives of housewives as privileged. Working-class women faced discrimination in the workplace and suffered from the absence of family benefits that would have made it possible to hold down a full-time job without causing great hardship to their families. In addition, hiring decisions were completely segregated by gender and race, down to the kinds of help-wanted ads that ran in the newspapers: "male help wanted" or "female help wanted". Jobs allotted to women offered lower wages and far fewer opportunities for advancement.

Once hired, women not only had to contend with discriminatory wages but also with the lack of maternity leave, child care and other family services that were becoming routine in the social democratic societies of Europe. Child care, which had been provided by

HELP WANTED—MALE

BARBER—White, for Saturday; $4.25. 1307 East Capitol st. 1*

MAN to attend stable, wash carriages, clean harness, and take care of horses; white. Apply at 707 22d, Apt. 12, after 7 p. m. 1

WASHMAN—Experienced, on shirts, collars, and family work. Apply BOX 316, Times office. 1*

WANTED—Men to learn barber trade; new method; wages after first month; steady position guaranteed. For particulars address MOLER BARBER COLLEGE, Dept. N, 207 Bowery, New York City. 1*

BUSHELMAN and coat maker. WATSON, 1306 G st. N. W. *

INSURANCE AGENTS—White and colored; one policy covers sick, accident and life; pays old age benefits; loans made on policies; old reliable company licensed to do business in the District of Columbia. Address BOX 311, Times office. 1*

MEN—Young, wanted to solicit subscriptions for Catholic magazine in Washington; producers can make big money. BOX 310, Times office. 1*

PRESSER—First-class, at once. Call 2504 14th st., J. KLEIN.

WHITE MAN—Active, to clean windows and help other work. Apply before 9 or after 5. ELLIOTT, 1400 U st. N. W.

HELP WANTED—FEMALE

GIRL—Good, for kitchen work. Call after 6 p. m., 7 H st. N. W. 1

GIRL—Good, to work in dining room, also one to do chamberwork, will pay good wages to right party, room and board; no colored need apply. Call 201 Eye st. N. W.

GIRL—Colored, for general housework; reference. 221 3rd st. N. W.

WAITRESS—Experienced; good wages. 610 9th st. N. W. No other need apply. AMERICAN LUNCH. 1

WOMAN—White, for cooking and housework in small family; leave city for summer. 8821 Woodly road. 1

A typical job listing in the early 1900s

the state for women workers in the defense industry, was taken away after the war. The loss of this essential benefit was one factor that pushed post-war women workers out of the labor force and into the home. Most of these social services continue to be withheld by the U.S. government — which refuses to raise taxes on the rich to pay for such programs, or cut into the gigantic military budget.

Black women, who were concentrated in agricultural and domestic occupations, suffered the additional discrimination and resulting hardship of having been excluded from Social Security. (Their exclusion had been one of the conditions demanded by Southern lawmakers in exchange for voting for New Deal legislation.) Many of the exclusions were ended in the 1950s.

Not all women of the era went along with the movement. Many preferred the role of family homemaker. It was traditional, could have its rewards and was in tune with the dominant ideology passed down through the state, the Church and the mass media. For financial reasons far fewer women today are in the position to choose whether or not to work — and far fewer prefer to stay at home, thanks to the cultural shifts and breakthroughs into the labor force that can be traced to the gains of the Second Wave period.

The accomplishments of the Second Wave were significant and far-reaching. (See Chapter 8.) The changes that benefited women reached deeply into society, and were brought about by a mass, independent feminist movement, which occurred both inside and outside the electoral system and independently of the major political parties. The movement's primary tactics were street demonstrations, direct actions and small-group consciousness-raising, as well as grassroots community organizing, and interventions against the mass media, popular culture and the courts. Feminist ideas flowed into the mainstream, as women saw gains in law and public policy, private life and popular culture.

The Second Wave of feminism was a truly mass movement that included women of all backgrounds and oppressed communities, as well as political backgrounds, from liberal to communist. The large white middle-class segment had the widest reach into the mass media and the general public, and continues to receive much more visibility in the historical presentations of the era in films and academic works. Unfortunately, this has left a somewhat distorted picture in the minds of many of today's activists, who are unaware that there was such a large left-wing and revolutionary sector.

This is a glance at the activity and goals of some of the constituencies active in the Sixties, and had a continuing influence in the following decades. (Note that the contemporary women's movement and its various groups will be mentioned in Chapter 10.)

LIBERAL FEMINISM

Liberal feminism emerged from the historical women's rights movement. It consisted largely of white middle-class women including a professional sector that made demands on federal and state institutions to end the discrimination that women experienced in the workforce. These women also tended to be married mothers, and their demands reflected the experiences and dissatisfaction of many housewives.[2]

The goal of this current was to open up the existing political and economic system to women and to achieve political, legal and social equality with men. Activists' political lives centered on political parties, unions and other institutions where they engaged in coalition building, electoral politics and union organizing, while working with male allies. They did not challenge the capitalist system and sought reform from within.

As this current grew, it developed closer ties with the Democratic Party and stressed lobbying and electoral politics as primary political strategies. The Democratic Party, in turn, made room to absorb these elements into its party machinery as a new loyal and influential constituency. Liberal feminists led and continue to lead campaigns for important legislative and policy changes.

The federal government began to pay new attention to women's equality issues in the early 1960s, thanks to the pressure brought by women activists and the growing visibility and successes of the civil rights movement. The U.S. Women's Bureau urged President John F. Kennedy to create the President's Commission on the Status of Women. The President appointed the commission in 1961 and selected Eleanor Roosevelt to chair it. Based on the Commission's recommendations, President Kennedy in 1962 ordered federal government agencies to stop discriminating against women employees.[3]

The Commission's first report, called "American Women" and issued in 1963, contained some progressive recommendations

President John F. Kennedy with American Association of University Women members, signs the Equal Pay Act of 1963.

that have since been enacted, such as more equitable employment practices, legal treatment and property rights for women. But half a century later, many of the core reforms that the Commission recommended still have not been realized, including pay equity across occupations and expanded services for working women, such as paid maternity leave, home services for working mothers and child care.

The report also addressed the oppression caused by poverty and racism as well as gender inequity, noting that the racial discrimination that deprived Black men of opportunities for employment created additional economic responsibilities for women: "Such women are twice as likely as other women to have to seek employment while they have pre-school children at home; they are just beginning to gain entrance to the expanding fields of clerical and commercial employment; except for the few who can qualify as teachers or other professionals, they are forced into low-paid service occupations." The report pointed out the similar situations and discrimination faced by Native Americans and Latinas.

NATIONAL ORGANIZATION FOR WOMEN

The most important popular manifestation of liberal feminism was and is the National Organization for Women (NOW), which became the largest mass-membership feminist organization in the country with a reported half-million members today.[4] It was

Organized by NOW, the Mobilization for Women's Lives
drew 150,000 to Washington D.C., November 12, 1989.

founded in 1966 by feminist activists, with Betty Friedan as president, in part in response to the fact that Title VII of the 1964 Civil Rights Act, which banned discrimination in employment, was not being consistently enforced. According to its statement of purpose the organization intended "to take action to bring women into full participation in the mainstream of American society now, exercising all the privileges and responsibilities thereof in truly equal partnership with men." The statement criticized the Equal Employment Opportunity Commission (EEOC) for not taking seriously enough the discrimination faced by women and the double discrimination suffered by Black women.

The organization took on the legal issues of wage discrimination; the dearth of women in the professions, government and higher education. It also stressed the need for policy to catch up to changing realities in the family: women were chafing against their unequal position in marriage. In addition, they were outliving their child-raising years, thus removing a major rationale for limiting them to the realm of the home.

In its early years, the NOW leadership was hostile to lesbian activists and issues, and had a weak position on abortion rights. Friedan herself made statements against the "lavender menace." Internal struggles led the group to become more inclusive over time, so that by 1971, amid the explosion of the lesbian and gay liberation movement and the growth of radical feminism, it embraced lesbian members and their cause, and gave strong support to abortion rights.

NOW's bill of rights, passed in 1967, called for enforcement of laws banning sex discrimination; maternity leave rights in employment and in social security benefits; tax deductions for home and child care expenses for working parents; child care centers; equal and integrated education; equal opportunities for job training and housing, and family allowances for women in poverty. That year also saw NOW's endorsement of legalized abortion.

Although the majority of its members were white, NOW was racially integrated from the start, and some of its charter members were veterans of the civil rights movement who saw the need to address discrimination on the basis of race and gender at the same time. Pauli Murray, civil rights worker, lawyer, feminist activist and the first Black woman to be ordained as an Episcopal priest, wrote: "The Negro woman can no longer postpone or subordinate the fight against discrimination because of sex in the civil rights struggle but must carry on both fights simultaneously. She must insist upon a partnership role in the integration movement."[5]

Pauli Murray

NOW had close ties to leading labor unions and for its first year its office was in the United Auto Workers (UAW) Solidarity House in Detroit. The UAW also contributed financial support to help it get started. Among NOW's founding members were members of UAW, CWA and the United Packing House Workers — including Addie Wyatt, a founder of the Coalition for Labor Union Women (CLUW).

NOW engaged in street actions, lawsuits, boycotts, lobbying and electoral campaigns. Petition drives against the EEOC, supported by sit-ins at the agency's field offices, helped bring about an end to sex-segregated job ads.

The organization also campaigned hard in 1972 for the presidential run of Shirley Chisholm, a NOW member and the first African American woman elected to the U.S. House of Representatives. Chisholm wrote in 1970: "The harshest discrimination that I have encountered in the political arena is anti-feminism, both from males and brain-washed, Uncle Tom females. When I first announced that I was running for the United States Congress, both males and females advised me, as they had when I ran for the NY State Legislature, to go back to teaching — a woman's vocation — and leave the politics to the men."[6]

BRING U.S. TOGETHER

VOTE **CHISHOLM** 1972
UNBOUGHT AND UNBOSSED

Chisolm campaign poster

OTHER LIBERAL
FEMINIST PROJECTS

Ms. Magazine was an important manifestation of the rise and impact of liberal feminism. The publication was founded by Gloria Steinem and others in 1972 with the goal of promoting feminism without having to compromise to the management of anti-woman advertisers and editors.

Steinem was a journalist and feminist activist who had first gained recognition by working undercover in a Playboy club and writing about the unfair conditions endured by Playboy bunnies. She was a co-founder of the Women's Action Alliance, the Coalition of Labor Union Women and Choice USA, among other organizations. The magazine was criticized by radical feminists for working within the traditional publishing world, featuring mostly white, straight middle-class professional women, and for promoting Steinem as a spokesperson of the movement. Nonetheless, Ms. broke several feminist ideas into the mainstream, openly discussing, for instance, women's sexuality and publishing the names and stories of women who had abortions — in a magazine that was on newsstands across the country.

In 1967, Steinem had admitted to working with the CIA as a student activist in the 1950s and early 1960s, but denied the allegations of radical feminists that she continued her collaboration. In early 2016, Steinem made headlines for quite an anti-feminist comment in a television interview that young women were supporting Bernie Sanders because "that's where the boys are." She soon apologized and said she had misspoken.

Ms. Magazine is now published quarterly, with a circulation of 100,000, by the Feminist Majority Foundation (FMF), another liberal group. Its co-founder, Eleanor Smeal, was a president of NOW. By the time the FMF was founded, in 1987, opinion polls showed that 56% of U.S. women considered themselves feminists. The organization conducts research, education and training program to influence policy and supports grass-roots and student activism for women's equality, reproductive health, social justice and nonviolence. It also supports worker union rights, pay equity and an end to sweatshops.

FMF generally supports the Democratic Party, intervenes in the electoral process and endorses liberal pro-woman politicians and legislation. It has also set up a national network of campus affiliates to promote its liberal feminist outlook and strategy.[7]

Another important liberal group, still active today, is the National Women's Political Caucus, founded in 1971 by Gloria Steinem and others to help elect women to public office. Addressing the founding meeting of the NWPC, Steinem said: "This is no simple reform. It really is a revolution. Sex and race, because they are easy visible differences, have been the primary ways of organizing human beings into superior and inferior groups, and into the cheap labor on which this system still depends. We are talking about a society in which there will be no roles other than those chosen or those earned. We are really talking about humanism."

While liberal feminists occasionally used this sort of radical rhetoric for sweeping social equality — even revolution — as we have laid out above, their ideology and program were solidly reformist in orientation. Other trends criticized the limited horizons of this brand of feminism, and became significant forces on college campuses at the grassroots level.

RADICAL FEMINISM AND WOMEN'S LIBERATION

Radical feminism emerged from several sources including the feminist wing of the New Left in the later 1960s. It was the current of the mass movement that was developed mostly by young, single women, many of whom were working low-paying day jobs to support their movement work. Many were college educated as well, and had exposure to a wide spectrum of radical ideas and movements percolating on college campuses. They gained their activist experience — direct action, mass protest and community organizing — in the civil rights movement, especially the Student Nonviolent Coordinating

Twenty thousand women took to the streets of
New York to strike for equality, August 1970.

Committee (SNCC), the campus-based New Left of Students for a
Democratic Society (SDS), and in anti-Vietnam war activism.

Many rejected electoral politics as a means of attaining their
goals. It was this wing of the feminist movement that coined the word
"sexism."[8] Radical feminists identified their movement as "women's
liberation," a name that ultimately took hold in the public mind to
describe the larger women's movement.

It must be noted that in the beginning of the Second Wave in the
mid-'60s, many left-wing men in these various Sixties organizations,
such as aforementioned SDS and SNCC harbored patriarchal attitudes
toward movement women, and put them down and mocked their
demands for total equality. The women did not back down. They built
their own dynamic movement and by the end of the 1960s most male
leftists (though not all) in the various components of the uprising
accepted or championed women's equality. That was a big victory,
and it has lasted in the political left. Here are two examples of male
chauvinism in the Sixties written by movement women:

Lindsey German provides this gem in an article in Counterfire,
Feb. 2, 2013:

> The background to the emergence of the women's
> movement in the U.S. in the late '60s was a level of sexism

and indifference [within the movements] to the question of women which is quite shocking to look back on. The student movement was quite disconnected from the Old Left. ... Women were told that their oppression was of the least importance, and told so in the most contemptuous and elitist way. At the National Conference for the New Politics held in August 1967, where a radical minority of women tried to formulate demands on women's liberation, drawing on the politics of black power, they were derided by most of the men at the conference. [Radical feminist] Shulamith Firestone was patted on the head by one of the male leaders and told 'move on little girl; we have more important issues to talk about here than women's liberation.' Such experiences shaped the early women's movement, which defined itself as dissatisfied with the behavior of the male left.

Frances M. Beal from Third World Women's Alliance New York wrote in 1969:

Unfortunately, there seems to be some confusion in the Movement today as to who has been oppressing whom. Since the advent of black power, the black male has exerted a more prominent leadership role in our struggle for justice in this country. He sees the system for what it really is for the most part. But where he rejects its values and mores on many issues, when it comes to women, he seems to take his guidelines from the pages of the Ladies Home Journal.

Women's liberation rebelled against subordination in the mass movement and fought for equality and for recognition of women's concerns within the movement, as well as for women's rights in the larger society. For them, equality with men in an unequal and racist society was too small a goal. They rejected male status and achievement as the standard to which women should aspire. They took on issues dealing with housework, interpersonal relationships, sexual relations, family arrangements, as well as inequality and injustice in the larger world.

In an interview for this book, Amy Kesselman, feminist historian and founding member of the Chicago Women's Liberation Union,
remembers the origins of the CWLU and describes how women came
together in the early years of women's liberation:

> Our group emerged from a conference put on by
> the National Conference for New Politics, which was in
> 1967. There were some thoughts of a left third party,
> which didn't materialize. A group of us started talking
> about women's issues being part of the left and we came
> up with some things that we wanted to incorporate into
> whatever document emerged from this conference. Shuli
> Firestone went up to say that we'd like to present this,
> and she was told that they had more important things to
> do. So we started meeting at this conference and came
> up with a bunch of ideas and soon after formed a group
> called the West Side Group. We were all left-identified and
> had been involved in the antiwar and civil rights move-
> ments and were full of pent-up ideas.... When I was active
> in the antiwar movement, the men in that movement —
> we had a sit-in and there were nine men and me on the
> steering committee — and I felt sort of trivialized and
> challenged and invisible and I think a lot of people felt
> that way. There were a number of things that were written
> that expressed those feelings. So we had a lot to say. We
> absolutely thought of ourselves as part of the left, but we
> also felt that we needed to have an independent women's
> movement, so that we could be in coalitions with other
> groups, but we would control our own movement. And
> not everybody felt that way....
>
> The group wrote a play. We were going to start an
> independent women's movement, a women's union in
> Chicago, and there were women on the left who were
> against it and we were afraid they were going to subvert
> the conference, so we made this play to bring people
> together. And it worked! So we started the Chicago
> Women's Liberation Union. Part of the inspiration for

the Chicago union was from the Vietnamese. One of the women in our group had represented the peace movement on a trip to Vietnam and met the women in the Vietnamese women's union. She was very impressed about the importance they felt in having an independent women's organization. And she brought that back.

We made a couple of mistakes though. One was that we felt it was important, since we had experienced having our issues treated as secondary, to focus on women's issues and experiences. We were worried about women for whom the experience of being a woman was not the primary focus. And I think we did not understand how other groups of women could not put gender as primary, how they had to look at their identities through race and class. So we talked a lot about wanting to connect with African American women and Latina women, but we did not understand that they couldn't place gender above race....

The other mistake is that we developed theory and consciousness-raising groups based on our experience, which didn't represent everybody's experience, although we talked about it as a universal experience. So we learned that that we were not going to be able to create an inclusive movement if we insisted that everybody put gender first....

We certainly tried very hard to connect with women of color and always saw class as important but felt like the theory and practice that we were developing needed to be incorporated into a broad left that addressed everybody's issues.

Unlike the liberal feminists, radical feminists believed that only a total transformation of society, and not elections or reforms within the existing system, could bring about real freedom for women and ensure that the differences that existed between women and men did not lead to oppression.

The radical feminist trend in the women's liberation movement opened up many new lines of theoretical inquiry, many of which were quite provocative and stimulating, and helped lay bare the sexist stereotypes that pervaded society in every area.[9] Feminist scholar Christine Stansell wrote, "Women's liberation generated countless pressure points of agitation, a myriad of ad hoc campaigns to change sexual mores, manners, men's expectations of women, women's expectations of themselves, and the very language of gender."[10]

While radical feminists had diverse views among themselves, as a trend they moved away from Marxism and class analysis. Like the socialist and communist feminists, they believed in the necessity for a radical change of the society, but they saw their primary enemy as patriarchy and male supremacy, not capitalism, and women's oppression as the primary oppression (as opposed to class exploitation or national oppression). Some promoted a view that men had primarily used biological differences to overthrow matriarchy and institute patriarchy, and this remained the core of women's oppression.

Among their solutions to women's oppression was a current that promoted separation from men. Despite this current's origins in the left, a strong thread of anti-communism, along with opposition to leaders and to hierarchical forms of organization, developed within it.

The radical feminists largely took the form of small collectives, with very intense internal dynamics that produced many splits and only a few organizations that have survived to the present.

At the same time, their influence on feminist thought and culture was profound. A key organizer and theorist in this trend was Shulamith Firestone (1945-2012). Raised in an orthodox Jewish family, she broke with her family to become a painter and early leader of the radical feminist movement. In 1969 she co-founded Redstockings, which held the first public speak-outs on abortion, and later New York Radical Women. Firestone believed that the oppression of women had its basis in biology itself, and that women would not be truly liberated until they were freed from the biological imperative of giving birth, to be replaced by artificial reproduction outside the womb. She wrote several books, the best known of which was The Dialectic of Sex, which claimed that the sexual class system was the primary social divide. In a way, the splits and factionalism that plagued radical feminism led to Firestone's own departure from the movement in the early

1970s. She remained isolated from the movement for the rest of her life and suffered from schizophrenia until her death at age 67.

The Marxist feminists contested certain radical feminist views, while often supporting their actions on behalf of women's liberation. The main Marxist critique explained that it was incorrect to maintain that the fundamental contradiction in society is patriarchy or male supremacy. The Marxist view is that the main problem is capitalist exploitation and oppression, which will be discussed further directly below. Moreover, while biology undoubtedly influenced and gave shape to the overall experience of women's oppression in patriarchal class society, what primarily gave rise to women's oppression was the development of private property relations.

SOCIALIST AND MARXIST FEMINISM

The 1960-75 rebellions resembled a big coming-out party for the political left after years of isolation and government crackdown on dissidents. For feminists, after a decade of intense government and media pressure upon women to cherish the role of a housewife, subordinate to her husband, following gains achieved during World War II, it was a liberation struggle well worth waging.

The U.S political left begins where liberals and the left wing of the Democratic Party leave off. Included in this category are social democrats, socialists, communists, various radicals, anti-imperialists and anarchists.

The left wing of the socialist movement and various communist groups embraced Marxism and several Marxist-oriented feminist formations were quite active during the Second Wave in protests. Among these groups at the time were Radical Women (affiliated with the Freedom Socialist Party), Chicago Women's Liberation Union, Bread and Roses in Boston, the Combahee River Collective, and others.

The main criticism of Marxism by some feminist organizations during the period of social uprisings was that the theory was ill equipped to fight against gender oppression in the here and now because it held that women's liberation would arrive when capitalist class society was abolished.

This was called reductionism for "reducing" the oppression of women to a class issue to be resolved by anti-capitalist revolution. Marx argued in the mid-1800s that gender oppression would dissolve

The revolutionary socialist current in the 1970s women's liberation movement is often overlooked in mainstream histories.

when class oppression was defeated. Actually as soon as the Bolsheviks seized power in Russia in 1917, and the Communist Party of China took over in 1949, both quickly extended women's rights. Socialist revolutions in Korea, Cuba and Vietnam followed suit.

Up into the 1960s the two leading communist organizations in the U.S., the Communist Party and the Socialist Workers Party, tended to subsume resolution of the "woman question" in practice to that of overthrowing capitalism. Smaller and newer Marxist groups already recognized the necessity to fight for reforms to alleviate the plight of women and all oppressed people.

In February of 1970, women members of one such communist organization, Workers World Party, formed an activist and educational female caucus within a party-organized group named Youth Against War and Fascism. The women wrote at the time: "Our caucus is made up of Black, Latin, Asian and white women. We are workers, mothers, and students — gay and straight." They participated in a multitude of women's activities and also "educated ourselves while at the same time raising the consciousness and sensitivity of the men in the organization to the oppression of women."

A leader of Worker's World Party, Dorothy Ballan, wrote in 1970: "The women's struggle is not subordinate to the class struggle. It is itself a form of class struggle, especially if consciously conducted against the bourgeoisie" (i.e., against the capitalist class who own most of society's wealth and means of production).

According to left feminist Barbara Epstein:

> In the 1960s and early 1970s the dominant tendency in the women's movement was radical feminism. At that time the women's movement included two more or less distinct tendencies. One of these called itself Socialist Feminism (or, at times, Marxist Feminism) and understood the

oppression of women as intertwined with other forms of oppression, especially race and class, and tried to develop a politics that would challenge all of these simultaneously. The other tendency called itself Radical Feminism. Large-R Radical Feminists argued that the oppression of women was primary, that all other forms of oppression flowed from gender inequality. .... Though the liberal and radical wings of the women's movement differed in their priorities, their demands were not sharply divided. ...

The radical feminist vision became stalled, torn apart by factionalism and by intense sectarian ideological conflicts. By the latter part of the 1970s, a cultural feminism, aimed more at creating a feminist subculture than at changing social relations generally, had taken the place formerly occupied by radical feminism. ... Ordinarily, such sectarianism occurs in movements that are failing, but the women's movement, at the time, was strong and growing. The problem was the very large gap between the social transformation that radical feminists wanted and the possibility of bringing it about, at least in the short run.

Socialists worked to build unity between the emerging gay liberation and women's liberation movements, which took off in tandem.

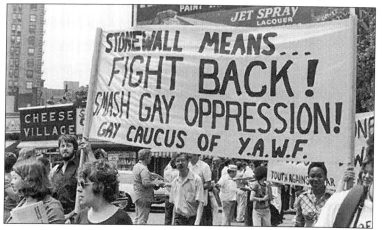

I think that radical feminism became somewhat crazed for the same reasons that much of the radical movement did during the same period. In the late 1960s and early 1970s many radicals not only adopted revolution as their aim but also thought that revolution was within reach in the United States. Different groups had different visions of revolution. There were feminist, black, anarchist, Marxist-Leninist, and other versions of revolutionary politics, but the belief that revolution of one sort or another was around the corner cut across these divisions. The turn toward revolution was not in itself a bad thing; it showed an understanding of the depth of the problems that the movement confronted. But the idea that revolution was within reach in the United States in these years was unrealistic."[11]

As Epstein indicates above, the belief in pending revolution generated intense enthusiasm for organizing, militancy in the streets and stimulating theoretical discussions about how patriarchy could actually be eliminated — qualities that are often lacking today. To the extent that revolutionaries developed an unrealistic sense of immediate revolution, however, this made the movement's decline more difficult to endure, leading to widespread disappointment and demoralization.

Writer, investigative journalist and feminist Barbara Ehrenreich is one of the most well-known advocates of socialist feminism, especially for her 1976 essay "What is socialist feminism?" The essay appeared in the publication of the social democratic New American Movement, which was hostile to Marxist-Leninist parties. In it she wrote:

We have to differentiate ourselves, as feminists, from other kinds of feminists, and, as Marxists, from other kinds of Marxists. ...

The trouble with radical feminism, from a socialist feminist point of view, is that it doesn't go any farther. It remains transfixed with the universality of male supremacy — things have never really changed; all social systems are patriarchies; imperialism, militarism, and capitalism are all simply expressions of innate male aggressiveness. And so on. ... The problem with this, from a socialist feminist point of view, is not only that it leaves out men (and the possibility of reconciliation with them on a truly human and egalitarian basis) but that it leaves out an awful lot about women. For example, to discount a socialist country such as China as a 'patriarchy' — as I have heard radical feminists do — is to ignore the real struggles and achievements of millions of women. ...

As feminists, we are most interested in the most oppressed women — poor and working class women, third world women, etc., and for that reason we are led to a need to comprehend and confront capitalism. I could have said that we need to address ourselves to the class system simply because women are members of classes. But I am trying to bring out something else about our perspective as feminists: there is no way to understand sexism as it acts on our lives without putting it in the historical context of capitalism."

Ehrenreich went on to criticize "mechanical Marxists" or "economic determinists" who view capitalism strictly through an economic lens while "We, along with many, many Marxists who are not feminists, see capitalism as a social and cultural totality. ...We have room within our Marxist framework for feminist issues which have nothing ostensibly to do with production or 'politics,' issues that have to do with the family, health care, 'private' life."[12]

Writing in Monthly Review in January 2011, Marxist Richard Levins noted:

Feminism is a refreshing influence on Marxism. Early feminist writings in the 18th and 19th centuries, beginning with Mary Wollstonecraft, called for women's equality and rejected any religious or biological justification for the subordination of women. They sometimes attributed the suppression of women to a hypothesized patriarchal revolution.

This was a view that was carried over into classical Marxism in Engels's 'Origin of the Family, Private Property and the State,' which referred to 'the world historical defeat of the female sex.' The emergence of bourgeois feminism [in the 1920s] was used to justify the [left's] rejection of feminism as a diversion from the class struggle. But in the 1940s, a core of strong proto-feminist women emerged in the Communist Party USA just at the time when McCarthyism was making all red organizing difficult. Many of the pioneers of Second Wave feminism in the United States had roots in communist and socialist movements and the unions.

The Marxist-oriented Combahee River Collective issued an important statement on socialism and Black feminism in 1977:

> We realize that the liberation of all oppressed peoples necessitates the destruction of the political-economic systems of capitalism and imperialism as well as patriarchy. We are socialists because we believe that work must be organized for the collective benefit of those who do the work and create the products, and not for the profit of the bosses. Material resources must be equally distributed among those who create these resources. We are not convinced, however, that a socialist revolution that is not also a feminist and anti-racist revolution will guarantee our liberation. ... Although we are in essential agreement with Marx's theory as it applied to the very specific economic relationships he analyzed, we know that his analysis must be extended further in order for us to understand our specific economic situation as Black women.

Jane Cutter, a post-Second Wave Marxist feminist and member of the Party for Socialism and Liberation (PSL), said in an interview for this book:

> People still need to hear voices that are concerned with building class unity. That's one of the contribu-

tions that was made by leftist feminists. We understand unity — not just among women but also between women and men.

Our movement is not a zero sum game, where if someone gets ahead, someone else falls behind. We need to reject negative and shame-based ways of dealing with each other. It weakens a movement when members are afraid to express their opinions and debate the different ways to move forward. Many Second Wave feminists had lively, passionate debates.

I believe women should care about socialism. The material basis for women's oppression has its origins in class society. We don't have to go back to ancient history to see that capitalists are profiting by paying women less, profiting off our unpaid labor that's necessary for the maintenance of the working class as a whole. Lots of women have no maternity leave and have to go right back to work after giving birth. Women make sacrifices — working part time, taking lower paying jobs with more flexible schedules to be able to take care of their children. They do the unpaid childcare labor and household labor for the maintenance of their families, so that other family members can work and the children will eventually become workers. The system is profiting off of this.

BLACK FEMINISM

Most activists who called themselves specifically "feminist" in the 1960s were white and middle class.[13] However, the movement for women's liberation was being organized among all races, and activists published each other's writings, organized actions and attended meetings together, and influenced each other's thinking from the beginning.

Black women in large numbers supported the goals of the women's movement. In a 1971 Harris poll, 60% of African American women said they supported efforts to strengthen women's status in society, compared to only 37% of white women. In 1972, in the first ever survey to ask directly about the women's movement, 67% of

Black women said they supported "women's liberation," compared to 35% of white women.[14]

Black women had a complex relationship with the feminist movement, despite being among the most enthusiastic proponents of women's equality. Their liberation was obviously tied to the liberation of all Black people, shaped by a common historical experience of national oppression and resistance alongside Black men even though the legacy of slavery and Jim Crow affected Black women in particular ways. They had to deal with sexism within the Black liberation movement and with white racism in the feminist movement. Differences between heterosexual and lesbian feminists also appeared in the Black feminist movement, with lesbians assuming leadership of prominent segments of the movement.

Women of color generally criticized radical feminists for their separatist elements and for declaring a universal sisterhood, based on their particular experiences, which indicated a lack of understanding of the different experiences of women from different races and classes. They also rejected the practice of putting gender first, ahead of class or race.[15]

Black and white women belonged to both racially mixed and separate organizations and no single organizational form or view could claim hegemony within the movement or any particular sector of women. There were also Third World caucuses within racially mixed organizations. In some of these caucuses issues of economic inequality and class stratification became more prominent.[16]

One of the first Black feminist organizations grew out of SNCC's women's caucus, which formed in 1968. Merging with a Puerto Rican women's organization, they called themselves the Third World Women's Alliance (TWWA), with an anti-capitalist critique of both the Black liberation movement and the largely white feminist movement. It lasted from 1970 to 1977, after which a sizable number went on to join Marxist-Leninist organizations.

The National Black Feminist Organization (NBFO), founded in 1973, sought to combine the fights against racism and sexism. To charges that they were undermining the struggle for Black liberation, they responded that they represented more than half the Black population and that for all Black people to be free, they needed to organize around the needs of Black women. Among the issues they stressed were domestic workers, welfare, reproductive freedom and the situation of unwed mothers. The NBFO operated as a national organization until 1977.[17]

The Combahee River Collective, noted above, was founded by Barbara Smith and others in 1975, when the Boston chapter of the NBFO separated from the national. With Black lesbians in the leadership, the collective presented an early theory of identity politics that consisted of the interlocking identities of gender, race and class, opposed the separatism of segments of radical, Black and lesbian feminism, and promoted coalition politics. The Collective declared itself to be socialist and called for the destruction of capitalism and imperialism as well as patriarchy, as a prerequisite for the liberation of all oppressed peoples. In addition they declared that a socialist revolution must also be feminist and antiracist.[18]

ASIAN AMERICAN FEMINISM

Asian American women formed grassroots groups throughout the country.

Many Asian American women felt marginalized within the mainstream feminist movement. They struggled against stereotypes and what they felt was the lack of interest among white feminists in learning about the issues of importance to Asian American women. Like many Black feminists, Asian American women stressed the importance of combatting racism as well as sexism, both in the larger society and in the mass movement, and in promoting women's rights in the context of their own communities.[19] Activists established the first Asian American women's center in Los Angeles in 1972.

Asian American working-class women struggled with issues of immigration as well as workplace discrimination. In the hotel industry, for example, they fought against the wage gap between higher paying skilled jobs and those of cleaners, dishwashers and other low paying and less visible jobs. In the late 1970s they conducted a two-year labor action that won a significant pay increase from management, as well as more respectful treatment from management.[20]

LATINA FEMINISM

Women in the Latina community were also in motion.

Latina farmworkers, led by Dolores Huerta and Cesar Chavez, were active with the United Farm Workers, which involved women from its founding in 1962. These women faced multiple oppressions: As mothers, they watched their children suffer from malnutrition born of poverty. Yet they had to work to earn income for their families and often had to bring their children out into the fields. At home they suffered from domination by their traditional husbands, who asserted the right to rule the family. All of this took place in the context of agricultural workers' exclusion from New Deal labor legislation that would have established better working conditions, higher pay and benefits. Women were instrumental in organizing — and winning – farm worker strikes.[21]

In 1971 the First National Chicana Conference — La Conferencia de Mujeres por la Raza — was held in Houston, Texas. Six hundred young Mexican American women passed resolutions that asserted their right to a positive attitude toward sex; rejected the Catholic Church as an oppressive institution; and called for the equality of women and men in every respect. They also called for free legal abortion and birth control for the Chicana community, "controlled by Chicanas," freedom from unwanted medical experiments and double standards about sex, 24-hour child care, and opportunities for political, educational and economic advancement. They also sought equal pay for equal work.[22]

Latina women in other parts of the country also led struggles against forced sterilization. (These struggles are covered in Chapter 8)

Revolutionary and socialist organizations began to develop and organize in the Chicano and immigrant communities as well, considerably to the left of the UFW.

LESBIAN FEMINISM

Lesbians have had a long history of activism in the women's movement. Unlike other movement activists, their very being at the time was illegal and marked by public ostracism. Laws prohibiting sexual acts between consenting adults of the same sex were in force in every state until 1962. In some states it was even a violation to wear the clothing of the opposite sex. Only in 2003 did the Supreme Court, in striking down Texas' "sodomy" law, rule in essence that all such state laws violated due process of consenting adults.[23] The Supreme Court's freedom to marry decision did not arrive until June 26, 2015.

The Daughters of Bilitis, the first lesbian rights organization, was founded in San Francisco in 1955 by four lesbian couples, with the goal of overcoming social isolation and prejudice, and promoting equality, education, research, and changes in penal codes as they pertained to homosexuality.[24] The DoB described itself as "A woman's organization for the purpose of promoting the integration of the homosexual into society."[25] It lasted 14 years, during which time it published a magazine called The Ladder, which was a communications link for many lesbians. A number of readers and members joined the feminist uprising in the mid-'60s.

The mass movements gave impetus to the growing movement for lesbian and gay rights, but even within the feminist movement, lesbians had to fight to have their concerns recognized. They also had to fight against the male dominated gay liberation movement, which marginalized lesbians.

The lesbian and gay liberation movement reached a turning point with the Stonewall rebellion, a historic fight-back action against police repression in June of 1969 at a gay bar in New York's Greenwich Village. Police raids against lesbians, gays, drag queens and transgender people were common at the time, but the patrons of the Stonewall on that evening had had enough.

Night after night, patrons and their allies engaged in violent struggle against the police, as they also sought legitimate and legal places to meet. The larger community was divided; there was some support but also rejection and opposition toward people who were considered outcasts from "respectable society." Stonewall propelled a whole generation of struggle, which has not ended to this day, and has been commemorated annually in Pride marches all across the country and Pride caucuses within unions and the AFL-CIO, called "Pride at Work."

As the more liberal feminists rejected open lesbianism, more radical feminists pushed it forward in actions and in new theory. NOW changed its attitude toward lesbians in 1971. Phyllis Lyon and Del Martin, founders of the DoB, were NOW members and Martin was the first out lesbian elected to its national board. (Lyon and Martin were also the first same-sex couple to marry in San Francisco after 50 years of commitment.)

In the Compton Cafeteria Riot of 1966,
transgender and lesbian youth in San Francisco
fought back against police harassment and violence.

Radicalesbians, an organization of "women-identified women,"
called lesbians the true feminist radicals.[26] They regarded lesbianism
as more of a political choice than a predetermined sexual orientation,
a stance that was challenged both within and outside the feminist
movement. Others turned to separatism, not only from men but also
from heterosexual feminists.

Some early radical lesbians saw heterosexuality as key to
male-dominated society and patriarchy and believed that it was necessary to embrace lesbianism in order to overthrow the misogynist
social order and create a more just society. They also sought to change
patriarchal culture, creating new forms of language (womyn, wimmin)
and religion (paganism, goddess worship), as well as engaging in creative and bold direct action, founding arts and performance programs

and women's bookstores, and laying the groundwork for new gender theories in the budding women's studies discipline.[27]

Among the early creative forces of this movement were poets Audre Lorde and Adrienne Rich; Barbara Smith, socialist feminist organizer and co-founder of the Combahee River Collective; and theologian Mary Daly.

In the aggregate, lesbian activists contributed significant energy and resoluteness to the feminist movement and they were strengthened in turn by the larger feminist movement. They played a key role in fighting against violence against women and for reproductive rights; created LGBTQ centers in cities across the country for education, social and cultural events and community organizing; fought against discrimination in the military, in educational and religious institutions, and in business; pushed for recognition of lesbian unions, leading up to the marriage equality movement; and fought against discriminatory laws.

Feminist theory and activism contributed to expanded visions of gender identity that are continuing to develop in the current LGBTQ movement, which has both expanded and challenged certain aspects of feminist thought.

LABOR FEMINISM

As the women's movement grew in the 1970s, labor feminists worried that the concerns of poor and working women would be set aside. Along with Black women, working-class feminists were among those who differed with liberal feminism's claims of universal sisterhood. With different class and racial backgrounds, experiences, relationships with and attitudes toward men, positions in their communities, and overall political orientations, many activist women rejected the claims of the mainstream feminism movement to represent all women. Many also rejected what they saw as the movement giving short shrift to the caregiving and "self-sacrifice" parts of women's lives. Instead, these women valued these aspects of their lives and wanted them to be recognized and valued by the movement.[28]

At the same time, working-class women, while often excluded from popular accounts of the mass women's movement, were inspired by the movement to open up opportunities for women in the trades and other nontraditional occupations. As "Sisters in the

Brotherhoods" tells it: "They faced daunting obstacles entering these occupations. On the job they endured unrelenting, often vicious harassment. They also received support from men who taught them their trades and helped them navigate unfamiliar territory."[29]

Individual women got jobs as firefighters, carpenters, electricians, mechanics and union organizers. They were helped by such organizations as Nontraditional Employment for Women (NEW), which was founded in 1978 to help break gender barriers in skilled unionized trade jobs; CLUW, and several unions.[30] In particular, the UAW and UE committed themselves to training women and opening up their hiring practices, bargained for benefits for women, and worked to combat sexism within the union. Union women fought for pay equity and for policies that would relieve them of the "double day," the unpaid second shift of housework and childcare.[31] ☐

Chapter 8
A movement that transformed society

DESPITE different approaches and views, taken together the struggles of all the various tendencies within the Second Wave feminist uprising pushed the movement forward. Some of the biggest achievements were in reforms won. Most important were the changes in the thinking of the people, seeding the political landscape for future victories. Many progressive and left movements and organizations underwent major changes in their attitudes and policies when they were sharply challenged by women members.

The major victories in the 1960s and '70s were in reproductive freedom and justice, educational opportunity, challenging domestic violence, sexual harassment and discrimination, and reshaping the country's culture, shattering old norms and opening up society to new ideas and ways of living. On an intellectual level the movement essentially introduced the concept of gender itself to the larger public, which previously understood the socialized behaviors and expectations for men and women as reflections of "human nature" and biology rather than social and historical development.

REPRODUCTIVE FREEDOMS
The subordination of women has been effected most insidiously through the enforcement of a double standard of sexual mores and laws that impose oppressive restrictions on women in their most private lives. As a consequence, the struggle for women's rights has been fought at the most basic levels of human life: the woman's place in the family and in society, the integrity of the body, the right to privacy, and all the ramifications in public, private and work life related to bearing and raising children.

Struggles for reproductive freedom and justice — for women to be able to plan their lives, their families and their health care — have always been tied up with the fight against racism, sexism and poverty. Yet the legitimate desires of women to control their reproduction were often confronted by the state, religious institutions, the medical profession and private pharmaceutical corporations, which not only intruded on the decision-making rights of women but also tested drugs and performed surgeries on unsuspecting poor and oppressed women. Therefore, the struggle for reproductive rights and freedoms was a cornerstone of the feminist mass movement.

BIRTH CONTROL, EXPERIMENTS AND STERILIZATION

The Food and Drug Administration (FDA) approved the birth control pill in 1960, giving women the ability to reliably control their fertility for the first time in history. Before "the pill," women had no reliable means of birth control apart from abstinence, and other forms of birth control were harder for women to conceal, thus risking the wrath of one's husband. While this scientific advance made reproductive choices technically possible in ways that were previously impossible, the political system held fast to its control of reproductive rights in two important ways.

On the one hand, women had inadequate access to the birth control methods that existed and no access to legal abortion. Restrictions on distribution of contraception were remnants of Victorian era vice and obscenity laws. While federal restrictions were overturned in the 1930s, some state laws remained on the books until a 1965 Supreme Court decision, *Griswold v. Connecticut,* gave married couples the right to access birth control, ruling that it was protected in the Constitution as a right to privacy. However, millions of unmarried women in 26 states were still denied access. Only a 1972 Supreme Court decision, *Baird v. Eisenstadt,* legalized contraception for all, regardless of marital status.[1]

Women quickly jumped at the opportunities to assert a modicum of power over their family size, sexual lives and the planning of their futures. By 1970, a stunning 60 percent of adult women in the United States were using birth control.[2]

The other attack on reproductive freedom was the widespread use of forced sterilization of poor women especially in the Black,

Mexican, Native and Puerto Rican communities. In the case of Puerto Rico, this included experiments on poor rural Puerto Rican women to develop the birth control pill. The experimental pill carried three times the amount of hormones of today's pill. The women, some of them desperate for some form of birth control, were not told that the pill was experimental and that they were in effect guinea pigs. Side effects were ignored, and the deaths that occurred were never investigated nor was anyone punished for carrying out the uninformed testing.

U.S. colonialism further imposed grotesque laws against Puerto Rican women, denying public assistance to those who refused sterilization procedures. This practice was an overt form of colonial control, operating under the guise of solving population problems and unemployment. From the 1930s and continuing until the 1970s, some 35 percent of Puerto Rican women were sterilized without their knowledge or consent. During the 1960s other state legislatures considered passing legislation authorizing the sterilization of poor women with too many "illegitimate" children. These efforts were unsuccessful, but the fact

Women in the Puerto Rican community mobilized to stop the genocidal practices of forced sterilization.

that they were seriously proposed reflected the deeply sexist and racist approach of the ruling class towards oppressed women.[3]

The women of the revolutionary socialist Young Lords Party in the United States were the first to draw public attention to the high levels of sterilization of Puerto Rican women. According to author Nancy MacLean, "The practice of sterilization in Puerto Rico goes back to the 1930s when doctors pushed it as the only means of contraception. In 1947-48, 7 percent of the women were sterilized; between 1953 and 1954, four out of every 25; and by 1957 the number had increased to about one out of three women."[4]

Latina activists were leaders of the movement against sterilization abuse. Dr. Helen Rodriguez-Trias, a prominent Puerto Rican activist, founded the Committee to End Sterilization Abuse (CESA) in New York City in 1973. CESA and its allies fought for a waiting period of up to 30 days that would give women the time they needed to protect themselves against coercion, avail themselves of unbiased counseling, and receive accurate information in their preferred language. In response, New York City instituted reforms in all city hospitals in 1975, with federal guidelines following in 1979.[5]

Similar struggles were waged by Chicana and Mexican activists in the Southwest and California, where doctors in overcrowded public hospitals routinely carried out sterilizations of women without their consent immediately after childbirth.

For Southern Black women, sterilization abuse was a civil rights issue. In the 1950s and early '60s, these women were subjected to what were called "Mississippi appendectomies," hysterectomies performed by white doctors without the women's consent when they entered the hospital for other procedures. These abuses were most prevalent in communities with an active civil rights movement. In 1961, civil rights activist Fannie Lou Hamer was subjected to this abuse.[6]

Native American women, some as young as 15, were targets of this form of population control in huge numbers — at least 25 percent of Native American women in the 1970s alone.[7] Federal funds were funneled through the states and also the Indian Health Service to pay for tubal ligations and hysterectomies.[8]

Some of these cruel approaches were justified as a form of controlling the population, some cited poor women's "dependence" on state services; others used paternalist arguments that it was in poor women's best interests. Whatever the rationale, this massive abuse of poor and oppressed women is hard to overstate. When civil rights and radical activists charged the government and the ruling class with a form of genocide against oppressed people, it was no exaggeration — it was policy.

THE IMPORTANCE OF ABORTION RIGHTS

The struggle to legalize abortion was the most visible of the reproductive rights campaigns waged by the women's movement. As with restrictions on birth control, restrictions on abortion were carried out through an alliance between political leaders and the medical profession that was intended to restrict women's rights and suppress their growing independence.

Abortion was legal in the U.S. until the mid-19th century. By 1880 medical and political establishments combined to outlaw it in most states except to save the mother's life. During this same period, the medical establishment — almost entirely a "boys' club" — took a strong stand against midwives, edging them out of their positions as providers of childbirth and abortion services.

Outlawing abortion did not end its practice. Before legalization, some one million abortions were performed each year in the United States. The annual death toll from illegal and self-induced abortions ranged from the hundreds to over 1,000. Serious infections and injuries forced women into hospital emergency rooms. Sympathetic doctors joined women's rights activists in calling for legalization. Others, bowing to hospital policy, refused treatment of women until the patient revealed the identity of the doctor who had carried out the abortion.

Deaths from illegal abortions were most prevalent among the poor and women of color. In 1969, 75 percent of the women who died from abortions (most of them illegal) were women of color. Of all legal abortions in that year, 90 percent were performed on white private patients.[9]

Legalization, without broad access to abortion services, did not in itself resolve this class dynamic as the procedure in a private clinic was quite costly.

According to a Guttmacher report, "Even in the early 1970s, when abortion was legal in some states, a legal abortion was simply out of reach for many. Minority women suffered the most. ... From

1972 to 1974, the mortality rate due to illegal abortion for nonwhite women was 12 times that for white women."[10]

Until the late 1960s efforts to legalize abortion took place in state legislatures, focusing on modifying, rather than overturning, restrictions. In the 1950's, Dr. Dorothy Brown, the first Black female surgeon in the South and a Tennessee State legislator, was the first state legislator in the United States to introduce a bill to legalize abortion in cases of rape or incest, beyond saving the life of the mother. In response to charges that abortion amounted to genocide of Black people, Dr. Brown responded: "We should dispense quickly the notion that abortion is genocide, because genocide in this country dates back to 1619."[11]

In 1969 the radical feminist group Redstockings conducted the first speak-out on abortion in New York City. Women spoke of their own experience with unwanted pregnancy, illegal and sometimes life-threatening abortions, and carrying a pregnancy to term only to give up the baby for adoption. This was followed by other speak-outs around the country and marked a turning point in the debate on legalizing abortion, from reforming existing restrictive laws to overturning them entirely. At first only the most radical feminists raised the issue, but soon liberal feminists joined in as well. A broad section of women began to demand access to safe, legal abortion as a key element of equality and freedom.

Advocates of legal abortion conducted marches, demonstrations at medical conventions, and sit-ins at hospitals. Feminists in Chicago organized an underground abortion service, called "Jane," that arranged for more than 11,000 abortions, "with a safety record that rivaled private clinics."[12]

Lawsuits challenging anti-abortion laws were filed in several states, and radical feminists played an important role in finding plaintiffs and educating local communities about the importance of legal abortion and the discriminatory nature of laws that forbade it.[13] Ultimately, a case brought by a plaintiff using the name Jane Roe to challenge a Texas law outlawing abortion was appealed to the Supreme Court. In 1973, the Court handed down a decision in *Roe v. Wade* that protected a woman's right to an abortion in the early stages of pregnancy, before the viability of the fetus, using the right to privacy that was affirmed in the 1965 *Griswold* decision.

Roe v. Wade was an exceptional victory for women, especially given the strong opposition from the religious right and conservatives in general. Legalization and the growing consciousness of women's needs brought better and safer abortion services. For the women who had access to legal abortion services, severe infections, fever and hemorrhaging from illegal or self-induced abortions became a thing of the past. Women health care workers improved their abortion techniques. Some commercial clinics hired feminist abortion activists to do counseling. Local women's groups set up public referral services, and women in some areas organized women-controlled nonprofit abortion facilities. These efforts turned out to be just the beginning of a longer struggle to preserve legal abortion and to make it accessible to all women.

The *Roe* decision did not totally satisfy the demand of the feminist movement who called for "abortion on demand," meaning no waiting period or having to first prove a special circumstance (such as rape). Most fundamentally, by not guaranteeing access, in terms of availability of clinics and in terms of cost, many women would still have to travel to another state or county, or pay exorbitant prices. These were very real restrictions — amounting to de facto prohibitions — for low-income women in particular and those in rural areas.

Since 1976, Congress has attached the "Hyde Amendment" in one form or another to federal budget bills, preventing the use of Medicaid funds for abortion services. It is the only medical procedure ever banned under Medicaid and has a devastating impact on access for young women and women in poverty. The pro-choice movement has been criticized for not mobilizing sufficiently against passage of this measure at that time, the first post-Roe victory for anti-abortion forces.

It is noteworthy that while the federal government will not pay for abortions, it has not stopped paying for the voluntary sterilization of poor women.

The Supreme Court was not full of feminists when it issued its *Roe* ruling. In fact, it was generally reactionary and conservative. It was a sign of the movement's strength, the pressure from below that had resonated through and shaken all of society.

Over the years, federal courts, state legislators and the Supreme Court has repeatedly chiseled away at the *Roe* ruling. In a 1992 decision, *Planned Parenthood v. Casey,* while the court upheld the right to abortion, it gave states the right to impose restrictions that did not create an "undue burden" on the woman seeking abortion. This decision has been tested repeatedly, as 27 states have passed laws with severe restrictions on abortion. These restrictions include waiting periods, parental consent, mandated counseling and the prohibition of state Medicaid dollars to fund abortion. According to a Guttmacher Institute report, a total of 1,074 abortion restrictions have been passed in the decades since Roe. Of these, 288 (27 percent) were enacted between 2010 and 2015.

There are those who believe that granting abortion rights on the basis of the constitutional right to privacy is a weakness of the *Roe* decision. Had the case been decided on the basis of equal rights, such as the one legalizing same-sex marriage, it may have been harder to challenge and chip away.

While all feminists supported a woman's right to choose, how the issue has been framed and presented was the subject of considerable debate and tension within the movement. There have been, on the one hand, ideological differences between liberal and radical feminists, and also between white and Black feminists, who tended to put the struggle for abortion rights in the context of the many forms of oppression facing Black women.

In the modern era, this extends to those who focus on "reproductive rights" or "reproductive justice." The latter has especially been advanced by Black feminists — as well as Latina and other women of color organizations —who understood the central importance of winning the legal struggle but were critical of the women's movement's single-issue focus on the issue. This tended to exclude or subordinate other aspects of the struggle, such as access to reproductive health care, the battles over sterilization, as well as economic and social rights. Some of these groups also use different language and points of emphasis when discussing abortion.(See Chapter 10)

Black feminists were also critical of forces in the Black liberation movement that campaigned against family planning. The Nation of Islam, the Pittsburgh chapter of the NAACP, Whitney Young of the Urban League and others actually reversed positions that had been in favor of family planning in the 1960s. A 1967 Black Power conference organized by Amiri Baraka passed an anti-birth control resolution. (Baraka at that point was a cultural nationalist; he became a communist in the 1970s and changed his previous positions on women's liberation.)

The Black Panther Party supported free abortion and contraceptives on demand. But there was tension within the party on abortion and family planning, with some male members trying to shut down family planning clinics in New Orleans and Pittsburgh.

According to Kathleen Cleaver, who was the party's information minister at the time, "In order for women to obtain liberation, the struggles [Black liberation and women's rights] are going to have to be united." The women of the Panthers, along with Angela Davis — all of whom were held in high esteem throughout the radical movement — also played a vital role in introducing and merging socialist and anti-colonial concepts with the women's movement. African American women, of course, have a long history in the struggle to obtain abortions. In the 1950s and '60s, Black midwives and doctors had to be underground to carry out their operations, as the practice remained illegal. According to reproductive justice leader Loretta Ross, "African American women exerted a dynamic and aggressive influence on the family planning movement. They

Kathleen Cleaver, 2008

constituted the largest single bloc of support for family planning and were so visible that politicians in some states began to see them as a potential political force." [14]

African American Rep. Shirley Chisholm, D-N.Y., wrote in 1970: "To label family planning and legal abortion programs 'genocide' is male rhetoric, for male ears. It falls flat to female listeners and to thoughtful male ones. Women know, and so do many men, that two or three children who are wanted, prepared for, reared amid love and stability, and educated to the limit of their ability will mean more for the future of the [B]lack and brown races from which they come than any number of neglected, hungry, ill-housed and ill-clothed youngsters."

THE WOMEN'S HEALTH MOVEMENT

All of these struggles at the grassroots and legal level contributed to the growing women's health movement, which challenged the medical and pharmaceutical fields from within, and reached into women's everyday lives.

In one important example, feminists challenged the safety of high-dose oral contraceptive pills at well-publicized congressional hearings in 1970. As a result, the formulation of the pill was changed and the package insert for prescription drugs came into being.

Also in 1970 the Boston Women's Health Collective published the groundbreaking "Our Bodies, Ourselves," a handbook on women's health, reproduction and sexuality, which contained a trove of facts, diagrams and instructions for women's enlightenment and self-care. [Working at Monthly Review in 1969, I remember seeing the galley proofs passed around and the women's joy and excitement at seeing this unprecedented resource for gaining power over our bodies and our health care. — D.G.]

According to Dr. Helen Rodriguez-Trias, the women's health movement changed the way many women and practitioners thought about women's health and medical care:

> Women brought a feminist perspective to health issues affecting women. They examined power relationships among individuals and between individuals and systems....
>
> The specialty of obstetrics gynecology created folks very geared toward surgical solutions. This was one reason why cesarean section rates were going up. This didn't necessarily respect women's wishes regarding childbearing or other issues. The only way to effect change was for more women to go into the professions and instill a different perspective—a more human touch and a more respectful relationship with patients.

At the same time, the gaps in health care continue to be caused by massive and growing economic and social inequality.[15]

FIGHTING DISCRIMINATION IN THE WORKPLACE

The "family wage system" has been an ideal in the United States since the early years of the 1900s. It is based on a male worker earning enough to maintain his wife and two or more children in relative economic security. One of the unspoken purposes was to remove women from the labor market, which they had begun to enter in the later 1800s, and more importantly to insure the continuation of the nuclear family with a male head of household — the convention of the day.

The unions initiated and fought for this "family wage," improving the lives of tens of millions of workers over the years, particularly in manufacturing and the public sector.

Of course, the family wage was never available to a large segment of the U.S. population. Women heads of household, low-skilled and low-wage workers, and most Black, Latino and Asian American families found it impossible to survive on a single income.

The family wage system began gradually declining in effectiveness in the middle 1970s when capitalist corporations stopped raising wages in correlation with increases in productivity. The result has been the general stagnation of working-class wages and jobs, and a significant decline in the union movement.

Every struggle by women in labor included a fight against low pay. Women were not expected to earn enough to support themselves, let alone a family. That was the man's job, and employers used the excuse of men's traditional role as breadwinner and head of household to keep female wages down.

While everyone knows about the mythological feminist "bra burners," most do not know about this example of female superexploitation in the workplace: In 1971 garment worker organizer Anne Draper, a Marxist and independent socialist, testified at the California Industrial Welfare Commission on behalf of raising the minimum wage. She held up a torn Woolworths bra. Many working women could afford one bra every several years, and the torn one had lasted only six months. "It was time for a raise," she testified.[16]

Congress passed the Equal Pay Act (EPA) in 1963, as a result of pressure from women's rights activists. The Equal Pay Act amended the 1938 Fair Labor Standards Act to prohibit sex discrimination in wages and called for equal pay for equal work. Over 50 years later the pay gap still exists, of course, but this was the first legal defeat for sexism in the workplace. The act kept in place the exclusion of certain agricultural, domestic workers and home health aides, occupations that were also excluded from Social Security and other New Deal federally mandated benefits for workers.[17]

A year later, the cause of women's equality received a major boost from the Civil Rights Act of 1964, which was fundamentally a product of the Black freedom struggle. That struggle always has, historically and today, boosted the rights of all oppressed and exploited people in this country. The bill banned discrimination not only on the basis of race, but also religion, national origin and sex in public accommodation and other areas. Title VII of the act dealt with employment, expanding the rights of women in employment beyond wage equity to include hiring, firing and promotion. Title VII also set up the Equal Employment Opportunity Commission (EEOC) to enforce employment-related anti-discrimination laws.

These regulations, combined with executive orders, were enforced most effectively in the public sector, opening up government jobs for women — and especially women of color — in local, state and federal agencies.

But the legal victories in the women's and the civil rights movements did not produce equality. Their real impact was to create an improved legal environment to carry out the struggle for equality. These laws did not, of course, address the fundamental problem of declining and low wages — which affected many men as well as women.

For working women of the 1960s-'70s there was a critical need to transform the workplace: to expand the choices of jobs; to earn a living wage by increasing women's real wages and by abolishing the pay gap between men and women workers; and to have access to more union jobs. This amounted to a fight for the right to economic independence and autonomy, but one that would also improve the standing of the entire working class.

Women led this struggle, many working within the labor movement. As an example of the cross fertilization between the two movements, Chicago Women's Liberation Union campaigned in 1971 to get female janitors equal pay with male janitors. Under the banner of their organization, Direct Action for Rights in Employment (DARE), they marched on the mayor's office and eventually won their campaign.

The Coalition of Labor Union Women (CLUW) is the country's only national organization for union women. Its founding in 1974 was the result of pressure by women within AFL-CIO combined with the influence of the feminist movement.[18] At its founding convention in Chicago, CLUW adopted four basic goals of action: to promote affirmative action in the workplace; to strengthen the role of women in unions; to organize the unorganized women; and to increase the involvement of women in the political and legislative process.[19]

In addition to union concerns, CLUW concerns itself with women's health, reproductive freedom and gay rights, among other social justice issues.

Labor women won some important victories during this period. In 1969, 400 hospital workers in Charleston, S.C., won a 116-day strike after the firing of 12 Black aides for attending a grievance meeting. In a 1972-74 labor action of garment workers against Farah Company of El Paso, 4,000 Chicana workers struck, headed up a national boycott, and won union recognition.

Women office workers formed a unique alliance of grassroots activists, the union movement and popular culture. In 1973 a grass-roots collective of Boston office workers formed Boston 9to5 to advocate for higher pay and opportunities for advancement. In 1975 the group won a class-action lawsuit against several publishing companies, awarding plaintiffs $1.5 million in back pay. That same year, the group teamed up with the Service Employees International Union (SEIU) to form Local 925 to help win collective bargaining rights for office workers in Boston. This alliance inspired the 1980 hit movie "9 to 5," starring Jane Fonda, Lily Tomlin and Dolly Parton.

The organization went national in 1981, focusing on pay equity, medical leaves, the effects of automation, and racial and sexual harassment and discrimination. Calling itself the National Association

Women in organized labor have been on the front lines of struggle.

PHOTO: COALITION OF LABOR UNION WOMEN

of Working Women, the organization became the largest membership organization of working women in the United States[20]

In other campaigns, working-class women fought for child care, garbage collection, crossing guards, parks, playgrounds, and swimming pools. They also fought against toxic waste dumping. In 1978 a Niagara Falls working-class mother, Lois Gibbs, whose son's school was built on a toxic waste dump, founded the Love Canal movement, which led to the creation of Superfund for toxic waste cleanup.

Labor feminism was an arena where women built up organizational and activist experience that they contributed to the larger feminist movement. The struggle for women's equality in the workplace of course continues today.

The women's movement waged a strong fight against economic inequality and, as with other inequities, brought the problem into the open. Progress was made in opening more sections of the labor force to women, some modest closing of the pay gap and some inroads in breaking the glass ceiling. But with more women in the workforce, more women at the bottom of the pay scale, no improvement in family benefits for working mothers and the safety net in shreds, the great bulk of improvements were left for later movements to win.

FIGHTING FOR EQUALITY IN THE SCHOOLS

Sex discrimination in public education was not included in the 1964 Civil Rights Act. It took an amendment to the 1965 Higher Education Act, called Title IX and passed by Congress in 1972, to ban discrimination in education on the basis of sex. Agitation by the women's movement played a key role in getting the amendment passed, but in the years since then, more agitation is needed to ensure that the law is enforced.

Title IX is best known for ending discrimination in sports. In the early 1970s, when the bill was passed, only one out of every eighteen high school athletes were girls; by 1980 the number was one out of three — a six-fold increase. Title IX also protects students in programs receiving federal funds from other forms of discrimination: helping pregnant and parenting students, young women in the STEM fields, and protection against sexual harassment and violence on campuses.

These years of struggle saw a huge increase in the percentage of young women enrolling in college. In 1960, less than 38 percent

The movement forced the government to create and expand athletics programs for young women in public schools and colleges.

of high school graduates went on to college; in 1985, almost 57 percent did. (Figures for male students were 54 percent in 1960 and 59 percent in 1980.)

The number of women with graduate degrees also increased during this period, as well as the number admitted to professional programs such as those in medicine, law and nursing. At the same time, job segregation by gender remained, and even as women were admitted into the higher echelons of the labor market, they continued to earn less than men.

In the universities, increasing numbers of women faculty were hired, thanks to anti-discrimination suits. These faculty members mentored female students who went on to become the next generation of educators.

Women also fought to change what was taught in school. Feminists created Women's Studies courses and programs in universities beginning in 1969. Women's Studies as a discipline also influenced the growing inclusion of women's perspectives and experience in other liberal arts and science disciplines. Often from within women's studies came LGBTQ scholarship and programs.

Feminist trends in education were not limited to universities. Women also flocked to new courses in auto mechanics, self defense, truck driving and other trades. During the period of an active and militant mass feminist movement, these programs increased rapidly. But their existence could not be taken for granted; as the movement has waned, many of the programs have been threatened, suffering from reduced funding and political attacks.

MAKING SEXUAL HARASSMENT ILLEGAL

Sexual harassment has long been a fact of life in the workplace, thriving in an environment of wage discrimination and patriarchal subordination of women. It has only been illegal since the passage of Title VII of the Civil Rights Act of 1964. But, like abortion, sexual harassment was not discussed in public. This was an indignity that was suffered in private.

A 1975 speak-out in Ithaca, N.Y., held by a group called Working Women United, revealed the extent of this harassment on the job, as well as the indignity and suffering that it caused.[21] A Supreme Court decision in 1986 held that sexual harassment created a discriminatory and hostile workplace that was illegal under Title VII. This went all the way to the Supreme Court in part because the term "sexual harassment" did not appear in the language of Title VII.[22] Subsequent court decisions expanded on workers' rights to be free of sexual harassment.

The practice, of course, has not been eliminated, but it has been considerably reduced from the early 1960s, and women now have a legal framework — and often internal company practices and policies — to strike back against sexual harassment.

OTHER LEGISLATIVE GAINS

In the early 1970s Congress passed more legislation for women's rights than ever before or since. Both houses passed the Equal Rights Amendment (which was then defeated by the states), provided tax breaks for working parents, and approved Title IX of the Higher Education Act. The EEOC upped its enforcement of laws against sex discrimination in employment and included women in affirmative action programs designed to ensure equal hiring and pro-motion opportunities.[23]

Laws were passed against sex discrimination in consumer credit and home mortgage lending. Up until 1974, banks could refuse women credit cards in their own names if they did not have their husbands' consent. This practice was deemed illegal. In 1975 the Supreme Court overturned the exclusion of women from serving on juries. (Again, it is incredible to think that such a practice existed not so long ago!)

All of these changes were directly or indirectly brought about by the struggle for women's equality and liberation.

ECONOMIC RIGHTS FOR POOR WOMEN

What about the women with children who couldn't work, or whose work didn't earn enough for their dependents? While Aid to Families with Dependent Children (AFDC) — the federally funded income program for the poor — saved families from homelessness and starvation, it imposed increasingly strict and humiliating restrictions on recipients. That program was ended under Democratic President Bill Clinton in 1996, and his replacement, the Personal Responsibility and Work Opportunity Reconciliation Act, was even more draconian. (See Chapter 1.)

But women fought back. In 1966 grass roots activists and groups representing poor people and welfare recipients organized the National Welfare Rights Organization (NWRO) as part of the civil rights and women's movements. At its peak it included more than 20,000 women.

NWRO activists pushed for grants beyond rent and utilities, to include such items as school, clothes and household appliances. They also won the right to due process and fair hearings and fought the intrusions into their privacy by welfare departments. Welfare rights activists developed a political consciousness and actions that were explicitly feminist.[24]

Johnnie Tillmon, NWRO executive director, wrote in Welfare is a Women's Issue in 1972: "AFDC is like a supersexist marriage. You trade in a man for *the man*. But you can't divorce him if he treats you bad. He can divorce you, of course, cut you off anytime he wants. But in that case, he keeps the kids, not you."[25] Tillmon, a sharecropper's daughter, had been a union shop steward in an industrial laundry until illness forced her to quit her job and go on welfare.

NWRO advocated for a guaranteed income, which would eliminate all categories for aid, such as gender and family, except

The National Welfare Rights Organization
held a march to end hunger in 1968.

economic need. This demand has resurfaced in other campaigns for
the rights of the poor, since the NWRO went out of existence from
bankruptcy in 1975.

The need for such a movement remains just as urgent today. In
1973, women headed 45.4 percent of poor families. By comparison,
in 2015, women headed more than 50 percent of poor families, and
64 percent of minimum wage earners were women.

THE EQUAL RIGHTS AMENDMENT

The sharp splits over the ERA that existed since it was introduced in the early 1920s were resolved 50 years later in 1970 as the
feminist struggle was escalating. As explained in Chapter 5, equal
rights feminists opposed the special protections for women workers
that social justice feminists defended. In the 1970s, ERA proponents
revisited the amendment, this time with assurances to safeguard
protections for working women. The Democratic Party, labor unions,
liberal feminist groups and some forces on the left joined together
to renew the struggle for a Constitutional amendment so that rights

cannot be denied or abridged on account of sex. They then joined with the League of Women Voters, the YWCA of the U.S., the Unitarian Universalist Association, the UAW, and the National Education Association. The signal actions of the ERA movement were Women's Strike for Equality demonstrations and the state boycotts.

Both houses of Congress actually passed the ERA: the House in 1971 and the Senate in 1972, but the amendment was never able to get the required number of states to be ratified, and at the 1979 deadline, the measure was still three states short of the 38 states needed. After an extension to 1982 the measure still did not pass in the additional states, and the amendment failed. The defeat spurred many women to run for office and defeat anti-ERA incumbents.

The fight for the Equal Rights Amendment was among NOW's most important campaigns, and the organization played a leadership role in campaigning for state ratifications, including organizing boycotts of states that had not ratified. In August 1970 NOW organized nationwide demonstrations, called the Women's Strike for Equality, in honor of Women's Equality Day, commemorating the 50th anniversary of women's suffrage. Demands of the march included passage of the ERA, as well as equal opportunity in employment and education, the right to abortion, and the right to child care.[26] The demonstration's most memorable slogan was "Don't iron while the strike is hot."

The ERA is still not a U.S. law, but was reintroduced in the 114th Congress.

FOR UNIVERSAL CHILD CARE

As a consequence of the militant and dynamic women's movement, as well as the concurrent social struggles in other areas, significant reforms were introduced at the Congressional level.

New York Democratic Reps. Shirley Chisholm and Bella Abzug introduced a comprehensive childcare act in Congress in 1971. A somewhat less expansive bill, sponsored by Minnesota Sen. Walter Mondale and Indiana Rep. John Brademas, passed both houses of congress that same year. The Comprehensive Child Development Act called for a nationwide network of nationally funded, locally administered childcare, which would provide education, nutrition and medical services to children on a sliding scale.

The movement demanded, and nearly won, universal free day care, which would have transformed the lives of working-class women in particular.

Despite broad public support for childcare — including among Republican women — the bill was vetoed by President Richard Nixon, who red-baited the move as "communal" and anti-family child raising. This campaign for universal child care unleashed a right-wing backlash that railed against the "Sovietization" of child-rearing.

That left women on their own to find and fund child care. In one creative action, in 1972 women students and faculty at the University of Massachusetts conducted a sit-in, with children, in the president's office. They had fought for daycare for two years with no response. At the sit-in, mothers threatened to give children "crayons – but not paper. That grabbed his attention, and before long there was a daycare center."[27]

Child care remains an essential unmet need for working mothers and creates significant financial stresses for working-class families nationwide. The lack of guaranteed child care, all these decades later, places the U.S. near the bottom of any international survey of women's status in society.

CHALLENGING SEXUAL VIOLENCE AGAINST WOMEN

For all the ways in which U.S. culture still condones and pro-motes sexual violence — and secures so few convictions of rapists —

before the women's movement of the 1960s and 1970s the situation was even worse. Few people remember today just how archaic and backward U.S. laws were with respect to rape, domestic violence and other abuse. The term "domestic violence" did not even exist prior to the women's movement and the concept of being raped by one's husband was considered a legal impossibility.

The feminist movement led the fight to eliminate rape, violence against women and domestic violence. The first struggle was just to define these as major social problems to begin with. Among the changes achieved by the movement was defining rape as a crime of power and control as opposed to just a sexual act.

The ability to prosecute rape was expanded. Previous rules requiring corroborating witnesses to the crime were thrown out. The courtroom also changed, and the practice of blaming the victims and aggressively grilling them about their sexual history was officially ended with rape shield laws that prohibit defendants from questioning rape victims about their prior sexual history or publishing their identity. In practice, of course, different forms of victim-blaming, invasive questioning and shaming has continued in many cases.

Rape crisis centers and hotlines, along with battered women's shelters, were established for the first time by feminist activists. Ultimately, these services became part of the law enforcement response. The medical establishment was pressured into changing the way it interviewed and treated rape survivors. Feminists were instrumental in creating self-defense programs for women and education programs for the public about sexual violence.

While the statistics changed little, the issues were brought out of the shadows. Law enforcement was challenged to take seriously the allegations of women and treat victims with respect. This struggle is ongoing, especially because the police's top priorities are, by design, to protect state power and private property. Violence against women is no threat to state power and to those who direct the workings of the police. Periodically activists have tried to introduce community alternatives to replace the inadequately trained or sexist law enforcement agents, but much more is needed.

Actions initiated by feminists increased public awareness and fight-back against sexist violence with demonstrations, rallies, speakouts, clothesline displays in honor of murdered women and tables for men to sign pledges against sexist violence. Take Back the Night marches were held in San Diego in 1973 and Philadelphia in 1975 and have been held every year since in many venues throughout the world, including in small towns.

For instance, after a wave of assaults against women in the small upstate village of New Paltz, N.Y., demonstrators marched through town, stopping and raising their voices to a roar at all the places where women were denied justice: the bars where drunken patrons assaulted or refused to come to the aid of women; the police station, where women's complaints were not taken seriously; and the courthouse, where perpetrators were set free. Students at the nearby state university have continued the annual marches.

Until the 1970s, rape was commonly considered to be a crime against women committed by strangers. Feminists fought for and won the criminalization of marital rape, which first became a U.S. crime in 1975 in South Dakota, and in every state since. The last state to outlaw marital rape was North Carolina in 1993.

Domestic violence was forced out of its hallowed position as a private matter and criminalized, along with marital and acquaintance rape. But even with new laws, enforcement is low, police responses often lack sensitivity and the prevalence of violations has not diminished much, considering the drop in other forms of violent crime nationwide. These factors have contributed to a very low percentage of victims reporting sexual violence to law enforcement.

WEAKENING PATRIARCHAL FAMILY NORMS

More than any other mass movement, feminism challenged conventional family life. The political and social significance of mass changes in family relations cannot be overstated. After all, while ruling-class bourgeois ideology is taught and reinforced in the school system and in the corporate-owned media, it is also often reproduced through hierarchical and oppressive relations in the home.

Gloria Steinem, in one of her more astute observations, wrote that family "is where we are trained to believe that we are human beings or that we are chattel, it is where we are trained to see the sex and race divisions and become callous to injustice even if it is done to ourselves, to accept as biological a full system of authoritarian government."

The 1970s sitcom 'All in the Family' portrayed the crass, sexist father figure Archie Bunker in constant outrage about the changes overtaking the country, and his home.

The principal material basis for a change in the family structure was the erosion in the "family wages" of men, combined with increasing opportunities for women to work outside the home and the highly inadequate — and always eroding — government social safety net. But social perceptions of family life — and the actual gender relations within the home — were slow to change. The women's movement challenged these perceptions along with the reality.

With more married women in the workforce came an increased need for help with housework and childcare. Women increasingly insisted that men were equally capable of doing housework and caring for children. In many families, these responsibilities began to be shared by husbands and partners. However, this was an individual solution, with each family figuring out how to get the work done. There was no support from Washington for childcare, cooking, laundry or any of the other tasks now performed by two-worker families. With the increase in families headed by single mothers, the burden on such women was even greater still. (See Chapter 2 for a description of the changing nature of the family)

Grassroots feminist groups came up with creative collective solutions — daycare and food co-ops and cooperative housekeeping groups, some of which lasted for years. But these experiments were temporary, usually relying on voluntarism, and the majority of married working women continued to work a double shift: one for inadequate pay and one for free.

As the feminist movement asserted a woman's right to her own sexuality, including the right to have sex outside of marriage, public attitudes about women's sexuality in particular began to change. The incidence of single motherhood began to rise, and the social stigma associated with it diminished, although it has not been eliminated. For hundreds of years, however, single motherhood — not to mention premarital or non-marital sex — had been scorned in the extreme, often resulting in outright social ostracism and daily abuse.

Before the feminist movement brought the issues of oppression in the home to light and fought for reforms, there were no laws protecting women from economic oppression, violence, and even rape within their own homes and by their own intimate partners.

The women's movement of the 1960s and 1970s confronted family crises head-on, setting up domestic violence shelters and rape crisis centers, conducting demonstrations and sit-ins, writing and publishing. By getting into the law enforcement, legal, medical and public health professions, the movement saw to it that these issues were dealt with as public health crises, as well as law enforcement ones. The legal system has been slow to enforce new laws, and the culture and education system have yet to catch up to the needs of women to be free of intimate oppression. The struggle for women's rights within their own homes and families, aside from the oppression suffered at the hands of the state, remains an essential one to defend women's humanity.

The very first freedom to exercise of course was the freedom to divorce — to leave unhealthy and unhappy home situations. While that right had long existed in different forms, the women's movement fought the stigma around it, and started fighting for no-fault divorces in the late 1960s. Previously, the process was considerably more difficult to have the state allow a divorce, requiring one party to prove in court the "fault" of the other.

In 1965, the divorce rate stood at 2.5 per 1,000 people — more or less unchanged from the preceding 25 years. By 1975 — just ten years later — the number of divorces had doubled. The record-level rate of divorces continued for some time, with women initiating proceedings in two-thirds of cases. Since the 1980s, divorce rates have gradually declined. Today, the overall marriage rates have also declined; as women have become more economically independent, and unmarried co-habitation become more acceptable, marriage has become much more of an emotional and personal decision, for both parties, than an economic necessity.

Finally, women no longer had to be identified in terms of their marital status — the honorific "Ms." replaced "Miss" and "Mrs." Married women also no longer had to assume their husbands' last names, though most continued to do so. These linguistic changes were significant assertions of women's individuality and independence.

Higher divorce rates and declining marriage rates have also contributed to the increase in single-mother households over the same period. But the capitalist state and corporate bosses did not make adjustments for this new reality, instead punishing female heads of household by shredding the social safety net, holding wages down, outsourcing jobs and leaving single women with children to bear the brunt of increasing poverty.

Arch-reactionary Phyllis Schafly sporting a "Stop ERA button."

Challenges to the conventional nuclear family did not always produce the changes that women sought but invariably brought the wrath of the right wing and religious conservatives.

CHANGING THE CULTURE

The most far-reaching changes occurred in the culture, as the women's movement brought the feminist agenda into the mainstream. However the mass media distorted or mocked the aims of feminism, it was no longer acceptable to describe women in blatantly sexist or sexual terms. No longer could news media, literature and public speech use male pronouns as generic human descriptors, with the excuse that saying "his or her" took too long. It was no longer acceptable to call a middle-aged or elderly woman "girl."

Feminists established women's institutions, such as bookstores, music festivals, coffeehouses, athletic teams, and publishers.[28] Women became very visible in mainstream media, as more and more were hired as reporters, anchors, editors, and columnists.

The popular culture reflected these changes, with more literature and articles by women of all races and ethnicities being published, and television taking on themes such as strong women, single women, divorce, sexual relationships outside of marriage, and single parenthood. Hollywood showed some improvement in its roles for women, but continues to lag behind in themes, acting roles and directorships.

In the fine arts, which continues to be a cultural holdout, Judy Chicago's installation "Dinner Party" in 1979 featured a table set with plates decorated with vagina-like images. Eve Ensler's 1996 "Vagina Monologues" became an annual phenomenon. (See Chapter 10) Chicana muralists in Los Angeles, such as Judy Baca and Barbara Carrasco, were known for their bold depictions of feminist themes, as well as of the Japanese internments during World War II, the farmworkers movement, and the anti-Vietnam war protests.[29]

Feminism itself expanded to include gender identity, the LGBTQ struggle, and the struggle of lesbians for equality within feminism and within the gay liberation movement.

Women's centers cropped up all over the country. One of the most prominent was set up by Bread and Roses, a socialist women's organization in Boston in 1971. The center became a place for women to gather, get information, discuss their experiences growing up as girls in a sexist society, and struggle together on issues of employment, welfare, rape and violence. It set up educational programs ranging from anti-racism to auto mechanics, as well as writing, art, international women's struggles, lesbianism and Marxism.[30]

Girls' and women's participation in athletics skyrocketed at the school, university and professional levels. Religious women pushed for ordination and changes in theology. As with previous periods of feminist action, women branched out into other areas: antiwar, environmental justice, housing rights, the LGBTQ struggle and the training of other women to organize.[31]

In the workplace, schools and out in public, dress codes changed dramatically, as dresses, corsets and heels were often replaced by pants and comfortable shoes.

The women's health care movement saw a huge rise in the education and hiring of women doctors with a feminist orientation. For the first 70 years of the century, only 4 percent of physicians were women; in 2011 48 percent were. As with other gains this was the result of struggle, including a 1970 class action lawsuit brought by women against every medical school in the country.[32] This also influenced changes in medical and pharmaceutical research to begin including women subjects — although women are nowhere near equity with men — where the default had always been men. Child-birth practices were also transformed, with more women insisting on giving birth with the aid of midwives, hospitals developing birthing centers, and fathers becoming involved in the birth process.[33]

Finally, women asserted the right to define their own sexuality. As the fear of pregnancy was diminished by the availability of birth control and abortion, single as well as partnered women asserted the right to determine sexual pleasure on their own terms. They challenged the double standard that entitled men to have sexual freedoms that were denied to women, and explored their own erotic desires and feelings.

They also sought out and engaged in research about the biology of sex, learning about female sexual organs and orgasms. They challenged the notion of the heterosexual as the norm of sexual behavior.

They fought against the objectification of women in advertising and mass media and the stereotypes of female passivity and surrender, as opposed to assertiveness, in their sex lives. These explorations of the erotic took place on a mass scale, and were reflected in pamphlets and other writings, music and arts.

WOMEN IN POLITICS

Women's political participation increased considerably thanks to the feminist movement, at the local, state, and federal level. It still remains paltry compared to many countries around the world, as documented in Chapter 2.

In 1964 Hawaii Representative Patsy Mink became the first Asian-American woman and the first woman of color in Congress; In 1968 Shirley Chisholm of New York, became the first African-American woman elected to Congress. In 1973 three more African American women were elected: Yvonne Burke of California, Cardiss Collins of Illinois, and Barbara Jordan of Texas.

Women held 14 seats (2.6 percent) in the U.S. Congress in 1965; 11 seats (2.1 percent) in 1970; 17 seats (3.2 percent) in 1980, and 31 seats (5.8 percent) in 1990. In 2015 women hold 104 seats (19.4 percent) in Congress.

In the U.S. Senate, the progress was much slower; there were no women senators from 1973 to 1978 and at least one in each year after that. Women's participation increased markedly after the 1991 confirmation of Clarence Thomas to the Supreme Court (See Chapter 11). Four new women were elected the next year to the Senate.

Women held about 7 percent of statewide elected offices in 1971, increasing to about 27 percent in 1999.

Women in elected office have had some influence on committees and in introducing pro-woman legislation. After all, the women legislators of the Second Wave era often carried a bit of the crusader spirit into the halls of power — and a liberal feminist reform program.

But today women in positions of power are considerably less progressive or feminist in their orientation than those early trailblazers. The political establishment and both major parties have shifted far to the right since the 1970s and the electoral system is dominated by corporate money and ruling-class connections top to bottom. Women officeholders, just like men, are fundamentally beholden to their parties and the same lobbyists and donors on matters of foreign policy, military spending, abortion, and other issues.

The ruling class fought for centuries to preserve the white male power club, but once the winds of change became unstoppable, they quickly learned to reorient their sails. Both parties began to increase their recruitment and training of new women leaders and people of color, finding new faces to carry out the same basic program.

This is not to say that the gender and racial composition of the halls of power is no longer consequential, or can never create meaningful contradictions that progressive and revolutionary-minded activists can utilize. Ruth Bader Ginsburg, who was appointed to the Supreme Court in 1993 by Bill Clinton, had been an important feminist advocate with the American Civil Liberties Union before becoming a justice and consistently took feminist positions on the Court. In 2014 Ginsburg told a Women's History Month meeting in Washington:

"If I could choose an amendment to add to this Constitution, it would be the Equal Rights Amendment."

All three women in the Court in 2016 are clearly influenced by the tradition of liberal feminism, and have continuously opposed anti-choice measures passed at the state level. On other critical issues facing poor and working-class people — including tens of millions of women — they have lined up with their conservative male colleagues.

THE MOVEMENT'S BROAD ACTIONS AND TACTICS

Using direct action, speak-outs, publications, street theater, and disruptions of more moderate feminist actions, radical and socialist feminists challenged the legitimacy of the nuclear family, pushed for recognition of lesbians, demanded universal abortion rights and agitated for equal opportunity supported by government child care. In some cases, radicals promoted celibacy and other dramatic changes in sexual and family relations.

In the context of a militant mass movement and a vibrant counter culture, women's liberation caught the public's attention. Among the first widely publicized actions was the protest at the 1968 Miss America pageant in Atlantic City, New Jersey,

Advertisements that exploited, objectified and offended women were often covered up.

when radical feminists displayed a "Freedom Trash Can," into which they hurled "hair curlers, false eyelashes, girdles, and bras." This was the source of the enduring epithet "bra burner."[34]

In response to crowds of men who routinely gathered to ogle women on Wall Street, a crowd of women in 1970 staged a Wall Street "Ogle-In," hooting at and mocking men in front of the Stock Exchange.[35] And no ad campaign was safe from attack by the women's liberation movement. Subway ads and billboards that commodified women's sex appeal to sell products were covered with stickers declaring "This ad insults women" — or just torn down.

A practice most closely associated with women's liberation was consciousness raising (CR). Through small-group speak-outs, women spoke from their own lived experience, bringing into the open their private thoughts with respect to their subordinate place in society. They discussed their attitudes toward and relationships with men, their sexual experiences, identities, and the realization that the misogyny around them was real, pervasive and experienced by multitudes of other women. These discussions helped women to understand patriarchy and power relations and to create strategies to transform society through collective action.[36]

CR was adapted from tactics used in other movements: in the civil rights movement, in the Chinese revolution ("speaking bitterness"), and in the Marxist movement (unlearning "false consciousness").

New York Radical Women pioneered its use in the feminist movement. According to Kathie Sarachild, "Our role was not to be a 'service organization,' we decided, nor a large 'membership organization.'...We would be the first to dare to say and do the undare-able, what women really felt and wanted. The first job now was to raise awareness and understanding, our own and others — awareness that would prompt people to organize and to act on a mass scale."

CR was seen as an authentic way to build a movement based on the real needs of women, who would "have to see the fight of women as their own, not as something just to help 'other women,' that they would have to see this truth about their own lives before they would fight in a radical way for anyone."[37] It was successful in spreading awareness of women's oppression, in breaking taboos about referencing women's real lives. From housework to sex to the workplace to discriminatory treatment at school, women began to see and challenge sexism everywhere.

As a spur toward activism, CR had a mixed record. Some groups never really progressed politically and open-ended discussions could go anywhere. Others, however, provided the impetus to turn consciousness into a fight for change. Some anti-feminist critics of the practice tried to pressure women to bypass CR and identify their political goals and programs the way more conventional groups did. This is not unlike how some have tried to criticize the Occupy Wall Street and Black Lives Matter movements in the more recent era.

Many trends in the women's liberation movement also promoted the formation of all-women's organizations. In part this was an ideological decision and an expression of women's autonomy. It was also a pragmatic decision, in response to the sexism within the activist movement.[38]

SUMMARY

The Second Wave uprising resulted in a considerable number of accomplishments and outright victories for women and tens of millions of families, while striking a dent in patriarchal norms across society. Legislative victories created significant changes in the workplace and in schools. Cultural breakthroughs radically altered family life, popular culture and political representation. Grassroots organizing created new women-led institutions dealing with child care, protection from violence, raising political consciousness, and more. The movement, directly and indirectly, empowered women to take control of their lives, their sexuality, their bodies and their relationships— to no longer accept a second-class status as "just the way things are."

Most people today probably have little idea how these progressive changes came about. Even many feminists today seriously underestimate the role of movement activism in advancing the cause of women.

This is not an accident or a problem of individual ignorance. It is part of a continuous historical pattern in which the capitalist ruling class, after strenuously fighting people's movements, then attempts to erase their significance once they succeed at making change. The main historical lesson that the textbooks, media and politicians like to impart is that "the country made positive changes" — as if this happened on account of the enlightened elite or some magical progressive force floating in the air. The main historical lesson they are afraid of is the real one: that all progressive change has come from struggle.

It is up to today's activists to recover and study this history of the women's movement, so the right lesson is drawn. ☐

Chapter 9
The right-wing backlash and continued attacks

Largely coinciding with the end of the Vietnam War in 1975, most of the varied activist movements, including feminists, began to fade away or already had done so earlier in the decade.

The decline was caused by several factors. A number of organizations were undermined and disrupted by the FBI's extensive Counterintelligence Program and by considerable police action around the country. The government spied on and sought to disrupt dozens of groups, particularly the antiwar movement, the left and militant organizations such as the Black Panthers and others.

With the end of the Vietnam War, the U.S. ruling class was able to stabilize its rule and heal some of its deep internal contradictions. The dramatic defeat U.S. militarism suffered in Southeast Asia inspired oppressed people worldwide to intensify their struggle, but it coincided with a deep split within the socialist camp that allowed U.S. imperialism to reverse its fortunes. The creation of what ultimately became a U.S.-China alliance against the Soviet Union demoralized and confused class-conscious workers, and put imperialism on firm footing again.

At the same time, because this broad movement was so incredibly diverse — each group with a different main objective, levels of political agreement, solidarity and internal problems — it could not unite as one in defense against the combined pressures of government subversion, negative media coverage and hostile institutional opinion (including certain labor unions and liberal groups), opposition from both "official" political parties, and a resurgent right-wing grassroots movement. Many groups in the broader movement broke apart from within due to intense factional differences. Others were exhausted and participants dropped away. Several rested on their laurels after gaining victories. A militant rank-and-file workers movement started to take off in the 1970s — encouraging many activists and leftists to get jobs in the factories — but it ultimately fell to a united ruling class bent on destroying the power of unions.

The feminist movement, which of course continues in different forms to this day, moved away from its militancy. Although a left current of the movement called for radical transformation of society, in practical terms most of the battles were for legislative reforms. As with many such movements, once a reform was won, activists who had limited goals ceased to fight. With this came a shift to electoral politics, a decline of street activism and, for many, a move toward the Democratic Party just at the time when the party itself was gravitating toward the right. The goal that many activists put forward of influencing and capturing the Democratic Party from within was flipped the other way around; the activists were themselves influenced and captured by the Democratic establishment.

NOW's two mass rallies in the modern period, in 1992 and 2004, demonstrated the continued feminist spirit among millions of women, but these activist moments were exceptions to the rule.

As this process was underway, right-wing criticism of the 1960-75 uprisings was transforming into a powerful backlash against the reforms and progressive changes in popular attitudes that emerged from this extraordinary period. One resurrected conservative objective was putting women "back in their place." As Nancy MacLean writes, "Just as the feminist surge built on the foundations of earlier decades, so did the antifeminist backlash."[1]

Conservative and traditionalist opposition to the prospect of greater freedoms for women has always been present. The main thrust of the reactionaries became aimed at abortion rights, and the right wing has been making big gains in various states in recent years.

Right-wing women have been enthusiastic participants in this movement to take back women's gains. Phyllis Schlafly, an experienced activist of the right, campaigned against the ERA in the 1970s, after the women's movement had finally unified around it, using "family values" stereotypes to defend traditional feminine roles. Since then, conservative women in large numbers have been active in the "right to life" and anti-LGBTQ movements, capitalizing on the fears that traditional ways of life were endangered.[2]

The backlash was strengthened with the election of conservative Republican President Ronald Reagan in 1980. During his eight-year watch, reactionary Republican and religious forces launched a veritable war on women, unleashing economic policies that keep women at the bottom of the economic ladder, attacking abortion and other reproductive rights, trivializing the crime of rape, denying women access to defense against violence, demonizing single mothers, especially women of color, and crushing public sector unions, which for decades were a means to economic stability and progress, especially for women and African Americans.

In 2004, following Reagan's death, Martha Burk, the chair of the National Council of Women's Organizations, declared he was "the most anti-woman president of the 20th century."[3]

Reagan administration policies tied in with the economic counterattack launched in the mid-70s by the capitalist class to reduce the wages of the working class and lower-middle class. They ended the practice of increasing wages in relative proportion to hikes in productivity that existed in most industries since the end of World War II, and aggressively moved to outsource jobs and dismantle government regulations. This capitalist offensive had two main purposes: (1) to greatly increase profits for the owners of the means of social production and employers of labor and (2) to gravely weaken the union movement.

Big business triumphed on both accounts, as an examination of the situation today reveals: Depressed wages for the mass of the workers, skyrocketing inequality, higher unemployment, fewer assets for average families and a higher poverty/low-wage rate. Up to 5 million U.S. families lost their homes as a result of the 2008-2009 Great Recession. Meanwhile a much smaller union movement has lost power and militancy. At the same time, the top wealthiest 1 percent of Americans possess 40 percent of all the nation's wealth, surpassing the bottom 80 percent to 90 percent, which owns as low as 7 percent. The rest of the wealth is grabbed by the 9 percent behind the top 1 percent.

All working people and families have suffered as a result of these economic trends. The Republican Party openly champions the policies of inequality, while the Democrats have given lip service to the plight of the poor. But in reality, they have facilitated the rich man's economic stranglehold, working with Wall Street, the big corporations and the 1 percent oligarchs who collectively, through their

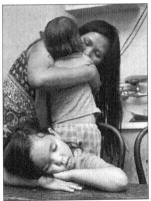

*The low-wage workforce
is mostly women.*

billions in bribes/donations, control the country's political system and direct the government bureaucracy.

Most women workers, who earned lower wages to begin with, have actually gone backward in this period. According to the National Women's Law Center: "Women make up 60 percent of the lower-paying workforce. ... Almost 30 percent of the female workforce is low-wage, in contrast to less than 20 percent of the male workforce. Of these women, three-fourths are white. The proportion of minority women is significantly higher than white women: 35.8 percent and 46.6 percent of African American and Latino women in contrast to 26.2 percent of white women." Average white family assets in 2013 (including house and car) amounted to $196,500; Black family assets: $10,000; Latino families: $13,700.

A healthy proportion of people have developed consciousness, and outrage, about these injustices in the years since the Great Recession which began in 2008. Even criticisms of the capitalist system — long suppressed or self-censored — are popping up with greater frequency than in the past. This accounts for the amazing size of the audiences that cheered Sen. Bernie Sanders (I-Vt.) in his primary campaign rallies for the Democratic presidential nomination — even though he describes himself as a socialist. Democratic liberals appear to have at least temporarily broken out of the political dungeons to which they were consigned by center-right presidents Bill Clinton and Barack Obama.

The demise of the Soviet Union in 1991 and the collapse of most of its socialist allies benefitted American capitalism and made the plight of U.S. workers worse. As the only remaining global superpower, the U.S. "inherited" previously unavailable international markets and brought most of the former socialist states of Eastern Europe into Washington's orbit. This meant the United States was free to expand its imperialist power and wars abroad with no worries about criticism or retaliation from its socialist rival. Without the

USSR looking over Uncle Sam's shoulder and shouting to the world its more serious shortcomings (as it did continuously about Jim Crow segregation, much to Washington's chagrin), the U.S. government has presided over a serious long-term attack on its own working class without criticism from significant international sources.

In 1993, under Democratic President Bill Clinton, Congress passed the North American Free Trade Agreement (NAFTA) over the objections of the labor movement, which had supported the election of Clinton and his party. NAFTA weakened worker rights in the United States, facilitated the trend of factory outsourcing, and destabilized the economies of Mexico and Central America, leading to a surge in immigration. Immigrant women became an increasingly significant population of working women in the United States. In the free trade zone set up on the Mexican side of the border, over 2,000 factories opened over the next ten years — with women filling the vast majority of the non-union and low-wage jobs. (By the early 2000s, many of these plants were again relocating to Asia.)

Since the terror attacks of Sept. 11, 2001, the "War on Terror" brought with it growing militarism in the United States, along with hyper-patriotism, an erosion of civil liberties and attacks on Muslim and South Asian communities.

In 2013, the U.S. military officially lifted its ban on women in combat units. This has been one of the few 21st century victories for women, taking into prominent consideration the unjust and illegal nature of America's wars in recent decades.

Despite the mainstream media's claims that we now live in a post-feminist era, implying women have met our goals of equality, feminism is actually on the defensive because of this relentless backlash.

Women's organizing on college campuses has declined. On some campuses, feminist groups begin each semester with a program called "the F-Word" (for feminist), seeking to debunk the negative stereotypes that have been attached to feminism by social conservatives and to promote the values of female equality.

Off campus it is the same story. Lauren Jacobs, a former student leader in the Feminist Majority Leadership Alliance, said in an interview for this book that after college she was shocked to see how much her co-workers had bought into the politics of the backlash — that racist and sexist oppression was a thing of the past:

A woman who led the mental health facility where I worked was opposed to family leave, saying 'women shouldn't be paid to stay home and have babies.' So now I'm fighting in a tiny area of the workplace.

I'm not seeing a coherent or national fightback. Not many people are thinking of transformation, mostly about reforms — getting access to services and support, fighting for prison reform, dealing with the burdens on mothers among the poor.

I see a lot of feminist discussion on social media, but it has limited capacity for social change. People aren't out on the streets, and that concerns me. Social media doesn't function the way it did in the Arab Spring — from the media to the streets. It doesn't make up for the lack of attention to social movements in the mainstream media. I think people aren't out in the street because they're afraid of the backlash.

Yet there are currents in the popular culture that are taking up the banner of feminism, as singers, actors and celebrities declare themselves to be feminists and supporters of women's empowerment. In a clear example of knee-jerk backlash — that backfired — Time Magazine conducted an absurd poll of "worst words" that should be banned in 2015. High on the list was the word "feminist." The magazine was forced to retract after thousands of feminists, male and female, raised their voices in protest.

REPRODUCTIVE FREEDOM

The right-wing backlash against women's progress has been harsh and unrelenting in its attacks on women's reproductive rights.

The birth control pill, IUD, surgical and medication abortion and other forms of contraception are scientific and technical advances that have revolutionized women's ability to plan their pregnancies. Part of the right-wing backlash of the late 20th and early 21st century has been to deny access to these advances, targeting abortion, contraception and the rights of pregnant women — and trans men — and this attack has taken many forms.

According to a recent Guttmacher report, "Anti-abortion groups are trying to coerce women's reproductive decision making by restricting access not only to abortion services, but by undermining private insurance coverage of contraceptives, defunding publicly supported family planning services and opposing com-

Pro-choice women protesting at the Supreme Court during the Burwell vs. Hobby Lobby hearings.

prehensive sex education, among other tactics. This approach stands in stark contrast to that supported by reproductive rights advocates, who have long pushed for policies grounded in voluntarism and informed consent that support all of a woman's pregnancy decisions."[4]

ABORTION RIGHTS

A major part of the right-wing attack is to shame women who have abortions, to make them feel isolated and intimidated. But the truth is that abortions remain quite common: as of 2014, 21 percent of all pregnancies in the U.S. (excluding those ending in miscarriage) are terminated by abortion.

Another myth is that only certain types of women have abortions. In fact, 18 percent are teenagers, more than half are in their 20s and the remaining are in their 30s and 40s. White women account for 36 percent of abortions; Black women account for 30 percent, Latina women account for 25 percent, and other races for 9 percent.

The majority of women who decide to abort their pregnancy already have children.

There are, of course, major economic factors that impact a woman's access to reproductive health care and decisions with respect to the size of their family. An estimated 42 percent of women obtaining abortions are poor and another 27 percent have incomes just above the poverty line. Yet Congress has prohibited Medicaid funds to be used to pay for abortions, except for cases of rape, incest or when the woman's life is endangered.[5] Because of the restrictions that keep piling up — lack of insurance funding, clinic closings, mandated physically invasive ultrasounds, "counseling" and other delays — abortion costs have risen and have become disproportionately less available to poor women. Poor women are six times as likely to have unplanned births.[6]

Opposition to abortion has ranged from legal challenges to street protests to violence. Campaigns to overthrow *Roe v. Wade* have taken place at the national, state and municipal level, seeking to chip away at abortion rights until the entire edifice collapses.

Restrictions on providers, limits on insurance coverage, outright bans on abortion well before fetal viability (the limit set by the *Roe* decision) and limitations on medication abortion are all part of the anti-abortion toolkit.

To fight the stigma, activists have again taken to holding abortion speak-outs. But at a recent campus speak-out reported to this author, the majority of testimonials came from older women. Students acknowledged that they declined to speak because of shame, a throwback to 1950s standards.

Legalizing abortion was a critical reform in an age of changing sexual mores in the 1960s and 1970s, with women's control of their own sexuality promoted as an absolute right detached from reproduction. Popular culture certainly has not returned to the era when women's sexuality was an absolutely forbidden topic; that has changed irreversibly. But the original political context for the open embrace of women's sexuality was the fierce struggle for women's equality and liberation in all spheres of life.

Today, majorities of people in this country continue to support the right to abortion, but the minority who oppose it are fighting hard, fighting dirty and winning battles. They are bold and unashamed in their nonstop attacks.

Extreme right-wing organizations have proliferated. Operation Rescue, founded in 1986 by Randall Terry, was one of the first of the Christian right anti-abortion groups. Its early tactics were to block access to abortion clinics. Through several splits and changes of leadership, Operation Rescue has been associated with violent tactics against abortion providers and also with trying to expand the reach of fundamentalist Christianity in the United States. With the religious

Planned Parenthood provides reproductive medical services in cities large and small, but also participates in social movements in those locations.

right, one of the key opponents of abortion, it is worth noting that 73 percent of women who have abortions are religiously affiliated.

Coalitions of Catholic and Evangelical Protestant groups organize to oust politicians who support abortion at both the federal and state level. There are 69 million Catholics and between 90-to-100 million Evangelicals (including children) in the United States. Of course, in all these religious communities there are many defenders of abortion rights — and some have organized to change the stances of their institutions and attended women's rights rallies.

Anti-abortion religious groups also set up "crisis pregnancy centers," which are publicly-funded facilities that purport to provide services to pregnant women, and attract women who are seeking abortions, but their real purpose is to shame women so they choose otherwise. They conceal their religious affiliations and then secretly proselytize for their churches.[7]

Legal challenges to *Roe* emerged shortly after the Supreme Court decision.

At the federal level, the most enduring restriction is the Hyde Amendment, passed in 1976, which prohibits the use of federal funds for abortion, leaving it up to the states to decide whether to use their own public funds. As of 2013 only 17 states used state funds to cover abortions for women on Medicaid. This denies abortions to poor women who depend on Medicaid for their health care. The Hyde Amendment is not a permanent law but serves as a rider to other laws and must be renewed every year, as it has been since its passage, including under President Obama's Affordable Care Act. Even as the Republican Party has been the most vociferous opponent of abortion, the Democrats have done far too little to introduce or defend pro-abortion legislation, as illustrated by the bipartisan acceptance of the Hyde Amendment.[8] [See Appendix 16] for "Five Facts You Should Know about the Hyde Amendment." Forces within the reproductive justice movement recently launched the All Above All campaign to defeat the Hyde Amendment once and for all.

A 1992 Supreme Court decision that weakened *Roe* was *Casey v. Planned Parenthood*, which upheld the constitutionality of provisions in a Pennsylvania law calling for a 24-hour waiting period before an abortion could be performed and for parental consent for minors wanting an abortion.

A 2007 Supreme Court decision, *Gonzales v. Carhart,* reversed an earlier decision and upheld a federal ban on "partial birth" abortion, in which a pregnancy, usually at 20-24 weeks, is terminated using a dilation and extraction method. The federal ban contains no exception for danger to the woman's health.[9] This decision provided ammunition for states to pass similar bans, even though late-term abortions are rare and are typically used only in medical emergencies, when the health or life of the mother is in danger.

In January 2015, the House of Representatives began to debate a bill to ban all abortions after 20 weeks and to require victims of rape or incest to have reported these crimes to the police to be exempt from the law. Congress members were forced to withdraw the bill after a number of Republican women denied their support. It was replaced with a bill that would make the Hyde Amendment permanent and also ban private funding of an abortion under the Affordable Care Act.[10]

In May 2015, the House passed the "Pain-Capable Unborn Child Protection Act", which prohibits abortions at 20 weeks, in a direct challenge to *Roe v. Wade,* which permits abortion before viability, usually 24 weeks. To get around the *Roe* rule, the bill relies on unproven assertions that a 20-week fetus can feel pain. In June 2015 Sen. Lindsey Graham (R-S.C.) introduced this bill in the Senate.[11]

Congress frequently inserts outrageous anti-abortion clauses into other bills, such as a 2015 anti-trafficking bill that attached funding rules, based on the Hyde Amendment, to prohibit federal funds from being used for the abortions of trafficking victims. The bill finally passed in April after a separate funding stream was found outside of federal funds.[12]

Abortion opponents have not succeeded in overturning *Roe* with federal legislation. What has been more effective is imposing restrictions at the state level, thus forcing abortion rights supporters to continuously battle their way through the courts. Between 2011 and 2014, states passed 231 abortion restrictions, and more than half of U.S. women of child-bearing age now live in states that are hostile to abortion.

In fact, more restrictions on abortion were enacted from 2011 to 2013 than in the entire previous decade. In 87 percent of U.S. counties there is not a single abortion provider, and four states — Mississippi, North Dakota, South Dakota and Wyoming — have only one statewide.[13]

By the end of the first quarter of 2015, 332 provisions seeking to reduce access to abortion were introduced in all but seven states; 53 of these provisions had been approved by at least one legislative chamber, and nine had been enacted.[14]

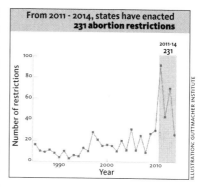

These restrictions include TRAP laws (Targeted Regulation of Abortion Providers) such as requirements that abortion clinics have hospital-like facilities and that abortion providers have admitting privileges at local hospitals, requirements that are not imposed on any other medical procedure, including ones that are far more dangerous. There are also limits or bans on medication abortions (as opposed to surgical); limits or bans on private insurance coverage of abortion; and pre-viability bans on abortion. Such restrictions have forced many clinics to close. An Arizona law that was upheld by the Supreme Court holds that providers of medication abortion must adhere to outdated FDA regulations that will greatly reduce women's access to this procedure.[15]

New York Times Supreme Court columnist Linda Greenhouse sounded an alarm in her October 15, 2015 article about the latest threat to legal abortion. The Supreme Court recently heard an appeal filed by several Texas abortion clinics that would be forced to close under a TRAP law — called HB2 — that was passed in 2013 and upheld in 2015 by the Fifth Circuit of the U.S. Court of Appeals. If the Supreme Court upheld the Fifth Circuit's decision, there would be only 10 abortion clinics in all of Texas, a state with 5.4 million women of reproductive age. A similar law in Louisiana was temporarily blocked by the Supreme Court.

The law's stated rationale to protect women's health has been repeatedly exposed as pure hypocrisy. In fact, state attorneys argued that without a single clinic in the western half of the state, women can simply cross the state line to New Mexico, which has no TRAP laws, for their abortions. "So," writes Greenhouse, "Texas' interest in protecting the health of its abortion patients evidently stops at the state line even as it sends women seeking abortions in West Texas across that line."[16]

The parts of the Texas TRAP law that required abortion clinics to be fitted out like ambulatory surgical centers and that required doctors to have admitting privileges at local hospitals were struck down by the Supreme Court in a 5-3 decision on June 27, 2016. The case, called *Whole Woman's Health v. Hellerstedt*, was decided on the grounds that these requirements constituted an "undue burden" on women seeking abortion, a principle laid down by the 1992 *Planned Parenthood v. Casey* decision. Since the *Whole Woman's Health* case was decided, a number of state restrictions and lawsuits to uphold restrictions have been withdrawn. But as we have seen in the past, one positive decision is not the end of the story. Opponents of women's reproductive rights will find other ways to challenge them, and women and their allies must be prepared not only to fight back but to seize the initiative and organize around holding on to — and expanding — their rights.

On the other side, more state measures were introduced (although not yet enacted) to expand or protect abortion access in 2014 than in any year since 1989.[17] And a federal appeals court struck down an Arkansas law that would ban abortion at 12 weeks of pregnancy, ruling that the law violated the precedent set by the Supreme Court that allows abortion before fetal viability, at 24 weeks.[18]

To protect women from running through a gauntlet of hostile protestors, Planned Parenthood and other groups have organized volunteers to escort women into the clinics. Some states have instituted laws to protect clinics, including setting up buffer zones around the buildings that are off limits

Escorts protect patients from anti-abortion protestors.

to pickets and harassers. This tactic suffered a serious blow when the Supreme Court in December 2014 struck down a 35-foot buffer zone around abortion clinics in Massachusetts.[19] In response NOW has circulated a petition demanding the removal of the Supreme Court's own buffer zone against protesters.

One immediate result of these attacks is that access to abortion is reduced, as fewer doctors are willing to perform the procedure. In addition defenders of abortion are forced to defend their rights on two fronts: the legality of abortion itself and the legality of defending clinics against violence.

These statewide abortion restrictions often reflect funding from wealthy conservatives who seek the erosion of women's reproductive rights. Since the Supreme Court's *Citizens United* decision, which removes all restrictions on political campaign contributions, money from the billionaire Koch brothers and right-wing corporate organizations, with support from American Legislative Exchange Council (ALEC) and leaders of the religious right, have poured in to state campaigns to restrict abortion.[20]

Among the rationales used by lawmakers to restrict abortion is the fraudulent notion that legal "personhood" begins at conception. This is intended to weaken *Roe's* requirement that abortion is allowed up to the time of viability — the ability of the fetus to live outside the womb. In essence these laws allow for the imposition of fetal rights that are in contradiction to, and at the expense of, the rights of the mother. It also opens the door for provisions that outlaw abortion early in pregnancy, even before a woman knows she is pregnant; assert that a fetus can feel pain and outlaw abortion on that ground; and penalize the pregnant woman for accidental harm that occurs to the fetus, including miscarriage.[21] We have already seen cases where private and district attorneys, supposedly acting "on behalf of unborn fetuses" — who hired them? — bring charges against pregnant women.

The anti-abortion forces now slickly cover their campaigns in supposed "concern" for the mother: because some women feel guilty about their abortions, and a mother's mental health can be damaged, they claim they are sparing women the stigma and shame of having had an abortion, and on and on. This is paternalistic, infantilizing logic in the extreme — the notion that male lawmakers have to protect women from making decisions about their own bodies. Whatever the rhetoric, the goal is to end abortion.

According to NARAL Pro-Choice America, "A campaign of violence, vandalism, and intimidation is endangering providers and patients and curtailing the availability of abortion services. Since 1993, eight clinic workers — including four doctors, two clinic employees, a clinic escort, and a security guard — have been murdered in the United States. Seventeen attempted murders have also occurred since 1991. In fact, opponents of choice have directed more than 6,800 reported acts of violence against abortion providers since 1977, including bombings, arsons, death threats, bioterrorism threats, and assaults, as well as more than 188,000 reported acts of disruption, including bomb threats, hate mail, and harassing calls."[22]

These murders are acts of domestic terrorism, and each act is the culmination of years of ever escalating violence and extreme anti-woman rhetoric. Yet these attacks are never described as terrorism in the hyper-sensationalist right-wing media that is obsessed with Islamic fundamentalist terrorism.[23] [See Appendix 17 for a brief listing of violent attacks and killings at some clinics.]

Another consequence of the right wing's heavy hand has been the tendency of some pro-abortion forces to water down their own message in order to make peace. In effect, they accept the right-wing arguments that women feel guilty and that ideally abortion would be rare, but women should have the individual right to choose and be safe. But the anti-abortion forces are not interested in making peace. Their goal is to stop abortion, and they have never backed down.[24]

The right wing tried to deprive Planned Parenthood of all federal funds in summer/fall of 2015 after producing a manipulated video purporting to show that that this extremely important health organization was cynically selling fetal tissue from abortions for profit. In September the House voted to defund Planned Parenthood but the conservatives did not prevail in the Senate. In retaliation, the Republicans threatened to shut down the government if this funding made its way into the final budget bill. Although there are some other clinics that provide similar services, they cannot pick up all the slack if Planned Parenthood clinics are forced to close.[25]

In a fitting twist, the man who engineered the Planned Parenthood video scandal was himself charged with one second-degree felony charge of tampering with a governmental record and a misdemeanor charge related to the prohibition of the purchase and sale of human organs.

This is not the first time conservatives and the religious right have sought to defund Planned Parenthood, which is already prohibited from using federal funds for abortions. The organization is a perennial target for defunding attempts by Congress and state legislatures, some of which have already been successful (Texas, Kansas), while most fail. Despite the fact that Planned Parenthood offers many non-reproduction-related health services, including breast cancer screenings, in 2012 the Susan B. Komen organization, a leading breast cancer charity, moved to end its funding of Planned Parenthood. A flood of opposition forced the group to reverse its decision almost immediately, and subsequently forced a change in Komen's leadership.

BIRTH CONTROL: A CENTRAL TARGET OF THE RIGHT

Birth control has always been at the heart of the attacks on abortion even though the use of contraceptives reduces the need for abortion. Accompanying the prohibitions and attacks on abortion is a fundamental attack on birth control in and of itself. The real target is women's control over reproduction. That is why feminists have demanded for decades that women have the right to "control over our own bodies."

Despite the rhetoric that equates abortion with murder, right wing forces target all forms of pregnancy prevention, birth control,

WORD (Women Organized to Resist and Defend) and other organizations staged actions across the country to put Plan B on pharmacy shelves, instead of behind the counter.

and family planning, including Plan B emergency contraception, which, thanks to public protest and constant legal battles, is finally available over the counter to all women.

Why do religious conservatives in particular — a significant proportion of the American population — oppose birth control methods? It reflects the teachings of long-dominant trends within organized religion, based historically in feudalism, that say it is "immoral" to have sex for pleasure and not for attempting to bear a child. The Catholic Church is the most powerful opponent of birth control, but the great majority of Catholic women who are at risk of an unintended pregnancy use birth control. Only 2 percent of Catholic women use church-sanctioned natural family planning.[26]

Right-wing religious forces and other conservative elements, many of whom would also prefer to keep women at home in their traditional role of dependent wife and mother, fund and mobilize for politicians that restrict reproductive rights and access to care. All the political energy spent on regulating pregnancies disappears, however, once the baby is born. There is no government mandated and publicly funded child care. In the private sector, it is up to each company to provide child care, and very few do so. The United States, more than any other industrialized capitalist country, does not finance maternity or family leave, child care or post-natal care.

Poor women and women of color suffer most for these racist and anti-worker policies. They have the fewest resources to get the treatments, medications and care they need on their own.

For example, Native American women were restricted to only partial access to Plan B emergency contraception for two years after the FDA, under federal court order, approved the drug for over the counter distribution in 2013. The Indian Health Service (IHS), a U.S. government agency charged with running pharmacies that are used by many Native people, dragged its feet for two years before finally signing a written agreement to adhere to FDA regulations making it available to all ages without prescription.[27]

Because the absurd notion of fetal personhood is so unpopular with the U.S. public, anti-abortion forces have resorted to other tactics. One is to conflate abortion and contraception, falsely claiming that certain contraception methods are actually abortifacients. These include IUDs and emergency contraception. Others deceptively claim that policies that guarantee insurance coverage for contraception are actually policies that mandate that women have abortions. Among the most prominent groups promoting these distortions and outright lies are the Susan B. Anthony List, Americans United for Life, U.S. Conference of Catholic Bishops, American Association of Pro-Life Obstetricians and Gynecologists and the Heritage Foundation.[28]

The biggest legal challenge to birth control in recent years was the suit initiated by the Hobby Lobby corporation to prohibit its employees from using company insurance for contraception under the Affordable Care Act. This prohibition was upheld by the Supreme Court in 2014 on so-called "religious freedom" grounds.[29] In fact, it imposed the religious beliefs of a small group of corporate bosses onto the decision-making of Hobby Lobby's 16,000 workers — the very opposite of religious freedom. Since then, many corporations with right-wing executives have followed Hobby Lobby's precedent.

In her vigorous dissent, Justice Ruth Bader Ginsburg pointed out that the burden of this ruling would fall unfairly on poor women.

For example, "The cost of an IUD is nearly equivalent to a month's full-time pay for workers earning the minimum wage," she wrote.[30]

Opponents of contraception also campaign for limiting school sex education programs to abstinence, omitting comprehensive education and contraception.[31] Only 22 states and the District of Columbia require sex education in the schools, and only 13 insist that the information be medically accurate!

In a July 20, 2015 article on the Jacobin website, Katha Pollitt pointed out: "Abortion opponents promote abstinence-only education despite strong evidence that it has no long-term positive effects. It may delay sex for younger teens, but not by much, and when those kids do have sex they are less likely to use condoms or contraception. Texas has the nation's third highest rate of teen pregnancy, but in 2011 anti-abortion stalwart Gov. Rick Perry prevented the health department from applying for millions of dollars in federal funds aimed at preventing teen pregnancy through birth control alongside abstinence education. In 2013, however, Texas spent $1.2 million of federal money on a website to promote abstinence before marriage."

RIGHTS OF PREGNANT WOMEN

Another blow in the war on reproductive freedom is the erosion of pregnant women's rights. For all that abortion opponents claim to advocate for pregnancy and childbirth, the consequences of their policies and actions are to rob women of their reproductive agency whether they wish to end or go through with their pregnancies. Claiming the personhood of fetuses, they deprive women of their own personhood.

In 2014 Tennessee became the first state to pass a law that would jail women for certain pregnancy outcomes. Women who have used illegal drugs while pregnant are especially targeted, and poor women will be most burdened. There is a serious lack of drug treatment centers in the state; methadone and other treatments considered to be safest for pregnant women are banned by this law; and Tennessee has refused the extension of Medicaid offered by the Affordable Care Act.[32]

The group National Advocates for Pregnant Women has documented and intervened in a trove of cases in which pregnant women are deprived of their rights in favor of the presumed rights of their fetuses. Attacks on the rights of pregnant women cover a wide range of additional issues: Forced medical interventions such as Cesarean sections; arrests, with subsequent abuse such as shackling in prison; penalizing women for alcohol and drug use; prosecutions for still-births, and piling on abuses of poor women and women of color who are pregnant.[33]

In some cases, such as shackling of pregnant immigrant detain-ees in U.S. Immigration and Customs Enforcement facilities, the abuses are violations of law.[34] In other cases, such as imprisonment for miscarriage or stillborn births, they are enforcing the law.

In June 2015, both houses of the New York State legislature passed an anti-shackling bill, which prohibits the restraining of preg-nant women in prisons throughout their pregnancies and for eight weeks post-partum. Pressure from the non-profit Correction Associ-ation of N.Y. and its Women in Prison Project, was instrumental in getting the law passed. A 2009 law that prohibited shackling during labor and delivery and limited shackling during travel to and from the hospital for childbirth, has been violated in some 85 percent of cases. Nationwide anti-shackling laws and policies are routinely vio-lated. Gov. Cuomo finally signed the New York State bill into law in December 2015.

According to Lynn Paltrow, Founder and Executive Director of National Advocates for Pregnant Women, "it's not just reproductive rights that are under attack, it is the personhood of people who can get pregnant.... that women's pregnancies are now becoming the subject of policing, prosecution and severe sentences in an age of mass incarceration."

Paltrow was referring to a case, among others, in which Purvi Patel, an Indiana woman, who had suffered a miscarriage, was sen-tenced to 20 years in prison. She was accused of taking drugs to induce an abortion, although no drugs were found in her system; as well as for neglect of the stillborn baby, who, the prosecutors alleged, without proof, had been born alive. Indiana is one of 38 states that have feticide laws. Paltrow went on to say that "if there is any doubt among people that the result, and perhaps intent, of the antiabortion, anti-fairness efforts in this country will be women becoming part of this system of massive incarceration, they should end those doubts. ... They could use their feticide law to re-criminalize abortion and punish women who have miscarriages."[35] She was released in September 2016 following the overturning of her conviction.

VIOLENCE AGAINST WOMEN

Violence against women is pervasive and worldwide — a vestige of the ancient history of male ownership of women as property. Its most extreme form is femicide, the deliberate killing of women and girls because of their gender. According to the World Health Organization, 35 percent of the murders of women worldwide are committed by intimate partners. In the United States, battering is the single largest cause of injury to women.[36]

The Centers for Disease Control (CDC) reported in 2011 that nearly 1 in 5 U.S. women have been raped at some point in their lives. An intimate partner committed more than half of those rapes. One in 6 U.S. women has been victims of stalking at some point during their lifetime and two-thirds of these were stalked by a current or former intimate partner. More than 1 in 3 women in the United States has experienced rape, physical violence, and/or stalking by an intimate partner in their lifetime, and 69 percent of these women experienced this violence for the first time before the age of 25.

Between 1995 and 2005 there was a general decline in violent crime, with violence against women declining 64 percent. However, during that period, rates of rape and sexual assault remained unchanged. Only about a third of these crimes are reported to law enforcement, and only 12 percent result in arrest. A recent news report quotes Mary P. Koss, a University of Arizona public health professor: "The 12 percent figure should puncture the public's illusion that rape victims can achieve justice through reporting to law enforcement."

One reason that many rape survivors do not trust law enforcement is the lax way in which law enforcement operates in cases of rape. Thanks to the women's liberation movement of the 1960s and '70s, police departments and hospitals instituted the practice of gathering evidence into rape kits that could be used in prosecutions. Nationwide, however, 400,000 rape kits have been found to be stored and untested, in many instances for decades. Activists are agitating to eliminate the backlog in rape kits and get repeat perpetrators off the streets.[37]

Poor women are the most vulnerable to domestic violence because of economic dependence. Access to an independent income, child care, transportation and affordable housing are primary considerations for women who seek to escape violence at home.

The federal Violence against Women Act (VAWA), which was meant to give some relief to victims through the criminal justice system, has a mixed record. While VAWA has increased prosecutions of domestic violence cases, and has provided for police training in how to handle cases of domestic violence, it has not reduced the incidence of this violence. The mandatory arrests of abusive partners under the act have reduced the number of women who are compelled to take self-defense into their own hands, but the number of women killed has not diminished, nor do these arrests give poor women an alternative to losing the family breadwinner. The act does not address the social and economic conditions that contribute to domestic violence, nor does it offer — and fund — a mandatory education program for both boys and girls on male-female equality, or self defense for girls, or affordable and safe housing or a secure income for women who want to flee their abusers.

The 2013 renewal of the act was held up by Congress members' reluctance to extend the act's protections to Native American women on reservations and to LGBTQ persons.

SEXUAL VIOLENCE IN THE MILITARY

Sexual violence by armed soldiers is also a near-universal and historic feature of war. Rape remains pervasive in military contexts. Deaths and injuries of civilians far outnumber those of combatants, and the majority of these victims are women. But military violence is not visited only on the enemy. It is foisted in epidemic proportions upon women within the perpetrators' own military service. Many of these crimes are committed by commanding officers and repeat offenders.

According to a report in Mother Jones: "Women in the U.S. military are being raped and sexually assaulted by their colleagues in record numbers. An estimated 26,000 rapes and sexual assaults took place in the military in 2012 [including a substantial number of rapes of men by other men].... Only one in seven victims reported their attacks, and just one in ten of those cases went to trial."[38] A 2014 survey conducted by the Defense Department with the Rand Corporation found somewhat lower overall numbers, but a greater percentage of these were violent, forcible attacks, as opposed to "unwanted sexual contact." Not only are these crimes seriously underreported, but the great majority of women who do report them are retaliated against and shunned.[39]

Prosecution for these crimes is conducted through the military chain of command, yet commanders themselves are frequently the perpetrators of sexual crimes. Efforts in the U.S. Senate to remove these prosecutions from the chain of command have failed to garner enough votes. In addition to military service women, civilian spouses of service members and civilian women who live near military bases are also targets of sexual assault, yet their numbers are not included in Pentagon tallies of sexual assault.

These crimes are a reflection of a culture of militarism that has escalated along with America's endless wars. The connection between militarism and violence against women in the home has a long history. Writer Ann Jones cites John Stuart Mill, who, "writing in the nineteenth century,... connected the dots between 'domestic' and international violence. But he didn't use our absurdly gender-neutral, pale gray term 'domestic violence.' He called it 'wife torture' or 'atrocity,'.... Arguing in 1869 against the subjection of women, Mill wrote that the Englishman's habit of household tyranny and 'wife torture' established the pattern and practice for his foreign policy. The tyrant at home becomes the tyrant at war."

The epidemic of sexual assault on campus
is finally starting to receive national attention.

PHOTO: WOLFRAM BURNER

Jones continues: "Some 3,073 people were killed in the terrorist attacks on the United States on 9/11. Between that day and June 6, 2012, 6,488 U.S. soldiers were killed in combat in Iraq and Afghanistan, bringing the death toll for America's war on terror at home and abroad to 9,561. During the same period, 11,766 women were murdered in the United States by their husbands or boyfriends, both military and civilian.[40]

SEXUAL VIOLENCE ON U.S. CAMPUSES

A surge in reporting about sexual assault on campus has taken place in recent years. Many surveys have shown that between 20 percent and 25 percent of college women are sexually assaulted on campus. These figures are not unusual; what is new is the level of publicity and the fightback conducted by campus women — against the attacks and against the impunity with which the perpetrators are rewarded.

As of April 2015, more than 100 campuses are under federal investigation for inadequately addressing sexual assaults under Title IX of the federal civil rights law that prohibits sex discrimination in education. These include elite private colleges, public colleges and at least one religious institution. In New York, Gov. Cuomo has ordered the State University of New York system to institute new policies to combat sexual assault.

In general the remedies targeted for reform are law enforcement behavior, which is often seen as disparaging and dismissive of rape victims, and campus disciplinary procedures, which serve to protect the campus' public profile by understating the occurrences of sexual assault.

A Huffington Post article reported in 2014: "The reason this issue has gotten so much attention ... is because students started speaking out and criticizing how their colleges and universities handled their sexual assault cases. ... Their focus was on soft punishments, disparaging comments college officials made to survivors, fraternities making rape jokes and alleged retaliation for criticizing their schools on these issues. ...The focus on campus sexual assault ... is about students who said they were wronged by their schools after they were raped — in some cases saying that was worse than the assault itself."[41] For these reasons, as in the military, students tend to underreport cases of sexual assault.

It is important to note that women ages 18-24 who are not in school suffer from sexual assault at an even higher rate than college students.

WOMEN AND MASS INCARCERATION

Men make up 13 of every 14 prisoners in the United States, but before the era of mass incarceration (starting in the 1970s), the proportion of women in prison was even smaller (one out of every 24 prisoners). According to a recent Truthout report: "Since 1980, the rate of women's incarceration has increased 518 percent. Less than 13,000 women were in prison in 1980. By the end of 2012, that number had risen to over 108,000 (not including the 102,000 women in local jails). Black women were the most targeted by the mass incarceration machine in its initial decades, with prison rates over six times women of other communities. In the last decade, more white and Latina women have fallen into the clutches of the criminal justice system. The Bureau of Justice Statistics found that Black women still had an imprisonment rate of nearly three times that of white women. The incarceration rate for Latinas is nearly twice that of white women."[42]

According to the ACLU, a million women in one way or another are under the supervision of the criminal justice system. Of this number, a reported 85-90 percent have a history of domestic and sexual abuse. Their involvement in this system leaves many incarcerated women vulnerable to re-victimization. A majority of women in prison are mothers. Once in prison many are reported to suffer sexual violence by prison guards with little chance of receiving justice.[43]

The Coalition of Women Prisoners, a project of the Correctional Association of New York (composed of former prisoners, social service workers, lawyers and others) has called for a Domestic Violence Survivors Justice Act, which would allow judges to take a history of domestic violence into account in sentencing decisions. It also calls for lower sentences and alternatives to incarceration.[44]

Among girls in the juvenile system, the picture is even worse. A report called "The Sexual Abuse to Prison Pipeline: The Girls' Story" found that while far fewer girls than boys were incarcerated, many — 80 percent-90 percent in some states and 30 percent nationwide — have a history of physical or sexual abuse, and many have been trafficked. Most girls in the system are not violent offenders, and although the crime rate among girls has not increased in 20 years, the number of arrests has increased. These girls are disproportionately poor African Americans, Latinas and Native Americans.[45]

A large percentage of incarcerated women are caught up in the war on drugs, imprisoned for nonviolent drug offenses and serving long mandatory sentences. A federal bipartisan move to reform sentencing guidelines in 2014 was halted before any progress was made. Another large percentage consists of immigrant women who, with their children, are detained as criminals in family detention centers — often privately owned — as they wait for asylum hearings. Others are imprisoned for fighting back against violent attacks.

A story in the Feminist Wire in June 2015 described the discriminatory punishments suffered by Black girls and women by police, a legacy of both Jim Crow racism and misogyny. The article cites the assault by a white policeman on a teenage black girl at a pool party in McKinney, Texas, and the beating of a Black homeless woman by a white police officer in Los Angeles. Both attacks were videotaped, but while the Texas officer was suspended and the Los Angeles officer was fired, neither faced criminal charges.[46]

Studies also show that Black girls face harsh disciplinary measures, including criminalization of school misbehavior, at a rate far higher than for white girls — six times higher nationally, 10 times higher in New York City, 11 times in Boston. (The gap between Black and white boys is three times nationally.)[47]

A New York Magazine article, April 20, 2015, reported that women constitute 20 percent of the unarmed people of color killed by police between 1999 and 2014. Women and girls face not only the state violence suffered by males but also rape and sexual assault.[48]

When President Obama launched his program My Brother's Keeper, aimed at providing support and services for Black boys, two public letters were written to the president in spring 2014, one by "200 Concerned Black Men" and the other by more than 1,600 women of color, urging the inclusion of girls in the program.

The men's letter read in part: "[I]n lifting up only the challenges that face males of color, MBK — in the absence of any comparable initiative for females — forces us to ask where the complex lives of Black women and Black girls fit into the White House's vision of racial justice?"

The women's letter included the following: "Girls and young women must be included in all our efforts to lift up the life chances of youth of color. To those who would urge us to settle for some separate initiative, we need only recall that separate but equal has never worked in conditions of inequality, nor will it work for girls and women of color here."[49]

The backlash consists of many elements in addition to right-wing efforts to reduce women's rights, including oppressive state and national government policies as well as the absence of affirmative new policies. For example why is it that the U.S. government will not initiate and finance a well directed and effective legal and educational program nationally to seriously reduce the plague of violence and rape against women in the country?

Women's oppression is social, not biological or innate, and it can be stopped by popular activism and substantial social, political and economic transformation. The continuing attacks on women's lives and rights, as well as the lack of progress in extending those rights, is all the worse because it has occurred based on reversing a strong women's movement that won many victories. After a period of relative passivity and disunity, women and their allies must mobilize again with collective action, primarily in the streets, workplaces and campuses, while also using the courts and legal system. It will take a massive and organized fightback to defeat the backlash against women's rights, and to move forward again. □

MOVING FORWARD

Chapter 10
The women's movement today: 1990-2016

TODAY'S women's movement has plenty to fight for, but there is no sustained and militant feminist upsurge as seen in previous periods of U.S. history. Those women's organizations with national capacity are consumed with largely defensive battles and orient towards building relationships within the Democratic Party. The coalitions they form with labor unions and civil rights groups are almost entirely of a top-down and bureaucratic nature, aimed at the passage of specific legislation rather than mobilizing the base or spreading feminist consciousness throughout society.

The fighting spirit remains at the grassroots level but has been reduced mostly to localized responses that are little match for the centralized, well-funded and coordinated attacks on women's rights from the religious right, conservative think tanks and capitalist politicians. While many activists have a critique of the political strategy of national women's organizations, these atomized feminist groups have been hampered by insular organizational practices, postmodern ideological perspectives and the weakness of the political left to provide a coherent alternative.

The "NGO-ization" of resistance — in which social justice organizations turn to liberal foundations to sustain themselves — affects all layers of the women's movement, not just the big organizations. No group should be faulted for trying to build professional-level organization — all movements need that to defeat well-organized adversaries. Nor is the pursuit of grants in and of itself a decisive question. The problem is the nature of the NGO deal — the strings and political limitations that come with funding and institutional support. Organizations become accountable fundamentally to their donors, forced to conform to their politics, language and planning — breeding a "single-issue" and territorial political culture that obstructs boldness of action, tactical flexibility and political transformation.

The narrowness of this organizational reality is in contradiction with the now-universal rhetorical insistence on intersectionality — the multi-layered reality of oppression. The more that foundation-funded organizations put intersectionality into practice, expanding their vision and reach, the more they find themselves "stepping on the toes" of others, competing for grants, moving in on "their issue," etc. Moreover, such groups find themselves self-censoring and pulling back from the fundamental questions — how do we win a new system and what would such a system look like — because doing so would lead to anti-capitalist and socialist solutions. The capitalists will surely cut off their stipend to those who advocate their overthrow.

To say all this is not to gripe, which achieves nothing, nor is it to "throw shade" at non-profit organizers. To the contrary, such organizations have attracted thousands of self-sacrificing young people who want to change the world and fight oppression — and who will undoubtedly play a significant role in the mass movements to come. It is necessary for radical and militant women to understand these contradictions and weaknesses because it structures the political terrain on which we fight. Similarly, every class-conscious worker must understand both the purpose of labor unions, and also their built-in limitations under capitalism.

Moreover, these weaknesses are, of course, only one part of the story. There are more than a few glimmers of hope. In fact, women's participation and leadership in social justice organizing — not to mention many other areas of life — is perhaps at an all-time high. Women's leadership has become an unmistakable characteristic of a range of campaigns and movements — from the organizing against sexist harassment and objectification in daily life, combating police violence, halting the war machine, protecting and extending reproductive justice, educating around the climate crisis, and organizing low-wage workers, immigrants and LGBTQ people. Among the young people turning towards radical and socialist organizing, there is a strong trend towards women's leadership and feminist consciousness.

In other words, there is the basis for, if not yet the reality of, a broad national activist women's movement struggling to safeguard our threatened rights and build upon past gains.

A large part of the feminist ferment that currently exists across the country is visible online. But it has not yet manifested in mass street and direct action, and certainly not in any sort of sustained way. The remnants of the last wave of struggle take the form of court and legislative battles, and in scattered publications. There is also the electoral arena, but simply voting every two or four years for the lesser evil candidate will not build a genuine women's liberation movement.

On the Marxist left, the Party for Socialism and Liberation (PSL), founded in 2004, has been working to revive a left-wing feminist movement. The group has held conferences on women and socialism and demonstrations and meetings on minimum-wage working women, immigration, police brutality, and violence against women and reproductive rights.

In 2012 PSL founded Women Organized to Resist and Defend (WORD) in response to the Republican party's misogynistic elections campaign that year. In the dozen or so cities and towns where it is organized, WORD has staged hard-hitting simultaneous protests on Women's Equality Day and International Women's Day over the years, and in support of women who are suffering from poverty, war, racism, and police brutality. [See Appendix 15]

Nathalie Hrizi, a PSL member and WORD activist, told us about the need for a new movement:

> Women are very conscious of attacks and oppression. There is no lack of understanding of what we're up against, how women are mistreated and regularly harassed. I know women who make their social media pictures unattractive just so creepy men won't harass them. What's lacking in the movement is an organization to pull in women and show that the current reality can be fought against and changed.

> We don't believe WORD can substitute itself for the movement, or make it appear out of thin air. We're a relatively small group of activists and there are 157 million women in the country. But every time we do a WORD action or speak-out, women stop, look, listen and sign up. They're interested in the idea of a movement in which

204 WOMEN FIGHT BACK

women will decide what to fight for and how to fight for it. They're impressed to see women who are unafraid to boldly speak up, chant, and march. It gives a glimpse of our collective power. They're not getting this in the groups that are close to the Democratic Party — NOW, Planned Parenthood and others. While the Democrats are able to contribute resources to these groups that work on behalf of abortion rights and contraception, fighting domestic violence and so on, they can't lead an independent women's movement.

The movement needs to change society. It needs to bring women and their allies to the next level, to create new leaders. Militant movements have existed in the past, but we don't yet have a real mobilization that would bring out millions of women, who I think would come out. Right now many potential activists are fearful of right-wing attacks and are hopeful that electoral change will change the situation.

Non-unionized low-wage working women are increasingly taking collective action, in some cases supported by unions and other groups and coalitions.

A GALVANIZING EVENT

The 1990s opened with a wake-up call for the feminist movement.

This was the 1991 confirmation hearing of the African American judge Clarence Thomas to the Supreme Court. Anita Hill, an African American lawyer and professor, and Thomas' former assistant, had charged him with sexual harassment. Hill was required to testify at the Senate hearing, which mirrored the humiliation she had felt at work. Her credibility and reputation were maligned.

The hearing unleashed some of the same debates that had dogged the anti-racist and feminist movements for decades. Was it racist to hold this Black judge to account for his sexist treatment of a woman subordinate? Should Hill have remained silent in order to preserve Black unity in the face of racist abuse by the white establishment? Was it sexist to confirm Thomas despite allegations of mistreatment from a woman on his staff? The hearing became a rallying point for women who refused to be bound by a false choice between accepting racism and accepting sexism.

Thomas was confirmed, but the issue of sexual harassment exploded onto the national consciousness. Feminists were appalled at the male-only coterie of senators that confirmed Thomas. Anti-racists were appalled at the cynicism with which this all-white Senate committee deter-

Prof. Anita Hill,
Harvard Law School, 2014

mined, in essence, that any conservative Black man would suffice to fill the late progressive Justice Thurgood Marshall's seat. Some Black feminists criticized their white sisters for being insensitive to the contradictory pressures Black women felt at the time.[1]

In response, more than 1,600 African American women signed a statement called "African American Women in Defense of Ourselves," which appeared as a full-page ad in the New York Times on Nov. 17, 1991, and in seven African American newspapers. The statement read in part:

> This country, which has a long legacy of racism and sexism, has never taken the sexual abuse of black women seriously.... As Anita Hill's experience demonstrates, Black women who speak of these matters are not likely to be believed.... We pledge ourselves to continue to speak out in defense of one another, in defense of the African American community and against those who are hostile to social justice, no matter what color they are. No one will speak for us but ourselves.[2] [See Appendix 12 for the complete text.]

Thus, in effect, began feminism's Third Wave, declared individually by a young African American woman, Rebecca Walker, in a 1992 article in Ms. Magazine. She stated: "I write this as a plea to all women, especially the women of my generation: Let Thomas' confirmation serve to remind you, as it did me, that the fight is far from over. Let this dismissal of a woman's experience move you to anger. Turn that outrage into political power. Do not vote for them unless they work for us. Do not have sex with them, do not break bread with them, do not nurture them if they don't prioritize our freedom to control our bodies and our lives.... I am not a post-feminism feminist. I am the Third Wave."[3]

During this same time, coalitions were building around abortion rights, organized primarily by liberal feminists. One of most visible manifestations was the impressive April 1992 March for Women's Lives in Washington D.C. The march, organized by NOW, drew some 750,000 people.

THE THIRD WAVE

Third Wave feminism was led by young women, many born in the 1960s and '70s, who had benefitted from the legal rights and protections won by the struggles of earlier feminists. In fact, many had grown up with feminism, with mothers who had been active in the Second Wave. They critiqued certain aspects of the Second Wave and also set out to complete what they saw as its unfinished work.[4]

There are various definitions for Third Wave feminism. Many highlight that it is the most diverse, broadly inclusive and yet also

Women's groups around the country mobilized nationwide in support of Marissa Alexander, imprisoned in Florida for defending herself from domestic abuse.

individualistic phase of feminism. It has been geared less towards particular reform struggles, electoral politics or collective action than previous phases. Centered on college campuses above all, it has focused on challenging certain assumptions of Second Wave feminism, exploring women's complex identities and carving out spaces to highlight typically marginalized voices.

According to University of Maryland Professor Patricia Hill Collins: "What is called Third Wave feminism is generally associated with feminist politics and movements that began in the 1980s and continue on to today.... Many feminists felt that earlier generations had over-generalized the experiences of white, middle-class, heterosexual women and ignored (and even suppressed) the viewpoints of women of color, the poor, gay, lesbian, and transgender people, and women from the non-Western world. Third-wave feminists have critiqued essential or universal notions of womanhood, and focus on issues of racism, homophobia, and Eurocentrism as part of their feminist agenda."[5]

Elements of Third Wave politics can be summed up in the 13-point agenda of the Third Wave Manifesta, written in 1999 by Jennifer Baumgardner and Amy Richards. Manifesta called for a feminist movement that includes a visible voting block of 18- to 40-year-olds; reproductive justice; equality between men and women in sexual behaviors, family planning responsibilities, child care, and eliminating violence against women; women's and feminist history taught universally, to men as well as women; recognition of the work and value of queer women in the feminist movement; establishing a balance between the self and community; equal access to health care; acceptance of women in all aspects of the military; liberation of adolescents from "slut-bashing," sexual harassment and violence; a fair workplace with equal pay, a living wage and family benefits; equality for women and the power of women to make their own choices, despite disparate trends of feminism; and passage of the Equal Rights Amendment.[6] (The full text of the 13-point agenda is in Appendix 13)

As early as the 1980s, writings by Black feminists called for a more inclusive feminism than the dominant, white-led currents of the Second Wave. Books such as "This Bridge Called My Back: Writings by Radical Women of Color," by Cherrie Moraga and Gloria Anzaldua, and "Home Girls" by Barbara Smith, decried the separatist trends that divided men from women and lesbians from heterosexual women. They called for a feminism that included upfront the fight against racism and capitalist exploitation.

POSTMODERNISM

Some leading figures of Third Wave feminism identified individually as socialists and Marxists, but in general the underlying theoretical basis for the broad trend has been postmodernism. This philosophical outlook rejects universal narratives of truth, including in science, in favor of subjective, differential explanations of reality depending on one's experience, identity and station in life. In politics this amounts to denying the validity of overarching explanations of society, such as a historical materialist framework, and typically involves reluctance to collective struggle, in favor of individualized, localized forms of resistance and changes to oneself. Marxism was the primary theoretical target of the postmodernist academic wave and remains so today.

Postmodernism amounts to a rejection of progressive thinking that was ushered in by the 18th century Enlightenment, which is characterized by rationalism, science and the search for objective truth.

Beyond introducing a difficult and often vague vocabulary, in terms of organizing, postmodernism also introduced a new style of politics that focused more on the dissection of language, symbols and culture. This, according to postmodernism, is where social power really operates, not at the level of the ruling class and the state. Therefore, as their primary activity, activists under the influence of postmodernism battle primarily to liberate "spaces" from oppressive language, discourse and practices. These battles replaced what were the primary subjects of debate for the previous generation of activists: how to achieve power, how to strategically organize against the state, how to base-build and construct larger political alliances, how to build people's power and make a revolution to reorganize all of society top to bottom.

The postmodern worldview, seeing in society only a spectrum of difference and privilege, rather than the counter-examples of unity and solidarity, considers such revolutionary projects unattainable and fanciful.

Many new activists and radicals in the student and social movements are deeply influenced by postmodern ideological concepts without even knowing it, think of themselves as "not ideological," and are unaware of the important theoretical and strategic differences with Marxism. This is a reflection of postmodernism's current dominance but also shows the need for Marxists to persuasively present their views to such activists.

INTERSECTIONALITY

The Third Wave also incorporates the principles of intersectionality, a term coined in 1989 by Kimberle Crenshaw, which describes the interlocking oppressions of race, gender and class. Crenshaw's original article on the subject was written in the context of discrimination law, not as an overall new theoretical framework to understand identity. She revealed how Black women, if they could not prove they were discriminated against specifically "as women" or "as Black," had no legal standing to challenge their discrimination; employers could point to the employment of white women or Black men to avoid accountability. As such, the discrimination law itself was constituted in such a way that erased and discredited the unique experiences and "intersecting" oppressions of Black women.

In more recent years, the term has taken on a life of its own. In general, it is used to affirm that activists, including feminists, must take into account the complex and layered oppressions of individuals, and address all forms of oppression together. The theory recognizes that these oppressions are not suffered separately and should therefore be fought together.

Sam Lacovara, a queer activist who coordinates the Feminist Collective on the SUNY New Paltz campus, described for this book how their group incorporates intersectionality.

> In our mission statement we say that we are a student advocacy organization that believes that the first step to revolution is understanding intersectionality. We're non-hierarchical and believe that the most effective growth and change comes through collective effort. Our weekly meetings focus on consciousness-raising discussions, and our goal is to communicate and cooperate with other on- and off-campus activists in order to build coalitions against all systems of oppression.

We identify ourselves as an intersectional feminist organization, so rather than just focusing on sexism, the way that a lot of feminist organizations do, we focus on the ways that sexism, classism, racism, and homophobia all kind of intersect and how even if we were a group of all women, which we're not, we wouldn't be able to organize around the goals of all the women in the group without also acknowledging their other identities. ...

The concept of waves is useful in teaching feminism chronologically, but I think if we really unpack the ways that feminists have been organizing throughout history, it becomes clear that it has always been continuous, and so if we are only focusing on the peaks, or the waves, everything that was happening in between to build that wave up kind of gets lost.

There is history to intersectionality in the Black feminist movement. In 1983 Barbara Smith wrote: "The feminist movement and the anti-racist movement have in common trying to insure decent human life. Opposition to either movement aligns one with the most reactionary elements in American society." She goes on to describe her own vision of feminism: "I have often wished I could spread the word that a movement committed to fighting sexual, racial, economic and heterosexist oppression, not to mention one which opposes imperialism, anti-Semitism, the oppressions visited upon the physically disabled, the old and the young, at the same time that it challenges militarism and imminent nuclear destruction is the very opposite of narrow."[7]

Similarly the Marxist left has a long history of uniting the struggles of all oppressed people and their allies in a movement for liberation. This unity is often resisted by some activists who want to keep issues separate, in some cases for territorial reasons (controlling "their issue"), and in some cases in order to avoid dealing with the problem of overturning capitalist system — which, once embraced, compels individuals to think about deeper unity, comradeship and revolutionary organization.

Marxist feminist anthropologist Eleanor Burke Leacock helped to formulate the concept of intersectionality in the early 1980s. Her efforts contributed to two core aspects of contemporary intersectional approaches to capitalism: (1) the acceptance of the intersectionality of oppression in all its forms — race, class, gender, sexuality, religion, etc., and (2) the general rejection of biological determinism as it relates to race, gender and class. Her work gives class a primary position.

'Reproductive justice' is a framework that connects women's legal rights with the fight for social and economic justice.

Anthropologist Catherine Hodge McCoid writes: "Leacock tested and found support for the Marxist hypothesis that humans once lived in a state in which men and women were equal partners. She explored and refuted biological determinist notions that (1) in all societies women have been subordinate to men (i.e., as a result of sexual biology), and she also refuted the idea that (2) basic features of capitalism (such as competition and private ownership of property) are found in all societies and individuals (i.e., are related to human 'nature'). Since so many of the contemporary forms of oppression — attacks on immigrants, the rise of religious 'fundamentalism,' the increasing use of rape and other torture as weapons of war, the coloring of prison populations, rising attacks on sexuality, as examples — are resurrecting the ideology of biological determinism and are class assaults with new faces, it is ever more urgent to use the tools Leacock helped to develop."[8]

This is not to say the Third Wave does not have an activist orientation. Such activism, however, differs from the mass street demonstrations of the past. Much of it tends to be local, decentralized and community oriented. Young feminists focus on racism, rape, sexual violence, the restrictions on abortion, LGBTQ discrimination and police violence against women, including trans women.

In the early 1990s Walker set up the Third Wave Direct Action Corporation, whose first project was "Freedom Summer '92," a voter registration drive that reached more than 20,000 new voters, mostly low-income young women of color.[9] In 1997 Walker and others set up

PHOTO: DAVID FENTON

Rebecca Walker

the Third Wave Foundation to fund social justice organizations. Among the causes they have funded are: Rise Up Georgia, which helped a local group pressure Coca Cola to divest from Confederate memorials; a bail fund for a Black trans woman in Brooklyn; Chicago Abortion Fund, which educates and engages low-income women to advocate for expanded access to reproductive services; and various training and leadership programs geared to youth of color and LGBTQ youth.[10]

Wazina Zondon, a young Afghan American Muslim woman, at work in Brooklyn, stresses the importance of education as a form of feminist activism:

I identify as a feminist. I work as a sexuality educator at an all-girls public middle and high school and teach through a sex-positive, intersectional, feminist, LGBTQ-affirming lens. I try to elevate feminist voices in the Afghan and Muslim community, in prayer spaces, study spaces.... The young feminists I work with want gender equality but they're also caught up in false definitions of feminism. Feminism is more than girl power. I try to get young women beyond individual expression. ...

Their issues are violence, harassment, negotiating sexual boundaries and their own desires: being unapologetic and also owning their own sexuality, their own bodies, and controlling who has access to them. Women rally around this. They're not yet thinking about reproductive health. ...

It's hard to be a person of color, hard to be sexually active without being shamed, hard to be poor. They need to understand that they're not alone and how to mobilize with others.

I have never lost hope. I want to see a movement that doesn't just rally around one celebrity or one issue but one that is totally intersectional, holistic and inclusive of not just women or those who identify as women. Something has to give. Gender equality, homophobia – it's essential to talk about feminism as a solution. ...

The core of activism is empathy. It's solidarity.

THIRD WAVE COMMUNICATIONS AND CULTURE

Current feminist activism also operates online and in social media. Books, zines, blogs and social networks disseminate feminist ideas frequently omitted from the mainstream media and serve as a form of consciousness-raising. Of course, the Internet is also used to organize street demonstrations.[11]

But social media has serious limitations as the basis of activism, transforming the individual and building a strong movement. As scholar and activist Barbara Ransby wrote:

> Leadership and organizing cannot be simply tweeted into existence. Movement building is forged in struggle, through people building relationships within organizations and collectives. Social media is only one part of a much larger effort.

> While the mainstream media is all abuzz about social media as if it were a stand-alone entity, it tends to ignore or render invisible the critical work of leader-organizers who are more focused on street action than virtual action. This bias toward social media work woefully distorts not only how we understand this evolving movement, but also how we see social movements in general.[12]

Some websites, such as everydayfeminism.com, use magazine-type articles such as "9 Helpful Tips for the Feminist First-Year College Student" to present a case for feminism, giving examples from everyday life, and validating a feminist point of view.

TheFBomb.org is a blog/community created for teenage and college women. The site describes itself as "loud, proud, sarcastic and passionate: everything young feminists are today." It provides feminist critiques of sexism in popular culture, promotes women in the arts and media, and publishes educational articles on various topics such as sexual violence and the *Hobby Lobby* Supreme Court case. In 2014 FBomb formed a collaboration with the Women's Media Center, which was founded by Jane Fonda, Robin Morgan and Gloria Steinem, prominent Second Wave feminists.

Online magazines such as Bitch, Bust, Bustle, Jezebel and Fusion. net, and blogs such as Feministing and Quirky Black Girls provide news and culture from a feminist point of view, as well as publishing young women writers. These publications and websites draw attention to the inequalities, oppression and exploitation faced by women, the LGBTQ community and people of color, as well as entertaining lifestyle and cultural content. In general, they educate readers about the issues but not about how to fight for social change, other than to change oneself and to encourage change through cultural means and in interpersonal and family relationships. These popular publications do not call for the kind of mass struggle conducted during the First and Second Waves.

A groundbreaking cultural event of its time was Eve Ensler's play The Vagina Monologues, first performed in 1996. It was a celebration of women's empowerment and an exploration of women's feelings about their bodies and about such topics as sexuality, birth and rape. The play is performed every year on campuses and in communities around Valentine's Day — V-Day — as an affirmation of women's right to control their bodies and as a protest against sexual violence. So-called "men's rights activists" and other reactionaries have targeted the play and Ensler for years, but recently, it has also drawn sharp critiques from feminist and trans rights circles.

Another cultural manifestation of bringing women's issues to the public is the international WOW (Women of the World) Festival. Panels on issues such as street harassment, women's health and domestic violence combine with musical performances. In 2015 the festival was held at New York's Apollo Theater, with discussion groups set up at other local venues.[13]

Celebrities such as Beyoncé and Taylor Swift, who have declared they are feminists, have helped bring the subject of feminism into the mainstream to audiences who have never been exposed to politics or a social justice movement. Comedians such as Amy Schumer bring direct expressions of women's rights into their performances. In one of her sketches, Schumer parodies pharmaceutical commercials: "Ask your doctor if birth control is right for you, then ask your boss if birth control is right for you. Ask your boss to ask his priest, find a Boy Scout and see what he thinks. ... Finally, ask yourself why you insist on having sex for fun."[14] Swift and Schumer represent a Hollywood celebrity brand of feminism, however, and both have been called out for displaying insensitivity and ignorance on questions of racial injustice and class inequality.

1 PERCENT FEMINISM

Then there is the feminism of the 1 percent. Lean In, a book by Facebook executive Sheryl Sandberg, exhorts women to achieve liberation and balance in their lives by not being afraid to assert themselves at work. This obscures the roots of feminism as a social justice movement. According to Linda Burnham, writing in the blog Meeting Ground Online: "The fact that Sandberg has occupied so much space and is taken so seriously as the new voice of feminism is a sign of how intractably conservative the current political environment is. That's all the more reason to reassert the social justice roots of feminism, and to make sure that it does not become synonymous with leaning in."[15]

Damayan Migrant Workers Association in New York organizes Filipina domestic workers to fight the 1%.

PHOTO: DAMAYAN

The struggles of domestic workers for fair wages and working conditions and protection from violence exemplify the emptiness of 1 percent feminism. Who is minding their own kids and cleaning the house while the boss is leaning in? What is the nanny/maid/cook/laundress earning and with what benefits, and to whom can she turn if she is mistreated? And, as Catherine Rottenberg puts it: "If Sheryl Sandberg is serious about sparking a conversation, then perhaps she should start by asking who the cleaning women at Facebook are and how much money they take home every month. Do they have a viable pension plan? Do they receive paid holidays? And what kind of child-care services does Facebook offer them?"[16]

GENERATIONAL DIFFERENCES

What is referred to as an intergenerational conflict has manifested itself between young Third Wavers and their foremothers from the Second Wave. There are some parallels between today's generational conflicts in the women's movement with the interactions between First Wave feminists and the young women who immediately followed them, nearly a century ago.

When the First Wave of feminism declined, especially in the 1920s after suffrage was achieved, the level of explicitly women's struggle declined. At the same time, young women began to more openly assert their independence and sexuality — in how they dressed, spoke and went out in public. Because the political and cultural dynamics had shifted so quickly, a wide gulf in sensibilities separated women only twenty years apart. Many of the First Wave activists who had fought so hard, and risked so much, were horrified at what they saw as apolitical, self-centered and undignified behavior of women who seemed to take for granted their foremothers' sacrifices.

Many older feminists feel that the younger ones have eschewed activism for individualistic and cultural activities and identity politics and that they have rejected the feminist movement that yielded so many victories and benefits. Many young feminists have been extremely critical of the Second Wave for its white middle-class composition and for presuming to define a universal feminism that fits all women's experiences. A number of Third Wavers say they resent having to pay homage to their predecessors as they forge their own paths.

This conflict came to a head very publicly in the 2009 election for president of NOW. With the retirement of Kim Gandy, many had hoped that a younger woman would take charge and bring in new younger members. Latifa Lyles, a 33-year-old Black woman with years of experience as a NOW volunteer, staffer and leader, and who wanted to bring in a more diverse membership, was considered by many to be the top candidate. However near the end of the campaign, Terry O'Neill, 56, with the support of older members from the Second Wave, joined the campaign — and won. Her campaign focused on street activism and took a dim view of Lyles' strategy of social media organizing and "insider" Congressional politics.

O'Neill remains president in 2016.[17] The generational struggle in NOW occurred entirely within the orbit of liberalism and the Democratic Party establishment, however, and was not politically substantive. Lyles immediately became the director of the Women's Bureau of the Labor Department in the Obama administration. O'Neill's 7 years of leadership have not produced the promised surge of in-the-streets struggle and she campaigned aggressively for Hillary Clinton, a center-right war hawk, against Bernie Sanders and the party's left wing.

Instead of ideology — or political strategy — the current inter-generational conflict has largely taken the form of a cultural clash. Feminist scholar Astrid Henry has pointed out that current young feminists reclaim concepts that earlier feminism ardently rejected: use of language like "girl," not to mention the dreaded "b-word," as well as girlie styles, and traditional feminine culture. She writes that even though they are freely chosen, these concepts seem to her like a watered-down form of empowerment.[18]

The feminist upsurge of the 1960s and 1970s aggressively challenged certain sexist words and indeed forced a large section of society to rethink and abandon them. There was a hard-fought and non-stop war on sexist language. But some of today's feminists prefer to change the connotations of sexist words rather than censor them from speech. This idea inspired the first "SlutWalk," a public march of women partially dressed or adorned in "provocative" clothing in Toronto, Canada, in 2011 in response to a police officer who blamed rape on women who dressed like "sluts." A number of such events have taken place in various cities around the world.

The purpose of the SlutWalk was to draw attention to sexual violence against women and to bring home the reality that rapists cause rape, not women's clothing or appearance. It also seeks to "reclaim" this word that is a slur against women who are, or appear to be, sexually active. This does not work for everyone, and was not embraced across the spectrum of Third Wave feminists. However ironic or provocative the organizers of SlutWalks intended to be, many women, especially Black women, whose history of slavery, rape and shame is a constant presence, are offended by the claim that calling oneself a slut in empowering. This sentiment has been echoed by several other women's organizations based in Third World and migrant communities.

Among those who believe Third Wavers have traded in radical politics for identity politics and activism for academia, Second Wave theorist and activist Carol Hanisch has written:

> Academia itself has contributed greatly to replacing the language of struggle with the elitist and often inaccessible language of the academy, like postmodernism, binary, agency, deconstruct, complicate, and so on. Neither the words nor the concepts have much meaning to most women's real lives....

> If we compare the passionate and galvanizing demands of the late '60s and early '70s with what passes as feminism today, we see major changes in strategy and goals. The robust cry for women to unite for organized power to defeat male supremacy has all but disappeared.... The Women's Liberation Movement was the masses of women in motion seeking collective power to end our status as the second sex. ... Next we are told to seek personal empowerment — not the power of women uniting like a union to force social change — but to seek 'agency' — more choice — for individual women. If every woman just had enough choices and 'leaned in' in the right way, her dreams would come true, never mind that those choices are not good enough. Books and magazine articles urging women on to 'self-empowerment' have

replaced those early 'strident' feminist tracts against male
supremacy. Then came 'Third Wave' feminism full of more
of the same — 'empowerment,' 'expressing themselves,'
and seeking 'safe spaces' — not with changing the world.[19]

As such, Third Wave feminism, while naming the battles to be
fought and rights to be won, tends to not name an explicit adversary
or define a clear worldview. For radical feminists the enemy was
patriarchy or even men themselves; for liberal feminists it was sexist
politicians in Congress and the White House; for Marxist feminists,
socialist and communist, it was capitalism and the class system. But
according to Prof. Laura Brunell, third wavers themselves declare that
the creation of a unified agenda or philosophy is a goal that is not
only unrealistic but undesirable.[20]

One can question whether this manifestation of feminism can
be called a wave, a term that is generally used to describe a great
surge. What we are witnessing instead is a reframing of the theoretical
framework of feminism, along with small pockets of resistance and
rebellion, some around the same issues that were fought against in
the Second Wave: economic inequality, restrictions on reproductive
rights, rape and violence, racism, poverty, sexual repression, and
capitalism and imperialism. Other issues have gained currency since
the end of the Second Wave: the environment, immigration, gender
rights, and police brutality. The political system has failed to respond
to women's needs. The task of today is to build on what is out there
into a mass, militant united movement that will fight for transforma-
tional change, with the feminist movement an identifiable, independent component of this mass movement.

Here are some of the various issues of the day that U.S. feminists are involved in.

REPRODUCTIVE RIGHTS

The fight for reproductive rights is one of the most visible and
potentially unifying struggles in today's feminist movement, but there
has not been a truly massive national protest against the right-wing
attacks on abortion and contraception since 2004, when over a million
women demonstrated in Washington. Seven organizing groups led the
way then — NOW, American Civil Liberties Union, Black Women's

Health Imperative, Feminist Majority, NARAL Pro Choice America, National Latina Institute for Reproductive Health, and Planned Parenthood Federation of America. More than 1,400 organizations co-sponsored the event, from the NAACP to the National Association of Social Workers.

This was a spectacular turnout — even if the event's political orientation was constrained by liberal feminism. But that was 12 years ago and the large women's organizations did not build on the momentum to launch a new wave of grassroots struggle or call follow-up national actions. Since 2004, over a score of state legislatures have passed multiple anti-abortion laws, often backed with demonstrations by religious conservatives and right-wing supporters, as well as large annual anti-abortion protests in Washington D.C. Public opposition is left to relatively small numbers of people in each state. The significant resources and compelling message of the women's organizations have been devoted largely to lobbying and getting "pro-women" Democratic Party officials elected.

A glimmer of a resurgent women's movement was in 2013 when Texas state senator Wendy Davis conducted an 11-hour filibuster against proposed legislation that would have severely restricted abortion in Texas. Women around the country supported her with money, mailings, petitions and social media, but eventually the legislation passed. Attempting to direct all that grassroots energy and national attention into an electoral route, Davis, a Democrat, subsequently waged an unsuccessful campaign for governor.

Also in 2013 a coalition of feminist activist groups caused the defeat of a ballot initiative in Albuquerque, N.M., that would have banned abortions after 20 weeks of gestation. This was the first attempt to pass anti-abortion legislation at the municipal level. Before the activist campaign, polls had predicted passage of the bill, but it was defeated by persistent door-to-door organizing. Women from all over the country traveled to Albuquerque to help their sisters fight against the bill.[21]

Pro-choice laws were introduced or passed in California, Connecticut, Arizona and other states in 2014 and 2015, and intense public pressure helped defeat or overturn restrictive laws in North Dakota, Maine, Virginia and Wisconsin. In New York state a measure to place the provisions of the *Roe v. Wade* decision into state law was

*Albuquerque women organizers celebrate the defeat of a proposed
municipal ban on abortion after 20 weeks, November 2013.*

defeated two years in a row by the Republican State Senate, despite
the work of a huge coalition of liberal women's groups, unions and
Democratic Party activists.

In a recently published book, Katha Pollitt takes on the defen-
siveness of the progressive forces around the issue of abortion. Her
book, titled Pro: Reclaiming Abortion Rights, asserts that abortion is
a social good and not an agonizing choice. She notes that for women
who, before learning they were pregnant had no intention of having a
baby, abortion was not an ambivalent choice. They have been manipulated into feeling guilty over their abortions.[22]

In response to this manipulation, and to the Congressional
fights to defund Planned Parenthood, two young women started a
Twitter campaign with the hashtag #ShoutYourAbortion. The purpose
was to de-stigmatize abortion and to erase the shame and secrecy
associated with it.

One medical advance that helps women avoid abortion is
emergency contraception, or the "morning after pill." Reproductive
rights activists had agitated for years for this medication, which had

been available by prescription only, to be available over the counter, without prescription and for all ages. A federal court had ruled that this drug be made available, but the Obama administration appealed. In May 2013 National Women's Liberation (NWL), joined by WORD, staged actions in drugstores all over the country, placing the medication on pharmacy shelves and using bullhorns to explain their actions to workers and customers. In June 2013 the Obama Administration finally dropped its appeal.[23]

The movement for Reproductive Justice (RJ) was developed by African American feminists in the 1990s and popularized by the social justice group SisterSong. RJ, which has widespread support in today's women's movement, expands the battle for women's control over reproduction beyond birth control and abortion, and includes the right to give birth to and raise a child with the necessary social supports. RJ activists speak out against poverty and racism as obstacles to raising a family, and call for health care during and after pregnancy, the rights of pregnant workers, and other family benefits — an inclusive vision that goes beyond formal rights to the question of universal access to needed services.[24]

VIOLENCE AGAINST WOMEN

Violence continues to be a major area of feminist protest and activism, whether it is intimate partner violence, street violence or police violence.

The continuing epidemic of rape and sexual violence has been responded to with mass marches, including smaller annual Take Back the Night marches in a number of towns and cities, the controversial SlutWalks, and heroic individual acts. One such act drew a mass response on campuses.

Emma Sulkowicz, a student at Columbia University, was raped by a fellow student in 2012. After being unsuccessful in getting the university to expel her alleged rapist, Sulkowicz vowed to carry her dorm mattress on campus wherever she went in 2014 and the next year, as long as he remained at the school. She even carried it to her graduation. This act, called "Carry That Weight," became a performance piece that was her senior thesis for her visual arts degree. Campuses across the country staged "Carry that Weight" demonstrations in October 2014 in solidarity, with activists carrying mattresses around their campuses. Many campus sexual crimes are committed by repeat offenders, giving rise to the charge that there are sexual predators living on campuses and getting away with these assaults.

Two women who had been sexually violated on campuses produced a film called "The Hunting Ground" in 2015. The film showed the prevalence of rape on campus, the corresponding denial of justice to the victims, and the protection of perpetrators, many of whom are repeat offenders. The public outrage over campus rape finally grew loud enough for federal authorities to investigate more than 100 campuses.

In related actions, feminist organizations such as Feminist Majority Foundation's campus arm, Feminists United, along with Black Women's Blueprint, the National Women's Law Center and others have been engaged with the Office of Civil Rights to fight against campus-based sexual violence, filing complaints under Title IX. Schools stand to lose federal funding if they do not comply with Title IX's provisions against sex discrimination on campuses.[25]

In the small college town of New Paltz, N.Y., Mid-Hudson WORD has organized marches, rallies and public meetings of hundreds of students and community residents to protest violence, rape and the misogyny characterized by the political system. Speakers from the antiwar, labor, LGBTQ and student movements have spoken out in favor of a unified feminist response to the war on women.

An extraordinary global response to domestic violence was initiated by author and playwright Eve Ensler. Called "One Billion Rising," it is an annual day of public dancing by women throughout the world in many thousands of locations to draw attention to the one in three women who are raped or beaten in life — amounting to one billion worldwide. The event is an expression of global solidarity with women that reveals in stark terms the depth and regularity of sexist violence. Some have criticized the actions for their lack of a clear struggle orientation or strategy, but the day represents a refreshing turn towards physical action and its looseness allows grassroots women's groups to adapt the day to help build their local struggles. In 2015, the official theme of the One Billion Rising day was revolution — because, in Ensler's words, to take on violence, "it is the system that has to change — from neoliberal capitalism to patriarchy. People are interpreting revolution in different ways — from calls to oust their country's president to fighting against abuse in the family."

South African actress and activist Andrea Dondolo
standing up with One Billion Rising

Misogyny fuels murder as well as violence. In May 2014 a male
college student murdered six and wounded 14 near the University of
California, Santa Barbara to punish women who had rejected him sexually and men who were more successful with women. The murders
followed online misogynist videos he had posted. In reporting the
incident, mainstream media stressed that not all men hate women
and that the shooter was mentally ill. More than half a million women
responded online, mostly on Twitter, using the hashtag #YesAllWomen:
while not all men are murderers and abusers, all women are potential
targets of misogynist violence and all women worry about the measures they need to take to avoid violence, at home or out in public.[26]

Two cases of women who have served time for acting in self-defense — Marissa Alexander and CeCe McDonald — became flash-
points of struggle that dramatized this reality.

George Zimmerman, Trayvon Martin's killer, was acquitted on
the basis of "self-defense," an outrageous lie that spurred protests
nationwide. It also caused feminist and anti-racist activists to notice
the double standard used in prosecuting women and people of color
who defend themselves. The case of Marissa Alexander showed the
double standard explicitly. Alexander is an African American woman

who, in 2010 fired a warning shot in the vicinity of her abusive ex-husband. Denied the right to use Florida's Stand Your Ground law in her defense, she was sentenced to 20 years in prison, despite the fact that the shot neither hit nor hurt anyone. A massive national movement supported her, with demonstrations, rallies and petitions to free her. Granted a new trial, but with the threat of an even longer sentence of 60 years, Alexander eventually pleaded guilty to lesser charges and received a sentence of three years, time served, plus a period of house arrest. This case exemplified the impunity of male batterers and also the legal obstacles faced by women who try to fight back.

CeCe McDonald is a young Black transgender woman who, while walking with friends, was attacked on a Minneapolis street in 2011 by a group of people hurling homophobic, racist and transphobic slurs at her. McDonald's face was cut with broken glass, and in the brawl that followed one of the attackers was killed. McDonald was charged with second degree manslaughter. At her trial, the judge rejected her self-defense claim as well as evidence that her attacker wore a swastika tattoo and had three prior convictions for assault. Facing a sentence of 80 years, she too accepted a plea deal and was sentenced to 41 months. She was freed after 19 months, thanks at least in part to organized and coordinated public demonstrations.[27]

FIGHTING RACISM

Women have played a major role in creating the movement against mass incarceration and in forming the activist groups in the broad Black Lives Matter movement.

Michelle Alexander's 2010 book "The New Jim Crow: Mass Incarceration in The Age of Colorblindness," plus her many speaking engagements, spurred reading groups in cities and towns across the country. This led in turn to community organizing against mass incarceration, including educational programs, street demonstrations, lobbying at all levels of government, and a groundswell of vocal and militant activism against the prison industrial complex.

This new movement drew attention to the racial and class dimensions of mass incarceration, and led to demands for changes ranging from ending mandatory sentences and privatized prisons to calling for governments and employers to "ban the box" — to end the practice of requiring job applicants to check off a box indicating whether they have ever been arrested or convicted. The public has now been inundated with information, even in the mainstream media, about the injustices of the prison system and the racism and brutality toward inmates inside the prison system.

The "Black Lives Matter" slogan and loose organizational network was founded by three Black queer women, all experienced social justice activists, after the acquittal of George Zimmerman. They are Aliza Garza, who is a special projects director with National Domestic Workers Alliance; Patrice Cullors, a playwright and performance artist; and Opal Tometi, Executive Director of the Black Alliance for Just Immigration. The movement came to greater public attention after the August 2014 police killing of Black teenager Mike Brown in Ferguson, Missouri. It has grown to a national movement, with activists traveling around the country to show solidarity and build the movement in cities where these murders continue to take place.

Violence against women perpetrated by police is beginning to get the attention it deserves. Although the Black Lives Matter movement grew initially around the killings of Black men, the movement is also insisting on public awareness of the fact that women are also killed by police. In a Democracy Now interview, Kimberle Crenshaw explains the slogan called "Say Her Name":

> Black women experience police brutality in many of the same ways that black men do and also in some ways that are different. Many of the cases that we talk about... involve police literally coming into people's homes, into their bedrooms, and actually killing them.... And we're finding that not only are black women killed by police, they're also subject to some of these same historical problems of sexual abuse. So they're women that many people don't believe. .... They're women that are not empathized with or seen as sympathetic or women in need. And so that, in turn, prompts a certain kind of coercive or violent response to them or an effort to abuse them, knowing that no one will believe them.[28]

#SayHerName is a nationwide project to draw attention to the growing numbers of Black women and girls who are victimized by police and heretofore overlooked by the "Black Lives Matter" movement. Sandra Bland was a young Black woman who died in custody in Texas after being brutally arrested for changing lanes without signaling. Rekia Boyd, 22 years old, was shot by an off-duty policeman in Chicago who had fired into a crowd. He was acquitted. Michelle Cusseaux, 50, was shot at close range by a police officer in Phoenix who had been called to take Cusseaux to a mental health facility.

The faces of women who have been killed by police appear on long banners at demonstrations. The text, running across the lines of photographs, reads: "Black Women Are Killed by the Police Too. Say Their Names. Remember Their Faces. The Movement is About Them Too." Other demonstrators carry four-foot high posters, each with a name, description, photograph and date of death.

The website Truthout reports on the resistance movement going on among women in prisons. Because of their inability to gather in public, women prisoners resort to other means to fight against the limitations of incarceration — individual actions that add up. For example, jailhouse lawyers have filed suits to protect incarcerated mothers' custody of their children. Others have filed suits to get the same educational and vocational training programs for female as for male prisoners. Some of these suits have led to policy changes. Getting information on prison conditions out to the public is another struggle, and, in the face of prohibitions, an act of resistance.

The sexual violence perpetrated on inmates by prison guards is a major issue, and fighting back often leads to further violence. Yet some women do report this abuse and some prison guards lose their jobs or go to prison themselves. Trans women are routinely placed in male prisons, denied their hormone treatments, and suffer physical and sexual violence. Some individual cases have led to policy changes. Several feminist publications are distributed in the prisons and some publish the works of imprisoned women. Black & Pink, an organization of LGBTQ prisoners and their allies, sends their newspaper into prisons throughout the United States. The California Coalition for Women Prisoners sends their publication, The Fire Inside, to California prisoners. Ms. Magazine is sending its publication into prisons and domestic violence shelters, as well as initiating reading programs. Networks of formerly incarcerated women are forming to advocate for those still inside.[29]

WOMEN FIGHT BACK AGAINST LOW WAGES

The one piece of federal legislation passed during the Obama administration that protects women workers is the Lily Ledbetter Fair Pay Act, which extends the statute of limitations for workers to sue an employer for wage discrimination. Although most people focused on gender discrimination, the Ledbetter act applies to discriminatory pay practices based on all protected categories, including race, age, disability, national origin and religion.

However, women are fighting for more than the right to sue, and the new act still requires women workers to be able to prove the discriminatory "intent" of their bosses, to know the pay of their colleagues and to be able to afford a lawyer. While the act has helped workers advance individual cases, it is no surprise that it has not substantially changed the pay gap. What is needed are social and collective solutions rather than just individual legal ones.

Women are at the forefront of the "Fight for Fifteen," the struggles of immigrant women and domestic workers, the fight against trafficking and other low-wage working-class movements. Women in these super-exploited jobs are fighting together for higher wages and better working conditions, illustrating the connection between feminist and worker struggles.

Among worker centers, many of which focus on highly vulnerable immigrant workers, women now feature prominently in

PHOTO: RINGO CHIU

leadership. While labor union presidents tend to still be mostly men, this too has shifted from decades ago. A few examples include Mary Kay Henry, president of the Service Employees International Union (SEIU); Karen Lewis, president of the Chicago Teachers Union (CTU); Saru Jayaraman of Restaurant Opportunities Center (ROC) United, a workplace justice organization for restaurant workers; Bhairavi Desai of the New York Taxi Workers Alliance; and Ai-Jen Poo of National Domestic Workers Alliance, among others.

This does not mean these individual women leaders necessarily have revolutionary or militant feminist politics. Mary Kay Henry, for instance, has functioned as a close ally of the Obama administration and Hillary Clinton. Karen Lewis, by contrast, led the bold teachers' strike against Rahm Emanuel and Chicago's Democratic machine. Ai-Jen Poo has been criticized by other women from within the domestic worker movement for emphasizing largely symbolic legislative victories over bottom-up worker organizing.

What it does reflect, however, is the overall presence of women within labor, who have brought their own experiences and demands into the movement in a more central way. In addition to wages and workplace conditions, many unions now organize for work-family issues, racial and gender equality, and access to child care. In a 2014 Nation article, Bryce Covert cites research that shows that "the win rate in National Labor Relations Board campaigns for female lead organizers averages 53 percent, more than 10 points ahead of male ones, and that shoots up to 69 percent for women of color....This effect is compounded when the race and gender of the organizer aligns with the workers; women of color who organize units with over three-quarters women of color have a win rate of 89 percent."[30]

"Fight for 15" is a movement of low-wage workers who are organizing and agitating for a federal minimum wage of $15 per hour — plus a union. The movement started with fast-food workers, backed by organizing and financial support from SEIU. Workers have conducted mass demonstrations and one-day strikes. The movement has quickly spread to home health aides and other industries. Three cities and New York State have passed laws that will raise the minimum wage to at least $15 within the next six years: San Francisco, Seattle and Los Angeles. Chicago, Oakland and Washington, D.C. have raised theirs to $13, $12.25 and $11.50 respectively.[31] In

2014-2015, 14 states and the District of Columbia haves raised their minimum wages, but none to the level of $15 per hour.[32]

At the federal level, the minimum wage, which needs Congressional action to be changed, has been raised only three times in the last 30 years. The tipped minimum wage has not changed for 25 years. Because women workers are clustered at the lower end of the pay scale, raising the minimum wage will reduce the gap between female and male workers.[33]

Among the low-wage workers whose plight is just beginning to be noticed by the general public are nail salon workers, 97 percent of whom are women, largely from Korea. Many are undocumented. They suffer wage theft, physical and verbal abuse, racial discrimination and exposure to toxic chemicals. Worker-rights activists have been fighting for these workers for many years, and finally, after a year-long investigation, the New York Times published a series of articles in 2015 exposing the horrifying working conditions endured by nail salon workers. New legislation in New York calls on salons to provide protective gear for workers; worker advocates call on salons to ban the toxic chemicals completely. Customers are asked to get involved by not patronizing salons that violate safety regulations. New York salons will be required by law to post a workers bill of rights.[34]

With all these progressive labor reforms dealing with the most vulnerable sectors of the working class, the main question will be enforcement. The capitalist state provides few mechanisms to force compliance from employers, the punishments for violating labor law are generally minimal, and labor departments are far too weak. That is why so many restaurant owners consider it a worthwhile risk to flout the minimum-wage law. The only thing that can make these reforms real is the level of organization among the workers themselves, and ultimately unionization.

WOMEN FIGHT BACK IN THE PUBLIC SECTOR

The public sector, which is suffering major budget cuts, layoffs and union-busting, has been an important arena for women, especially women of color, to rise up in the workforce. Wisconsin's breaking of public sector unions in 2011, the Chicago teachers strike of 2012, the ongoing struggle of the postal workers against privatization, the battles to save public hospitals, the teacher-parent-

*A bright spot in labor militancy nationwide
has come from teachers' unions, whose
membership are three-quarters women.*

community solidarity around saving public schools against the
encroachment of corporate business — all these are examples of the
prospects for unity between women's groups and workers, between
male and female workers, and between women workers and local
communities that must grow even stronger as part of a new mass
workers movement and feminist movement.

The Chicago Teachers Union (CTU) went on strike in 2012
not only for wages and benefits but also as a revolt against school
closings and privatization of public schools. Not only did nearly 90
percent of teachers approve the strike, but also two-thirds of parents
supported it. The union, 87 percent female, was led by an African
American woman, Karen Lewis. The teachers' union was excoriated
as "greedy" in the mainstream media, a common response to public
sector workers, who already earn less than those of the private sector
and who are fighting against privatization. The teachers were also
demonized as women, and yet teaching became a women's career
decades ago because they could be hired for less money than men.

While there was public support for the Chicago teachers by
other teachers and workers, what should have been a natural alliance
with the feminist movement did not materialize.[35] The contract settlement contained many victories but was a compromise nonetheless,

and the city and school board continue to cut funding, lay off teachers and close public schools.[36]

A teachers' strike in Seattle in September 2015, the largest since the Chicago strike, addressed some of the same issues: wages and benefits and also standardized tests. This strike was supported by the Seattle City Council, with the visible leadership of socialist council member Kshama Sawant, and presented itself as a women's rights issue and anti-racist struggle.[37] The strike settlement was a win for the teachers' union not only on wages but also on the testing and race and equity issues that the union fought for.

DOMESTIC WORKERS

The National Domestic Workers Alliance (NDWA), is an organization that represents domestic workers, nannies and caregivers to the elderly. Its affiliate organizations' memberships are virtually all women, including rank-and-file members, staff and leaders.

Through lawsuits, demonstrations, public outreach campaigns and community organizing, the NDWA raises public awareness of the caring work done mostly by women, and the need for these workers to earn fair wages and benefits. A recent federal appeals court ruling granted domestic workers the right to a minimum wage and overtime protections granted to other workers under the Fair Labor Standards Act, a right that NDWA had agitated for.

At the state level, domestic workers are fighting an uphill battle. In 2015 Oregon became the fifth state to grant protections to domestic workers in a Domestic Workers Bill of Rights, which includes overtime pay, rest periods, paid time off and protections against sexual harassment and retaliation. New York State has a similar law. California's much weaker law was passed after an initial veto by Democratic Gov. Jerry Brown. According to Sarah Jaffe, "even in 2012, the year of the 'war on women' as Democratic politicians reminded us in fundraising emails... [Brown] felt safe vetoing protections for mostly-women workers."[38]

Among NDWA's member organizations is Damayan, a worker-led organization of Filipina immigrant women, who organize and educate women to fight for their rights to fair wages, working conditions, unionization and against trafficking. One of the problems faced by domestic workers is the isolation they experience working in individual homes.

Damayan organizers find domestic workers in the neighbor-hoods where they work and bring them together for education, sol-idarity and fightback. In addition, Damayan also organizes "against the labor export program of the Philippines and exposes corporate neoliberal economic policies in the country as the primary root of the chronic poverty and widespread unemployment that push Filipinos, mostly women, to migrate to foreign lands in search of a livelihood. Currently 12 million Filipinos, over 10 percent of the country's popu-lation, are overseas as migrant workers in about 200 countries around the globe. Last year, they sent home $20.1 billion in remittances to support their families, thus propping up the Philippines' economy while working in conditions of widespread poverty and abuse."[39]

INDEPENDENT ELECTIONS

The Democratic Party remains unwilling to promote major changes to enhance the position of working women and the poor. To the contrary, the Clinton and Obama administrations both oversaw drastic cuts of programs that benefit women and children in the name of bipartisan compromise with Republicans. Both parties eagerly embraced the Wall Street bailout, the military-industrial complex and a constant barrage of reforms that have facilitated the accumulation of capital by a tiny billionaire class.

It is no surprise then that millions of people are now registering as independents and oppose all establishment politics, even if the rigged electoral system ends up giving them only two "viable" can-didates, from that very establishment, on Election Day. Independent parties are entering the electoral arena to give voters a choice and to present them with a politics of equality. Women candidates routinely run for high office in these parties.

The PSL has offered women candidates in every election since its founding, for U.S. president and for statewide and municipal elec-tions. The 2016 candidate was Gloria La Riva, an experienced socialist activist and union leader who ran on a platform of ending U.S. wars, defending the environment, reproductive rights for all women and immigrant rights.[40] Previous PSL candidate Peta Lindsay ran on a similar platform in 2012.

For two election cycles the Green Party has nominated Jill Stein to run for president of the United States. Stein runs on a platform of environmentalism, economic equality, peace and removing wealth from the electoral system.

While these campaigns are not going to change the structure of U.S. electoral politics, let alone win, they are indicators of how the next upsurge of a radical and left-wing movement will undoubtedly feature women's leadership as a key feature.

LGBTQ LIBERATION AND DEBATES OVER GENDER IDENTITY

Long after most of the movements of the 1960s and '70s had slowed down, the LGBTQ movement has continued with increasing visibility and militancy. From the Stonewall rebellion in 1969, to annual Pride marches all across the nation, to pressuring the state to end the discrimination against gays and lesbians in the military, to coverage of gay and lesbian issues in the mainstream media — this movement never stopped. In the latest victory, same sex marriage, or marriage equality, was approved by the Supreme Court in 2015. While this does not erase discrimination in employment, housing or any other rights or benefits, it is a significant step forward for the civil rights of the LGBTQ community.

Likewise the movement for transgender rights has been operating in full force for years. Trans women suffer disproportionate levels of violence, employment discrimination, abuse in prison, lack of healthcare, public shaming and even suicide. Their exclusion from certain currents of feminism is regarded as bigoted and narrow, in contradiction to feminist values of equality and inclusion.[41]

Other activist movements have incorporated the cause for transgender rights and equality within their own organizations, including Black Lives Matter, and the prison reform movements. The New York Times in 2016 ran five important editorials on transgender life and rights.

Feminist consciousness and women's organizing these days is often far more outspoken on LGBTQ oppression and organizing than in decades past.

At first glance, the women's and LGBTQ movements are clear natural allies. After all, it was the advance of feminism that focused society on the problems of patriarchy, that destabilized conventional concepts of masculinity, femininity, the family and sexuality and that pointed to a new world where people could dress, love and live as they like, with political, social and economic equality.

The early LGBTQ liberation movement was deeply influenced by the women's liberation movement. Today, there is a wide basis for common struggle against a common reactionary enemy. Among activists in both movements today there remains considerably more solidarity and support between them than there is among general society. In the recent struggles over marriage equality, anti-LGBTQ discrimination and the odious "bathroom bills," which were about much more than bathroom access, targeting trans people, many women's organizations were on the front lines showing their support for the LGBTQ movement. Likewise, LGBTQ organizations have consistently supported women's groups fighting sexual violence, attacks on reproductive rights and pay inequality.

Nonetheless, a considerable area of debate and controversy has opened up over theoretical and language questions, which have a direct bearing on day-to-day politics. The debate generally takes the form of the same generational struggle within feminism discussed earlier.

These debates do not make the women's movement and the trans movement permanent enemies, even though the tenor of the discussions, especially on the fringes of both sides, often makes it appear so.

Protest in North Carolina against the HB2 bathroom bill prohibiting people from using the bathroom that coincides with their gender.

PHOTO: PILAR TIMPANE

One of the most intense debates in recent years has revolved around the definition of womanhood itself. These are not entirely new questions — having long occupied women's studies and gender studies departments in academia in particular — although they have been taken in new directions.

Some who consider themselves feminists have stopped using the term "woman" except with modifiers such as "transwoman" and "ciswoman." But to suggest that the standalone phrase "woman" is suddenly meaningless, or should not be used, is to deny the lived reality and consciousness of half the human race, and cannot be an acceptable element in the struggle for liberation.

In large part, the LGBTQ movement has accepted the definition of gender advanced by Third Wave feminism itself. In an Encyclopedia Britannica entry that, significantly, was endorsed by Rebecca Walker, a pioneer of Third Wave feminism, Prof. Laura Brunell writes:

> Influenced by the postmodernist movement in the academy, third-wave feminists sought to question, reclaim, and redefine the ideas, words, and media that have transmitted ideas about womanhood, gender, beauty, sexuality, femininity, and masculinity, among other things. There was a decided shift in perceptions of gender, with the notion that there are some characteristics that are strictly male and others that are strictly female giving way to the concept of a gender continuum.

From this perspective each person is seen as possessing, expressing and suppressing the full range of traits that had previously been associated with one gender or the other. For third-wave feminists, therefore, 'sexual liberation,' a major goal of second-wave feminism, was expanded to mean a process of first becoming conscious of the ways one's gender identity and sexuality have been shaped by society and then intentionally constructing (and becoming free to express) one's authentic gender identity.[42]

In short, this approach boils down gender to individual identity and self-description. As an inherently subjective question, it does not possess any particular social or biological characteristics that can be defined objectively. This contrasts with long-standing understandings of gender and womanhood from both the radical feminist and Marxist traditions. These emphasized historically defined forms of oppression and experiences that shaped women's reality from the moment of being categorized as girls at birth — regardless of identity and sense of self — and growing up thereafter in patriarchal society.

Feminist theorist Judith Butler, whose work draws heavily from postmodernism, takes issue with the idea that a single notion of "woman" exists, and therefore rejects any such notion as the foundation of feminist politics and thought.[43]

In the spirit of this view on gender — that it "cannot be defined by anyone other than the individual" —New York Gov. Cuomo announced in September 2015 that the students in the 64 four-year and two-year colleges of the State University system could now select from seven different options to identify their gender and eight for sexual orientation on college application forms. According to press reports, a New York student can self-identify as a man, woman, trans man, trans woman, genderqueer (a person who identifies with neither, both, or a combination of male and female genders), gender-fluid (a person who may at any time identify as different genders, or any other non-binary identity) and questioning or unsure. Or they can simply write in another identity of their own choice. Facebook offers 58 different gender options so far — reflecting the diverse, and increasing, list of gender identities currently in use.

While many feminists and other progressives applaud such changes as a democratic advance for an oppressed community, others are indignant at the possibility of self-determined gender identity that contradicts a person's sex assignment at birth.

Adding another layer to the tension, a small but influential element of Third Wave feminists and LGBTQ advocates, who are active mainly in academia and social media, has waged a constant battle primarily against the language and slogans of women's organizations as implicitly transphobic (or cissexist.) This has often gone beyond criticizing the weaknesses and problems in the women's movement and far beyond attacking the explicit transphobes in the women's movement, who should be called out and rejected. It seems to assume that trans visibility and liberation can be won by waging war against all of Second Wave or "mainstream" feminism as the main enemy of progress.

Some of these writers have asserted that for the women's movement to focus on abortion rights and access as core organizing issues was inherently oppressive because it "excluded," and supposedly alienated, trans women who cannot become pregnant.

From another angle, critics asserted that describing the assault on abortion rights and access as part of a "war on women" in fact "erased" trans men who also can become pregnant and who face unique challenges and discrimination inside the reproductive health care system.

An article by Lauren Rankin in Truthout explained:

How do we adequately address and include those who have abortions but are not women [referring to trans men]? We must acknowledge and come to terms with the implicit cissexism in assuming that only women have abortions. (Cissexism is defined as "the appeal to norms that enforce the gender binary and gender essentialism, and then used in the oppression of gender variant [non-binary] and trans identities.) Transmen have abortions. People who do not identify as women have abortions. They deserve to be represented in our advocacy and activist framework.

'Stand with Ohio Women' and the 'War on Women' may be great rallying cries, but they also very clearly reiterate the notion that abortion is both solely a women's issue and that only women have abortions. This can make those in the trans community feel excluded, and it can deter them from both seeking the abortion care they may need or becoming actively involved in abortion rights advocacy.[44]

Giving an opposing view in The Nation, Katha Pollitt wrote:

I'm going to argue here that removing 'women' from the language of abortion is a mistake. We can, and should, support transmen and other gender-non-conforming people. But we can do that without rendering invisible half of humanity and 99.999 percent of those who get pregnant. ... The primary sources of abortion data in the U.S. — the CDC and the Guttmacher Institute — don't collect information on the gender identity of those who seek abortion, but conversations with abortion providers and others suggest the number of transgender men who want to end a pregnancy is very low. I don't see how it denies 'the existence and humanity of trans people' to use language that describes the vast majority of those who seek to end a pregnancy.

Pollitt was sharply criticized by two prominent Third Wave foundations that fund reproductive rights nonprofits. In a follow-up article, she responded:

"I never said trans men and other gender-non-conforming people should not be mentioned. I simply think we can include them without barring the word 'women.' We can use 'women and other pregnant people,' 'women and gender-nonconforming people,' or similar terms. That would make crystal clear to those who don't identify as women that they are welcome, a point that vague words like 'people,' 'callers,' and 'anyone' convey only indirectly.

Indeed, the right-wing attack on abortion rights flows from the historical subjugation of women, the control of women's bodies and sexuality, as an oppressed social sector since the beginning of patri-archal, class society.

The vast majority of women who are outraged by the attacks on abortion access and birth control understand deeply and intuitively that these are anti-woman attacks. The historic breakthrough of the feminist project has been to instill precisely such collective conscious-ness among women and to organize women, for the first time, as a political subject on that basis. That is why the insistence of dropping women-specific language in cases such as these strikes such a raw nerve among many feminists — as it appears to be an undoing of that project, a step backwards, and an erasure of women.

Condemning women's organizations for using slogans and language that speak broadly to the experiences of women — an oppressed group that represents the majority of humanity and is under persistent attack — has not been productive for building the solidarity needed to push forward the movements for women's and LGBTQ liberation.

The language of social movements can and will evolve over time according to the practical needs of the struggle. In fact, struggle and collaboration is what most compels people to change their language — out of respect for those they wish to organize alongside. Almost all the online articles about "how to be a better ally" focus exclusively around terminology rather than participation in the struggle itself. But real comradeship is ultimately built through such shared sacrifice, the experience of practical solidarity — not just one's command over language. That is the road for uniting the women's and trans movements as well. Only a small number of women in the country, let alone the world, are even aware of these issues and debates, but for years they have consumed much of the internal life of women's, LGBTQ and trans organizations. These groups are naturally poised to provide guidance as a new generation enters the struggle against patriarchy. It is critical that we find a way to build solidarity.

In terms of theory, to lay a foundation for deeper unity between these movements, more analysis must be provided from a scientific socialist and historical materialist perspective on the actual history of women's oppression, the gender division of labor and the social relations that are tied to the control of reproduction. There is a deep and inextricable link between this history and the history of LGBTQ oppression. This history has to be the starting point, rather than abstract definitions of womanhood, from either a biological essentialist or postmodern outlook.

There is also a proud history of common struggle that is often erased with blanket dismissals and over-simplifications about both feminism and the LGBTQ movement. For instance, the 1960s and 70s movement for reproductive rights was strengthened immeasurably by the solidarity of the heterosexual and gay men who marched alongside their sisters. In the 1980s the women's movement was a key ally of ACT-UP when it led direct actions against Catholic Church leaders who were promoting bigoted views on abortion, homosexuality and AIDS.

There are many more examples that must be highlighted to show that solidarity — not division — is the norm between these two struggles.

In day-to-day organizing, certain best practices can be respected from both sides of the debate, and these practices should be judged on whether they move the struggle for liberation forward. The most progressive elements of both the women's and trans movements must seek to maximize inclusiveness and solidarity for the liberation of all women and all oppressed people.

Moreover, in building unity between oppressed groups — which include all LGBTQ people and all women, among others — extreme care must be taken around questions of who is "more oppressed." The principle of solidarity — "an injury to one is an injury to all" — has to be the guiding principle instead. The key to genuine unity is to respect, listen to and appreciate the different experiences with oppression, which give people a shared interest in fighting for a new system. □

Chapter 11
What kind of movement for the Trump era?

THE election of Trump was a game changer. With this blatant sexist and his hard right-wing cabinet occupying the White House, all the gains of the women's movement for the last 50 years are in grave danger. It is urgent to build a militant, broad and united women's movement to fight back.

The 2016 election campaign brought into sharp focus the state of U.S. politics, culture and thought. Many believed that the Republican Party was too conservative and bigoted to ever win another presidential election among an increasingly diverse and progressive electorate. Many assumed that the loud-mouth bigot would be defeated by the more refined and nominally "inclusive" campaign of Hillary Clinton, whose election as the first woman president would score some symbolic victory for feminism as well. This whole line of thinking was disproven and it is important to understand why.

The election revealed a widespread disillusionment with the economic and political system — similar to the growing crisis of legitimacy for the liberal democratic order across Western Europe. That sentiment is shared across Democratic, Republican and independent voters, but the Democratic Party selected a candidate that, despite her gender, was seen as the ultimate representation of the status quo.

What is the status quo? It is an economy based on gross inequality and rampant poverty. It is a political system that is widely seen as corrupt, undemocratic and dominated by big-money donors; where both parties' establishments are widely distrusted by their own membership.

Since the 2008-2009 recession, some 58 percent of all wealth has accrued to the richest 1 percent of Americans, and corporate profits have more than doubled, while the working class has suffered

Rampant poverty and income inequality were largely ignored by Hillary Clinton, while Trump gave the impression he would improve conditions.

stagnant wages, lost pensions, rising health care costs, and crushing, lifelong student debt.[1]

Internationally, U.S. wars and military threats continue throughout the Middle East, southern Asia and northern Africa, with the United States imposing its will as the world's hegemon. Unsolvable global crises fill the airwaves, the future looks increasingly dark and much of the country believes that life is getting harder and the nation is "declining." This was the sentiment that Trump mobilized and then utilized — falsely promoting rejuvenation, like rising far-right movements across Europe, Latin America, Asia and elsewhere.

THE ELECTION OF DONALD TRUMP

Trump won a stunning upset victory over Clinton, gaining 306 electoral votes to Clinton's 232. Clinton received nearly 3 million more votes than Trump and in effect won the popular election — but that is not how it works in America. The elitist Electoral College provides for the indirect election of the president in a way that disproportionately favors smaller states and converts the national elections essentially into 50 state elections in which even narrow winners take all the electors from a given state. Four presidential candidates in history, including Clinton in 2016 and Al Gore in 2000, have lost with numerical majorities. The undemocratic nature of the U.S system is well known and should be changed.

Liberation News analyzed Trump's victory the day after the election:

> The economies of 93 percent of counties nationwide are at or below where they were in 2008. The stock market has tripled in value since Obama first took office, but wages are stagnant and economic polarization is well documented. These were the conditions that powered the Bernie Sanders rebellion within the party, but the Democratic National Committee put it down. Then Clinton ran to the right and ever since the entire election cycle has been devoid of any meaningful discussion about the core issues facing working-class and poor people in the United States.[2]

Trump blamed immigrants, people of color, the poor and Muslims for this economic disaster. Vermont Sen. Bernie Sanders pointed his arguments directly at Wall Street and the 1 percent and put forward a number of liberal and social democratic proposals. Clinton copied some of his ideas to conceal her own center-right political orientation, but her flip-flops on immigration, health care, the minimum wage, the Trans Pacific Partnership and mass incarceration — combined with other scandals — left many unconvinced. Sanders amassed a large primary vote but Clinton's deep institutional connections and big early primary wins, when Sanders was less known, were insurmountable.

In the debates, Clinton generally outsmarted and out-talked bullyboy Trump, his sexist performance and swaggering insults. But she remained an unpopular public figure and her program simply did not address the extreme economic and social tribulations confronting a large sector of the U.S. population. Clinton could not inspire a large turnout from poor and working-class Democratic Party voters, or from young voters looking for social transformation.

Trump's campaign was openly sexist from the beginning. During the primary season, he used misogynist slurs to describe women who opposed him. After he was nominated, a leaked 2005 video tape showed Trump bragging about his ability to get away with sexual assault because he was a star. After that, more than a dozen women came forward with allegations against Trump of sexual abuse. This caused a temporary decline in his poll numbers, but he quickly regained momentum as the FBI launched new investigations of Clinton's State Department emails.

The recording was only one example of Trump's sexist insults toward women, which have been documented for years.

In 2006 he called comedian Rosie O'Donnell fat, a slob, ugly, disgusting. In 2008 he claimed women throw themselves at him, "They'll flip their top, and they'll flip their panties." In 2011 he called breastfeeding disgusting. In 2011 he called journalist Gail Collins a dog. In 2013 (to a Celebrity Apprentice contestant) he said, "Isn't that a woman's place in the boardroom — on her knees?" In 2016 he insulted the physical appearance of Carly Fiorina, his one female opponent in the Republican primary.

His attitude and public behavior toward Clinton, the first woman candidate for president from a major party in U.S. history, was clearly sexist. During the debates he constantly interrupted her and talked over her, and famously declared her "a nasty woman."

Until he was elected, Trump did not have the support of the ruling class or the political establishment of the Republican Party. Trump rebelled against his own party's leadership and focused his attention on winning angry white working- and middle-class Republicans and independents to his program.

The capitalist system, big corporations and banks were ignored in his rhetoric, while he blamed Blacks and Latinos, Muslims, immigrants, refugees and women' rights for social problems. White men were Trump's most vocal supporters, but 53 percent of white women — including 62 percent of those without college degrees and 45 percent with college degrees — voted for Trump.

Oxfam America recently reported on the decline of "good jobs" across the country:

> Today, millions of Americans do arduous work in jobs that pay too little and offer too few benefits. They serve food, clean offices, care for the young and elderly, stock shelves, and deliver pizza. They work these jobs

year after year, while caring for their children and parents, trying to save for college, and paying their bills. And yet despite their best efforts, these low-wage workers fall further and further behind.

> In the past 35 years, the very rich have seen an astronomical increase in income, while the middle class and low-wage workers have seen their wages stagnate or even decline. As this divide has grown, the wealthiest people and companies have gained disproportionate power in our economy and our government; low-wage workers have seen their access to power and their ability to influence dwindle.[3]

Trump promised to halt trade deals that took away American jobs and to launch a trillion dollar infrastructure plan, as well as other proposals that conveyed the impression he would take steps to improve conditions. Trump never projected any real plans, but conveyed himself as a strong decisive builder who would take a wrecking ball to an inept weak political class. Clinton had no massive jobs plan, and declared that "America is already great."

Trump's "working-class" imagery is utter nonsense. He is a lifelong enemy of the working class. He exploited discontent to attain power for himself. In the process, he appealed to every vulgar instinct possible, declaring the main problems of working people were from a decline in "traditional" America. Appealing to racism, Trump said the decline, during the eight years of a Black president, stemmed from workers of color, from Latino immigrants, from Muslims, from Syrian and other refugees. He also blamed the decline on the struggle for women's rights.

While only 43 percent of white women voted for Clinton, 80 percent of women of color overall voted for her, with Black women at 95 percent and Hispanic women at 70 percent. These groups voted for Obama in slightly larger numbers in 2012. Across the board then, women's voting patterns were not greatly affected by a woman's candidacy or the blatant sexism of her opponent.

Furthermore, despite his own vulgarity and scandal-ridden personal life, Trump garnered the vast majority of the right-wing religious vote. This was largely motivated by his anti-abortion stance, in which he advocated punishing women who have abortions and promised to appoint Supreme Court justices that would overturn *Roe v. Wade*. While he later reversed himself on punishing women, he declared that doctors who performed abortions should be punished. Trump's running mate Mike Pence, former governor of Indiana, is deeply connected to the religious right. He vehemently opposes abortion rights and has pushed for the defunding of Planned Parenthood.

Commenting on the racial divide, UCLA professor Robin Kelley wrote in Boston Review:

> Trump's followers are not trying to redistribute the wealth, nor are they all 'working class' — their annual median income is about $72,000. On the contrary, they are attracted to Trump's wealth as ... an American dream that they, too, can enjoy once America is 'great' again — which is to say, once the country returns to being 'a white MAN's country'. ....[They are] convinced that the descendants of unfree labor or the colonized, or those who are currently unfree, are to blame for America's decline and for blocking their path to Trump-style success. For the white people who voted overwhelmingly for Trump, their candidate embodied the anti-Obama backlash.[4]

THE POST-ELECTION RESPONSE

Yet after the election, President Obama — the target of so much of Trump's venom — issued a conciliatory statement wishing Trump a "successful" presidency. He stated, "We are now all rooting for his success in uniting and leading the country." In a later press conference, Obama told Trump that he and his staff would "do everything we can to help you succeed because if you succeed, then the country succeeds." One wonders which elements of Trump's reactionary, racist, Wall Street program were most deserving of "success."

Those threatened by Trump's attacks on the oppressed and exploited have begun to come together, and a new feminist movement must unite with others around broader issues of concern to women.

Within hours of Trump's election, demonstrators across the country poured into the streets.

Demonstrations happened immediately after the election throughout the United States, with protestors numbering in the tens of thousands. Student walkouts took place in high schools and colleges across the country. Over 100 schools declared themselves sanctuary campuses to protect immigrants, Muslims, people of color and other targets of the Trump right wing.

The Trump election requires a broad struggle not just against the Trump administration, but also, as *Liberation* wrote, "the extreme reactionary forces his campaign has emboldened" who "will not be appeased by his taking the White House. The Trump campaign has facilitated the rise of a new right-wing trend in U.S. politics that has as its defining characteristics open racism and misogyny coupled with anti-establishment rhetoric and conspiracy theories."

These far-right forces grew and recruited heavily during the Obama administrations. Now they feel more confident than ever with Trump's victory and his subsequent cabinet choices.

FEMINIST RESPONSES TO THE ELECTION

In the aftermath of the vote, the Internet was flooded with accusations of betrayal from African-Americans and Latina women who noted that they and not white women had voted for Clinton by large majorities.

Feminist opinion, whether for or against Clinton, was of course universally against Trump.

Mahroh Jahangiri, executive director of Know Your Nine, wrote on Feministing.com about her frustration over the assumed support for Clinton, "It is often grounded in little to no knowledge of her policy stances on issues that impact women (and men and gender nonconforming folks and other human beings) outside of abortion rights."[5] She pointed out Clinton's policy stances in support of Israel's military attacks on Gaza, U.S. sanctions against Iran, the Iraq war, and U.S. drone attacks on civilians, all of which have brought misery and death to the women and children she claimed to defend.

Other feminists encouraged a Clinton vote largely because of fear of what Trump might bring. Juliana Britto Schwartz, a Latina feminist writer and Feministing.com contributor, while critical of Clinton's foreign policies, wrote:

> For so many marginalized folks, four years of Trump means four (more) years of fighting for basic human rights.... Let's be clear: people of color, queer and trans people, immigrants, Muslims, women, and folks with disabilities are extremely vulnerable right now. The most important thing right now is to show up, commit to their work, and if you're able, support them....Fellow feminists, especially White [sic] women, we have work to do.[6]

Patricia Williams, legal scholar, expert on critical race theory and Nation columnist, blasted Trump for his racism and sexism:

> Trump began his political career more than 20 years ago by taking out a full-page ad in the New York Times, calling for the execution of five teenagers wrongly accused of raping and beating a young white stockbroker who became known as the Central Park Jogger. Although

DNA evidence pinned the crime to another man, Trump has never backed down from his assertion that he was right. ... Trump holds great appeal to those who were only recently forced to remove the Confederate flag from government buildings, and, in a profoundly felt sense, have never conceded that the American civil war is over.[7]

Most feminists and left-liberal writers portrayed the election as fundamentally a referendum on racism and sexism. Patricia Hill Collins, African American feminist scholar on race, gender and class, wrote:

> This was no ordinary campaign. I had hoped that the country could confront the hatred that many of its citizens seemingly feel for black people, Latinos, Muslims, undocumented migrants and women. I had hoped that an eminently qualified white woman would escape the protracted vitriol that confronted our first sitting black president. Perhaps Clinton's race would protect her from the insults she endured, in large part, because of her gender. I was wrong.[8]

Among feminists online, several graphics went viral comparing Clinton's loss to the workplace phenomenon of more qualified women being passed over for less qualified men.

HILLARY CLINTON'S CANDIDACY

Many saw the prospect of the first woman president as a triumph for feminism. Americans in both major parties have long been open to a woman president.

Placard at a New York Trump protest

In 1999 the Gallup poll found that 92 percent of Americans said they would vote for a woman. When Gallup first asked that question in 1937 the figure was 33 percent.[9]

What would a Clinton presidency really have meant for women, and how accurate were the hopes of many women that she represented a win for feminism?

The election of the first woman president would be an important breakthrough, especially considering the dismal record of the United States in electing women to leadership positions, including below that of president.

But voting in a woman head of state to administer an otherwise oppressive government is not enough to bring about core changes in the economic or political system or to transform the lives, conditions and opportunities for the vast majority of women.

In Britain, Margaret Thatcher launched an extreme anti-labor offensive that ravaged the working class. In Germany, Chancellor Angela Merkel has supervised the devastating austerity program imposed on the rest of Europe and put down the widespread Greek resistance to it. The colonial-settler state of Israel when led by Golda Meir in 1969 was no less brutal to the indigenous Palestinian people. The presence of women secretaries of state in the United States — Madeleine Albright, Condaleezza Rice and then Hillary Clinton — did not make U.S. foreign policy any more humane or less militaristic. Certainly, the election of the McCain-Palin ticket in 2008 would not have meant anything truly positive for women, even though it would have meant the election of the first woman vice-president.

The question then is: What would a Clinton victory have truly meant for women?

For millions of self-declared feminists, Clinton was presented as their champion. NOW's president Terry O'Neill commented just before the election that Clinton's detractors "just can't stand it that the U.S. is on the verge of electing its first woman president — a woman, moreover, who is an unapologetic feminist and proud to champion women's equality in all walks of life." Lena Dunham, creator and star of the TV series "Girls," spoke of Clinton as a "true feminist," who has survived sexism and misogynist anger directed toward ambitious and accomplished women.

For sure, compared to the women candidates of the Republican right wing, Clinton embraced certain women's rights causes and gave voice to them from her positions of influence. For instance, as first lady, Clinton represented the United States at the U.N. Fourth World

Conference on Women in Beijing in 1995, giving a talk "Women's Rights are Human Rights" that won her extensive praise from women's rights groups at the time. The speech named as human rights violations many of the problems facing women — low wages, violence, lack of health care, religious persecution, sex trafficking, rape, genital mutilation — and strongly advocated the right to family planning, a clean environment and benefits for older women.

As a Senator, Clinton generally had a liberal record on the few women's rights issues that arose during her tenure. She voted the Democratic Party line, and never risked any political capital on such causes. Instead, she ingratiated herself with the defense establishment, positioning herself as a hawk on Iraq and military spending, while cementing friendships among her Wall Street "constituents" with an eye towards her first presidential run. When it came to progressive movements, she sought a centrist course, for instance opposing the demand for complete marriage equality until 2013, after it had long been mainstream and right before it was about to win at the Supreme Court

Likewise, as secretary of state, Clinton called for ratification of the U.N.'s Convention on the Elimination of All Forms of Discrimination Against Women in 2011. The U.S. has yet to sign the agreement. But her priorities clearly lay elsewhere, as described below.

During the 2016 presidential campaign, she called for a raise to the minimum wage, but not to the $15 per hour advocated by the low-wage workers movement and by Sanders. Also, during the campaign she defended legalized abortion as guaranteed by the 1973 Supreme Court decision in *Roe v. Wade*. She also expressed support for wage equality between men and women and extensive family leave benefits that would allow women to achieve equity in the workplace. Whether such campaign planks would have translated into actual policy is another matter, of course. Barack Obama made practically all the same promises in 2008. The formal platform of Democratic candidates generally bears little resemblance to their priorities in office.

Clinton was also the preferred candidate of Wall Street, the fossil fuel and pharmaceutical industries and a militaristic foreign policy establishment. These ruling-class groupings poured money into her campaign. In the general election she dropped much of the progressive rhetoric of the primary season that would have impacted the profit margins of her corporate backers.

As secretary of state, Hillary Clinton was largely responsible for the destruction of Libya and overthrow of Muammar Gaddafi.

In an Aug. 4 column in TomDispatch.com, titled "The Decay of American Politics," Andrew J. Bacevich wrote of Clinton:

> Even by Washington standards, Secretary Clinton exudes a striking sense of entitlement combined with a nearly complete absence of accountability. She shrugs off her misguided vote in support of invading Iraq back in 2003, while serving as senator from New York. She neither explains nor apologizes for pressing to depose Libya's Muammar Gaddafi in 2011, her most notable 'accomplishment' as secretary of state. 'We came, we saw, he died,' she bragged back then, somewhat prematurely given that Libya has since fallen into anarchy and become a haven for ISIS.

> The essential point here is that, in the realm of national security, Hillary Clinton is utterly conventional. She subscribes to a worldview (and view of America's role in the world) that originated during the Cold War, reached its zenith in the 1990s when the United States proclaimed itself the planet's 'sole superpower,' and persists today remarkably unaffected by actual events. On the campaign trail, Clinton attests to her bona fides by routinely reaf-

firming her belief in American exceptionalism, paying fervent tribute to the world's 'greatest military,' swearing that she'll be 'listening to our generals and admirals,' and vowing to get tough on America's adversaries. These are, of course, the mandatory rituals of the contemporary Washington stump speech, amplified if anything by the perceived need for the first female candidate for president to emphasize her pugnacity.[10]

Her campaign also engaged in shameful hyper-patriotism. The Democratic National Committee leadership instructed Clinton delegates to drown out Sanders delegates if they began chanting anti-war slogans. On July 28, during a speech by retired Marine Corps General John Allen, a number of delegates began chanting "No More War" and were quickly made inaudible by the insistent and DNC-directed ultra-nationalist chant "USA, USA, USA!"

Activists in Honduras have held Clinton personally responsible for facilitating the coup and death squad government that assassinated leaders of the social justice movement there, including Berta Cáceres.

On the campaign trail, many in the Black Lives Matter movement confronted Clinton for her outspoken support of mass incarceration policies and the gutting of welfare in the 1990s, which tore apart so many families in Black and poor neighborhoods.

In the immigrant rights movement, activists pointed to her complicity in the Obama administration's mass deportation machine, questioning her campaign promises.

There is no question that Clinton was up against a hateful misogynist whose administration presents a serious danger to women — and all oppressed people — if he is not stopped. But the Democratic Party is not up to the task of fighting back, and will only give voice to progressive causes to harness dissent for their own ends and to facilitate the smoother functioning of the capitalist status quo. What we need is a broad, independent and militant movement to fight against the Trump administration and prevent the far right from gaining additional traction.

THE TWO-PARTY 2016 ELECTION

In the aftermath of the 2016 election, both major parties are undergoing a profound analysis of the upset in their base. Both were the subjects of populist uprisings, one from the left and one from the right. According to an article in the Hudson Valley Activist Newsletter, populism arises in distressed societies where there is considerable discontent and opposition to the national leadership and its economic and political programs. In this case, neither party had any intention of improving the appalling plight afflicting over half the population.

Left-wing populism, such as the liberal uprising in the Democratic Party led by Sanders, generally seeks to improve the lot of all the people in multinational America with social and economic programs financed in part by taxing the extraordinary wealth of the ultra-rich. It is not an anti-capitalist movement — to the contrary it seeks to curtail the "excesses" of capitalism — but insofar as it highlights the problems of the economic system, it gives space for anti-capitalist and socialist ideas to grow.

Right-wing populism, such as the anti-liberal uprising in the Republican Party, seeks to improve the lot of white Americans — both middle-class people who fear the erosion of privileges and stability, and workers who indeed have been exploited and pushed around for decades. This movement, however, shows no concern for the many millions of non-white workers experiencing even worse conditions. It is heavily imbued with racism, with colossal misogyny, contempt toward immigrants and refugees of color, abhorrence toward the LGBTQ community, and with Christian prejudice against Muslims and a touch of anti-Semitism, among other grave dangers. There are certainly voters for Trump who did not personally share these negative values but who decided this bigotry would not affect them, and that Trump might improve their living conditions, or was simply the "lesser evil" compared to a status quo candidate.

A national poll conducted by NORC/University of Chicago in May 2016 found that only 13 percent of Americans say the two-party system for presidential elections works. Some 38 percent believe the system is seriously broken, and just under half say it could work with some improvements. The same poll found that only 29 percent of Democrats and 16 percent of Republicans have a great deal of confidence in their party, and similar percentages have faith in their party's nominating process. Majorities in both parties believe their party is not open to the views of ordinary voters.[11]

The two-party lock on U.S. politics gives voters little choice but to vote for one evil or another, and any hope for "change" can only come from the other major party.

With such disaffection with the two major parties, millions voted for third party candidates, but their votes did not disrupt the outcome. More significant, 48 percent of eligible voters stayed home.

Of the alternative party candidates, the Green Party's Jill Stein garnered 1,207,000 votes or 1 percent of the popular vote. Her total was nearly triple the number she won in 2012, when she won 0.36 percent of the votes. Libertarian candidate Gary Johnson won more than four million votes or 3.2 percent of the total. Gloria La Riva, who ran on the Peace and Freedom ticket in California and Party for Socialism and Liberation (PSL) in seven other states, brought in more than 70,000 votes, more than any socialist ticket since 1976.

PSL candidate Gloria La Riva

Stein wrote after the election:

> The anti-establishment revolt we're witnessing is driven by very real suffering in our country. High real unemployment, falling real wages, lack of affordable healthcare and education have devastated our communities, while both establishment parties have pushed corporate trade deals, wars for oil and Wall Street bailouts to enrich the elite. The anger at economic inequality is easily manipulated to divide the people against each other. We must revive American democracy, if we are to stop our descent into authoritarianism.[12]

In an extensive interview with Mint Press News just after the Democratic National Convention, Gloria La Riva analyzed the problems with the two-party system. Here are some excerpts:

The fundamental difference is that the Republicans and Democrats are capitalist parties, and we are a socialist party. Capitalist parties are beholden to Wall Street and the monopoly banks and the giant multinational corporations who possess extreme wealth and influence. Our party is at its core diametrically different because we are a working-class party, beholden only to the greater good of all workers and oppressed peoples here and around the world.

Republican politicians continuously push legislation to attack women and immigrants' rights. They are a right-wing conservative party. ...The Democratic Party presents itself as a more liberal and friendly option for people, but it was the Democratic Party who put through free trade policies like NAFTA which destroyed thousands of jobs in the U.S. and ripped apart the Mexican economy, causing mass impoverishment there.

While we are constantly propagandized that we live in the 'greatest democracy ever,' the reality is that we live under the dictatorship of big capital. Real power is in the hands of the banks, monopoly corporations and the military-industrial complex. Fundamental change requires taking that power out of their hands and putting it in the hands of the people. That is why, while we fight for every reform that benefits the working class and the population as a whole, we know that what is ultimately needed is revolutionary change and the reorganization of the economy and society on a socialist basis.[13]

WHAT LIES AHEAD

However one voted in or understood the 2016 election, with the election of Trump, the priority must become building a broad movement to fight against the anti-woman laws that are sure to come.

The election of the misogynist, racist, xenophobic billionaire Donald J. Trump handed women's liberation its most direct and malicious challenge in more than 100 years. The moment will not allow for the gradual buildup of new rights and shedding of old customs

*The women's movement was part of an all-around social upheaval.
A 1972 protest against the Vietnam war includes banners demanding
freedom for Angela Davis and a halt to deportations, among other causes.*

of the earlier phases of the movement. Instead, this new phase will require the most vigorous defense of victories already won, as well as an expansion of rights into new areas. Trump and his minions rode to victory on all the most pernicious aspects of the conservative backlash discussed in the previous chapter. They threaten all the advances, big and small, that women, in their unity and strength and defiance, have won. They must not and will not get away with it.

The biggest gains women in the United States have made since winning the right to vote in 1920 were the result of the activism of women and their allies, particularly during the period of radical social and cultural transformation from 1965 to 1975. Even a quick review of where women are today and where they were before that uprising is a validation of that struggle.

Tens of millions of previously unorganized women were speaking out, taking action and engaging with radical ideas for the first time. But the presence of highly committed women organizers and organizations, most of whom had experience in the Black freedom, working-class and anti-war movements, played a pivotal role. They turned women's seething resentment against sexism into a call to action, and forcefully showed that women could self-organize, could be militant, unafraid and fight back. Millions of women rallied to the call when it was finally made audible to them.

Justly aggrieved women, some with no previous political engagement at all, formed groups with differing political viewpoints throughout the United States. There was no overall leader of this movement. Liberal women were represented in significant number but so were radical and left-wing women, including Marxists.

Despite differences over how to organize, with whom to organize and what sort of system could guarantee women's liberation, the struggle continued apace even without any formal coalition embracing all or most of the participating groups. For some, the goal was to smash patriarchy. Some sought to end capitalist class exploitation, oppression and the subordination of women through social revolution. Others fought for abortion rights. Many demanded equal pay, to be treated respectfully in all areas of life, to break down all occupational barriers, to stop the sexist harassment in schools, jobs and streets, and to shake up, if not abolish, the patriarchal family.

For all this diversity, the notion that women were in any sense inferior to men was no longer intellectually, socially or politically sustainable. The fighting force of women of all walks of life had given male supremacy a black eye.

That phase of the fight ended 40 years ago, though elements of the women's movement have carried on to this day, and women's oppression has not gone away.

The legislative and social changes did not go far enough to enshrine women's equality. The cultural acceptance of sexist objectification has in some cases grown. Domestic and sexual violence is rampant and harassment is routine. The organization of domestic work and child rearing was not fundamentally transformed, continuing the patriarchal division of labor in home life, and thus, all of society. Many millions of low-wage and poor women, plus a majority of Black, Latina and Native American women have only partially enjoyed the gains of the last generation.

Women are still far from true liberation and equality. Anyone who dares dispute that fact must be challenged with the following questions.

What about unequal pay for almost all women and the pitifully low wages for the whole working class? What about the beatings, the rapes, the harassments and the fear of walking down a lonely street in the dark? What about the continuing though more limited existence of male supremacy in the culture, the economy and the business world? What about having a government that hardly seems to care about the destitute, the hungry, the women with children receiving shamefully inadequate social benefits and the women who must go back to work a month after childbirth?

What about the accelerating successful right-wing attacks on abortion in state after state, and on local and national groups that offer women's health care including effective contraception and abortion services? This list could go on, but the point is clear. There is a lot more to do for women in the United States and too few are doing it with mass activism, community organizing, mass disruption and protest demonstrations — the proven methods of confronting power. What is required is a new upsurge to defend and extend women's rights for all women.

The next wave of struggle cannot simply replicate the tactics, strategies and perspectives of previous ones. The world is different — in part because of what has been achieved but also because of the newest male supremacist threat. Certain lessons are absolutely clear. Women's breakthroughs in the 1960s and 1970s were not the product of years of writing letters to Congress, or trying to elect less sexist Democrats. Although many did do these things, in some cases this created a more favorable environment for reform. However, this was not the spirit of the era, and these moderate tactics were an entirely secondary factor to the social and cultural revolution underway.

The principal factor was that millions of women came together, voiced their ideas and pent-up anger at male domination and took risks to challenge their own subordination. They did so publicly in the streets, classrooms, workplaces and meeting halls, and they did so at home. Quite simply, they would not take it anymore.

That movement had its own internal weaknesses and ideological shortcomings, elaborated in previous chapters. But the fundamental reasons for its decline, and the ongoing oppression of women, are not its imperfections. Fundamentally, that movement was born as part of a radical all-round upheaval, and a whole period of worldwide struggle, which took aim at the ruling order from every angle.

In the 1960s, millions of Black people were in motion, fixed on tearing down Jim Crow segregation and shaking the country's racist foundation. The supposedly invincible U.S. military was losing a war in Vietnam, but the ruling class, with the Democratic Party firmly in control of both houses of Congress and the White House until 1969, refused to end the suffering. Anti-capitalist ideas, long suppressed by McCarthyite anti-communism, came roaring back. Social revolution and national liberation appeared to be the dominant trend across the globe, leading a large section of humanity to question the existing order, dream of another world, and then fight for it. New economic competitors were rising to challenge U.S. industrial supremacy, and the country's economic base was being revolutionized by the advent of microprocessor and computer technologies.

The ruling-class counteroffensive — aimed at re-stabilizing U.S. imperialism abroad, beating back the rebellions at home and ensuring a new period of profitability — created a whole new period in which counterrevolution became the norm. The social movements were repressed, demoralized and atomized. New victories were few and far between. Many progressive reforms were reversed. Class inequality took off, and new forms of racist and sexist oppression were devised. Most critically, the notion of thinking and dreaming big, of fighting for a whole new world, of revolutionary transformation being achievable through struggle, was deemed invalid and antiquated.

IS A NEW UPSURGE POSSIBLE?

A new stage of rebellion is clearly in the making; it is beginning within the context of this reactionary era and made more urgent by the election of Trump.

There are millions of self-declared feminists who are not engaged in organizing and struggle at all. Of those who are organized, they fall into three main categories. Together they are known loosely as the "the women's movement" but we must question the extent to which there is really a "movement" orientation.

One category is mainstream feminism, which is anchored by the liberal powerhouse NOW. The organization's main activities in 2015-16 were to secure the presidency for Clinton and to elect women as well as male Democrats to Congress. This corresponds in general to the organization's main activity — pressuring Congress and the White House.

*Millions of people took to the streets on January 21, 2017,
to oppose the Trump agenda of misogyny and bigotry.*

The NOW leadership assiduously backed Clinton against Sanders, whose program represented the left wing of the Democratic Party. Sanders' program included many of the social-democratic reforms that NOW backs in theory, which would help working-class women most of all. Young women voters overwhelmingly supported him against Clinton's status quo campaign. But NOW backed Clinton with the false line that she has been a champion for women's rights and directed anger at Sanders supporters for potentially ruining the chances of electing the country's first woman president.

Of course, from the standpoint of basic democracy, it is past time for a woman president, just as it was past time for a Black president, for both historical and psychological reasons. Barack Obama, however, did very little concretely for the Black masses, nor, as we have seen, could Clinton legitimately hold up the banner for feminism.

NOW and its numerous allies, such as Feminist Majority Foundation, may constitute up to half of the organized women's movement. Their members are well-intended, but the organizations themselves, and their top leadership, have become essentially the "women's lobby" inside the Democratic Party establishment. They cannot provide the leadership or the boldness of action or the muscle for a productive and radical new wave of struggle.

Many liberal-thinking women were active in Second Wave protests, of course, and many more will take part when and if a mass activist movement once again takes to the streets on behalf of women's equality.

A second category of the movement is organizationally fragmented. It is largely composed of young and somewhat older women who came to consciousness during the Third Wave. Grounded in academic and university settings primarily, many adhere to post-modern theories, focusing on localized campaigns and expending considerable energy on the language and practices used in organizing spaces. Post-modernism is a dead end as a guide for effective political struggle against the ruling class and forging deep, long-lasting unity between oppressed and working-class communities. Post-modernism grew in tandem with the suppression and decline of the socialist left, which has a proud history of fusing together and leading the fights against oppression, discrimination and class exploitation. A resurgent socialist movement will undoubtedly pose fresh ideological and organizational debates about how to most effectively fight for women's liberation.

There is room for unity in action here, but many participants in the Third Wave seem to shun larger organizations and political systems, as well as working with the political left. Individuals in this milieu tend to support and give time to particular campaigns that resonate with them, but do not commit to becoming sustained cadres or to larger organizations. This could change, but it will take real effort on the part of those who understand the need for unity, organization and activism to bring this about. If we are talking about real change, think of what transpired after a decade of radical struggle in the streets, meeting halls, and campuses by various groups of women that were fed up with second-class citizenship.

The third category with big organizing potential are the many women who are involved in the ranks of other movements — from climate justice to anti-war activism, from opposition to drones to excoriating racism, from electoral reform to fighting mounting inequality, from marching against Monsanto to building socialism. If serious feminist activism were on the agenda, given the opportunity, many of these activist women would devote time to a women's movement that showed signs of real dynamism.

The political left could play a major role in a revitalized women's movement that was willing to take strong steps to fight against inequality, oppression, discrimination, male supremacy, exploitation and the right-wing war on women.

While the emancipatory vision and ideological horizons of the feminist movement have been limited in recent decades, it is likely that a revitalized women's movement will go hand in hand with a revitalized interest in socialism and revolutionary politics. The resonance of Bernie Sanders' self-declared "democratic socialist" and feminist platform among young women, who largely rejected Clinton in the primaries, points to such a political opening.

Hopefully, a revitalized movement would also include direct action to disrupt the far-right functionaries who will be dominating government in the near future and the staging of innovative protests in the face of congressional and White House reaction. Thousands of women could be trained to speak up at public meetings throughout the country. All this would be part of a much-needed, large, diverse and activist-oriented feminist movement which would defend past gains and destroy obstacles remaining in the way of total equality.

Is this pie in the sky? Look at it this way: In the early 1960s many women hoped for basic equality but few indeed believed it would happen in their lifetimes.

It was still quiet in early 1965 when two young women — Casey Hayden and Mary King, both white — wrote what they termed "a kind of memo." According to the Chicago Women's Liberation Union (CWLU), they "circulated this paper to women in the civil rights movement based on their experiences as Student Nonviolent Coordinating Committee volunteers. It is widely regarded as one of the first documents of the emerging women's liberation movement."

At the time, the CWLU women drew parallels between the treatment of African Americans and all women in society. They identified both forms of oppression as part of a caste system, which "uses and exploits women." The memo was important because it foreshadowed the issues that would be taken up by the feminist movement: women's subordinate position in the movement, in the workplace and in their personal and family relationships, and the legitimacy of these concerns as topics for a transformative political movement.

In the last paragraph the women wrote: "Objectively, the chances seem nil that we could start a movement based on anything as distant to general American thought as a sex-caste system."

Few anticipated it would begin in a matter of months, and that over the course of 10 years, so much would be accomplished.

Under the political circumstances women now face, it is incumbent on them to join together and fight the misogynist in the White House and prevent the right from destroying what previous movements have built up. A new militant women's movement must carry on this work. The call to action is once again loud and clear. The time to act is right now. We won't go back. □

APPENDICES

Appendix 1

U.S. women's rights timeline

1837-39	The Anti-Slavery Convention of American Women holds the first nationwide gatherings of women in the United States. The conventions are racially integrated.
1848	First women's rights convention, Seneca Falls, N.Y. Declaration of Sentiments outlines grievances, sets the agenda for women's rights movement. Resolutions call for equal treatment of women and men under the law and voting rights for women.
1850	First National Women's Rights Convention, Worcester, Mass., attracting more than 1,000 participants. National conventions are held yearly (except for 1857) through 1860.
1855	The Missouri Supreme Court rules that an enslaved Black woman, Celia, is legally property and has no right to defend herself against rape by her master.
1863	Women's National Loyal League formed to push for a Congressional amendment fully abolishing slavery. The group involves all the leading figures of the women's movement and collects nearly 400,000 petitions to abolish slavery, the largest petition drive in U.S. history at that time.
1869	A debate over the Fifteenth Amendment, which extended voting rights to all men regardless of "race, color or previous condition of servitude," splits the women's suffrage movement. Susan B. Anthony and Elizabeth Cady Stanton oppose the passage of the amendment as written and form the National Woman Suffrage Association. Their primary goal is to achieve voting rights for women by means of another congressional amendment to the Constitution.

Lucy Stone, Henry Blackwell and others form the American Woman Suffrage Association, which supports the passage of the Fifteenth Amendment. The AWSA subsequently focuses exclusively on gaining voting rights for women through amendments to individual state constitutions. The territory of Wyoming passes the first women's suffrage law. The following year, women begin serving on juries there.

1870 The Fifteenth Amendment to the U.S. Constitution establishes universal suffrage for male citizens, including formerly enslaved Black men, but not to women.

1872 Susan B. Anthony registers and votes in Rochester, N.Y. and is arrested along with 15 other women. Sojourner Truth is turned away at a Michigan voting booth. Victoria Woodhull runs for U.S. president, the first woman to do so, as the candidate of the Equal Rights Party.

1873 Congress adopts the Comstock Act, which prohibits the importation or mailing of "obscene matter," including contraceptives and information about contraception — which had previously been legal.

1888 The first national study on divorce finds more women making use of changes in divorce law. One in 15 marriages, an unprecedented number, end in divorce. All but one state, South Carolina, allow divorce and all but six allow divorce on grounds of cruelty. South Carolina does not permit divorce until 1949.

1889 Jane Addams and Ellen Gates Starr co-found Hull House in Chicago, the first settlement house in the United States.

1890 The National Woman Suffrage Association and the American Woman Suffrage Association merge to form the National American Woman Suffrage Association (NAWSA). As the movement's mainstream organization, NAWSA wages state-by-state campaigns to obtain voting rights for women.

1893 Colorado is the first state to adopt an amendment granting women the right to vote. Utah and Idaho follow suit in 1896, Washington in 1910, California in 1911, Oregon, Kansas, and Arizona in 1912, Alaska and Illinois in 1913, Montana and Nevada in 1914, New York in 1917, and Michigan, South Dakota, and Oklahoma in 1918.

1896 The National Association of Colored Women is formed, bringing together more than 100 Black women's clubs. Leaders in the Black women's club movement include Josephine St. Pierre Ruffin, Mary Church Terrell and Anna Julia Cooper.

1900 All states finally grant married women the right to own property in their own name.

1903 The National Women's Trade Union League is established to advocate for improved wages and working conditions for women.

1909 The first Women's Day is held on Feb. 28 in New York, commemorating the women's garment strike of the previous year. The Socialist Party organizes the event.

1911 International Workers' Day is recognized for the first time with coordinated mass marches and events in multiple countries. Six years later, the IWD march in Russia for "Bread and Peace" sparks the February Revolution.

In New York City, 3,000 people march for women's suffrage.

1913 Alice Paul and Lucy Burns form the Congressional Union to work toward the passage of a federal amendment to give women the vote. Members picket the White House and practice other forms of civil disobedience. Working with NAWSA, Alice Paul organizes the largest women's suffrage parade to date on the eve of Wilson's inauguration. Approximately 10,000 people march down Pennsylvania Avenue in Washington, D.C., enduring police and mob violence. Black women in the parade protest attempts to segregate them to the back.

1915 The American Medical Association admits its first women members. The Woman's Peace Party is organized in Washington, D.C., in response to the outbreak of World War I in 1914.

1916 Margaret Sanger opens the first U.S. birth control clinic in Brooklyn, N.Y. Although the clinic is shut down 10 days later and Sanger is arrested, she eventually wins support through the courts and opens another clinic in New York City in 1923.

Alice Paul and others break away from the NAWSA and form the National Woman's Party.

Montana elects suffragist Jeannette Rankin to the House of Representatives. She is the first woman elected to the U.S. Congress.

1918   In *New York v. Sanger,* the New York Court of Appeals allows doctors to advise married patients about birth control for health purposes. It takes another 47 years to overturn all the state prohibitions on contraceptive prescriptions for married couples.

1919   The 19th Amendment to the U.S. Constitution, known as the federal woman suffrage amendment, granting women the right to vote is introduced in Congress in 1878. The amendment, which was originally written by Susan B. Anthony, was passed by the House of Representatives and the Senate. It is then sent to the states for ratification.

1920   The 19th Amendment is signed into law. The Women's Bureau of the Department of Labor is formed to collect information about women in the workforce and safeguard good working conditions for women. Wife-beating is outlawed nationwide.

1921   Margaret Sanger founds American Birth Control League, which later becomes Planned Parenthood Federation of America.

1927   Supreme Court upholds compulsory sterilization of the "unfit," including those with mental disabilities, in *Buck v. Bell.*

1933   Frances Perkins becomes first woman appointed to the U.S. Cabinet and serves as Secretary of Labor until 1945.

1935   Mary McLeod Bethune organizes the National Council of Negro Women, a coalition of Black women's groups that lobbies against job discrimination, racism and sexism.

1938   Federal ban on dissemination of contraceptive information is lifted.

1941   Jeanette Rankin, Republican and pacifist, is the only
        member of Congress to vote against declaring war on Japan
        following the attack on Pearl Harbor.

1946   Congress of American Women is founded, bringing together
        radical women who link the women's struggle with struggles
        for labor rights, Black freedom and peace. It is destroyed
        four years later by the anti-communist witch hunt, but many
        of its activists become leaders and mentors in the women's
        upsurge of the 1960s and 1970s.

1955   The Daughters of Bilitis, the first lesbian organization in the
        United States, is founded in San Francisco.

1960   The Food and Drug Administration approves birth control
        pills.

        Student Nonviolent Coordinating Committee is founded
        after lunch counter sit-ins. Mentored by Ella Baker, SNCC
        produces a large number of women leaders and organizers
        across the South.

1961   President Kennedy establishes President's Commission
        on the Status of Women, appointing Eleanor Roosevelt
        as chairwoman. Women Strike for Peace builds national
        mothers' campaign against nuclear war.

1962   Students for Democratic Society issues Port Huron
        Statement, a manifesto for student activists.

1963   Betty Friedan, who had ties to the Old Left, publishes "The
        Feminine Mystique," which describes the dissatisfaction
        felt by middle-class American housewives with the narrow
        role imposed on them by society. The book becomes a best-
        seller and galvanizes the modern women's rights movement.
        The report of the Presidential Commission on the Status
        of Women is issued. It documents discrimination against
        women in the workplace. It makes recommendations for
        improvement, including fair hiring practices, paid maternity
        leave and affordable child care. Congress passes the Equal
        Pay Act, making it illegal for employers to pay a woman less
        than what a man would receive for the same job.

1964   The Civil Rights Act is passed. Title VII bars discrimination in
        employment on the basis of race or sex, and establishes the

Equal Employment Opportunity Commission to investigate complaints and impose penalties.

1965   In *Griswold v. Connecticut,* the Supreme Court strikes down the one remaining state law prohibiting the use of contraceptives by married couples. The ruling established the right to privacy for married couples. Phrase "women's liberation" is coined at the Students for a Democratic Society conference.

1966   The National Organization for Women is founded. National Welfare Rights Organization is formed.

1967   New York Radical Women is formed. First public speak out against abortion laws is held in New York City.

1968   "No More Miss America" protest against sexism and racism is held at Miss America Pageant. Shirley Chisholm becomes the first African American woman elected to Congress.

1969   The Stonewall Rebellion in Greenwich Village leads to the founding of the Gay Liberation Front. Members of Redstockings disrupt a New York State legislative hearing on abortion laws where the panel of witnesses is 14 men and a nun. Chicago activists organize clinic "Jane." The National Association for the Repeal of Abortion Laws is founded.

Faith Seidenberg and Karen DeCrow, who were refused service at McSorley's Old Ale House, then an all-male establishment in New York City, sued for discrimination and won on 14th Amendment equal protection grounds. California becomes the first state to adopt a "no fault" divorce law, which allows couples to divorce by mutual consent. By 1985, every state has adopted a similar law. Laws are also passed regarding the equal division of common property.

1970   The first women's studies program in the United States is established at San Diego State University after a year of intense organizing. The first issue of "Women and Their Bodies," the precursor to "Our Bodies, Ourselves," is published. A sit-in at the offices of the Ladies' Home Journal protests "women's magazines" as sexist. On Aug. 26, tens of thousands of women across the nation participate in the Women's Strike for Equality on the 50th anniversary of obtaining the vote.

Congress enacts Title X of the Public Health Service Act, the only federal program devoted to the provision of family planning services nationwide. President Richard Nixon vetoes a bill for federally funded childcare centers throughout the U.S., calling it anti-family and communistic. In *Schultz v. Wheaton Glass Co.*, a federal U.S. Court of Appeals rules that jobs held by men and women need not be "identical" — but instead "substantially equal" — to fall under the protection of the Equal Pay Act.

1971   The first annual Women's Equality Day is celebrated on Aug. 26.

1972   The Equal Rights Amendment is passed by Congress and sent to the states for ratification. Originally drafted by Alice Paul in 1923, the amendment reads, "Equality of rights under the law shall not be denied or abridged by the United States or by any State on account of sex." The amendment fails to gain ratification in three-fourths of the state legislatures (38 states), and dies in 1982. First rape crisis centers and battered women's shelters are established. Ms. Magazine begins publication. In *Eisenstadt v. Baird* the Supreme Court rules that the right to privacy includes an unmarried person's right to use contraceptives. Title IX of the Education Amendments bans sex discrimination in schools. The National Conference of Puerto Rican Women and the Asian American Women's Center are founded.

1973   The Supreme Court, in *Roe v. Wade*, establishes a woman's right to safe and legal abortion, overriding the anti-abortion laws of many states. The National Black Feminist Organization is founded. The Supreme Court upholds Equal Employment Opportunity Commission rule outlawing sex-segregated help wanted ads. The American Psychiatric Association ceases classifying homosexuality as a disorder. The first shelter for battered women opens.

1974   The passage of the Equal Credit Opportunity Act prohibits discrimination in consumer credit practices on the basis of sex, race, marital status, religion, national origin, age, or receipt of public assistance. In *Corning Glass Works v. Brennan*, the U.S. Supreme Court rules that employers cannot justify paying women lower wages because that is what they traditionally received under the "going market rate." A wage differential occurring "simply because men would not work at the low rates paid women" is deemed unacceptable. The Committee to End Sterilization Abuse is founded. The Mexican American Legal Defense and Education Fund launches the Chicana Rights Project. The Coalition of Labor Union Women is founded. Women of All Red Nations is formed by Native American women.

1975   United Nations declares the "Decade for Women." Joan Little, an African American woman who was raped by a white prison guard while in a North Carolina jail, is acquitted of murdering her abuser. The case established a precedent for self-defense against the charge of murder in cases of rape. The first "Take Back the Night" march is held in Philadelphia.

1976   The first marital rape law is enacted in Nebraska, making it illegal for a husband to rape his wife. Organization of Pan Asian American Women is founded. Congress passes the Hyde Amendment, denying Medicaid funding for abortion to poor women, significantly cutting access to the rights gained from *Roe v. Wade*.

1977   Pauli Murray becomes the first African American woman to be ordained as an Episcopal priest in 1977. The National Women's Conference is held in Houston. Some 20,000 women from all over the country pass a National Plan of Action.

1978   The Pregnancy Discrimination Act bans employment discrimination against pregnant women. President Carter institutes affirmative action for women in construction in response to a feminist lawsuit against the government; women enter "non-traditional" blue collar jobs in much larger numbers.

1979   First National March on Washington for Lesbian and Gay Rights is held with more than 100,000 marchers. Supreme Court rules in *Bellotti v. Baird* that teenagers do not have to secure parental consent to obtain an abortion. Judy Chicago's art installation "The Dinner Party," which features 39 elaborate place settings for mythical and historical women, is first displayed; it eventually is viewed by 15 million people worldwide.

1980   Gerda Lerner creates America's first Ph.D. program in women's history at the University of Wisconsin-Madison.

1981   Sandra Day O'Connor becomes the first woman to serve as a justice of the U.S. Supreme Court.

1982   ERA fails to gain ratification.

1984   Geraldine Ferraro is chosen as the vice presidential nominee of the Democratic Party, the first woman candidate of a major party.

1986   The Supreme Court rules in *Meritor Savings Bank v. Vinson* that sexual harassment is a form of illegal job discrimination.

1989   In *Webster v. Reproductive Health Services,* the Supreme Court upholds a Missouri law that imposed restrictions on the use of state funds, facilities, and employees in performing, assisting with, or counseling on abortions, restrictions thought to be forbidden under *Roe v. Wade.* In response, the National Organization for Women organizes the largest rally in Washington, D.C. history, bringing 600,000 people to the March for Women's Lives in April and another 350,000 in November.

1991   Anita Hill accuses U.S. Supreme Court nominee Clarence Thomas of sexual harassment; he was confirmed to the Supreme Court. In response to the Anita Hill sexual harassment case, feminist Rebecca Walker publishes an article in Ms. Magazine entitled Becoming the Third Wave. American feminist Susan Faludi publishes "Backlash," about the conservative reaction to feminism in the 1980s.

1992   In *Planned Parenthood v. Casey,* the Supreme Court reaffirms the validity of a woman's right to abortion under *Roe v. Wade* and establishes the standard of "undue burden" in evaluating restrictions on abortion. Freedom Summer '92, the inaugural project of the Third Wave Foundation, registers 20,000 new voters.

1993   The Family and Medical Leave Act becomes law. Janet Reno becomes the first female U.S. Attorney General. Ruth Bader Ginsburg becomes Supreme Court Justice. Marital rape is outlawed nationwide.

1994   The Violence Against Women Act tightens federal penalties
        for sex offenders, funds services for victims of rape and
        domestic violence, and provides for special training of
        police officers.

1995   UN World Women's Conference is held in Beijing. Around
        200,000 march in Washington, D.C., the first and largest
        mass action to stop violence against women.

1996   The feminist play "The Vagina Monologues," written by
        American playwright Eve Ensler, premieres in New York. In
        United States v. Virginia, the Supreme Court rules that the all-
        male Virginia Military School has to admit women in order
        to continue to receive public funding. It rules that creating a
        separate, all-women's school will not suffice.

1997   Madeleine Albright becomes the first woman to serve
        as U.S. Secretary of State and quickly earns an equal
        reputation to her male counterparts as a war criminal.
        Performing genital mutilation on girls in the United States
        is outlawed.

1999   A federal law specifically provides that "a woman may
        breastfeed her child at any location in a federal building
        or on federal property, if the woman and her child are
        otherwise authorized to be present at the location."

2000   The Supreme Court strikes down a Nebraska law criminalizing
        "partial-birth abortion[s]" without regard for the health of the
        mother. The Third Wave Manifesta is published.

2003   A federal law is enacted prohibiting a form of late-term
        abortion that the law misleadingly calls "partial-birth," a
        procedure referred to in medical literature as intact dilation
        and extraction.

2004   The March for Women's Lives is held in Washington, D.C.,
        to support the right to abortion, access to birth control,
        scientifically accurate sex education, prevention and
        treatment of sexually transmitted infections, and to show
        public support for mothers and children.

2007   The Supreme Court upholds the 2003 ban on the "partial-
        birth" abortion procedure. It is the first ruling to ban a
        specific type of abortion procedure. Justice Ruth Bader

Ginsburg, who dissents, calls the decision "alarming" and says the ruling is "so at odds with our jurisprudence" that it "should not have staying power."

2009 President Obama signs the Lilly Ledbetter Fair Pay Restoration Act, which allows victims of pay discrimination to file a complaint with the government against their employer within 180 days of their last paycheck. The Supreme Court had previously ruled that such lawsuits must be made within 180 days of the employer's original wage decision.

2013 American military leaders remove the military's ban on women serving in combat, overturning a 1994 rule prohibiting women from being assigned to smaller ground combat units. After a prolonged grassroots struggle, the U.S. Food and Drug Administration is ordered to make the Plan B One-Step morning-after birth control pill and its generic versions available to people of any age without a prescription.

2014 In *Burwell v. Hobby Lobby,* the Supreme Court rules that closely held for-profit corporations, based on their owners religious beliefs, are exempt from the contraceptive mandate under the Affordable Care Act which had required employers to cover certain contraceptives for their female employees. The Supreme Court strikes down Massachusetts' 35-foot buffer zones around abortion clinics to protect those entering the clinic from harassment by anti-choice forces.

2015 A policy update required all pharmacies, clinics and emergency departments run by the Indian Health Services to have Plan B One-Step in stock, and to distribute it to any woman (or her representative) who asked for it without restrictions. California and Oregon pass laws to allow for birth control pills, patches and rings to be sold by pharmacists without a doctor's prescription.[1]

Appendix 2
The anti-slavery convention of American women

THE Anti-Slavery Convention of American Women took place annually from 1837 to 1839. Less well known than the 1848 Seneca Falls Convention for Women's Rights, it was groundbreaking, nonetheless, as the first national gathering of women ever held in the United States. Established with the encouragement of abolitionist William Lloyd Garrison, the meetings drew 175 delegates from 10 states. Garrison had written that the participation of women was essential to the abolition movement, despite the tendency of male abolitionists to "overlook or depreciate" their influence and of women to undervalue their own power. Garrison wrote of the one million women held in bondage and asked, "When woman's heart is bleeding, shall woman's voice be hushed?"[2]

The women's anti-slavery conventions were racially integrated, and incorporated members of hundreds of local and state anti-slavery groups from around the country.

The conventions passed radical resolutions, which included: calling for women to use their role as mothers to teach their children to oppose slavery; denouncing northern complicity in the slave trade, including enforcement of the fugitive slave laws; denouncing northerners who marry slaveholders; condemning churches for soliciting donations from slaveholders; boycotting the products of slave labor; promoting racial integration in education; calling on abolitionists to give employment to Black people; and calling on their churches to preach anti-slavery sermons. The delegates also rejected resolutions for better treatment of slaves — nothing short of abolition would suffice.

The 1838 convention, held in Philadelphia, was met by mob violence, and the Pennsylvania Hall, where some of the meetings were to be held, was burned to the ground.

These conventions chose Lucretia Mott and others as delegates to attend the World Anti-Slavery Convention in London in 1840. The women's exclusion from the London convention was a precipitating event that led ultimately to the 1848 Seneca Falls Convention, which produced the Declaration of Sentiments and Resolutions on the Rights of Women.

After the 1839 meetings, women were granted the right to take part in the American Anti-Slavery Society and the Women's Convention was disbanded.

The conventions resulted in the publication and dissemination of important anti-slavery pamphlets and petitions, the acceptance of women as speakers in mixed male/female assemblies, an increase in collaborative activism between Black and white women, increased communication and organizing among women who were geographically separated, and the political experience that would be necessary to conduct the suffrage and other women's rights struggles to come. As Ira Brown wrote, "they deserve to be remembered as one of the sources of American feminism."[3] ☐

Appendix 3
Lucy Stone:
Selected quotations

LUCY Stone (1818-1893) was one of the most important leaders of the nineteenth century women's rights, abolition and temperance movements. While no recordings exist of her renowned oratory, the power of her words still resonates in written form. Here are a few selected quotations.

- "'We, the people of the United States.' Which 'We, the people'? The women were not included."
- "A wife should no more take her husband's name than he should hers. My name is my identity and must not be lost."
- "We want rights. The flour-merchant, the house-builder and the postman charge us no less on account of our sex; but when we endeavor to earn money to pay all these, then, indeed, we find the difference."
- "I expect to plead not for the slave only, but for suffering humanity everywhere. Especially do I mean to labor for the elevation of my sex."
- "If, while I hear the shriek of the slave mother robbed of her little ones, I do not open my mouth for the dumb, am I not guilty? Or should I go from house to house to do it, when I could tell so many more in less time, if they should be gathered in one place?"
- "If a woman earned a dollar by scrubbing, her husband had a right to take the dollar and go and get drunk with it and beat her afterwards. It was his dollar."
- "In education, in marriage, in religion, in everything disappointment is the lot of women. It shall be the business of my life to deepen that disappointment in every woman's heart until she bows down to it no longer."

- "The idea of equal rights was in the air. The wail of the slave, his clanking fetters, his utter need, appealed to everybody. Women heard. Angelina and Sara Grimke and Abby Kelly went out to speak for the slaves. Such a thing had never been heard of. An earthquake shock could hardly have startled the community more. Some of the abolitionists forgot the slave in their efforts to silence the women. The Anti-Slavery Society rent itself in twain over the subject. The Church was moved to its very foundation in opposition."

- "You may talk about Free Love, if you please, but we are to have the right to vote. Today we are fined, imprisoned, and hanged, without a jury trial by our peers. You shall not cheat us by getting us off to talk about something else. When we get the suffrage, then you may taunt us with anything you please, and we will then talk about it as long as you please."[4] ☐

Appendix 4

Profile: The Grimke sisters of South Carolina

The Grimke sisters of South Carolina, Sarah (1792-1873) and Angelina (1805-1879), were born into an upper-class slaveholding family, but ended up playing a unique role in the abolition movement. With firsthand knowledge of the atrocities of the slave system, they forsook the privileges of wealth and power and devoted their lives to ending slavery. They were among the first women to speak before mixed audiences of men and women and the very first to testify before a state legislature (Massachusetts) on the evils of slavery and the rights of African American people. Both sisters left the South, joined the Quaker movement and lived in Philadelphia, New York and Massachusetts. Angelina was one of the speakers who participated in the 1838 Anti-Slavery Convention of American Women, during which Pennsylvania Hall was burned down. They fought for racial equality as well as the abolition of slavery.[5]

ANGELINA GRIMKE, SELECTED QUOTES

- "I want to be identified with the negro; until he gets his rights, we shall never have ours."
- "Hitherto, instead of being a help meet to man, in the highest, noblest sense of the term, as a companion, a co-worker, an equal, she has been a mere appendage of his being, an instrument of his convenience and pleasure, the pretty toy with which he whiled away his leisure moments, or the pet animal whom he humored into playfulness and submission."
- "Abolitionists never sought place or power. All they asked was freedom; all they wanted was that the white man should take his foot off the negro's neck."

- "Slavery always has, and always will, produce insurrections wherever it exists, because it is a violation of the natural order of things."
- "Women ought to feel a peculiar sympathy in the colored man's wrong, for, like him, she has been accused of mental inferiority, and denied the privileges of a liberal education."
- "I trust the time is coming, when the occupation of an instructor to children will be deemed the most honorable of human employment."
- "What man or woman of common sense now doubts the intellectual capacity of colored people? Who does not know, that with all our efforts as a nation to crush and annihilate the mind of this portion of our race, we have never yet been able to do it."
- "The denial of our duty to act in this case is a denial of our right to act; and if we have no right to act, then may we well be termed the white slaves of the North, for like our brethren in bonds, we must seal our lips in silence and despair."
- "We Abolition Women are turning the world upside down."
- "Can you not see that women could do and would do a hundred times more for the slave, if she were not fettered?"[6] □

Appendix 5

Black women in the suffrage movement

While American history has remembered the white leaders of the woman suffrage movement, Black women leaders played a prominent role.

Angela Davis writes: "Of the eight million women in the labor force during the first decade of the twentieth century, more than two million were Black. As women who suffered the combined disabilities of sex, class and race, they possessed a powerful argument for the right to vote. But racism ran so deep within the woman suffrage movement that the doors were never really opened to Black women. The exclusionary policies of the NAWSA did not deter Black women from demanding the vote. Ida B. Wells, Mary Church Terrell and Mary McLeod Bethune were among the most well-known Black suffragists."[7]

PROFILE: IDA B. WELLS (1862-1931)

Ida B. Wells, who was orphaned as a teenager in Mississippi, took on the responsibility of raising five younger siblings, making her living as a teacher. She became an anti-racist activist at a young age, suing a railroad for discrimination at the age of 22.

Wells became co-owner of a local Black newspaper in Memphis, The Free Speech and Headlight, in which she wrote editorials against anti-Black violence, disenfranchisement and poor schools, as well as the reluctance of many Black people to fight for their rights. After three close friends were lynched, the paper became a strong voice against lynching. The cause would consume Wells for the rest of her life. She traveled throughout the United States and Europe to organize solidarity campaigns against lynching.

Wells was an organizer of the National Association of Colored Women in 1896 and of the NAACP in 1909. Her article called, "How

Enfranchisement Stops Lynching" fused the two issues for the public. Realizing that Black women lacked both the vote and any experience with the political system, Wells, along with a white colleague, Belle Squires, co-founded the Alpha Suffrage Club, the largest Black women's suffrage organization in Illinois. This group helped pass a state women's suffrage law and organized to elect the first Black alderman in Chicago. Her defiance of the NAWSA's attempt to force Black suffragists to march at the back of the 1913 suffrage parade gave heart to other Black suffragists and helped unite the causes of universal suffrage and race and gender equality. Wells remained an activist up to her death in 1931.[8]

PROFILE: MARY CHURCH TERRELL (1863-1954)

Mary Church Terrell, the daughter of a former slave who had inherited considerable wealth from her father, was considered the most important leader in the Black women's club movement. According to Angela Davis, "few could equal Mary Church Terrell as an advocate of Black Liberation through the written and spoken word. She sought freedom for her people through logic and persuasion. An eloquent writer, a powerful orator and a master at the art of debate," Terrell championed the causes of Black equality, women's suffrage and the rights of working people. She marched for justice and against racism until the age of 89.[9]

Among her most famous quotations: "And so, lifting as we climb, onward and upward we go, struggling and striving, and hoping that the buds and blossoms of our desires will burst into glorious fruition ere long. With courage, born of success achieved in the past, with a keen sense of the responsibility which we shall continue to assume, we look forward to a future large with promise and hope. Seeking no favors because of our color, nor patronage because of our needs, we knock at the bar of justice, asking an equal chance."

PROFILE: MARY MCLEOD BETHUNE

Mary McLeod Bethune (1875-1955) was the 15th of 17 children, born on a rice and cotton farm in Sumter County, S.C. Although born free, her parents and most of her siblings had been enslaved, and her mother worked for her former master. Educated in a one-room Black schoolhouse, to which she walked five miles every day, McLeod went on to become a teacher.

With few resources but an abundance of nerve, she built a Black girls' school from the ground up, and then rallied supporters and donors to set up a network schools and hospitals across the South. In 1904, she founded Bethune-Cookman University, a historically Black college in Florida, which she created with small donations and volunteers on a former garbage dump, ultimately serving some 4,000 students per year and graduating more than 16,000 students.

Bethune's work on behalf of the vote benefited both women and men. Even after passage of the 15th Amendment, African American men were essentially blocked from voting by Jim Crow laws. After women's suffrage was ratified in 1920, Bethune held classes to prepare women and men for the literacy tests held in the South and raised funds for the nefarious poll taxes, measures which were meant to prohibit Black citizens from voting. Despite intimidation from the Ku Klux Klan, she bravely led a procession of African Americans to the polls.

Bethune was also the founder and president of the National Association of Colored Women's Clubs and the National Council of Negro Women, with over 1 million members. She was appointed special advisor to President Franklin D. Roosevelt on minority affairs. In 1936 she became director of the Division of Negro Affairs of the National Youth Administration, the first Black person to hold such a federal office. She also held honorary degrees and other offices at the federal level and was a consultant at the Conference to Draft a United Nations Charter.[10] ☐

Appendix 6
Rose Schneiderman's memorial speech
to protest the Triangle Shirtwaist Factory fire

Rose Schneiderman's memorial speech given at the Metropolitan Opera House to the New York Women's Trade Union League to protest the Triangle Shirtwaist Factory Fire, April 2, 1911.

"I would be a traitor to these poor burned bodies if I came here to talk good fellowship. We have tried you good people of the public and we have found you wanting.

"The old Inquisition had its rack and its thumbscrews and its instruments of torture with iron teeth. We know what these things are today; the iron teeth are our necessities, the thumbscrews are the high-powered and swift machinery close to which we must work, and the rack is here in the firetrap structures that will destroy us the minute they catch on fire.

"This is not the first time girls have been burned alive in the city. Every week I must learn of the untimely death of one of my sister workers. Every year thousands of us are maimed. The life of men and women is so cheap and property is so sacred. There are so many of us for one job it matters little if 146 of us are burned to death.

"We have tried you citizens; we are trying you now, and you have a couple of dollars for the sorrowing mothers, brothers and sisters by way of a charity gift. But every time the workers come out in the only way they know to protest against conditions, which are unbearable, the strong hand of the law is allowed to press down heavily upon us.

"Public officials have only words of warning to us — warning that we must be intensely peaceable, and they have the workhouse just back of all their warnings. The strong hand of the law beats us back, when we rise, into the conditions that make life unbearable.

"I can't talk fellowship to you who are gathered here. Too much blood has been spilled. I know from my experience it is up to the working people to save themselves. The only way is through a strong working-class movement."[11] ☐

Appendix 7
Elizabeth Gurley Flynn (1890-1964)

ELIZABETH Gurley Flynn was a labor organizer, feminist and communist.

A rebel from a young age, she was expelled from high school at 16 for her political activities, including a speech called "What Socialism Can Do for Women." At 17, she became a full-time organizer with the Industrial Workers of the World, leading strikes of garment workers, earning the nickname Rebel Girl. In 1919, she chained herself to a lamppost as part of the Spokane, Washington, free speech fight, where labor agitators were being jailed simply for speaking out. She was a founder of the American Civil Liberties Union (ACLU) the following year, where she aided in the defense of Sacco and Vanzetti; supported access to birth control and women's suffrage; and was a critic of male-dominated unions.

Gurley Flynn joined the Communist Party in 1936, an act that led to her expulsion from the ACLU board of directors, and was elected national chair of the CPUSA in 1961. During the anti-communist McCarthy era, Flynn served two years in prison for violating the Smith Act (the 1940 law which made it a criminal offense to advocate the violent overthrow of the government or to organize or be a member of any group or society devoted to such advocacy).[12]

Flynn and her co-defendant conducted their own defense at their 1952 trial. Following are selected quotes from her defense:

"I have ... been chairman of the Women's Committee of the Communist Party since 1945, which ... carries on the struggle for equal rights for women in shops, unions, and all organizations, even including our own party when necessary.

"We have ... helped organize women for full equality, both politically and economically, for the building of movements for peace,

consumers' councils, parent-teachers' organizations, and similar organizations, for the unity of Negro and white women, and to overcome
the exploitation of Negro women as workers, as women, as Negroes.

"We will demonstrate to you how constructive and beneficial
is the nature of our work among women, inspiring them to greater
self-confidence, greater comradeship with one another, greater participation in public affairs. ... [W]e have urged the organization of
women for political activity, not only on Election Day, but the year
around, in hearings, delegations, petitions and statements to all legislative and public bodies on such issues as child care, better schools,
better housing, a better standard of living, etc.

"We have written of the history of the women's movement in
our country, where every right we now enjoy has been won only by
organized struggle — the right of women to vote, to serve on juries,
protective labor legislation for women workers, mothers' pensions,
and so forth.

"We have directed our sharpest criticism to the virtual disfran-
chisement of the southern Negro women by force and violence and
through the poll tax, discrimination against women in factories, lack
of upbringing, etc.

"We have advocated socialism as a system of society best guaranteeing to women full equal rights in all spheres and insuring to
them the possibility of exercising these rights."[13] □

Appendix 8

'Rebel Girl'

In honor of Elizabeth Gurley Flynn

JOE Hill, the famous IWW labor leader who was executed in 1915, wrote the song "Rebel Girl" in honor of Flynn. The lyrics appear below.

There are women of many descriptions
In this queer world, as everyone knows.
Some are living in beautiful mansions,
And are wearing the finest of clothes.
There are blue blood queens and princesses,
Who have charms made of diamonds and pearl
But the only and thoroughbred lady
Is the Rebel Girl

CHORUS
That's the Rebel Girl, the Rebel Girl!
To the working class, she's a precious pearl.
She brings courage, pride and joy
To the fighting Rebel Boy
We've had girls before, but we need some more
In the Industrial Workers of the World.
For it's great to fight for freedom
With a Rebel Girl.

Yes, her hands may be hardened from labor
And her dress may not be very fine
But a heart in her bosom is beating
That is true to her class and her kind.
And the grafters in terror are trembling

When her spite and defiance she'll hurl
For the only and thoroughbred lady
Is the Rebel Girl.[14] ☐

Appendix 9

Mother Jones 1837-1930: Selected quotes

A huge investment in the working class

- "God Almighty made women and the Rockefeller gang of thieves made the ladies."
- "What one state could not get alone, what one miner against a powerful corporation could not achieve, can be achieved by the union."
- "I asked a man in prison once how he happened to be there and he said he had stolen a pair of shoes. I told him if he had stolen a railroad he would be a United States Senator."
- "In Georgia, where children work day and night in the cotton mills, they have just passed a bill to protect song birds. What about the little children from whom all song is gone?"
- "Sit down and read. Educate yourself for the coming conflicts."
- "Life comes to the miners out of their deaths, and death out of their lives."
- "I'm not a humanitarian. I'm a hell-raiser."
- "I would fight God Almighty Himself if He didn't play square with me."
- "I am not afraid of the pen, or the scaffold, or the sword."
- "Out of labor's struggle in Arizona came better conditions for the workers, who must everywhere, at all times, under advantage and disadvantage work out their own salvation."[15] □

Appendix 10
Ella Baker's legacy

AMONG the recurrent themes in today's women's movement are leadership development among the most oppressed and how to convert online activism into stronger "real-life" relationships and fighting organizations. Although she died decades ago, Ella Baker's legacy has important lessons for 21st century activists with regard to both these matters.

Ella Baker (1903-1986) had a profound influence on the civil rights and women's rights movements. She was an unparalleled organizer, but the legacy that most resonates for today's movement is her philosophy and practice of leadership — inspiring, recruiting and training activists to be leaders in many organizations and campaigns for African American people, the poor and women.

She was active in the NAACP, helped found the Southern Christian Leadership Conference (SCLC), and organized voter registration drives and consumer cooperatives in housing projects. She fought for equal pay for Black teachers, for job training and against lynching.

Inspired by the student sit-ins in Greensboro, North Carolina, she left the SCLC and called for a meeting with young student activists, a meeting that led to the founding of the Student Nonviolent Coordinating Committee (SNCC), a group that she continued to mentor.

In 1961, reacting to the murders of three volunteers, two white and one Black, with the SNCC-led Freedom Summer, Baker famously said, "The unfortunate thing is that it took this ... to make the rest of the country turn its eyes on the fact that there were other [B]lack bodies lying in the swamps of Mississippi. Until the killing of a [B]lack mother's son becomes as important as the killing of a white mother's son, we who believe in freedom cannot rest."

Her leadership principles were very specific: she rejected the stereotype of the charismatic all-knowing leader in favor of collective leadership, enlisting ordinary people in the hard work of movement building. Activist and scholar Barbara Ransby writes in a June 2015 ColorLines article that Baker had "a confidence in the wisdom of ordinary people to define their problems and imagine solutions. Baker helped everyday people channel and congeal their collective power to resist oppression and fight for sustainable, transformative change. Her method is not often recognized, celebrated or even seen except by many who are steeped in the muck of movement-building work."

In her later years, Baker worked on campaigns for school desegregation, Puerto Rican and African independence, and peace, allying herself with the Women's International League for Peace and Freedom.

In a September 2015 speech at Vassar College, Angela Davis, citing Ella Baker's legacy, described today's radical Black movement, which is often described as "leaderless," as instead "leader-full."

Ransby writes:

... [L]eadership and organizing cannot be simply tweeted into existence. Movement-building is forged in struggle, through people building relationships within organizations and collectives. Social media is only one part of a much larger effort.

While the mainstream media is all abuzz about social media as if it were a stand-alone entity, it tends to ignore or render invisible the critical work of leader-organizers who are more focused on street action than virtual action. This bias toward social media work woefully distorts not only how we understand this evolving movement, but also how we see social movements in general.[16] ☐

Appendix 11
Purpose of the Daughters of Bilitis (1955)
A huge investment in the working class

A **WOMEN'S** Organization for the Purpose of Promoting the Integration of the Homosexual into Society by:

1. Education of the variant, with particular emphasis on the psychological, physiological and sociological aspects, to enable her to understand herself and make her adjustments to society in all its social, civic and economic implications — this to be accomplished by establishing and maintaining as complete a library as possible of both fiction and nonfiction literature on the sex deviant theme; by sponsoring public discussions on pertinent subjects to be conducted by leading members of the legal, psychiatric, religious and other professions; by advocating a mode of behavior and dress acceptable to society.

2. Education of the public at large through acceptance first of the individual, leading to an eventual breakdown of erroneous conceptions, taboos and prejudices; through public discussion meetings aforementioned; through dissemination of educational literature on the homosexual theme.

3. Participation in research projects by duly authorized and responsible psychology, sociology and other such experts directed toward further knowledge of the homosexual.

4. Investigation of the penal code as it pertains to the homosexual, proposal of changes to provide an equitable handling of cases involving this minority group, and promotion of these changes through due process of law in the state legislatures.[17] ☐

Appendix 12

'African American women in defense of ourselves'

THE following is the text of the open letter that 1,600 Black women signed in 1991 to show solidarity with Professor Anita Hill, who was under non-stop attack for having spoken out before the Senate Judiciary Committee about the sexual harassment she endured from Judge Clarence Thomas.

We are particularly outraged by the racist and sexist treatment of Professor Anita Hill, an African American woman who was maligned and castigated for daring to speak publicly of her own experience of sexual abuse. The malicious defamation of Professor Hill insulted all women of African descent and sent a dangerous message to any woman who might contemplate a sexual harassment complaint.

We speak here because we recognize that the media are now portraying the Black community as prepared to tolerate both the dismantling of affirmative action and the evil of sexual harassment in order to have any Black man on the Supreme Court. We want to make clear that the media have ignored or distorted many African American voices. We will not be silenced.

Many have erroneously portrayed the allegations against Clarence Thomas as an issue of either gender or race. As women of African descent, we understand sexual harassment as both. We further understand that Clarence Thomas outrageously manipulated the legacy of lynching in order to shelter himself from Anita Hill's allegations. To deflect attention away from the reality of sexual abuse in African American women's lives, he trivialized and misrepresented this painful part of African American people's history. This country, which has a long legacy of racism and sexism, has never taken the sexual abuse of [B]lack women seriously. Throughout U.S. history [B]lack women have been sexually stereotyped as immoral, insatiable, perverse, the initiators in all sexual contacts — abusive or otherwise. The common assumption in legal proceedings as well as in the larger society has been that [B]lack women cannot be raped or otherwise sexually abused. As Anita Hill's experience demonstrates, [B]lack women who speak of these matters are not likely to be believed.

In 1991, we cannot tolerate this type of dismissal of any one Black woman's experience or this attack upon our collective character without protest, outrage and resistance.

We pledge ourselves to continue to speak out in defense of one another, in defense of the African American community and against those who are hostile to social justice, no matter what color they are. No one will speak for us but ourselves.[18] ☐

Appendix 13

Manifesta: A thirteen-point agenda

"**MANIFESTA:** Young Women, Feminism, and the Future" was a 1999 book by Third Wave feminist activists Jennifer Baumgardner and Amy Richards, which was a declaration of principles for young feminists. It set forth a 13-point agenda for Third Wave feminism, which appears below.

1. To out unacknowledged feminists, specifically those who are younger, so that Generation X can become a visible movement and, further, a voting block of eighteen- to forty-year-olds.

2. To safeguard a woman's right to bear or not to bear a child, regardless of circumstances, including women who are younger than eighteen or impoverished. To preserve this right throughout her life and support the choice to be childless.

3. To make explicit that the fight for reproductive rights must include birth control; the right for poor women and lesbians to have children; partner adoption for gay couples; subsidized fertility treatments for all women who choose them; and freedom from sterilization abuse. Furthermore, to support the idea that sex can be — and usually is — for pleasure, not procreation.

4. To bring down the double standard in sex and sexual health, and foster male responsibility and assertiveness in the following areas: achieving freedom from STDs; more fairly dividing the burden of family planning as well as responsibilities such as child care; and eliminating violence against women.

5. To tap into and raise awareness of our revolutionary history, and the fact that almost all movements began as youth movements. To have access to our intellectual feminist legacy and women's history: for the classics of radical feminism, womanism, mujeristas, women's

liberation, and all our roots to remain in print; and to have women's history taught to men as well as women as a part of all curricula.

6. To support and increase the visibility and power of lesbians and bisexual women in the feminist movement, in high schools, colleges and the workplace. To recognize that queer women have always been at the forefront of the feminist movement, and that there is nothing to be gained — and much to be lost — by down-playing their history, whether inadvertently or actively.

7. To practice "autokeonony" ("self in community"): to see activism not as a choice between self and community but as a link between them that creates balance.

8. To have equal access to health care, regardless of income, which includes coverage equivalent to men's and keeping in mind that women use the system more often than men do because of our reproductive capacity.

9. For women who so desire to participate in all reaches of the military, including combat, and to enjoy all the benefits (loans, health care, pensions) offered to it's members for as long as we continue to have an active military. The largest expenditure of our national budget goes toward maintaining this welfare system, and feminists have a duty to make sure women have access to every echelon.

10. To liberate adolescents from slut-bashing, listless educators, sexual harassment, and bullying at school, as well as violence in all walks of life, and the silence that hangs over adolescents' heads, often keeping them isolated, lonely and indifferent to the world.

11. To make the workplace responsive to an individual's wants, needs and talents. This includes valuing (monetarily) stay-at-home parents, aiding employees who want to spend more time with family and continue to work, equalizing pay for jobs of comparable worth, enacting a minimum wage that would bring a full-time worker with two children over the poverty line, and providing employee benefits for freelance and part-time workers.

12. To acknowledge that, although feminists may have disparate values, we share the same goal of equality, and of supporting one another in our efforts to gain the power to make our own choices.

13. To pass the Equal Rights Amendment so that we can have a constitutional foundation of righteousness and equality upon which future women's rights conventions will stand.[19] ☐

Appendix 14
National Welfare Rights Organization (1966-1975)

EXCERPTS from: "Revisiting the National Welfare Rights Organization" (From Colorlines, November 19, 2000)

The National Welfare Rights Organization (NWRO) made history by organizing tens of thousands of welfare recipients to demand income, clothing, food, and justice for their families. For the first time, U.S. welfare recipients rejected the welfare stigma and organized along class, race, and gender lines to challenge the system that kept them at the bottom of the economic ladder. At its peak in 1969, NWRO membership was estimated at 22,000 families nationwide, mostly [B]lack, with local chapters in nearly every state and major city.

NWRO was founded by George Wiley, a nationally recognized chemist and only the second African American on the faculty of Syracuse University. [A member of CORE (Congress of Racial Equality) in Syracuse, in 1964 he abandoned] academia and his scientific career to devote himself to the civil rights movement. The next year, striving to link civil rights with the burgeoning anti-poverty movement, he founded the Poverty/Rights Action Center, which evolved into NWRO.

NWRO ... leveraged tangible improvements in the welfare system and, in the process, changed the attitudes of thousands of women who joined the organization. Largely as a result of NWRO 'minimum standards' campaigns for furniture and clothing, welfare payments in New York City alone increased over 30-fold from $1.2 million in 1963 to $40 million in 1968, an income transfer that went directly into the pockets of the poor. By 1968, militant action taken by welfare recipients across the country had resulted in a changed atmosphere inside welfare offices, as these agencies established community relations departments, provided access to state welfare manuals, and began to treat recipients as clients rather than supplicants. For the first time, organized recipients negotiated with agency directors as peers.

NWRO's impact extended far beyond money and legal rights. By asserting that the right to welfare is akin to a civil right and that women and poor people deserve to be treated with dignity and respect, NWRO was the first movement to create a distinct political identity among poor [B]lack women, who comprised 90 percent of the organization's membership. It infused thousands with the sense that welfare was an entitlement, not a favor, ... that society has a responsibility to care for children, and that women raising children on welfare had the right to determine how to spend their benefit checks on their children's behalf, ...and [that women had a right] to adequate income, regardless of whether they worked in a factory or at home raising children. ... Being on welfare was a necessity created by the economic system, not the fault of individual women, and surviving on welfare was a badge of honor, not a symbol of shame.

The NWRO made historic contributions to the social justice movement in the U.S. ... It increased welfare benefits, developed legal and procedural rights, and created a movement of poor [B]lack women.[20] ☐

Appendix 15

Women Organized to Resist and Defend (WORD) organizing statement, 2012

WORD is a grassroots, feminist organization that is dedicated to building the struggle for women's rights and equality for all.

We formed because of the shocking number of attacks on the rights of women, through anti-abortion legislation, slashing of social services and new heights of misogyny in the rhetoric of the right wing. Now more than ever, a new, fighting women's movement is needed.

We believe in organizing and taking to the streets, independent of the politicians of either major party. Throughout history, the gains that women have made have been won through militant struggle. We want to revive this kind of struggle by uniting all women to defend our rights.

We fight for equality for all. We know that fighting racism, anti-LGBT bigotry and the oppression of the poor are part and parcel of our struggle. No woman can be free while others are oppressed.

WORD was initiated by women who have been active in the anti-war movement and the fight against racism, police brutality and in support of immigrant rights.

WHAT WE STAND FOR:

- Full reproductive rights now: Access to safe, legal abortion and birth control — on demand. We want healthcare that covers these services and access to it for all women. We want the information that we need to stay healthy, including an end to abstinence-only sex education in our schools.
- Defending women in the workplace: Closing the wage gap, providing maternity leave and ending penalties on working mothers. Ending sexual harassment at work.

- Stop the budget cuts: Cutting federal and state social services punishes poor women. We demand government funding for social services that millions of working and poor women depend on.
- We want full equality and respect now: Fight racism, sexism and anti-LGBT bigotry. Stop the exploitation and commercialization of women in mass media. An injury to one is an injury to all!

EXCERPTS FROM WORD MISSION STATEMENT:

Women's rights are under severe attack. Access to healthcare — including contraception and abortion — childcare, housing, welfare and other benefits are being slashed across the country. We are tired of politicians playing political football with our lives. It's time we take action, organize and fight back.

It has been 39 years since the Supreme Court's *Roe v Wade* decision that declared access to abortion to be a fundamental right. It was a victory for the women's movement, giving women the fundamental right of control over our own bodies. Since that time, abortion rights have been under attack.

We need to build a powerful new movement to defeat the right-wing attacks. We need to show the legislators, politicians and pundits that we will not let them take away our freedom and send us back to the dark days of back-alley abortions and social inequality.

We will defend the gains of the women's movement and push for greater justice for all women. We will fight for social programs that poor women and families depend on, for economic equality, and for an end to sexist discrimination. Women and men of all ages, nationalities and sexual orientations are invited to join in this campaign.[21] □

Appendix 16

Five facts you should know about the Hyde Amendment

THE Hyde Amendment, passed in 1976 and affirmed by the Supreme Court in 1980, prohibits federal funds from being used for abortions except in cases of rape, incest or endangerment to the life of the mother. The law effectively leaves the decision of funding abortion to the states, and most states, under the thumb of reactionary state legislatures and governors, choose not to. Here are five facts you should know about the Hyde Amendment:

1. The law primarily impacts poor women. The late Henry Hyde (R-IL), the conservative congressman who first proposed the amendment, acknowledged this reality during a Medicaid funding debate in 1977, when he told his colleagues, "I certainly would like to prevent, if I could legally, anybody having an abortion: a rich woman, a middle-class woman or a poor woman. Unfortunately, the only vehicle available is the ... Medicaid bill."

2. About 42 percent of women who have abortions live below the poverty line. The unintended pregnancy rate among poor women is five times the rates for higher-income women, as is the abortion rate. A key reason for the discrepancy is poor women's limited access to contraception.

3. By restricting Medicaid funding for abortion, one in four low-income women who would like to obtain abortions are instead forced to carry an unwanted pregnancy to term. Since the Hyde Amendment was enacted more than 35 years ago, over one million women have been unable to afford abortions.

4. Since the Hyde Amendment passed, only four states have voluntarily decided to use their funds to cover abortion. Another 13 states are required to do so by court order, just as they would other forms of health care. Thirty-two states and the District of Columbia

basically follow the Hyde Amendment as the congressman intended, with some small variations. One state, South Dakota, only pays for abortion when a woman's life is in danger, but not in cases of rape and incest — an apparent violation of federal law.

5. In order to assuage opponents of abortion in his own party, President Obama signed an executive order stating that the Affordable Care Act — which could expand Medicaid to cover as many as 21.3 million additional low-income Americans by 2022 — would maintain current Hyde Amendment restrictions.[22]

All* Above All, a coalition led by and primarily composed of reproductive justice organizations, has spearheaded a bold national campaign to overturn the Hyde Amendment. For years, more moderate and well-known organizations of the reproductive rights movement resisted the inclusion of this cause. Using public funding to guarantee abortion access for low-income women was considered too controversial or radical. In 2015 and 2016, however, many of these mainstream organizations, including Planned Parenthood, started committing more resources and attention to the struggle against Hyde, and credited the long-standing leadership of women of color organizations on this issue. Widely considered an unwinnable fight for years, the cause now has unprecedented momentum. □

Appendix 17

Martyrs of the women's rights movement

A short review of violent attacks at abortion clinics

- In 1993 Dr. David Gunn was murdered at a Pensacola, Florida, clinic after years of harassment and threats by Operation Rescue and others.
- In 1994 in Pensacola, Dr. John Britton and clinic escort James Barrett were murdered by a member of the right-wing Christian Army of God.
- Also in 1994 in Brookline, Massachusetts, Army of God terrorists killed receptionists Shannon Lowney and Lee Ann Nichols in a Planned Parenthood clinic.
- In 1998 Dr. Barnett Slepian was murdered in his New York State home by another right-wing Christian terrorist.
- In 1998 a bomb killed security guard Robert Sanderson in front of a Birmingham, Alabama, clinic and seriously injured a nurse, Emily Lyons.
- In 2009 Dr. George Tiller was assassinated at his church in Wichita, Kansas, by a right-wing Christian fundamentalist. The murder followed years of death threats, a firebombing of his clinic and a previous assassination attempt.
- A violent attack took place in March 2015 at the last remaining abortion clinic in Mississippi. A masked intruder attacked the Jackson clinic with a machete and seriously damaged equipment and the electrical system. The clinic stayed open, supported not only by the region's women's health activists but also by local law enforcement.
- A gunman killed three people and wounded nine at a Colorado Springs abortion clinic on Nov. 27, 2015. The killer was reportedly responding to the doctored videos purporting to show Planned Parenthood employees offering to sell fetal tissue for profit.[23] ☐

Appendix 18

Sampling of 2015-2016 abortion restrictions in various states

- In March 2015 the Arizona legislature passed a bill banning abortion coverage in health plans purchased through the federal exchange, and requires doctors to tell women they can potentially reverse a medication abortion despite the lack of any scientific evidence. In March 2016, Arizona law required women using medication abortion to use an outdated protocol. In May 2016, the medication provisions were repealed, but the restrictions on insurance were increased, as doctors who provide abortions are forbidden from receiving state Medicaid funds for other medical services.

- In March 2015 the Ohio House passed a bill that would ban abortion after a fetal or embryonic heartbeat is detectable, which happens in the earliest stages of pregnancy, before many women realize they are pregnant. Doctors who violate the law would face up to a year in prison. Ohio State Rep. Teresa Fedor spoke out against the bill, disclosing she had had an abortion after being raped while serving in the military. She declared, "You don't respect my reason, my rape, my abortion, and I guarantee you there are other women who should stand up with me and be courageous enough to speak that voice. What you are doing is so fundamentally inhuman, unconstitutional, and I've sat here too long. I dare every one of you to judge me. ... How dare government get in my business."[24]

- In April 2015 Kansas became the first state to ban the dilation and extraction procedure in the second trimester of pregnancy. The law provides for exceptions to save the life of the mother or to prevent irreversible damage to her health.

- In June 2015 North Carolina passed a 72-hour waiting period for abortion.
- In June 2015 the U.S. Fifth Circuit Court of Appeals upheld a Texas TRAP law that would result in the shutting down of all but nine abortion clinics in the state. The Texas law placed an "undue burden," prohibited by the *Roe* decision, on poor and rural women who depend on these clinics not only for abortions but also for breast exams, cancer screenings, HIV/STD tests, and birth control. On June 29, in a 5-4 ruling, the Supreme Court temporarily suspended that decision. On June 27, 2016, the Supreme Court struck down the Texas TRAP law provisions that called for doctors to have admitting privileges and for clinics to be outfitted like hospitals, setting a precedent for TRAP laws in other states to be struck down. In addition, the Court rejected appeals from some states whose TRAP laws had been rejected by lower courts.
- During January to June 2016, thirty-two states attempted to ban all or most abortions. Some have focused on late-term abortions, others on particular types of procedures, others on the reasons for abortion. Fourteen additional states have imposed new restrictions such as waiting periods, reduced access to medication abortion and new regulations on abortion clinics.
- On July 1, 2016, Mississippi banned Medicaid funding for non-abortion family planning services if the facility provides abortions (which already are not covered by Medicaid). ☐

Appendix 19

Paid maternity leave policies

In weeks, of 34 countries surveyed by the Organization for Economic Cooperation and Development (OECD)

Slovak Rep.	164	Netherlands	42
Hungary	160	Luxembourg	42
Finland	158.3	Ireland	42
Poland	126	France	42
Czech Rep.	112	UK	39
Estonia	82	Norway	36
Austria	81	Portugal	30.1
Latvia	71	Belgium	28
Lithuania	65	Iceland	26
Korea	64.9	Australia	17
Sweden	60	Greece	17
Japan	58	Turkey	16
Germany	57.3	Spain	16
Slovenia	52.1	Switzerland	14
Canada	52	New Zealand	14
Denmark	50	Mexico	12
Italy	47.7	U.S.	0[25]

Appendix 20
U.N. conferences
on women

FOUR global conferences on women were convened by the United Nations between 1975 and 1995. Women-led non-governmental organizations played a large role in winning recognition for women's rights to the workings of the United Nations. Beginning with a 1973 women's conference in Vienna, and continuing at a U.N. meeting in 1975, international women's rights groups won the establishment of the World Decade for Women. Even as the momentum of the U.S. feminist movement began to slow, the U.N. began to push for progress for women worldwide.

The first world conference on the status for women, called by the General Assembly, took place in Mexico City in 1975, to mark the opening of the Decade for Women. The conference focused on three objectives: full gender equality, the full participation of women in development and an increased contribution by women to the strengthening of world peace. The conference adopted a Plan of Action, with targets to be met by 1980, and called on member governments to set goals and strategies. The conference also saw unprecedented participation and leadership by women, and led to the establishment of a training institute for the advancement of women and a development fund for women.

The second conference met in Copenhagen in 1980, one year after the adoption of the U.N. Convention on the Elimination of All Forms of Discrimination against Women (CEDAW), informally known as the bill of rights for women. The United States is the only country in the Western Hemisphere and the only industrialized democracy that has not ratified this legally binding treaty.

Despite the progress manifested by the adoption of CEDAW, the Copenhagen conference revealed the disparity between official rights granted and the ability of women to exercise these rights. The conference called for an increase in political will among the countries' leaders to improve the lives of women, as well as more women in decision-making positions and services, and resources to support women's lives.

The third conference, referred to as the "birth of global feminism," was held in Nairobi in 1985. Reports to the conference revealed that the improvements in the status of women had benefited only a small minority of women worldwide, primarily in the developed world, and that the goals of the Decade for Women had not been met. The Nairobi conference sought to come up with new strategies to meet the goals of equality, development and peace. One advance was the declaration that all issues were women's issues and that women's equality, participation and leadership were essential in all institutions of society.

The Fourth World Conference on Women, held in Beijing in 1995, drew 17,000 attendees; a parallel NGO conference nearby drew an additional 30,000. The conference unanimously adopted the Beijing Declaration and the Platform for Action, an agenda for women's empowerment, which is considered the key global policy document on gender equality. It specifies 12 critical areas of concern that are the main obstacles to women's equality and which require concrete action by governments and civil society:

"Women and poverty, education and training of women, women and health, violence against women, women and armed conflict, women and the economy, women in power and decision-making, institutional mechanisms for the advancement of women, human rights of women, women and the media, women and the environment, and the girl-child."

Five-year progress reviews of the Beijing agenda have been held since 2000, upholding the commitments reached at Beijing and pledging further action to reach its goals.

The U.N. conferences, especially Beijing, were met with great enthusiasm and optimism by feminist activists in the United States and elsewhere. They provided an international forum for activists to meet and learn from each other, compare the needs and progress of their countries' movements, and to plan for future action. The U.N. conferences provided a framework and opportunity for internationalizing the women's movement and for raising the consciousness of activists.

The key limitation of government-sponsored conferences, both national and international, is that they are beholden to the political forces that rule member nations. The vast majority of the world's countries are under the thumb of global capitalism, which reinforces sexist ideas and the patriarchal division of labor, constantly undermines the existing social safety net, and pushes the international working class in a competitive race to the bottom.[26] □

Appendix 21
National Women's Conference 1977

THE National Women's Conference, held in Houston in November 1977, was the first and only national conference of women sponsored by the federal government. It was called by President Gerald Ford, a Republican, in 1974, in response to the U.N. proclamation that 1975 would be the International Women's Year. Congress approved $5 million for state and national conferences. In 1977, President Jimmy Carter appointed Congresswoman Bella Abzug to head the commission to oversee the conferences. The National Women's Conference was attended by 20,000 participants. Women athletes ran a relay from Seneca Falls, home of the suffrage movement, to Houston, carrying a lighted torch.

The real momentum pushing the presidential executive orders and the massive attendance of women from every state was the mass movement for women's liberation that had shaken the country.

In 1971, polls had found that a majority of Americans opposed "efforts to strengthen and change women's status in society." By 1975, 63 percent of the population supported women's equality, and Congress responded by allocating the funds for the Houston Conference.[27]

The gathering was the most diverse the United States had ever seen. Gloria Steinem wrote, "It was a constitutional convention for the female half of the country. After all, we had been excluded from the first one."

Not all the attendees were feminists. In some states the delegations were co-opted by religious fundamentalists and the Ku Klux Klan to oppose abortion, contraception and the multiracial gathering. Right-wing pickets and a counter conference organized by Phyllis Schlafly received significant media coverage.[28]

But the conference succeeded in passing a progressive pro-women's agenda, voting on and passing a 26-point Plan of Action [see below]. It also brought together women who had never before had the opportunity to meet together in person: Native American women from different parts of the country; women of all economic, racial and ethnic backgrounds; workers and students; and international observers. Resolutions were passed calling for equality in the workplace, affordable child care, vocational training for women in prison, and an end to discrimination against women of color and lesbians. Caucuses of Black, Latina, Asian and Native American women united around a "Minority Plank" calling for immigrant rights, a living wage and an end to bias in housing and other areas. In addition to women's equality, resolutions were passed in favor of disarmament and environmental protection.

The conference was not a lawmaking body and could only propose recommendations. The National Plan of Action of the National Women's Conference was submitted to the President and Congress in March 1978, after which President Carter established the National Advisory Committee for Women. The only concrete result was that the Senate granted a three-year extension for ratification of the Equal Right Amendment, which ultimately failed in 1982. No further action was taken by the administration or Congress on the conference recommendations, and, under political pressure, Carter fired Abzug from her position.[29]

The Plan of Action was ambitious, and over the years women have certainly made progress in many areas. But to see so many of the same issues on today's women's rights agenda is a clear indication of the need for a new independent mass movement. It also illustrates the limitations of such government-sponsored conferences, especially non-binding ones. In a society where a tiny corporate ruling class is the real power, including over the government, progressive proposals can be publicized with great fanfare one day but the funding can be eliminated the next, bringing them to a bitter and quick end. ☐

Appendix 22
Women's voices from the global climate justice movement

So far we have focused on the U.S. movement for women's rights, which, as we have seen, is part of an international movement for women's emancipation and human rights. The international movement for climate action and environmental justice has resounded with women, who have rallied to this cause and are in the front ranks of this crucially important movement.

Here are some of their voices:

Vandana Shiva is a world renowned advocate for the environment. Trained as a physicist at the University of Punjab, Dr. Shiva is an expert on agriculture, food, biodiversity, the unsustainability of industrial agriculture and a champion of women's rights. Some quotes follow:

> Nature shrinks as capital grows. The growth of the market cannot solve the very crisis it creates.

> Whenever we engage in consumption or production patterns which take more than we need, we are engaging in violence.

> We are either going to have a future where women lead the way to make peace with the Earth or we are not going to have a human future at all.

> As usual, in every scheme that worsens the position of the poor, it is the poor who are invoked as beneficiaries.[30]

326 WOMEN FIGHT BACK

Gloria La Riva was the 2016 presidential candidate for the Party of Socialism and Liberation. She spoke at a climate march in Oakland, California, on Nov. 21, 2015, leading up to the U.N. climate summit in Paris. Here are excerpts from her remarks:

> Capitalist production is what's destroying the planet. The pollution of the oceans, the oil drilling, fracking — everybody knows it's capitalism, and you can't control or reform capitalism. We need a real revolution. We need socialism. Cuba is the only country in the world that is considered sustainable, and there's a reason: They don't produce for profit. We have to dismantle the Pentagon, dismantle nuclear weapons. We need solar energy, sea energy, wind energy. We need to cut down on cars. We need public transport and bicycles. We need to save the planet. The media can be used to educate people about the crisis we're in right now. We need education. If people were truly educated about the climate crisis, they would become environmentalists. ... When everything runs on oil, when wars are carried out for oil, we need a revolution.[31]

Paige Murphy is an organizer with Red Nation from Albuquerque, New Mexico. In a September 2015 climate march through Hollywood, she spoke on the plight of indigenous people and their resources. She told the crowd, "We have faced violence and the destruction of our land and resources for over 500 years and for 500 years we have resisted. We continue this fight today as we take on Gold King, a mining company that has devastated our rivers with millions of gallons of toxic waste. We will fight until they clean it up and pay reparations to our people."[32]

Naomi Klein is the author of "This Changes Everything: Capitalism vs. the Climate." One of her key contributions is to bring the connection between the climate crisis and capitalism to the mainstream. Here are some quotes from her book:

> What is really preventing us from putting out the fire that is threatening to burn down our collective house?

I think the answer is far more simple than many have led us to believe: we have not done the things that are necessary to lower emissions because those things fundamentally conflict with deregulated capitalism, the reigning ideology for the entire period we have been struggling to find a way out of this crisis. We are stuck because the actions that would give us the best chance of averting catastrophe—and would benefit the vast majority—are extremely threatening to an elite minority that has a stranglehold over our economy, our political process, and most of our major media outlets.

By this point in history—after the 2008 collapse of Wall Street and in the midst of layers of ecological crises—free market fundamentalists should, by all rights, be exiled to a similarly irrelevant status, left to fondle their copies of Milton Friedman's "Free to Choose" and Ayn Rand's "Atlas Shrugged" in obscurity. They are saved from this ignominious fate only because their ideas about corporate liberation, no matter how demonstrably at war with reality, remain so profitable to the world's billionaires that they are kept fed and clothed in think tanks by the likes of Charles and David Koch, owners of the diversified dirty energy giant Koch Industries, and ExxonMobil.

Climate change detonates the ideological scaffolding on which contemporary conservatism rests. A belief system that vilifies collective action and declares war on all corporate regulation and all things public simply cannot be reconciled with a problem that demands collective action on an unprecedented scale and a dramatic reining in of the market forces that are largely responsible for creating and deepening the crisis.

The UN Climate Summit, COP21, took place in Paris from Nov. 30 to Dec. 12, 2015. There were only a handful of women among the official representatives of member nations. There was no mention of women's rights in the official agreement. Yet, women are doing the grassroots activist work in the countries that are most affected by climate change, and they made clear the connection between climate change and the lives of women.

Following are selected remarks from interviews at COP21 on democracynow.org, December 10 and 11, 2015:

May Boeve, Executive Director of the environmental group 350.org, announced that the international campaign for divestment from gas, oil and coal companies had reached a new milestone:

> The divestment movement is about something quite simple: if it's wrong to cause climate change, it's wrong to profit from causing climate change. And the divestment movement has taken off all over the world with this as its rallying cry.

> ... [A]s of today, total divestment commitments have passed the $3.4 trillion mark, that is $3.4 trillion of assets under management now fossil-free. That includes a combination of different types of commitments, both commitments to full divestment, which we define as divestment from coal, oil, and gas, and also partial divestment, which includes one of those fuels or some other combination.

> ... A growing number of investors representing a growing amount of capital do not want to be associated with this industry any longer. It is a rogue industry. And that is what these commitments represent. It demonstrates that investors are taking climate risk extremely seriously.

> ... Over 500 institutions have committed to divest, that includes, just today, 19 cities here in France, including Bordeaux, Saint-Denis, and Dijon. The French Parliament has endorsed divestment. And between last September, when we announced the $2.7 trillion mark, and today, Uppsala became the largest city in Sweden to divest from fossil fuels, Münster became the first German city to divest, Melbourne, Australia, second-largest city

committed, and the London School of Economics, another primary institution .... They have committed to divest.

This movement works because it is powered by tens of thousands of individuals who are powering these commitments forward. So we thank you, all of you who fought for divestment, and who will fight for reinvestment of where those resources go.

Priscilla Achakpa, a delegate from Nigeria, is a member of the Indigenous People's Caucus, the Women's Caucus and the Women and Gender Constituency at the U.N. climate summit. She is Executive Director of the Women Environmental Program in Nigeria. She spoke of the ways in which women bear the brunt of climate change:

[W]omen are affected differently because of their vulnerability, first and foremost, because of their reproductive system. And ... as caregivers, who take care of the elderly, who take care of the children, ... most of the time it's so difficult for them to bear the impact of this climate change. ... I come from Nigeria, and I will talk about Nigeria, and I will start from the issue of the Lake Chad, which in the past, was feeding over millions of people in the 1970s. Lake Chad river basin is now dried up. Hundreds of millions of people have been displaced as a result of the dried up of Lake Chad. And most of the people that are affected are women and children because the men are forced to migrate, but the women cannot leave because they have the children there to take care of. So the women, most of the times, are forced with the impact of climate change and they live with it daily. ...

[W]hen we're addressing the issues of Boko Haram we should look at the issues of environmental insecurity. ... Rivers are drying up, the source of livelihoods of most of the people who are dependent upon these rivers, including the Lake Chad, which is situated in the northeast part of Nigeria, and therefore, a lot of people have been displaced. There's poverty. Their source of livelihood is completely eroded. So when you take out the source of livelihood of these people and you leave them with no options, no alternatives, of course the tendency is that they resort into violence. ...

Our organization, Women Environmental Program is dealing very much with the issues of solar power. Solar dryers, particularly. ... Because we have a lot of perishable crops. ... First and foremost you have tomatoes, you have onions, you have pepper, you have oranges. Most of these crops have been destroyed because the women do not have the storage for them. And how to package them becomes impossible. ... [H]ow can we help the women to package some of these products that will be marketed even when it's off season, instead of throwing them away? And that was how we brought in the issues of solar dryers that we've been using very much. ... So even when it's off season, they still have tomatoes, they still have pepper, to be able to sell.

Maria Nailevu, from Fiji, is part of DIVA for Equality and represents women from the Pacific: "For women, we are the heartbeat of every household. We are the ones that worry about our daily living. We are the ones that sustain our life at home. So it doubles our workload. Where we used to find food is no longer there. Where we used to find the resources is no longer there. So, it has contributed a lot of workload on women, fast making them more vulnerable."

Majandra Rodriguez is a climate activist from Lima, Peru.

We are part of the most vulnerable countries to the impacts of climate change. We are not talking about 1.5 [degrees Celsius, maximum increase in climate temperature] to survive; we are talking about 1.5 to maybe have a chance at surviving, because we are already dying. We are here to demand that every single country take action. However, some countries need to take more action, because they have polluted our atmosphere for 200 years, and their wealth is based upon our poverty. ...

Peru is one of the most vulnerable countries to climate change. We are extremely biodiverse. Most of our territory is covered by the Amazon rainforest. The Amazon rainforest is extremely fragile. It's extremely interdependent, and so any change in any aspect of that environment affects the entire ecosystem. So we have to begin to recognize that we aren't separate from nature, we depend on nature. And, you know, it's the butterfly effect. I mean, a change in the Amazon rainforest in one part of the country at a very basic level — a change in precipitation, change in temperature levels, change in droughts, etc. — can have drastic impacts on other parts of the world.

Abeer Al Butmeh is a member of Palestine Friends of the Earth: "Palestine is affected by climate change — a water shortage and a high temperature during summer and the low temperature during the winter. The Israeli occupation makes the situation worse, because we cannot manage our water resources."

Kandi Mossett represents the Indigenous Environmental Network, North Dakota: "Prior to fracking, we had seven coal-fired power plants, so we're all dealing with mercury contamination and cancers from that. And then enter fracking around 2007, and what we're dealing with is a death by a thousand cuts. We have people that are literally on the front lines being killed by all of the semi traffic, by the increase in violence against women. Ever since we've had the oil industry enter, we've had these jobs that were created, but there were 11,000 jobs created and over 10,000 people that came into our state. And we've had violence against women increase by 168 percent, particularly in the area of rape. We have 14-, 15- and 16-year-old girls that are willingly going into man camps and selling themselves."

Ruth Nyambura is a Kenyan political ecologist and a member of the African Ecofeminist Collective:

We go back to the gender-ascribed roles that women have in the society. So, for example, globally, 70% of food production is by women. In some parts, 80% of food production is by women. Women are the majority of the food producers. Across the whole agricultural sector, they basically hold it down. We have the externalization of the costs of extractive industries. When you have pollution, when water is taken away from communities, goes to mining companies, goes to corporations, women have to spend even more time looking for water, you know, both because of patriarchy and because of the way the system has been organized. So, to have a text [the COP21 agreement] that says nothing around gender equality, that still proposes market solutions, that brought about the climate crisis—and knowing the function of the market in the capitalist system that we are in, women benefit the least, if at all. ☐

Endnotes

Introduction: Women advance through struggle

1 The word "Sixties" in this book, which will show up a number of times, refers to the 15-year period of collective uprisings over a variety of important causes in the U.S. from 1960 to 1975. Where we just mean the numerical decade we write "1960s." Second Wave activism took place from 1965 to 1975.

2 Sonia Pressman Fuentes,. "The Women's Rights Movement: Where It's Been, Where It's At" (Keynote Address, Women Lawyers of Utah 20th Anniversary Celebration/Retreat, Deer Valley, Utah, October 12, 2001), http://userpages.umbc.edu/ ~ korenman/wmst/womens_rights.html.

3 http://www.theatlantic.com/politics/archive/2016/04/a-sanders-surge-in-polling-if-not-delegates/477198/

4 Katha Pollitt, "Even if You Haven't Had an Abortion, You Owe Planned Parenthood," August 27, 2015, http://www.thenation.com/article/even-if-you-havent-had-an-abortion-you-owe-planned-parenthood/.

5 "Underpaid and Overloaded," National Women's Law Center, 2014, http://www.nwlc.org/sites/default/files/pdfs/executivesummary_nwlc_lowwagereport2014.pdf .

Chapter One: The status of U.S. women — USA is NOT number one

1 Bella DePaulo, "7 Stunning Ways Life Was Different in the 1960s," *Psychology Today (blog)*, Sept. 6, 2014,https://www.psychologytoday.com/blog/living-single/201409/7-stunning-ways-life-was-different-in-the-1960s.

2 Ibid.

3 Wendy Wang, Kim Parker and Paul Taylor, "Breadwinner

Moms," May 29, 2013, http://www.pewsocialtrends.
org/2013/05/29/breadwinner-moms/.

4   Jens Manuel Krogstad, "5 Facts about the Modern American
Family," April 30, 2014, http://www.pewresearch.org/fact-
tank/2014/04/30/5-facts-about-the-modern-american-family/.

5   Charles M. Blow, "Jeb Bush and Single Mothers," *New York
Times*, June 15, 2015, http://www.nytimes.com/2015/06/15/
opinion/charles-blow-jeb-bush-and-single-mothers.html.

6   Shane Ferro, "More work and less play for women around the
world," *Reuters (blog)*, March 12, 2014, http://blogs.reuters.
com/equals/2014/03/12/more-work-and-less-play-for-women-
around-the-world/.

7   Bryce Covert, "Putting a Price Tag on Unpaid Housework,"
Forbes, May 30, 2012, http://www.forbes.com/sites/
brycecovert/2012/05/30/putting-a-price-tag-on-unpaid-
housework/.

8   "Women's Employment During the Recovery," 2011, http://
www.dol.gov/_sec/media/reports/femalelaborforce/.

9   "20 Facts About U.S. Inequality that Everyone Should Know,"
http://web.stanford.edu/group/scspi/cgi-bin/facts.php.

10 National Women's Law Center, "Wage Gap Is Stagnant for
Nearly a Decade," September 23, 2015, http://www.nwlc.org/
resource/wage-gap-stagnant-nearly-decade.

11 Mark Brenner and Stephanie Luce, "Women and Class: What
Has Happened in Forty Years?," *Monthly Review*, July-August
2006, http://monthlyreview.org/2006/07/01/women-and-class-
what-has-happened-in-forty-years/.

12 National Women's Law Center, "The Wage Gap, State by State,"
September 17, 2015, http://www.nwlc.org/wage-gap-state-state.

13 National Women's Law Center, "Higher State Minimum Wages
Promote Fair Pay for Women," May 26, 2015, http://www.nwlc.
org/resource/higher-state-minimum-wages-promote-fair-pay-
women.

14 Sarah Jaffe, "Trickle-Down Feminism," *Dissent*, Winter 2013,
http://www.dissentmagazine.org/article/trickle-down-feminism.

15 Joseph Paul Brown, "The Dignity of Living: The U.S.'s Home Care
Aides," Truthout, June 20, 2015, http://www.truth-out.org/news/
item/31439-the-dignity-of-living-america-s-home-care-aides.

16 Michelle Chen, "What Fast-Food Workers Are Fighting For," *The Nation (blog)*, June 17, 2015, http://www.thenation.com/blog/210105/what-low-wage-workers-are-fighting#.

17 Latifa Lyles, "It's Time for Equal Pay Now," *U.S. Department of Labor Blog*, April 13, 2015, https://blog.dol.gov/2015/04/13/its-time-for-equal-pay-now/.

18 Jaffe, "Trickle-Down Feminism."

19 Women's Bureau, Department of Labor, "A Guide to Women's Equal Pay Rights," April 2012, https://www.dol.gov/equalpay/equalpay-employee.pdf.

20 David Cooper, Mary Gable and Algernon Austin, "The public-sector jobs crisis: Women and African Americans hit hardest by job losses in state and local government," *Economic Policy Institute*, May 2, 2012, http://www.epi.org/publication/bp339-public-sector-jobs-crisis/.

21 Patricia Cohen, "Public-Sector Jobs Vanish, Hitting Blacks Hard," *New York Times*, May 25, 2015, http://www.nytimes.com/2015/05/25/business/public-sector-jobs-vanish-and-blacks-take-blow.html.

22 Organisation for Economic and Co-operation and Development, "Length of maternity, paternity and parental leave," http://www.oecd.org/gender/data/lengthofmaternitypaternityparentalleave.htm.

23 http://timetocareny.org/coalition-partners/.

24 Jaffe, "Trickle-Down Feminism."

25 Claire Cain Miller, "The Motherhood Penalty vs. the Fatherhood Bonus," *New York Times*, September 6, 2014, http://www.nytimes.com/2014/09/07/upshot/a-child-helps-your-career-if-youre-a-man.html.

26 Nathalie Hrizi, "Parental Leave a Fantasy in the U.S., and Only 3 Other Countries," *Liberation News*, September 22, 2015, http://www.liberationnews.org/parental-leave-a-fantasy-in-the-u-s-and-only-3-other-countries.

27 Sharon Lerner, "The Real War on Families: Why the U.S. Needs Paid Leave Now," *In These Times*, August 18, 2015, http://inthesetimes.com/article/18151/the-real-war-on-families.

28 Christopher Ingraham, "Our infant mortality rate is a national embarrassment," *Washington Post (blog)*, September 29,

2014, http://www.washingtonpost.com/blogs/wonkblog/
wp/2014/09/29/our-infant-mortality-rate-is-a-national-
embarrassment/.

29 "Norway Ranks as World's Best Place to Be a Mother." http://
www.msn.com/en-za/news/other/norway-ranks-as-worlds-best-
place-to-be-a-mother/ar-BBjccWB.

30 Amnesty International, "Deadly Delivery: The Maternal Health
Care Crisis in the USA," May 7, 2011, http://www.amnestyusa.
org/research/reports/deadly-delivery-the-maternal-health-care-
crisis-in-the-usa.

31 Feminist Daily Newswire, "Detroit Maternal Death Rate is triple
the U.S. Average," July 21, 2014, https://feminist.org/blog/
index.php/2014/07/21/why-detroits-maternal-death-rate-is-three-
times-higher-than-the-us-average/.

32 Juliana Herman, Sasha Post and Scott O'Halloran, "The United
States Is Far Behind Other Countries on Pre-K," *Center for
American Progress*, May 2, 2013, https://www.americanprogress.
org/issues/education/report/2013/05/02/62054/the-united-
states-is-far-behind-other-countries-on-pre-k/.

33 Jane Mansbridge, "How Did Feminism Get to Be?," *American
Prospect*, December 19, 2001, http://prospect.org/article/how-
did-feminism-get-be.

34 Inter-Parliamentary Union, "Women in National Politics,"
accessed August 13, 2016, http://www.ipu.org/wmn-e/classif.
htm.

35 Alana Eichner, and Katherine Gallagher Robbins, "National
Snapshot: Poverty among Women & Families, 2014," *National
Women's Law Center*, September, 2015, http://www.nwlc.org/
sites/default/files/pdfs/povertysnapshot2014.pdf .

36 "LGBT Workers and the Minimum Wage," *Civilrights.org*, April
2014, http://civilrightsdocs.info/pdf/minimumwage/lgbt-
minimum-wage.pdf.

37 World Health Organization, "Global and regional estimates
of violence against women: prevalence and health effects of
intimate partner violence and non-partner sexual violence,"
2013, http://www.who.int/gender/violence/who_multicountry_
study/summary_report/chapter2/en/.

38 World Health Organization, "WHO Multi-country Study on

Women's Health and Domestic Violence against Women," 2005, http://apps.who.int/iris/bitstream/10665/43310/1/9241593512_eng.pdf.

39 Organisation for Economic and Co-operation and Development, "Gender Equality and Women's Rights in the Post-2015 Agenda: A foundation for sustainable development," http://www.oecd.org/dac/POST-2015%20Gender.pdf.

40 UN Women, "Commission on the Status of Women 2013," accessed August 13, 2016, http://www.unwomen.org/en/news/in-focus/csw57-stop-violence-against-women.

41 UN Women, "Facts and Figures: Ending Violence against Women: A pandemic in diverse forms," October 2014, http://www.unwomen.org/en/what-we-do/ending-violence-against-women/facts-and-figures.

Chapter Two: The origin of women's oppression

1 Karl Marx and Freiderich Engels, "The German Ideology," *Marxist Internet Archive, accessed August 22, 2016,* https://www.marxists.org/archive/marx/works/1845/german-ideology/.

2 Pat Brewer, "Feminism and Socialism: Putting the Pieces Together, Preface," resolution at the 14th National Conference of the Democratic Socialist Party, Australia, January 1992, http://www.dsp.org.au/node/18.

3 Jane Cutter, "Women's Oppression," (unpublished manuscript, 2014).

Chapter Three: Women in three socialist revolutions

1 "The Russian Revolution and the Emancipation of Women," *International Communist League (Fourth Internationalist), Spring 2006, accessed August 24, 2016,* http://www.icl-fi.org/english/esp/59/emancipation.html.

2 Jane Cutter, "Women's Oppression," Unpublished manuscript, 2014.

3 "Women and the Russian Revolution," http://www.bolshevik.org/1917/no7/no07wmru.html.

4 Cutter, *Women's Oppression.*

5 Cutter, *Women's Oppression.*

6   Mary Buckley, "Women in the Soviet Union," *Feminist Review* 8, no. 1 (1981): 79, http://www.palgrave-journals.com/fr/journal/v8/n1/full/fr198113a.html.

7   Cutter, *Women's Oppression.*

8   Joy Ziegeweid, "Justice for Russian Women? Russia Begins to Face Its Domestic Violence Problem," *Human Rights Brief,* November 2, 2014, http://hrbrief.org/2014/11/justice-for-russian-women-russia-begins-to-face-its-domestic-violence-problem/.

9   Yuhui Li, "Women's Movement and Change of Women's Status in China," *Journal of International Women's Studies* 1, no. 1 (2000): 30-40, http://vc.bridgew.edu/jiws/vol1/iss1/3.

10 "Women in the Chinese Revolution, 1921-1950," *People's March,* accessed August 24, 2016, http://www.bannedthought.net/India/PeoplesMarch/PM1999-2006/publications/women/china-1.htm.

11 Li, *Women's Movement and Change of Women's Status in China.*

12 "All-China Women's Federation," http://en.wikipedia.org/wiki/All-China_Women%27s_Federation.

13 Andrew Jacobs, "Taking Feminist Battle to China's Streets, and Landing in Jail," *New York Times,* April 5, 2015, http://www.nytimes.com/2015/04/06/world/asia/chinese-womens-rights-activists-fall-afoul-of-officials.html.

14 Cutter, *Women's Oppression.*

15 Cutter, *Women's Oppression.*

16 "Gender Equality and the Role of Women in Cuban Society," *American Association University Women,* February 2011, accessed August 24, 2016, http://www.aauw.org.

17 Cutter, *Women's Oppression.*

18 "The World Factbook," https://www.cia.gov/library/publications/the-world-factbook/rankorder/2091rank.html.

19 Cutter, *Women's Oppression.*

20 Mariela Castro, Interview by Edmundo García, trans. Walter Lippmann, http://www.walterlippmann.com/docs2294.html.

21 Ban Ki-moon, Opening remarks at press conference in Havana, January 28, 2014, https://www.un.org/sg/en/content/sg/speeches/2014-01-28/opening-remarks-press-conference-havana.

Chapter Four: A new movement is born: the 1800s

1 Emily Sunstein, *A Different Face: The Life of Mary Wollstonecraft* (New York: Harper & Row, 1975).

2 "Maria Stewart," Public Broadcasting System, accessed August 16, 2016, http://www.pbs.org/wgbh/aia/part4/4p4439.html.

3 Margaret Fuller, *Woman in the Nineteenth Century* (New York: The Norton Library, W.W. Norton & Co., 1971).

4 On October 16, 1859, John Brown, a white abolitionist, led 19 men in a raid on the federal armory at Harper's Ferry, West Virginia. The objective of the raid was to seize arms and initiate a slave revolt against the Southern slave system. The John Brown raid failed in its immediate aims but has been described as the opening salvo in the U.S. Civil War, which culminated in the revolutionary defeat of the slave system.

5 See: "Harriet Tubman," http://en.wikipedia.org/wiki/Harriet_Tubman; "Combahee River Collective (1974-1980)," http://www.blackpast.org/aah/combahee-river-collective-1974-1980; Angela Davis, *Women, Race and Class* (New York: Vintage Books, 1983), 32-40; "Frances Harper," http://en.wikipedia.org/wiki/Frances_Harper; "Sojourner Truth," http://en.wikipedia.org/wiki/Sojourner_Truth.

6 Davis, *Women, Race and Class,* 39.

7 "Seneca Falls Convention," http://www.historynet.com/seneca-falls-convention.

8 Eleanor Flexner, *A Century of Struggle* (Cambridge: The Belknap Press of Harvard University Press, 1975), 91.

9 "Elizabeth Cady Stanton Quotes." http://womenshistory.about.com/cs/quotes/a/ec_stanton.htm.

10 Flexner, *A Century of Struggle,* 86-88.

11 "Susan B. Anthony Quotes." http://womenshistory.about.com/cs/quotes/a/qu_s_b_anthony.htm.

12 "Lucy Stone Quotes." http://womenshistory.about.com/od/quotes/fl/Lucy-Stone-Quotes.htm.

13 Flexner, *A Century of Struggle,* 148.

14 Flexner, *A Century of Struggle,* 147.

15 Gerda Lerner, ed., *Black Women in White America: A Documentary History* (New York: Pantheon Books, 1972), 245.

16 Davis, *Women, Race and Class,* 115-116.

17 "A History of Women in Industry," National Women's History Museum, https://www.nwhm.org/online-exhibits/industry/womenindustry_intro.html; Lerner, *Black Women in White America*, 250.

18 Flexner, *A Century of Struggle*, 78, 134.

19 Flexner, *A Century of Struggle,* 197-198.

20 Flexner, *A Century of Struggle,* 198.

21 "Lowell Mill Women Create First Union of Working Women," AFL-CIO, http://www.aflcio.org/Issues/Civil-and-Workplace-Rights/Working-Women/Working-Women-in-Union-History/Lowell-Mill-Women-Create-First-Union-of-Working-Women.

22 Davis, *Women, Race and Class,* 139.

23 Flexner, *A Century of Struggle*, 135.

24 "Susan B. Anthony Quotes," http://www.brainyquote.com/quotes/authors/s/susan_b_anthony.htm.

25 Flexner, *A Century of Struggle*, 139-140.

26 Flexner, *A Century of Struggle*, 135.

27 Flexner, *A Century of Struggle*, 142-144.

28 "A History of Women in Industry," National Women's History Museum, https://www.nwhm.org/online-exhibits/industry/womenindustry_intro.html.

29 "Atlanta's Washerwomen Strike," AFL-CIO, http://www.aflcio.org/Issues/Civil-and-Workplace-Rights/Working-Women/Working-Women-in-Union-History/Atlanta-s-Washerwomen-Strike.

30 Ibid.

31 Flexner, *A Century of Struggle*, 198-199.

32 "Mary Harris 'Mother Jones'," National Women's History Museum, https://www.nwhm.org/education-resources/biography/biographies/mary-harris-mother-jones/.

33 Flexner, *A Century of Struggle*, 153-154.

34 Davis, *Women, Race and Class,* 140-142.

35 Flexner, *A Century of Struggle*, 144.

36 Flexner, *A Century of Struggle*, 202-104.

37 Flexner, *A Century of Struggle*, 65.

38 Davis, *Women, Race and Class,* 104-105, 109.

39 Loretta Ross, "Understanding Reproductive Justice," *Trust Black Women,* March 2011, http://www.trustblackwomen.org/our-

work/what-is-reproductive-justice/9-what-is-reproductive-justice.

40 Flexner, *A Century of Struggle,* 182-196.

41 Flexner, *A Century of Struggle,* 188.

42 Lerner, *Black Women in White America,* 448.

43 Flexner, *A Century of Struggle,* 196.

44 Davis, *Black Women in White America,* 436-437, 498.

45 Davis, *Race and Class,* 136.

46 "Ida B. Wells Quotes," http://www.inspirationalstories.com/quotes/t/ida-b-wells/.

47 Lerner, *Black Women in White America,* 442-443.

48 Davis, *Race and Class,* 134-136.

Chapter Five: Suffrage and social justice

1 Flexner, *A Century of Struggle,* 260 (see chap. 4, n. 7).

2 Ibid.

3 J.D. Zahniser, "Why Doesn't Everybody Know Who Alice Paul Was and What She Did?" *History News Network,* July 27, 2014, http://historynewsnetwork.org/article/156345.

4 Flexner, *A Century of Struggle,* 273 (see chap. 4, n. 7).

5 Sheridan Harvey, "Marching for the Vote: Remembering the Woman Suffrage Parade of 1913." http://memory.loc.gov/ammem/awhhtml/aw01e/aw01e.html#ack.

6 Davis, *Race and Class,* 125 (see chap. 4, n. 4).

7 Davis, *Race and Class,* 142-145 (see chap. 4, n. 4).

8 Amrita Basu, ed., The Challenge of Local Feminisms: Women's Movements in Global Perspective (Boulder: Westview Press, 1995), 438.

9 Lerner, *Black Women in White America,* 211-212 (see chap. 4, n. 14).

10 "As Study Finds 4,000 Lynchings in Jim Crow South, Will U.S. Address Legacy of Racial Terrorism?" *Democracy Now,* February 11, 2015, http://www.democracynow.org/2015/2/11/as_study_finds_4_000_lynchings.

11 Lerner, *Black Women in White America,* 472 (see chap. 4, n. 14).

12 Flexner, *A Century of Struggle,* 277 (see chap. 4, n. 7).

13 Flexner, *A Century of Struggle,* 295 (see chap. 4, n. 7).

14 Flexner, *A Century of Struggle*, 298 (see chap. 4, n. 7).

15 Flexner, *A Century of Struggle*, 316-318; "Southern Strategy." http://en.wikipedia.org/wiki/Women's_suffrage_in_the_ United_States#Southern_strategy.

16 Davis, *Race and Class,* 148 (see chap. 4, n. 4).

17 Dorothy Sue Cobble, Linda Gordon and Astrid Henry, *Feminism Unfinished: A Short, Surprising History of American Women's Movements* (New York: Liveright Publishing Corp, 2014), 5.

18 Dorothy Sue Cobble, *The Other Women's Movement: Workplace Justice and Social Rights in Modern America* (Princeton: Princeton University Press, 2004), 7-8.

19 Flexner, *A Century of Struggle*, 238 (see chap. 4, n. 7).

20 Flexner, *A Century of Struggle*, 236 (see chap. 4, n. 7).

21 Flexner, *A Century of Struggle*, 249 (see chap. 4, n. 7).

22 Flexner, *A Century of Struggle*, 255 (see chap. 4, n. 7).

23 Alicia Williamson, "The Working-Class Origins and Legacy of International Women's Day," *UE News,* February 28, 2014, http://www.ueunion.org/ue-news/2014/the-working-class-origins-and-legacy-of-international-women's-day.

24 Davis, *Race and Class,* 143 (see chap. 4, n. 4).

25 Flexner, *A Century of Struggle*, 267 (see chap. 4, n. 7).

26 Ann Schofield, "Rebel Girls and Union Maids: The Woman Question in the Journals of the AFL and IWW, 1905-1920,"*Feminist Studies* 9, no. 2 (1983): 335-58

27 Flexner, *A Century of Struggle*, 249 (see chap. 4, n. 7).

28 "Triangle Shirtwaist Fire," AFL-CIO, accessed August 20, 2016, http://www.aflcio.org/Issues/Civil-and-Workplace-Rights/Working-Women/Working-Women-in-Union-History/Triangle-Shirtwaist-Fire.

29 "National Women's Trade Union League of America Records," Schlesinger Library, Radcliffe College, Unpublished finding aid, http://ocp.hul.harvard.edu/ww/nwtul.html.

30 Flexner, *A Century of Struggle*, 252 (see chap. 4, n. 7).

31 Howard Zinn, *A People's History of the United States* (New York: Harper Colophon, 1980), 327.

32 Schofield, *Rebel Girls and Union Maids*, 348.

33 "Elizabeth Gurley Flynn (1890-1964)," http://laborquotes. weebly.com/f-g.html.

34 Flexner, *A Century of Struggle*, 298-299 (see chap. 4, n. 7).

35 Cobble, *Feminism Unfinished,* 51.

36 Dan Bryan, "The Great (Farm) Depression of the 1920s," *American History USA,* March 6, 2012, http://www.americanhistoryusa.com/great-farm-depression-1920s/.

37 Cobble, *Feminism Unfinished,* 23-24.

38 "Women and the Peace Movement," National Women's History Museum, https://www.nwhm.org/online-exhibits/progressiveera/peace.html.

39 "How Did Women Peace Activists Respond to Red Scare Attacks during the 1920s?," *Women and Social Movements in the United States, 1600-2000,* http://womhist.alexanderstreet.com/wilpf/intro.htm.

40 Loretta J. Ross, "African-American Women and Abortion: 1800-1970," in *Theorizing Black Feminisms: The Visionary Pragmatism of Black Women (New York: Routledge, 1993),* 149-150.

41 Davis, *Race and Class,* 215 (see chap. 4, n. 4).

42 Ross, *African-American Women and Abortion*, 146.

43 Ross, *African-American Women and Abortion*, 148.

44 Ashley Baggett, "It's Her Fault; It's Feminists' Fault: The Tie Between Victim Blaming and Scapegoating Feminists," *Nursing CLIO (blog),* July 21, 2012, http://nursingclio.org/2012/07/21/its-her-fault-its-feminists-fault-the-tie-between-victim-blaming-and-scapegoating-feminists/.

45 Sara Mayeux, "Redefining Rape: Talking to Estelle Freedman About Street Harassment and Intersectionality in the Early 20th Century," *Hairpin,* October 2, 2013, http://thehairpin.com/2013/10/redefining-rape/.

46 Lerner, *Black Women in White America*, 149 (see chap. 4, n. 14).

47 http://www.hup.harvard.edu/catalog.php?isbn = 9780674724846.

48 "Stop Street Harassment," http://www.stopstreetharassment.org/2013/10/redefiningrape2/.

49 Flexner, *A Century of Struggle*, 235-236 (see chap. 4, n. 7).

50 Cobble, *Feminism Unfinished,* 9-10.

51 Cobble, *Feminism Unfinished,* 4.

Chapter Six: War and postwar America

1   Sybil Lewis, in "The Homefront: America During World War II," by Mark Jonathan Harris, Franklin D. Mitchell, and Steven J. Schechter (New York: The Putnam Publishing Group, 1984).
2   "Army Nurse Corps in World War II," http://www.history. army.mil/books/wwii/72-14/72-14.htm.
3   "Institute on World War II/ African American," http://ww2.fsu. edu/African-American.
4   "The Postwar Period Through the 1950s." In Encyclopedia of American Social History, edited by Mary Kupiec Cayton, Elliott J. Gorn, and Peter W. Williams (New York: Charles Scribner's Sons, 1993. U.S. History in Context (accessed December 21, 2016). http://link.galegroup.com/apps/doc/BT2313026907/ UHIC?u = oldt1017&xid = 6851f7a0.

Chapter 7: Feminism and the mass movements

1   Betty Friedan, *The Feminine Mystique* (New York: W.W. Norton and Company, Inc., 1963).
2   Linda Nicholson, ed., *The Second Wave: A Reader in Feminist Theory* (New York and London: Routledge, 1997), 2.
3   Nancy MacLean, *The American Women's Movement, 1945-2000: A Brief History with Documents* (Boston, New York: Bedford/St. Martin's, 2009), 11-12, 66-69.
4   Ibid., 71.
5   Lerner, *Black Women in White America*, 599 (see chap. 4, n. 14).
6   Ibid.
7   http://feministmajority.org
8   Nancy MacLean, *The American Women's Movement*, 16-17; Christine Stansell, *The Feminist Promise: 1792 to the Present* (New York: The Modern Library, 2010), 234-236.
9   Nicholson, *The Second Wave*, 2.
10   Stansell, *The Feminist Promise*, 222.
11   Barbara Epstein, "What Happened to the Women's Movement?" *Monthly Review*, Volume 53, Number 1. May 2001. http:// monthlyreview.org/2001/05/01/what-happened-to-the-womens-movement/.
12   Barbara Ehrenreich, "What is Socialist Feminism?" *Marxist*

Internet Archive, accessed August 22, 2016, https://www.
marxists.org/subject/women/authors/ehrenreich-barbara/
socialist-feminism.htm.

13 MacLean, *The American Women's Movement,* 26.

14 Jane Mansbridge, "How Did Feminism Get to Be?" *American
Prospect,* December 19, 2001, accessed August 22, 2016,. http://
prospect.org/article/how-did-feminism-get-be.

15 MacLean, *The American Women's Movement,* 27.

16 Mansbridge, *How Did Feminism Get to Be?*

17 MacLean, *The American Women's Movement,* 121-124.

18 Zillah R. Eisenstein, ed., *Capitalist Patriarchy and the Case for
Socialist Feminism* (New York: Monthly Review Press, 1979),
362-372.

19 MacLean, *The American Women's Movement,* 142-146.

20 Ibid., 155-157.

21 Ibid., 19.

22 Ibid., 104-105.

23 Ibid., 11.

24 Ibid., 58-59.

25 "Daughters of Bilitis." https://en.wikipedia.org/wiki/
Daughters_of_Bilitis.

26 MacLean, *The American Women's Movement,* 101-103.

27 Ara Wilson, "1970s Lesbian Feminism," *The Feminist Ezine,*
accessed August 22, 2016, http://www.feministezine.com/
feminist/lesbian/1970s-Lesbian-Feminism.html.

28 Cobble, *Feminism Unfinished,* 62 (See chap. 4, n. 17).

29 "Sisters in the Brotherhoods," http://www.talkinghistory.org/
sisters/index.html.

30 ibid.

31 MacLean, *The American Women's Movement,* 8-9.

Chapter Eight: A movement that transformed society

1 Kirsten M.J. Thompson, "A Brief History of Birth Control in the
U.S.," *Ourbodies Ourselves,* December 14, 2013, http://www.
ourbodiesourselves.org/health-info/a-brief-history-of-birth-
control/.

2 MacLean, *The American Women's Movement,* 12 (see chap.
7, n. 3).

3   Ross, *African-American Women and Abortion*, 156 (see chap. 5, n. 40).

4   MacLean, *The American Women's Movement*, 93 (see chap. 7, n. 3).

5   Jessica Gonzalez-Rojas and Taja Lindley, "Latinas and Sterilization in the United States," *Women's Health Activist Newsletter*, May/June 2008, https://nwhn.org/latinas-and-sterilization-united-states; Joyce Wilcox, "The Face of Women's Health: Helen Rodriguez-Trias," *American Journal of Public Health* 92.4 (2002), 566-569, Print, http://www.ncbi.nlm.nih.gov/pmc/articles/PMC1447119/.

6   An interview with Rebecca Kluchin (Demanding the Right to Reproduce: Voluntary and Forced Sterilization in America), interview by Mandy Van Deven, *Rewire*, August 5, 2009, http://rhrealitycheck.org/article/2009/08/05/demanding-right-reproduce-voluntary-and-forced-sterilization-america/.

7   Jane Lawrence, "The Indian Health Service and the Sterilization of Native American Women," *The American Indian Quarterly* 24, no. 3 (2000): 400-419, accessed August 23, 2016,.http://muse.jhu.edu/login?auth = 0&type = summary&url = /journals/american_indian_quarterly/v024/24.3lawrence.html

8   Michael Sullivan DeFine, "A History of Governmentally Coerced Sterilization: The Plight of the Native American Woman," University of Maine School of Law, accessed May 1, 1997, http://whale.to/b/define.html

9   feminist.com

10 Rachel Benson Gold, "Lessons from Before Roe: Will Past be Prologue?," *The Guttmacher Report on Public Policy* 6, no. 1 (March 2003), https://www.guttmacher.org/pubs/tgr/06/1/gr060108.html#box.

11 Ross, *African-American Women and Abortion*, 151 (see chap. 5, n. 40).

12 MacLean, *The American Women's Movement*, 25 (see chap. 7, n. 3).

13 Amy Kesselman, "Women vs. Connecticut," in *Abortion Wars: A Half Century of Struggle*, 1950-2000, ed. Rickie Solinger (Berkeley: University of California Press, 1998), 43.

14 Ross, *African-American Women and Abortion,* 153-155 (see chap. 5, n. 40).

15 "The Face of Women's Health: Helen Rodriguez-Trias," http://www.ncbi.nlm.nih.gov/pmc/articles/PMC1447119/.

16 Cobble, *Feminism Unfinished*, 64 (See chap. 4, n. 17).

17 "The Equal Pay Act of 1963," http://www.eeoc.gov/laws/statutes/epa.cfm.

18 Linda Gordon, "The Women's Liberation Movement," in Cobble et al, 2014, 69-145.

19 CLUW.org.

20 Gordon, *The Women's Liberation Movement,* 133.

21 MacLean, *The American Women's Movement,* 131 (see chap. 7, n. 3).

22 Arlene Foy Reynolds, "Sexual Harassment and the Law," in *Women: Images and Realities, A Multicultural Anthology*, eds. Suzanne Kelly, Gowri Parameswaran and Nancy Schniedewind (New York: McGraw Hill, 2012), 203-204.

23 MacLean, *The American Women's Movement,* 24 (see chap. 7, n. 3).

24 MacLean, *The American Women's Movement,* 18-19 (see chap. 7, n. 3).

25 MacLean, *The American Women's Movement,* 107 (see chap. 7, n. 3).

26 MacLean, *The American Women's Movement,* 19 (see chap. 7, n. 3).

27 Gordon, *The Women's Liberation Movement,* 75.

28 MacLean, *The American Women's Movement, 23* (see chap. 7, n. 3).

29 Gordon, *The Women's Liberation Movement,* 138-142.

30 "We Raise Our Voices: Celebrating Activism for Equality and Pride in Boston's African American, Feminist, Gay and Lesbian, and Latino Communities," the online edition of a Northeastern University Libraries exhibition (Boston: Northeastern University Libraries, 2003), http://www.lib.neu.edu/archives/voices/w-intro.htm.

31 MacLean, *The American Women's Movement, 36*-39 (see chap. 7, n. 3).

32 Elizabeth C. Patterson, review of Doctors Wanted: No

Women Need Apply," by Mary Roth Walsh and "The Hidden Malpractice," by William Morrow, *American Scientist 66,* no. 4 (1978), http://www.americanscientist.org/bookshelf/pub/doctors-wanted-no-women-need-apply-and-the-hidden-malpractice.

33 Gordon, *The Women's Liberation Movement,* 121.

34 Stansell, *The Feminist Promise,* 228 (see chap. 7, n. 8).

35 Stansell, *The Feminist Promise,* 240 (see chap. 7, n. 8).

36 MacLean, *The American Women's Movement,* 16-17 (see chap. 7, n. 3).

37 Kathie Sarachild, "Consciousness Raising: A Radical Weapon," 1973 in *Women: Images and Realities,* ed. Kelly et al (New York: McGraw Hill, 2012), 567-568.

38 MacLean, *The American Women's Movement,* 20 (see chap. 7, n. 3).

Chapter Nine: The right-wing backlash and continued attacks

1 MacLean, *The American Women's Movement,* 33 (see chap. 7, n. 3).

2 MacLean, *The American Women's Movement,* 34-35 (see chap. 7, n. 3).

3 http://womensenews.org/2004/06/time-bury-reagans-legacy-women/

4 Joerg Dreweke," Contraception Is Not Abortion: The Strategic Campaign of Antiabortion Groups to Persuade the Public Otherwise," *Guttmacher Policy Review* 17, no. 4 (Fall 2014), http://www.guttmacher.org/pubs/gpr/17/4/gpr170414.html.

5 "U.S. Abortion Rates & Related Information," *Our Bodies Ourselves,* March 22, 2014, http://www.ourbodiesourselves.org/health-info/u-s-abortion-rates/.

6 "Fact Sheet: Induced Abortion in the United States, July 2014," *Guttmacher Institute,* accessed August 28, 2016, https://www.guttmacher.org/fact-sheet/induced-abortion-united-states.

7 Sarah Jones, "Crisis of Faith: Religious Facilities Rely On Misleading Tactics, Dupe Women," *Americans United,* September 19, 2014, https://www.au.org/blogs/wall-

of-separation/crisis-of-faith-religious-facilities-rely-on-
misleading-tactics-dupe-women.

8   Barry Sheppard, "United States: Attacks on abortion rights
     accelerate," *Green left weekly,* June 1, 2015, https://www.
     greenleft.org.au/node/59160.

9   Pew Research Center, "A History of Key Abortion Rulings of
     the U.S. Supreme Court," January 16, 2013, http://www.
     pewforum.org/2013/01/16/a-history-of-key-abortion-rulings-
     of-the-us-supreme-court/.

10   Natalie Villacorta, "House votes to block federal funding
     of abortion," *Politico,* January, 22, 2015, http://www.
     politico.com/story/2015/01/house-abortion-ban-federal-
     funding-114497.html.

11   Laura Bassett, " Lindsey Graham Reintroduces 20-Week
     Abortion Ban: 'I Am Dying For That Debate,'" *Huffington Post,*
     June 11, 2015, http://www.huffingtonpost.com/2015/06/11/
     lindsey-graham-abortion_n_7561410.html.

12   Jennifer Bendery, "Senate Passes Human Trafficking Bill with
     Abortion Restrictions on Victims," *Huffington Post,* April 22,
     2015, http://www.huffingtonpost.com/2015/04/22/sex-
     trafficking-bill-abortion_n_7120028.html.

13   Esme E. Deprez, "The Vanishing U.S. Abortion Clinic,"
     Bloomberg, January 7, 2015, http://www.bloombergview.com/
     quicktake/abortion-and-the-decline-of-clinics.

14   Guttmacher Institute, "Trends in the States: First Quarter 2015,"
     http://www.guttmacher.org/media/inthenews/2015/04/02/.

15   Heather D. Boonstra and Elizabeth Nash, "A Surge of State
     Abortion Restrictions Puts Providers—and the Women They
     Serve—in the Crosshairs," *Guttmacher Policy Review* 17, no. 1
     (Winter 2014), http://www.guttmacher.org/pubs/gpr/17/1/
     gpr170109.html; Adam Liptak, "Supreme Court Lets Decision
     on Arizona Abortion Law Stand," *New York Times,* December.
     15, 2014, http://www.nytimes.com/2014/12/16/us/politics/
     justices-let-stand-a-ruling-blocking-an-arizona-abortion-law.
     html; Rick Rojas, "Arizona Orders Doctors to Say Abortions With
     Drugs May Be Reversible," *New York Times,* March 31, 2015,
     http://www.nytimes.com/2015/04/01/us/politics/arizona-doctors-
     must-say-that-abortions-with-drugs-may-be-reversed.html/.

16   Linda Greenhouse, "Abortion at the Supreme Court's Door," *New York Times*, October 15, 2015, http://www.nytimes.com/column/linda-greenhouse.

17   "State Attacks on Women's Health," Planned Parenthood, accessed August 29, 2016, http://www.plannedparenthoodaction.org/issues/state-attacks-womens-health/.

18   "Appeals Court Rules Abortion Ban Past 12 Weeks Unconstitutional," *Feminist Daily Newswire*, May 28, 2015, http://feminist.org/blog/index.php/2015/05/28/appeals-court-rules-abortion-ban-past-12-weeks-unconstitutional/.

19   Adam Liptak and John Schwartz, "Court Rejects Zone to Buffer Abortion Clinic," *New York Times*, June 26, 2014, http://www.nytimes.com/2014/06/27/us/supreme-court-abortion-clinic-protests.html.

20   Adele Stan, "How the Koch Brothers Helped Bring About the Law That Shut Texas Abortion Clinics," *The American Prospect*, October 3, 2014, http://prospect.org/article/how-koch-brothers-helped-bring-about-law-shut-texas-abortion-clinics.

21   "New Congress, Same Old Attacks on Women's Rights," Women Organized to Resist and Defend, January 10, 2015, http://www.defendwomensrights.org/new_congress_same_old_attacks_on_women_s_rights.

22   "Anti-Choice Violence and Intimidation," *National Abortion and Reproductive Rigths Action League*, January 1, 2015, http://www.prochoiceamerica.org/media/fact-sheets/abortion-anti-choice-violence.pdf.

23   Alex Henderson, "America's 10 worst terror attacks by Christian fundamentalists and far-right extremists," *RawStory*, January 11, 2015, http://www.rawstory.com/rs/2015/01/americas-10-worst-terror-attacks-by-christian-fundamentalist-and-far-right-extremists/.

24   Jennifer Dalven, "Ohio Just Defeated an Extreme Abortion Ban, but Don't Get Too Comfortable," *ACLU*, December 14, 2014, https://www.aclu.org/blog/speakeasy/ohio-just-defeated-extreme-abortion-ban-dont-get-too-comfortable?redirect = blog/reproductive-freedom-womens-

rights/ohio-just-defeated-extreme-abortion-ban-dont-get-too-comfort.

25 Jennifer Frost and Kinsey Hasstedt, "Quantifying Planned Parenthood's Critical Role In Meeting The Need For Publicly Supported Contraceptive Care," *Health Affairs Blog,* September 8, 2015, http://healthaffairs.org/blog/2015/09/08/quantifying-planned-parenthoods-critical-role-in-meeting-the-need-for-publicly-supported-contraceptive-care/; Gail Collins, "The Fight for Unplanned Parenthood," *New York Times,* September 18, 2015, http://www.nytimes.com/2015/09/19/opinion/gail-collins-the-fight-for-unplanned-parenthood.html.

26 "Guttmacher Statistic on Catholic Women's Contraceptive Use," Guttmacher Institute, February 15, 2012, http://www.guttmacher.org/media/inthenews/2012/02/15/.

27 "IHS Expands Plan B Access for Native American Women," *Feminist Daily Newswire,* September 23, 2013, http://feminist.org/blog/index.php/2013/09/23/ihs-expands-plan-b-access-for-native-american-women/

28 Joerg Dreweke, " Contraception Is Not Abortion: The Strategic Campaign of Antiabortion Groups to Persuade the Public Otherwise," *Guttmacher Policy Review* 17, no. 4 (Fall 2014), http://www.guttmacher.org/pubs/gpr/17/4/gpr170414.html.

29 Adam Liptak, "Supreme Court Rejects Contraceptives Mandate for Some Corporations," *New York Times,* June 30, 2014, http://www.nytimes.com/2014/07/01/us/hobby-lobby-case-supreme-court-contraception.html.

30 Laura Bassett, "Ruth Bader Ginsburg Writes Scathing 35-Page Dissent In Birth Control Case," *Huffington Post,* June 30, 2014, http://www.huffingtonpost.com/2014/06/30/ruth-bader-ginsburg-write_n_5544111.html.

31 Dreweke, *Contraception is not Abortion.*

32 Katie McDonough, "Tennessee just became the first state that will jail women for their pregnancy outcomes," *Salon,* April 30, 2014, http://www.salon.com/2014/04/30/tennessee_just_became_the_first_state_that_will_jail_women_for_their_pregnancy_outcomes/.

33 http://www.advocatesforpregnantwomen.org; Lynn M. Paltrow and Jeanne Flavin, "Pregnant, and No Civil Rights,"

New York Times, http://www.nytimes.com/2014/11/08/
opinion/pregnant-and-no-civil-rights.html.

34 Audrey Quinn, "In Labor, in Chains: The Outrageous Shackling
of Pregnant Inmates," *New York Times*, July 26, 2014, http://
www.nytimes.com/2014/07/27/opinion/sunday/the-
outrageous-shackling-of-pregnant-inmates.html; Joanne
Lin, "End Near for Shackling of Pregnant Women," *ACLU*,
1/21/2014, https://www.aclu.org/blog/immigrants-rights-
reproductive-freedom/end-near-shackling-pregnant-women.

35 "20 Years in Prison for Miscarrying? The Case of Purvi Patel
& the Criminalization of Pregnancy," *Democracy Now*, April 2,
2015, http://www.democracynow.org/2015/4/2/20_years_
in_prison_for_miscarrying; Lynn Paltrow, "How Indiana Is
Making It Possible to Jail Women for Having Abortions," *The
Public Eye*, March 29, 2015, http://www.politicalresearch.
org/2015/03/29/how-indiana-is-making-it-possible-to-jail-
women-for-having-abortions/.

36 National Coalition Against Domestic Violence, http://www.
ncadv.org.

37 Kim Craig, "100 serial rapists identified after rape kits
from Detroit Crime Lab are finally processed," http://
www.reporternews.com/news/100-serial-rapists-identified-
after-rape-kits-from-detroit-crime-lab-are-finally-processed-
ep-347577-346083992.html.

38 Mary F. Calvert, "Photos: Women Who Risked Everything to
Expose Sexual Assault in the Military," *Mother Jones*, September
8, 2014, http://www.motherjones.com/politics/2014/09/
sexual-violence-american-military-photos.

39 Patricia Kime, "Incidents of rape in military much higher
than previously reported," *Military Times*, December 5,
2014, http://www.militarytimes.com/story/military/
pentagon/2014/12/04/pentagon-rand-sexual-assault-
reports/19883155/.

40 Ann Jones, "Men Who Kick Down Doors: Tyrants Home
& Abroad," *Tomdispatch*, March 21, 2013, http://www.
tomdispatch.com/post/175663/tomgram percent3A_ann_
jones,_the_war_against_women/.

41 Tyler Kingkade, "Sexual Assault Statistics Can Be Confusing, But

They're Not The Point," *Huffington Post,* December 15, 2014, http://www.huffingtonpost.com/2014/12/15/sexual-assault-statistics_n_6316802.html.

42   Victoria Law, "FreeHer: Formerly Incarcerated Women Demand an End to Mass Incarceration," *Truthout,* June 26, 2014, http://www.truth-out.org/news/item/24605-freeher-formerly-incarcerated-women-demand-an-end-to-mass-incarceration.

43   "Prison Rape Elimination Act of 2003," *ACLU,* accessed August 29, 2016, https://www.aclu.org/prison-rape-elimination-act-2003-prea?redirect = prisoners-rights-womens-rights/prison-rape-elimination-act-2003-prea.

44   http://www.dvsja.org

45   Timothy Williams, "History of Abuse Seen in Many Girls in Juvenile System," *New York Times,* July 9, 2015, http://www.nytimes.com/2015/07/09/us/girls-in-juvenile-facilities-often-abused-report-says.html.

46   Sikivu Hutchinson, "Police Criminals and the Brutalization of Black Girls," *The Feminist Wire,* June 9, 2015, http://www.thefeministwire.com/2015/06/police-criminals-and-the-brutalization-of-black-girls/.

47   Kimberlé Williams Crenshaw, Priscilla Ocen and Jyoti Nanda, "Black Girls Matter: Pushed Out, Overpoliced, and Underprotected," *African American Policy Forum,* http://static1.squarespace.com/static/53f20d90e4b0b80451158d8c/t/54dcc1ece4b001c03e323448/1423753708557/AAPF_BlackGirlsMatterReport.pdf.

48   Alex Ronan, "It's Time to Talk About the Female Victims of Police Brutality," *New York Magazine,* April 29, 2015, http://nymag.com/thecut/2015/04/black-women-and-girls-face-police-brutality-too.html.

49   "Why We Can't Wait: Women of Color Urge Inclusion in 'My Brother's Keeper,'" *African American Policy Forum,* June 17, 2014, http://www.aapf.org/recent/2014/06/woc-letter-mbk.

Chapter Ten: The women's movement today, 1990-2016

1   Nellie Y. McKay, "Acknowledging Differences: Can Women Find Unity Through Diversity?" in *Theorizing Black Feminisms: The Visionary Pragmatism of Black Women,* ed. Stalie M. James and

Abena P.A. Busia (London and New York: Routledge, 1993), 267-282.

2   "African American Women in Defense of Ourselves," https://www.tumblr.com/search/ African + American + Women + In + Defense + of + Ourselves.

3   Rebecca Walker, "Becoming the Third Wave" *Ms. Magazine, Spring 2002,* http://www.msmagazine.com/spring2002/ BecomingThirdWaveRebeccaWalker.pdf.

4   Elinor Burkett and Laura Brunell, "The Third Wave of Feminism," in *Encyclopaedia Britannica Online,* s.v., updated July 14, 2016, http://www.britannica.com/topic/feminism/ The-third-wave-of-feminism.

5   "Feminist Social Theory, "*Social Theory re-wired,* accessed August 30, 2016, http://routledgesoc.com/profile/feminist-social-theory.

6   Jennifer Baumgardner and Amy Richards, "Manifesta: Young Women Feminism and the Future," in *Women: Images and Realities, A Multicultural Anthology*, ed. Kelly, Suzanne, Gowri Parameswaran and Nancy Schniedewind (New York: McGraw Hill, 2012), 606-612.

7   Barbara Smith, ed., *Home Girls: A Black Feminist Anthology* (Kitchen Table: Women of Color Press, 1983), xxix.

8   Catherine Hoddge McCoid, "Eleanor Burke Leacock and Intersectionality: Materialism, Dialectics, and Transformation," *Race, Gender & Class* 15, no. 1/2 (2008).

9   Astrid Henry, "From a Mindset to a Movement," in *Feminism Unfinished: A Short, Surprising History of American Women's Movements,* Dorothy Sue Cobble, Linda Gordon and Astrid Henry (New York: Liveright Publishing Corp., 2014), 155.

10 http://thirdwavefund.org/grant-recipients.html.

11 Astrid Henry, "From a Mindset to a Movement," in *Feminism Unfinished: A Short, Surprising History of American Women's Movements,* Dorothy Sue Cobble, Linda Gordon and Astrid Henry (New York: Liveright Publishing Corp. 2014), 176-179.

12 Barbara Ransby, "Ella Taught Me: Shattering the Myth of the Leaderless Movement," *Colorlines,* June 12, 2015, http://www. colorlines.com/articles/ella-taught-me-shattering-myth-leaderless-movement.

13 Stacey Anderson, "Feminism at the Apollo: Women of the World Festival Debuts Stateside," *Newsweek*, June 8, 2015, http://www.newsweek.com/women-world-festival-comes-harlem-340843.

14 Audrey Bilger, "Inside and Out," *Ms. Magazine*, Summer 2015, 20.

15 Linda Burnham, "Feminism Almost Always Needs a Modifier," *Meeting Ground ONLINE*, May 28, 2014, http://meetinggroundonline.org/feminism-almost-always-needs-a-modifier/.

16 Catherine Rottenberg, "Hijacking Feminism," *Aljazeera, March 25, 2013,* http://www.aljazeera.com/indepth/opinion/2013/03/201332510121757700.html.

17 Susan Faludi, "American Electra: Feminism's Ritual Matricide," *Harpers Magazine,* October 2010, http://harpers.org/archive/2010/10/american-electra/.

18 Henry, *From a Mindset to a Movement,* 184.

19 "How to Defang a Movement: Replacing the Political with the Personal," *Meeting Ground ONLINE, April 6, 2014,* http://meetinggroundonline.org/how-to-defang-a-movement-replacing-the-political-with-the-personal/.

20 Burkett and Brunell, *The Third Wave of Feminism.*

21 Women Organized to Resist and Defend (WORD), "Speaking out against domestic violence," November, 17, 2015, http://www.defendwomensrights.org/statements?page = 3.

22 Sady Doyle, "Abortion Isn't a Necessary Evil. It's Great," *In These Times*, October 3, 2014, http://inthesetimes.com/article/17216/abortion_isnt_necessary_evil_its_great_pro_choice.

23 WORD, http://www.defendwomensrights.org/statements?page = 7.

24 Loretta, Ross, "Understanding Reproductive Justice," *Trust Black Women,* March 2011, http://www.trustblackwomen.org/our-work/what-is-reproductive-justice/9-what-is-reproductive-justice.

25 Gaylynn Burroughs and Debra S. Katz, "Won't Back Down," *Ms. Magazine*, Summer 2015, 24-29.

26 Alexandra Brodsky, "Roundup: Essential Feminist Writing on the Isla Vista Shooting," *Feministing*, accessed August 30,

2016, http://feministing.com/2014/05/27/essential-feminist-writing-on-the-isla-vista-shooting/.

27 WORD, http://www.defendwomensrights.org/statements?page = 3.

28 "Say Her Name: Families Seek Justice in Overlooked Police Killings of African-American Women," *Democracy Now,* May 20, 2015, http://www.democracynow.org/2015/5/20/say_her_name_families_seek_justice.

29 Maya Schenwar, "Women's Prisons as Sites of Resistance: An Interview with Victoria Law," *Truthout,* June 28, 2015, http://www.truth-out.org/progressivepicks/item/31461-women-s-prisons-as-sites-of-resistance-an-interview-with-victoria-law.

30 Bryce Covert, "How the Rise of Women in Labor Could Save the Movement," *The Nation,* January 10, 2014. http://www.thenation.com/article/how-rise-women-labor-could-save-movement/.

31 "Minimum Wage Laws and Proposals for Major U.S. Cities," Raise the Minimum Wage, updated April 27, 2015, http://www.raisetheminimumwage.com/pages/minimum-wage-laws-and-proposals-for-major-u.s.-cities.

32 "State Minimum Wages/2015 Minimum Wage by State," *National Council of State Legislatures,* updated July 19, 2016, http://www.ncsl.org/research/labor-and-employment/state-minimum-wage-chart.aspx.

33 "Higher State Minimum Wages Promote Fair Pay for Women," *National Women's Law Center,* May 26, 2015, http://www.nwlc.org/resource/higher-state-minimum-wages-promote-fair-pay-women.

34 Julia Robins, "Aesthetic Activism," *Ms. Magazine,* Summer 2015, 12.

35 Sarah Jaffe, "Trickle-Down Feminism," *Dissent,* Winter 2013, http://www.dissentmagazine.org/article/trickle-down-feminism.

36 "Chicago Teachers Picket City Hall," *Liberation News,* July 2, 2015, http://www.liberationnews.org/chicago-teachers-picket-city-hall/.

37 "Seattle Strike Enters Fifth Day as Teachers Protest Testing Policies, Racial Inequity & Low Wages," *Democracy*

Now, September 16, 2015, http://www.democracynow.org/2015/9/15/seattle_strike_enters_fifth_day_as.

38 Jaffe, *Trickle-Down Feminism.*

39 Damayanmigrants.org.

40 http://www.votepsl.org/program.

41 Tina Vasquez, "It's Time to End the Long History of Feminism Failing Transgender Women," *Bitch,* February 17, 2014, https://bitchmedia.org/post/the-long-history-of-transgender-exclusion-from-feminism.

42 Brunell, *The Third Wave of Feminism.*

43 "Feminist Social Theory," *Social Theory re-wired,* accessed August 30, 2016, http://routledgesoc.com/profile/feminist-social-theory.

44 Lauren Rankin, "Not Everyone Who Has an Abortion Is a Woman — How to Frame the Abortion Rights Issue," *Truthout,* July 31, 2013, http://www.truth-out.org/op-ed/item/17888-not-everyone-who-has-an-abortion-is-a-woman-how-to-frame-the-abortion-rights-issue.

Chapter Eleven: What kind of movement for the Trump era?

1 Josh Barro, "95% Of Income Gains Since 2009 Went To The Top 1% — Here's What That Really Means," Businessinsider.com, September 12, 2013, http://www.businessinsider.com/95-of-income-gains-since-2009-went-to-the-top-1-heres-what-that-really-means-2013-9.

2 "United States of Trump? What's at stake? The fight back begins!" *Liberationnews.org,* November 11, 2016, https://www.liberationnews.org/united-states-of-trump-whats-at-stake-the-fight-back-begins/.

3 "Working Poor in America," *OXFAM America,* 2014, https://www.oxfamamerica.org/static/media/files/Working-Poor-in-America-report-Oxfam-America.pdf.

4 Robin Kelley, "Forum Response: After Trump," *Boston Review,* November 15, 2016, http://bostonreview.net/forum/after-trump/robin-d-g-kelley-trump-says-go-back-we-say-fight-back.

5 Juliana Britto Schwartz, "Why these two feminists aren't voting for Hillary," *Feministing* (blog), April 4, 2016, http://feministing.com/2016/04/06/why-these-two-feminists-arent-voting-for-hillary/.

6   Juliana Britto Schwartz, "President Trump," *Feministing* (blog), November 9, 2016, http://feministing.com/2016/11/09/president-trump/.

7   Patricia J. Williams, "You're Fired! The Holman Rule Returns…" *Madlawprofessor* (blog), January 27, 2017, https://madlawprofessor.wordpress.com.

8   Patricia Hill Collins, "Panel: What does the US election result say about misogyny?" *The Guardian*, November 9, 2016, https://www.theguardian.com/commentisfree/2016/nov/09/us-election-result-misogyny-america-panel-woman.

9   Frank Newport, "Americans Today Much More Accepting of a Woman, Black, Catholic, or Jew As President," *Gallup*, March 29, 1999, http://www.gallup.com/poll/3979/americans-today-much-more-accepting-woman-black-catholic.aspx.

10 Andrew Bacevich, "Tomgram: Andrew Bacevich, Pseudo-Election 2016," *Tomdispatch.com*, August 4, 2016, http://www.tomdispatch.com/post/176172/tomgram%3A_andrew_bacevich,_pseudo-election_2016/.

11 "The Frustrated Public: Views of the 2016 Campaign, the Parties, and the Electoral Process," The Associated Press-NORC Center for Public Affairs Research, May 15, 2016, http://www.apnorc.org/projects/Pages/HTML%20Reports/the-frustrated-public-americans-views-of-the-election-issue-brief.aspx.

12 Jill Stein, "Unite and Fight: Empathy, Appreciation, and a Call to Action," *Jill2016.com*, November 9, 2016, http://www.jill2016.com/resisttrump2.

13 Robert Fantina, "Socialist Presidential Candidate Gloria La Riva: 'We Live Under The Dictatorship Of Big Capital,' " *MintPress News*, August 12, 2016, http://www.mintpressnews.com/exclusive-interview-with-socialist-presidential-candidate-gloria-la-riva/219394/.

Appendices

1   Ann-Marie Imbornoni, "Women's Rights Movement in the U.S.: Timeline of Key Events in the American Women's Rights Movement 1980–Present," http://www.infoplease.com/spot/womenstimeline1.html; "Timeline of Feminism in the United States," https://en.wikipedia.org/wiki/Timeline_of_feminism_

in_the_United_States; Nancy MacLean, *"The American Women's Movement, 1945-2000: A Brief History with Documents"* (Boston, New York: Bedford/St. Martin's, 2009), 175-180.

2   Ira V. Brown, "'Am I Not a Woman and a Sister?' The Anti-Slavery Convention of American Women, 1837-1839," https://journals.psu.edu/phj/article/viewFile/24363/24132.

3   Ibid.

4   "Lucy Stone Quotes," http://womenshistory.about.com/od/quotes/fl/Lucy-Stone-Quotes.htm.

5   Carol Berkin, "Angelina and Sarah Grimke: Abolitionist Sisters," https://www.gilderlehrman.org/history-by-era/slavery-and-anti-slavery/essays/angelina-and-sarah-grimke-abolitionist-sisters,

6   "Angela Grimke Quotes," http://www.brainyquote.com/quotes/authors/a/angelina_grimke.html; Jone Johnson Lewis, "Angelina Grimke Quotes," http://womenshistory.about.com/cs/quotes/a/angelina_grimke.htm.

7   Angela Davis, *Women, Race and Class* (New York: Vintage Books, 1983), 144.

8   Davis, *Women, Race and Class*, 135-6.; Wanda A. Hendricks, Paulette Pennington Jones and Careda Rolland Taylor, "Ida Wells-Barnett Confronts Race and Gender Discrimination," accessed September 12, 2016, http://www.lib.niu.edu/1996/iht319630.html; Richard Wormser, "The Rise and Fall of Jim Crow," access September 12, 2016, http://www.pbs.org/wnet/jimcrow/stories_people_wells.html.

9   Davis, *Women, Race and Class,* 135-6.

10 Gerda Lerner, ed., *Black Women in White America: A Documentary History* (New York: Pantheon Books, 1972), 134-146.

11 http://historymatters.gmu.edu/d/5480/

12 Tony Pecinovsky, "Women's history: Elizabeth Gurley Flynn, the Rebel Girl," *Peoples World,* March 19, 2010, http://peoplesworld.org/women-s-history-elizabeth-gurley-flynn-the-rebel-girl/.

13 "Elizabeth Gurley Flynn: Statement at the Smith Act Trial. Delivered April 24 1952," http://www.americanrhetoric.com/speeches/elizabethgurleyflynn.htm.

14 http://joehill2015.org/joe-hill/joe-hill-songs/the-rebel-girl/.

15 "Mary Harris Jones Quotes," http://www.brainyquote.com/
quotes/quotes/m/maryharris232149.html.

16 MacLean, *The American Women's Movement*, 59-62; Barbara
Ransby, "Ella Taught Me: Shattering the Myth of the Leaderless
Movement," *Colorlines*, June 12, 2015, http://www.colorlines.
com/articles/ella-taught-me-shattering-myth-leaderless-
movement.

17 MacLean, *The American Women's Movement*, 58-59.

18 http://racialicious.tumblr.com/post/43158287342/we-are-
particularly-outraged-by-the-racist-and.

19 Jennifer Baumgardner and Amy Richards, "Manifesta: Young
Women Feminism and the Future," in *Women: Images and
Realities, A Multicultural Anthology*, ed. Suzanne Kelly, Gowri
Parameswaran and Nancy Schniedewind (New York: McGraw
Hill, 2012), 606-12.

20 Mark Toney, "Revisiting the National Welfare Rights
Organization," *Colorlines*, November 29, 2000, http://www.
colorlines.com/articles/revisiting-national-welfare-rights-
organization.

21 http://www.defendwomensrights.org/about-word.

22 Jonh Light, "Five Facts You Should Know About the Hyde
Amendment," January 25, 2013. http://billmoyers.com/
content/five-facts-you-should-know-about-the-hyde-
amendment/.

23 "Anti-Choice Violence and Intimidation." http://www.
prochoiceamerica.org/media/fact-sheets/ Click on "Anti-
Choice Violence and Intimidation," January 1, 2015; "Masked
Intruder Attacks Last Abortion Clinic Standing in Mississippi,"
Feminist, March 25, 2015, http://feminist.org/blog/index.
php/2015/03/25/masked-intruder-attacks-last-remaining-
mississippi-abortion-clinic/; Julie Turkewitz, and Jack
Healy, "3 Are Dead in Colorado Springs Shootout at Planned
Parenthood Center," *New York Times*, November 27, 2015,
http://www.nytimes.com/2015/11/28/us/colorado-planned-
parenthood-shooting.html.

24 Catherine Candisky, "House passes 'heartbeat bill' after
emotional debate," *Dispatch*, March 26, 2015, http://www.

dispatch.com/content/stories/local/2015/03/25/Ohio-House-heartbeat-abortion-bill.html.

25 Nadja Popovich,"The US is still the only developed country that doesn't guarantee paid maternity leave," *The Guardian,* December 3, 2014, http://www.theguardian.com/us-news/2014/dec/03/-sp-america-only-developed-country-paid-maternity-leave.

26 "World Conferences on Women," http://www.unwomen.org/en/how-we-work/intergovernmental-support/world-conferences-on-women; "The Four Global Women's Conferences 1975 - 1995: Historical Perspective," http://www.un.org/womenwatch/daw/followup/session/presskit/hist.htm.; MacLean, *The American Women's Movement,* 40, 167-9.

27 MacLean, *The American Women's Movement,* 1

28 Gloria Steinem, *My Life on the Road* (New York: Random House, 2015), 54-58.

29 "1977 National Women's Conference," https://en.wikipedia.org/wiki/National_Women%27s_Conference; "Sisters of '77," http://www.pbs.org/independentlens/sistersof77/conference.html.; Steinem, *My Life on the Road.*

30 https://www.goodreads.com/author/quotes/144748.Vandana_Shiva

31 Gloria La Riva, "Gloria La Riva at Climate March in Oakland, Ca.," *Liberation News,* December 5, 2015, video, http://www.liberationnews.org/video-gloria-la-riva-at-climate-march-oakland-2015/.

32 "Marching though Hollywood: Planet and People Over Profits!" *Liberation News,* September 16, 2015, http://www.liberationnews.org/marching-hollywood-planet-people-profits/.

Bibliography

BOOKS

Ballan, Dorothy. *Feminism and Marxism*, New York: World View Publishers, 1978.

Baxandall, Rosalyn and Linda Gordon, Eds. *Dear Sisters: Dispatches from the Women's Liberation Movement*, New York: Basic Books, 2000.

Basu, Amrita, Ed. *The Challenge of Local Feminisms: Women's Movements in Global Perspective*, Boulder: Westview Press, 1995.

Bennett, Judith M. *History Matters: Patriarchy and the Challenge of Feminism*, Philadelphia: University of Pennsylvania Press, 2006.

Cobble, Dorothy Sue. *The Other Women's Movement: Workplace Justice and Social Rights in Modern America*, Princeton: Princeton University Press. 2004

Cobble, Dorothy Sue, Linda Gordon and Astrid Henry. *Feminism Unfinished: A Short, Surprising History of American Women's Movements*, New York: Liveright Publishing Corp. 2014.

Crittenden, Ann. *The Price of Motherhood: Why the Most Important Job in the World is Still the Least Valued*, New York, Henry Hold & Co., 2001.

Cutter, Jane. *Women's Oppression*. Unpublished manuscript. 2014

Davis, Angela. *Women, Race and Class*, New York: Vintage Books, 1983.

Eisenstein, Zillah R., Ed. *Capitalist Patriarchy and the Case for Socialist Feminism*, New York: Monthly Review Press, 1979.

Flexner, Eleanor. *A Century of Struggle*, Cambridge: The Belknap Press of Harvard University Press., 1975.

Friedan, Betty. *The Feminine Mystique*, New York: W.W. Norton and Company, Inc., 1963.

Fuller, Margaret. *Woman in the Nineteenth Century*, New York: The Norton Library, W.W. Norton & Co., 1971.

James, Stalie M. and Abena P.A. Busia, Ed. *Theorizing Black Feminisms: The Visionary Pragmatism of Black Women*, London and New York: Routledge, 1993.

Kelly, Suzanne, Gowri Parameswaran and Nancy Schniedewind, Eds. *Women: Images and Realities, A Multicultural Anthology*, New York: McGraw Hill, 2012.

Lerner, Gerda, Ed. *Black Women in White America: A Documentary History*, New York: Pantheon Books, 1972.

MacLean, Nancy. *The American Women's Movement, 1945-2000: A Brief History with Documents*, Boston, New York: Bedford/St. Martin's, 2009.

Nicholson, Linda, Ed. *The Second Wave: A Reader in Feminist Theory*, New York and London: Routledge, 1997.

Smith, Barbara, Ed. *Home Girls: A Black Feminist Anthology*. Kitchen Table: Women of Color Press, 1983.

Solinger, Rickie, Ed. *Abortion Wars: A Half Century of Struggle*, 1950-2000, Berkeley: University of California Press, 1998.

Stansell, Christine. *The Feminist Promise: 1792 to the Present*, New York: The Modern Library, 2010.

Steinem, Gloria. *My Life on the Road*. New York: Random House, 2015.

Sunstein, Emily. *A Different Face: The Life of Mary Wollstonecraft*, New York, Harper & Row, 1975.

Weigand, Kate. *Red Feminism*, Baltimore: The Johns Hopkins University Press, 2001.

Zack, Naomi. *Inclusive Feminism: A Third Wave Theory of Women's Commonality*, Lanham, MD: Rowman & Littlefield Publishers, Inc., 2005.

Zinn, Howard. *A People's History of the United States*, New York, Harper Colophon, 1980.

ESSAYS, ARTICLES

"20 Facts About U.S. Inequality that Everyone Should Know." http://web.stanford.edu/group/scspi/cgi-bin/facts.php .

"20 Years in Prison for Miscarrying? The Case of Purvi Patel & the Criminalization of Pregnancy." April 2, 2015. http://www.democracynow.org/2015/4/2/20_years_in_prison_for_miscarrying .

"35% of Puerto Rican Women Sterilized." https://www.uic.edu/orgs/cwluherstory/CWLUArchive/puertorico.html .

"A Guide to Women's Equal Pay Rights." https://www.dol.gov/equalpay/equalpay-employee.pdf .

"A History of Key Abortion Rulings of the U.S. Supreme Court." January 16, 2013. http://www.pewforum.org/2013/01/16/a-history-of-key-abortion-rulings-of-the-us-supreme-court/.

"A History of Women in Industry." https://www.nwhm.org/online-exhibits/industry/womenindustry_intro.html.

"Abortion Surveillance — United States, 2009." Centers for Disease Control and Prevention, November 23, 2012. http://www.cdc.gov/mmwr/preview/mmwrhtml/ss6108a1.htm .

Adewunmi, Bim: "Kimberlé Crenshaw on Intersectionality: 'I wanted to come up with an everyday metaphor that anyone could use.'" *New Statesman*, April 2014. http://www.newstatesman.com/lifestyle/2014/04/kimberl-crenshaw-intersectionality-i-wanted-come-everyday-metaphor-anyone-could.

"African American Women in Defense of Ourselves." https://www.tumblr.com/search/African + American + Women + In + Defense + of + Ourselves .

"Aid to Dependent Children: The Legal History." The Social Welfare History Project. http://www.socialwelfarehistory.com/programs/aid-to-dependent-children-the-legal-history/ .

"Alice Paul Quotes." http://www.brainyquote.com/quotes/authors/a/alice_paul.html.

"All-China Women's Federation." http://en.wikipedia.org/wiki/All-China_Women%27s_Federation.

"American Women: Report of the President's Commission on the Status of Women, 1963." http://www.dol.gov/wb/American%20Women%20Report.pdf ()

Anderson, Stacey. "Feminism at the Apollo: Women of the World Festival Debuts Stateside." http://www.newsweek.com/women-world-festival-comes-harlem-340843 .

"Angela Grimke Quotes." http://www.brainyquote.com/quotes/authors/a/angelina_grimke.html.

"Anti-Choice Violence and Intimidation." http://www.prochoiceamerica.org/media/fact-sheets/ Click on "Anti-Choice Violence and Intimidation." January 1, 2015.

"Appeals Court Rules Abortion Ban Past 12 Weeks Unconstitutional."
    May 28, 2015. http://feminist.org/blog/index.php/2015/05/28/
    appeals-court-rules-abortion-ban-past-12-weeks-unconstitutional/.

"Army Nurse Corps in World War II." http://www.history.army.mil/
    books/wwii/72-14/72-14.htm .

Aronowitz, Nona Willis. "Raising the Baby Question." http://www.
    thenation.com/article/raising-baby-question May 25, 2009.

"As Study Finds 4,000 Lynchings in Jim Crow South, Will
    U.S. Address Legacy of Racial Terrorism?" February
    11, 2015. http://www.democracynow.org/2015/2/11/
    as_study_finds_4_000_lynchings.

"Atlanta's Washerwomen Strike." http://www.aflcio.org/Issues/
    Civil-and-Workplace-Rights/Working-Women/Working-Women-
    in-Union-History/Atlanta-s-Washerwomen-Strike .

"Background Information on Sexual Violence used as a Tool of
    War." http://www.un.org/en/preventgenocide/rwanda/about/
    bgsexualviolence.shtml .

Baggett, Ashley. "It's Her Fault; It's Feminists' Fault: The Tie
    Between Victim Blaming and Scapegoating Feminists." July 21,
    2012. http://nursingclio.org/2012/07/21/its-her-fault-its-feminists-
    fault-the-tie-between-victim-blaming-and-scapegoating-feminists/.

Baldwin, Katherine. "Canada Best G20 Country to be a Woman,
    India Worst." http://in.reuters.com/article/2012/06/13/g20-
    women-idINDEE85C00420120613 .

Bassett, Laura. " Lindsey Graham Reintroduces 20-Week Abortion
    Ban: 'I Am Dying For That Debate'" June 11, 2015. http://
    www.huffingtonpost.com/2015/06/11/lindsey-graham-
    abortion_n_7561410.html .

Bassett, Laura. "Ruth Bader Ginsburg Writes
    Scathing 35-Page Dissent In Birth Control Case."
    June 30, 2014. http://www.huffingtonpost.
    com/2014/06/30/ruth-bader-ginsburg-write_n_5544111.
    html?ncid = fcbklnkushpmg00000046&ir = Women.

Baumgardner, Jennifer and Amy Richards. "Manifesta: Young Women
    Feminism and the Future." *Women, Images and Realities*. 606-12.

Beal, Frances M. "Black Women's Manifesto; Double Jeopardy: To
    Be Black and Female." 1969. http://www.hartford-hwp.com/
    archives/45a/196.html.

Bendery, Jennifer. "Senate Passes Human Trafficking Bill with Abortion Restrictions on Victims." April 22, 2015. http://www.huffingtonpost.com/2015/04/22/sex-trafficking-bill-abortion_n_7120028.html .

Berkin, Carol. "Angelina and Sarah Grimke: Abolitionist Sisters." https://www.gilderlehrman.org/history-by-era/slavery-and-anti-slavery/essays/angelina-and-sarah-grimke-abolitionist-sisters .

Bilger, Audrey. "Inside and Out." *Ms Magazine*, Summer 2015. 20.

"Black Girls Matter: Pushed Out, Overpoliced, and Underprotected." http://static1.squarespace.com/static/53f20d90e4b0b80451158d8c/t/54dcc1ece4b001c03e323448/1423753708557/AAPF_BlackGirlsMatterReport.pdf .

"Black Youth-Organized Millions March NYC Draws Tens of Thousands in Movement's Biggest Protest Yet." http://www.democracynow.org/2014/12/15/black_youth_organized_millions_march_nyc .

Blow, Charles M. "Jeb Bush and Single Mothers." June 15, 2015. http://www.nytimes.com/2015/06/15/opinion/charles-blow-jeb-bush-and-single-mothers.html?partner = rssnyt&emc = rss&_r = 1 .

Boonstra, Heather D. and Elizabeth Nash. "A Surge of State Abortion Restrictions Puts Providers—and the Women They Serve—in the Crosshairs." *Guttmacher Policy Review,* Winter 2014, Volume 17, #1. http://www.guttmacher.org/pubs/gpr/17/1/gpr170109.html.

Brenner, Mark and Stephanie Luce. "Women and Class: What Has Happened in Forty Years?" July-August 2006. http://monthlyreview.org/2006/07/01/women-and-class-what-has-happened-in-forty-years/ .

Brewer, Pat. "Feminism and Socialism: Putting the Pieces Together, Preface." 14th National Conference of the Democratic Socialist Party, Australia, January 1992.

Brewer, Pat. Introduction to *Engels: The Origin of the Family, Private Property and the State.* 2004. http://readingfromtheleft.com/PDF/EngelsOrigin.pdf .

Brodsky, Alexandra. "Roundup: Essential Feminist Writing on the Isla Vista Shooting." http://feministing.com/2014/05/27/essential-feminist-writing-on-the-isla-vista-shooting/ .

Brown, Ira V. "'Am I Not a Woman and a Sister?' The Anti-Slavery Convention of American Women, 1837-1839." https://journals. psu.edu/phj/article/viewFile/24363/24132 .

Brown, Joseph Paul. "The Dignity of Living: The U.S.'s Home Care Aides. June 20, 2015. http://www.truth-out.org/news/ item/31439-the-dignity-of-living-america-s-home-care-aides .

Brunell, Laura. "The Third Wave of Feminism." http://www. britannica.com/topic/feminism/The-third-wave-of-feminism .

Bryan, Dan. "The Great (Farm) Depression of the 1920s." March 6, 2012. http://www.americanhistoryusa.com/ great-farm-depression-1920s/.

Buckley, Mary. "Women in the Soviet Union." *Feminist Review* 1981. http://www.palgrave-journals.com/fr/journal/v8/n1/full/ fr198113a.html .

Bufkin, Sarah. " Domestic Workers Bill Killed in California by Jerry Brown Veto." http://www.domesticworkersunited.org/index.php/ en/pressroom/dwu-in-the-news/item/112-domestic-workers-bill-killed-in-california-by-jerry-brown-veto .

Burnham, Linda. "Feminism Almost Always Needs a Modifier." May 28, 2014. http://meetinggroundonline.org/feminism-almost-always-needs-a-modifier/ .

Burkett, Elinor. "What Makes a Woman?" June 6, 2015. http://www. nytimes.com/2015/06/07/opinion/sunday/what-makes-a-woman. html?_r = 1.

Burroughs, Gaylynn and Debra S. Katz. "Won't Back Down." *Ms Magazine*, Summer 2015, 24-29.

Calvert, Mary F. "Photos: Women Who Risked Everything to Expose Sexual Assault in the Military." Sept. 8, 2014 http://www. motherjones.com/politics/2014/09/sexual-violence-american-military-photos .

"Cancer Patient Married to Undocumented Man Among 100 Women Who Marched 100 Miles to See Pope." http://www. democracynow.org/2015/9/23/cancer_patient_married_to_ undocumented_man .

Candisky, Catherine. "House passes 'heartbeat bill' after emotional debate." March 26, 2015. http://www.dispatch.com/content/ stories/local/2015/03/25/Ohio-House-heartbeat-abortion-bill.html .

Catalano, Shannan. "Intimate Partner Violence, 1993–2010."
November, 2012. http://www.bjs.gov/content/pub/pdf/ipv9310.pdf.

Chemaly, Soraya. "50 Facts About Domestic Violence." November
30, 2013. http://www.huffingtonpost.com/soraya-chemaly/50-
actual-facts-about-dom_b_2193904.html .

Chen, Michelle. "The War on Planned Parenthood Is Also an
Assault on Poor Women of Color." August 3, 2015. http://www.
thenation.com/article/the-war-on-planned-parenthood-is-also-an-
assault-on-poor-women-of-color/.

Chen, Michelle. "What Fast-Food Workers Are Fighting For." June
17, 2015. http://www.thenation.com/blog/210105/what-low-
wage-workers-are-fighting# .

"Chicago Teachers Picket City Hall." July 2, 2015.
http://www.liberationnews.org/chicago-teachers-
picket-city-hall/?utm_source = facebook&utm_
medium = shared_article&utm_campaign = Liberation %20
News.

Chittal, Nisha. "How social media is changing the feminist
movement." 04/06/15. http://www.msnbc.com/msnbc/
how-social-media-changing-the-feminist-movement.

Cobble, Dorothy Sue. "More than Sex Equality." In Cobble, Dorothy
Sue, Linda Gordon and Astrid Henry. *Feminism Unfinished: A
Short, Surprising History of American Women's Movements,* New
York: Liveright Publishing Corp. 2014, pp. 1-67.

Cohen, Patricia. "Public-Sector Jobs Vanish, Hitting Blacks Hard."
May 25, 2015. http://www.nytimes.com/2015/05/25/business/
public-sector-jobs-vanish-and-blacks-take-blow.html?hp&ac
tion = click&pgtype = Homepage&module = second-column-
region&region = top-news&WT.nav = top-news&_r = 1.

Collins, Gail. "The Fight for Unplanned Parenthood."
September 18, 2015. http://www.nytimes.com/2015/09/19/
opinion/gail-collins-the-fight-for-unplanned-parenthood.
html?partner = rssnyt&emc = rss.

"Combahee River Collective (1974-1980)." http://www.blackpast.
org/aah/combahee-river-collective-1974-1980.

"The Combahee River Collective: A Black Feminist Statement."
In Eisenstein, Zillah R., Ed. *Capitalist Patriarchy and the Case*

for Socialist Feminism, New York: Monthly Review Press, 1979: 362-372.

Commission on the Status of Women 2013. http://www.unwomen. org/en/news/in-focus/csw57-stop-violence-against-women .

Cooper, David, Mary Gable and Algernon Austin. "The public-sector jobs crisis: Women and African Americans hit hardest by job losses in state and local governments." Economic Policy Institute, May 2, 2012 http://www.epi.org/publication/bp339-public-sector-jobs-crisis/.

Covert, Bryce. "How the Rise of Women in Labor Could Save the Movement." January 10, 2014. http://www.thenation.com/article/how-rise-women-labor-could-save-movement/ .

Covert, Bryce. "Putting a Price Tag on Unpaid Housework." http://www.forbes.com/sites/brycecovert/2012/05/30/putting-a-price-tag-on-unpaid-housework/.

Craig, Kim. "100 serial rapists identified after rape kits from Detroit Crime Lab are finally processed." http://www.wxyz.com/news/100-serial-rapists-identified-after-rape-kits-from-detroit-crime-lab-are-finally-processed .

Crenshaw, Kimberle. "Mapping the Margins: Intersectionality, Identity Politics, and Violence against Women of Color" *Stanford Law Review* Vol. 43, No. 6 (July 1991), pp. 1241-1299. http://www.jstor.org/discover/10.2307/1229039?uid = 3739832&uid = 21 34&uid = 2487529363&uid = 2&uid = 70&uid = 3&uid = 2487529353 &uid = 3739256&uid = 60&sid = 21105409916483 .

"Cuban same-sex couples 'wed' in march for LGBT rights led by Castro's daughter." May 9, 2015. http://www.theguardian.com/world/2015/may/09/cuba-gay-marriage-lgbt-mariela-castro .

Culp-Ressler, Tara. " The U.S. Is One Of The Only Countries In The World Where Maternal Deaths Are Rising." May 6, 2014. http://thinkprogress.org/health/2014/05/06/3434509/us-maternal-mortality/.

Dalven, Jennifer. "Ohio Just Defeated an Extreme Abortion Ban, but Don't Get Too Comfortable." December 14, 2014. https://www.aclu.org/blog/speakeasy/ohio-just-defeated-extreme-abortion-ban-dont-get-too-comfortable?redirect = blog/reproductive-freedom-womens-rights/ohio-just-defeated-extreme-abortion-ban-dont-get-too-comfort.

"Daughters of Bilitis." https://en.wikipedia.org/wiki/ Daughters_of_Bilitis.

"Deadly Delivery: The Maternal Health Care Crisis in the USA." May 7, 2011. http://www.amnestyusa.org/research/reports/ deadly-delivery-the-maternal-health-care-crisis-in-the-usa.

"Declaration of Sentiments and Resolutions, Woman's Rights Convention, Held at Seneca Falls, 19-10 July 1848." http:// ecssba.rutgers.edu/docs/seneca.html .

Define, Michael Sullivan. "A History of Governmentally Coerced Sterilization: The Plight of the Native American Woman." https://files.zotero.net/20220314746/A%20History%20of%20 Governmentally%20Coerced%20Sterilization%20The%20 Plight%20of%20the%20Native%20American%20Woman%20 By%20Michael%20Sullivan%20DeFine.pdf .

DePaulo, Bella. "7 Stunning Ways Life Was Different in the 1960s." Sept. 6, 2014. https://www.psychologytoday.com/blog/living-single/201409/7-stunning-ways-life-was-different-in-the-1960s .

Deprez, Esme E. "The Vanishing U.S. Abortion Clinic." January 7, 2015. http://www.bloombergview.com/quicktake/abortion-and-the-decline-of-clinics .

"Detroit Maternal Death Rate is triple the U.S. Average." July 21, 2014. https://feminist.org/blog/index.php/2014/07/21/why-detroits-maternal-death-rate-is-three-times-higher-than-the-us-average/.

"Domestic Violence Survivors Justice Act." http://dvsja.org .

Doyle, Sady. "Abortion Isn't a Necessary Evil. It's Great." *In These Times*, October 3, 2014. http://inthesetimes.com/article/17216/ abortion_isnt_necessary_evil_its_great_pro_choice.

Dreier, Peter. " What We Can Learn From Ella Baker In A Post-Ferguson Era." December 26, 2014. http://talkingpointsmemo. com/cafe/ella-baker-in-a-ferguson-era .

Dreweke, Joerg. " Contraception Is Not Abortion: The Strategic Campaign of Antiabortion Groups to Persuade the Public Otherwise." *Guttmacher Policy Review* Fall 2014, Volume 17, Number 4. http://www.guttmacher.org/pubs/gpr/17/4/ gpr170414.html .

Ehrenreich, Barbara. "Maid to Order." http://harpers.org/ archive/2000/04/maid-to-order/. April, 2000.

Ehrenreich, Barbara. "What is Socialist Feminism?" https://www.marxists.org/subject/women/authors/ehrenreich-barbara/socialist-feminism.htm 1976.

Eichner, Alana and Katherine Gallagher Robbins. "National Snapshot: Poverty among Women & Families, 2014." http://www.nwlc.org/sites/default/files/pdfs/povertysnapshot2014.pdf .

Elia, Nada. "Ending Zionism is a feminist issue." July 24, 2014. http://electronicintifada.net/content/ending-zionism-feminist-issue/13631 .

"Elizabeth Cady Stanton Quotes." http://womenshistory.about.com/cs/quotes/a/ec_stanton.htm .

"Elizabeth Gurley Flynn (1890-1964)." http://laborquotes.weebly.com/f-g.html

"Elizabeth Gurley Flynn: Statement at the Smith Act Trial. Delivered April 24 1952." http://www.americanrhetoric.com/speeches/elizabethgurleyflynn.htm.

Ensler, Eve. "I Never Defined a Woman as a Person With a Vagina" http://time.com/3672912/eve-ensler-vagina-monologues-mount-holyoke-college/ .

Epstein, Barbara. "What Happened to the Women's Movement?" *Monthly Review*, Volume 53, Number 1. May 2001. http://monthlyreview.org/2001/05/01/what-happened-to-the-womens-movement/ .

"The Equal Pay Act of 1963." http://www.eeoc.gov/laws/statutes/epa.cfm.

"Equal Pay and the Wage Gap." http://www.nwlc.org/our-issues/employment/equal-pay-and-the-wage-gap

"The Face of Women's Health: Helen Rodriguez-Trias." http://www.ncbi.nlm.nih.gov/pmc/articles/PMC1447119/.

"Facts about Violence." http://www.feminist.com/antiviolence/facts.html .

"Facts and Figures: Ending Violence against Women: A pandemic in diverse forms." October 2014. http://www.unwomen.org/en/what-we-do/ending-violence-against-women/facts-and-figures .

"Fact Sheet: Induced Abortion in the United States, July 2014." http://www.guttmacher.org/pubs/fb_induced_abortion.html#1a.

Faludi, Susan. "American Electra: Feminism's Ritual Matricide."
October 2010. http://harpers.org/archive/2010/10/
american-electra/.

"Femicide in Latin America." April 4, 2013. http://www.unwomen.
org/en/news/stories/2013/4/femicide-in-latin-america#edn2 .

Feminist Newswire. "Breaking: House Votes to Defund
Planned Parenthood." September 18, 2015. http://
feminist.org/blog/index.php/2015/09/18/
breaking-house-votes-to-defund-planned-parenthood/.

"Feminist Social Theory." http://routledgesoc.com/profile/feminist-
social-theory .

Ferro, Shane. "More work and less play for women
around the world." March 12, 2014. http://
blogs.reuters.com/equals/2014/03/12/
more-work-and-less-play-for-women-around-the-world/.

Fisher, J.A. "A Brief Look at Third-Wave Feminism." May 16,
2013. https://beingfeministblog.wordpress.com/2013/05/16/
todays-feminism-a-brief-look-at-third-wave-feminism/.

"The Four Global Women's Conferences 1975 - 1995: Historical
Perspective." http://www.un.org/womenwatch/daw/followup/
session/presskit/hist.htm.

"Frances Harper." http://en.wikipedia.org/wiki/Frances_Harper

Frost, Jennifer and Kinsey Hasstedt. "Quantifying Planned
Parenthood's Critical Role In Meeting The Need For
Publicly Supported Contraceptive Care." September
8, 2015. http://healthaffairs.org/blog/2015/09/08/
quantifying-planned-parenthoods-critical-role-in-meeting-
the-need-for-publicly-supported-contraceptive-care/?utm_
source = Master + List&utm_campaign = 9bca0f7c13-
NIC_HAB_Kinsey_PP9_8_15&utm_medium = email&utm_
term = 0_9ac83dc920-9bca0f7c13-257239617 .

Fuentes, Sonia Pressman. "The Women's Rights Movement:
Where It's Been, Where It's At." http://userpages.umbc.
edu/ ~ korenman/wmst/womens_rights.html .

Fulton, Deirdre. "Beyond Abortion and Equal Pay: Survey Highlights
Wide Scope of Women's Issues." August 26, 2015. http://www.
commondreams.org/news/2015/08/26/beyond-abortion-and-
equal-pay-survey-highlights-wide-scope-womens-issues .

Garcia, Saudi. "8 Shocking Facts About Sterilization in U.S. History." http://mic.com/articles/53723/8-shocking-facts-about-sterilization-in-u-s-history. July 10, 2013.

"Gender Equality and the Role of Women in Cuban Society." February 2011. http://www.aauw.org.

"Gender Equality and Women's Rights in the Post-2015 Agenda: A foundation for sustainable development." http://www.oecd.org/dac/POST-2015%20Gender.pdf.

"Gerda Lerner, Interviewed by Nancy MacLean." Voices of Feminism Oral History Project, September 12–13, 2003 Madison, Wisconsin, Sophia Smith Collection, Smith College Northampton, MA. http://www.smith.edu/libraries/libs/ssc/vof/transcripts/Lerner.pdf .

"Global, regional, and national levels and causes of maternal mortality during 1990–2013: a systematic analysis for the Global Burden of Disease Study 2013." September 13, 2014. http://www.thelancet.com/journals/lancet/article/PIIS0140-6736(14)60696-6/fulltext .

Goel, Taylor. "Communist Party, Turkey runs 550-woman ticket in elections." Apr 22, 2015. http://www.liberationnews.org/all-550-candidates-of-the-communist-party-turkey-for-the-upcoming-elections-are-women/.

Gold, Rachel Benson. "Lessons from Before Roe: Will Past be Prologue?" *The Guttmacher Report on Public Policy*. March 2003, Volume 6, Number 1. https://www.guttmacher.org/pubs/tgr/06/1/gr060108.html#box .

Goldberg, Michelle. "Feminism's Toxic Twitter Wars." *The Nation*. February 17, 2014. pp. 12-17.

Gonzalez-Rojas, Jessica and Taja Lindley. "Latinas and Sterilization in the United States." *Women's Health Activist Newsletter*, May/June 2008. https://nwhn.org/latinas-and-sterilization-united-states.

Gordon, Linda. "The Women's Liberation Movement." In Cobble et al, 2014, pp.69-145.

Gordy, Cynthia. "Who is Peta Lindsay?" February 15, 2012. http://www.theroot.com/articles/politics/2012/02/who_is_peta_lindsay_meet_the_black_woman_running_for_president.html?page=0,0 .

Greenhouse, Linda. "Abortion at the Supreme Court's Door."
October 15, 2015. http://www.nytimes.com/column/
linda-greenhouse.

"Guttmacher Statistic on Catholic Women's Contraceptive Use."
February 15, 2012. http://www.guttmacher.org/media/
inthenews/2012/02/15/.

"Harriet Tubman." http://en.wikipedia.org/wiki/Harriet_Tubman.

Harvey, Sheridan. "Marching for the Vote: Remembering the Woman
Suffrage Parade of 1913." http://memory.loc.gov/ammem/
awhhtml/aw01e/aw01e.html#ack .

Hayden, Casey and Mary King. "Sex and Caste: A Kind of Memo."
1965. https://www.uic.edu/orgs/cwluherstory/CWLUArchive/
memo.html .

Hellerstein, Erica. "Inside The Highly Sophisticated Group
That's Quietly Making It Much Harder To Get An Abortion."
Think Progress, December 2, 2014. http://thinkprogress.
org/health/2014/12/02/3597770/americans-united-life-
abortion/?elq = ~ ~ eloqua..type--emailfield..syntax--recipientid ~
~ &elqCampaignId = ~ ~ eloqua..type--campaign..campaignid--0..
fieldname--id ~ ~ .

Henderson, Alex. "America's 10 worst terror attacks by Christian
fundamentalists and far-right extremists." January 11, 2015.
http://www.rawstory.com/rs/2015/01/americas-10-worst-terror-
attacks-by-christian-fundamentalist-and-far-right-extremists/ .

Hendricks, Wanda A., Paulette Pennington Jones, and Careda
Rolland Taylor. "Ida Wells-Barnett Confronts Race and Gender
Discrimination." http://www.lib.niu.edu/1996/iht319630.html

Henry, Astrid. "From a Mindset to a Movement." In Cobble et al,
147-225.

Herman, Juliana, Sasha Post and Scott O'Halloran. " The United
States Is Far Behind Other Countries on Pre-K." May 2,
2013. https://www.americanprogress.org/issues/education/
report/2013/05/02/62054/the-united-states-is-far-behind-other-
countries-on-pre-k/ .

Hess, Amanda. "Why Women Aren't Welcome on the Internet."
January 6, 2014. http://www.psmag.com/health-and-behavior/
women-arent-welcome-internet-72170

"Higher State Minimum Wages Promote Fair Pay
    for Women." http://www.nwlc.org/resource/
    higher-state-minimum-wages-promote-fair-pay-women
"How Did Women Peace Activists Respond to Red Scare Attacks
    during the 1920s?" http://womhist.alexanderstreet.com/wilpf/
    intro.htm .
"How to Defang a Movement: Replacing the Political with the
    Personal." 2014. http://meetinggroundonline.org/how-to-defang-
    a-movement-replacing-the-political-with-the-personal/
Hrizi, Nathalie. "Parental Leave a Fantasy in the U.S., and
    Only 3 Other Countries." September 22, 2015. : http://
    www.liberationnews.org/parental-leave-a-fantasy-in-the-u-
    s-and-only-3-other-countries/?utm_source = facebook&utm_
    medium = shared_article&utm_campaign = Liberation%20
    News.
Hutchinson, Sikivu. "Police Criminals and the Brutalization of Black
    Girls." June 9, 2015. http://www.thefeministwire.com/2015/06/
    police-criminals-and-the-brutalization-of-black-girls/ .
"Ida B. Wells Quotes." http://www.inspirationalstories.com/
    quotes/t/ida-b-wells/.
"IHS Expands Plan B Access for Native American
    Women." Feminist Newswire, September 23, 2013.
    http://feminist.org/blog/index.php/2013/09/23/
    ihs-expands-plan-b-access-for-native-american-women/
Imbornoni, Ann-Marie. "Women's Rights Movement in the U.S.:
    Timeline of Key Events in the American Women's Rights
    Movement 1980–Present." http://www.infoplease.com/spot/
    womenstimeline1.html
Ingraham, Christopher. "Our infant mortality rate is a national
    embarrassment." September 29, 2014. http://www.
    washingtonpost.com/blogs/wonkblog/wp/2014/09/29/
    our-infant-mortality-rate-is-a-national-embarrassment/
"Institute on World War II/ African American." http://ww2.fsu.edu/
    African-American.
"Interview with Mariela Castro." http://www.walterlippmann.com/
    docs2294.html.
Jacobs, Andrew. "Taking Feminist Battle to China's Streets,
    and Landing in Jail." April 5, 2015. http://www.nytimes.

com/2015/04/06/world/asia/chinese-womens-rights-activists-fall-afoul-of-officials.html .

Jaffe, Sarah. "Trickle-Down Feminism." *Dissent*, Winter 2013. http://www.dissentmagazine.org/article/trickle-down-feminism .

Jervis, Lisa. "The End of Feminism's Third Wave." Winter 2004. http://www.msmagazine.com/winter2004/thirdwave.asp.

Jones, Ann. "Men Who Kick Down Doors: Tyrants Home & Abroad." March 21, 2013. http://www.tomdispatch.com/post/175663/tomgram%3A_ann_jones,_the_war_against_women/

Jones, Sarah. "Crisis of Faith: Religious Facilities Rely On Misleading Tactics, Dupe Women." Sept. 19, 2014. https://www.au.org/blogs/wall-of-separation/crisis-of-faith-religious-facilities-rely-on-misleading-tactics-dupe-women .

"Justice Dept.: Violence against women fell 64% over decade." http://www.cbsnews.com/news/justice-dept-violence-against-women-fell-64-over-decade/ .

Keith, Lierre and Derrick Jensen. "The Emperor's New Penis." June 21, 2013. http://www.counterpunch.org/2013/06/21/55123/

Kesselman, Amy. "Women vs. Connecticut." In Solinger, *Abortion Wars*, p.43.

Kessler-Harris, Alice. "What Happened to Second Wave Feminism?" Roundtable of American Historical Association. January 4, 2015. https://www.youtube.com/watch?v = cCnLktyNq18 .

Kliff, Sarah. "9 facts about violence against women everyone should know9 facts about violence against women everyone should know." Sept. 16, 2014. http://www.vox.com/2014/5/25/5748610/eight-facts-about-violence-against-women-everyone-should-know .

Kime, Patricia. "Incidents of rape in military much higher than previously reported." December 5, 2014. http://www.militarytimes.com/story/military/pentagon/2014/12/04/pentagon-rand-sexual-assault-reports/19883155/.

Kingkade, Tyler. "Sexual Assault Statistics Can Be Confusing, But They're Not The Point." 12/15/14. http://www.huffingtonpost.com/2014/12/15/sexual-assault-statistics_n_6316802.html .

Krogstad, Jens Manuel. "5 Facts about the Modern American Family." April 30, 2014. http://www.pewresearch.org/fact-tank/2014/04/30/5-facts-about-the-modern-american-family/ .

Kugler, Sara. "When You Remember the March on Washington, Remember Anna Hedgeman. http://cooperproject.org/march-on-washington-remember-anna-hedgeman/ August 21, 2013.

"Labour force participation rate by sex, 15 + ,15-64 and 15-24 years old." http://www.oecd.org/gender/data/labourforceparticipation bysex15and15-24yearsold.htm

Law, Victoria. "FreeHer: Formerly Incarcerated Women Demand an End to Mass Incarceration" June 26, 2014. http://www.truth-out.org/news/item/24605-freeher-formerly-incarcerated-women-demand-an-end-to-mass-incarceration.

Lawrence, Jane. "The Indian Health Service and the Sterilization of Native American Women." http://muse.jhu.edu/login?auth = 0&type = summary&url = /journals/american_indian_quarterly/v024/24.3lawrence.html .

Leacock, Eleanor. "Introduction to *Origin of the Family, Private Property and the State,* by Frederick Engels http://www.marxistschool.org/classdocs/LeacockIntro.pdf.

"Length of maternity, paternity and parental leave." http://www.oecd.org/gender/data/lengthofmaternitypaternityparentalleave.htm .

Lerner, Sharon. "The Real War on Families: Why the U.S. Needs Paid Leave Now." August 18, 2015. http://inthesetimes.com/article/18151/the-real-war-on-families.

"Letter from Gerda Lerner [to Betty Friedan]" 1963. http://schlesingerlibrary.omeka.net/items/show/55

"Letter of 200 Concerned Black Men Calling for the Inclusion of Women and Girls in 'My Brother's Keeper.'" May 28, 2014. http://www.aapf.org/recent/2014/05/an-open-letter-to-president-obama

Lewis, Jone Johnson. "Angelina Grimke Quotes." http://womenshistory.about.com/cs/quotes/a/angelina_grimke.htm .

Lewis, Sybill. "The Homefront: America During World War II." http://ic.galegroup.com/ic/uhic/PrimarySourcesDetailsPage/PrimarySourcesDetailsWindow?failOverType = &query = &proId = UHIC&windowstate = normal&contentModules = &display-query = &mode = view&displayGroupName = PrimarySources&limiter = &currPage = &disableHighlighting = false&displayGroups = &sortBy = &search_within_results = &p = UHIC&action = e&catId = &activityType = &scanId = &documentId = -

GALE%7CCX3428500080&source = Bookmark&u = silv39674&-jsid = bd0f553de554352e7fbb86fb31ab2941 .

"LGBT Workers and the Minimum Wage." http://civilrightsdocs. info/pdf/minimumwage/lgbt-minimum-wage.pdf .

Li, Yuhui (2000). "Women's Movement and Change of Women's Status in China." Journal of International Women's Studies, 1(1), 30-40. http://vc.bridgew.edu/jiws/vol1/iss1/3 .

Light, John. "Five Facts You Should Know About the Hyde Amendment." January 25, 2013. http://billmoyers.com/content/five-facts-you-should-know-about-the-hyde-amendment/ .

Lin, Joanne. "End Near for Shackling of Pregnant Women" 1/21/2014. https://www.aclu.org/blog/immigrants-rights-reproductive-freedom/end-near-shackling-pregnant-women.

Liptak, Adam. "Supreme Court Lets Decision on Arizona Abortion Law Stand." December. 15, 2014. http://www.nytimes.com/2014/12/16/us/politics/justices-let-stand-a-ruling-blocking-an-arizona-abortion-law.html.

Liptak, Adam. "Supreme Court Rejects Contraceptives Mandate for Some Corporations." June 30, 2014. http://www.nytimes.com/2014/07/01/us/hobby-lobby-case-supreme-court-contraception.html .

Liptak, Adam and John Schwartz. "Court Rejects Zone to Buffer Abortion Clinic" June 26, 2014. http://www.nytimes.com/2014/06/27/us/supreme-court-abortion-clinic-protests.html.

"Lowell Mill Women Create First Union of Working Women." http://www.aflcio.org/Issues/Civil-and-Workplace-Rights/Working-Women/Working-Women-in-Union-History/Lowell-Mill-Women-Create-First-Union-of-Working-Women .

"Lucy Stone and the Women's Rights Movement." http://www.pbs.org/wgbh/americanexperience/blog/2015/02/24/lucy-stone/.

"Lucy Stone Quotes." http://womenshistory.about.com/od/quotes/fl/Lucy-Stone-Quotes.htm.

Lueptow, Kelsey. "Feminism Now: What the Third Wave is Really About." January 10, 2014. http://everydayfeminism.com/2014/01/feminism-now/ .

Lyles, Latifa. "It's Time for Equal Pay Now." April 13, 2015. https://blog.dol.gov/2015/04/13/its-time-for-equal-pay-now/ .

"Lynching as Racial Terrorism." New York Times Editorial, 2/11/15. http://www.nytimes.com/2015/02/11/opinion/lynching-as-racial-terrorism.html?ref = opinion.

Mansbridge, Jane. "How Did Feminism Get to Be?" American Prospect, December 19, 2001. http://prospect.org/article/how-did-feminism-get-be .

"Maria Stewart." http://www.pbs.org/wgbh/aia/part4/4p4439.html.

"Marxism vs Post-Modernism." February 19, 2013. http://www.workerspower.net/marxism-vs-post-modernism .

"Mary Church Terrell Quotes." http://www.azquotes.com/author/43693-Mary_Church_Terrell.

"Mary Harris Jones Quotes." http://www.brainyquote.com/quotes/quotes/m/maryharris232149.html.

"Mary Harris 'Mother Jones'." https://www.nwhm.org/education-resources/biography/biographies/mary-harris-mother-jones/

"Masked Intruder Attacks Last Abortion Clinic Standing in Mississippi." Mar 25, 2015. http://feminist.org/blog/index.php/2015/03/25/masked-intruder-attacks-last-remaining-mississippi-abortion-clinic/.

Matthews, Dylan. "Everything You Need to Know about the War on Poverty." January 8, 2014. http://www.washingtonpost.com/blogs/wonkblog/wp/2014/01/08/everything-you-need-to-know-about-the-war-on-poverty/ .

Mayeux, Sara. "*Redefining Rape*: Talking to Estelle Freedman About Street Harassment and Intersectionality in the Early 20th Century." October 2, 2013. http://thehairpin.com/2013/10/redefining-rape/.

McCoid, Catherine Hodge. "Eleanor Burke Leacock and Intersectionality: Materialism, Dialectics, and Transformation." *Race, Gender & Class*. Vol. 15, No. 1/2. 2008.

McDonough, Katie. "Tennessee just became the first state that will jail women for their pregnancy outcomes." April 30, 2014. http://www.salon.com/2014/04/30/tennessee_just_became_the_first_state_that_will_jail_women_for_their_pregnancy_outcomes/?utm_source = facebook&utm_medium = socialflow .

McKay, Nellie Y. "Acknowledging Differences: Can Women Find Unity Through Diversity?" In James and Busia: 267-282.

Miller, Claire Cain. "The Motherhood Penalty vs. the Fatherhood Bonus." Sept. 6, 2014. http://www.nytimes.com/2014/09/07/upshot/a-child-helps-your-career-if-youre-a-man.html?abt = 0002&abg = 1&_r = 0 .

Mirashem, Molly. "What Young Feminists Think of Hillary Clinton." May 16, 2015. http://www.nationaljournal.com/s/27066/what-young-feminists-think-hillary-clinton.

"More State Abortion Restrictions Were Enacted in 2011–2013 Than in the Entire Previous Decade." January 2, 2014. http://www.guttmacher.org/media/inthenews/2014/01/02/index.html .

"Mother Jones (1837–1930)." http://www.aflcio.org/Issues/Civil-and-Workplace-Rights/Working-Women/Working-Women-in-Union-History/Mother-Jones-1837-1930 .

National Intimate Partner and Sexual Violence Survey: 2010 Summary Report Executive Summary. http://www.cdc.gov/violenceprevention/pdf/nisvs_report2010-a.pdf

"National Women's Conference." https://en.wikipedia.org/wiki/National_Women%27s_Conference

"National Women's Trade Union League of America." http://ocp.hul.harvard.edu/ww/nwtul.html

Neuman, Scott. "North Carolina Set to Compensate Forced Sterilization Victims." http://www.npr.org/blogs/thetwo-way/2013/07/25/205547272/north-carolina-set-to-compensate-forced-sterilization-victims. July 25, 2013.

"New Congress, Same Old Attacks on Women's Rights." January 10, 2015. http://www.defendwomensrights.org/new_congress_same_old_attacks_on_women_s_rights .

"Norway Ranks as World's Best Place to Be a Mother." http://www.msn.com/en-za/news/other/norway-ranks-as-worlds-best-place-to-be-a-mother/ar-BBjccWB .

"NY Women's Equality Coalition." http://nywomensequality.org/10-point-plan/ .

Olsen, Tillie. "I Stand Here Ironing." In *Tell Me A Riddle, Requa I, and Other Works*. 2013: University of Nebraska: 5-14.

"One Billion Rising Honors 'Revolution' as New Report Highlights Threats to Black Girls in U.S." Feb. 12, 2015. http://www.

democracynow.org/2015/2/12/one_billion_rising_honors_
revolution_as .

Paltrow, Lynn. "How Indiana Is Making It Possible to Jail Women for
Having Abortions." March 29, 2015. http://www.politicalresearch.
org/2015/03/29/how-indiana-is-making-it-possible-to-jail-women-
for-having-abortions/#sthash.7Kdd3ITY.dpuf .

Paltrow, Lynn M. and Jeanne Flavin. "Pregnant, and No Civil
Rights." http://www.nytimes.com/2014/11/08/opinion/pregnant-
and-no-civil-rights.html .

Patterson, Elizabeth C. *Doctors Wanted: No Women Need Apply*
and *The Hidden Malpractice*." http://www.americanscientist.org/
bookshelf/pub/doctors-wanted-no-women-need-apply-and-the-
hidden-malpractice.

Pecinovsky, Tony. " Women's history: Elizabeth Gurley Flynn,
the Rebel Girl." March 19, 2010. http://peoplesworld.org/
women-s-history-elizabeth-gurley-flynn-the-rebel-girl/.

Pickert, Kate. "What's Wrong with the Violence Against Women
Act?" February 27, 2013. http://nation.time.com/2013/02/27/
whats-wrong-with-the-violence-against-women-act/.

Pollitt, Katha. "The Anti-Abortion Vanguard."
https://www.jacobinmag.com/2015/07/
pro-choice-abortion-birth-control-pollitt/.

Pollitt, Katha. "Even if You Haven't Had an Abortion, You Owe
Planned Parenthood." August 27, 2015. http://www.thenation.
com/article/even-if-you-havent-had-an-abortion-you-owe-
planned-parenthood/ .

Pollitt, Katha. "Who Has Abortions?" March 13, 2015. http://www.
thenation.com/article/who-has-abortions/.

Popovich, Nadja."The US is still the only developed country that
doesn't guarantee paid maternity leave." December 3, 2014.
http://www.theguardian.com/us-news/2014/dec/03/-sp-america-
only-developed-country-paid-maternity-leave?CMP = edit_2221 .

"The Postwar Period Through the 1950s" http://ic.galegroup.com/
ic/uhic/ReferenceDetailsPage/DocumentToolsPortletWindow?dis-
playGroupName = Reference&u = oldt1017&u = oldt1017&jsid = -
347c2091a080fbd71aebaad95d411063&p = UHIC % 3AWHIC&ac-
tion = 2&catId = &documentId = GALE % 7CBT2313026907&zid =
dbaf8355e54c396b9af1f64d3a9cea8c.

"Prison Rape Elimination Act of 2003." https://www.aclu.org/
    prison-rape-elimination-act-2003-prea?redirect = prisoners-rights-
    womens-rights/prison-rape-elimination-act-2003-prea .

"Proof of the GOP War on Women." http://www.politicususa.com/
    proof-war-women-2.

Quinn, Audrey. "In Labor, in Chains: The Outrageous Shackling
    of Pregnant Inmates" July 26, 2014. http://www.nytimes.
    com/2014/07/27/opinion/sunday/the-outrageous-shackling-of-
    pregnant-inmates.html.

Rankin, Lauren. "Not Everyone Who Has an Abortion Is a Woman
    - How to Frame the Abortion Rights Issue" July 31, 2013. http://
    www.truth-out.org/op-ed/item/17888-not-everyone-who-has-an-
    abortion-is-a-woman-how-to-frame-the-abortion-rights-issue

Ransby, Barbara. "Ella Taught Me: Shattering the Myth of the
    Leaderless Movement." June 12, 2015.

http://www.colorlines.com/articles/
    ella-taught-me-shattering-myth-leaderless-movement

Ravitz, Jessica. "The new women warriors: Reviving the fight for
    equal rights." April 16, 2015. http://www.cnn.com/2015/04/02/
    us/new-womens-equal-rights-movement/

"Redefining Rape and Street Harassment: 1880-1920s." 10/3/13.
    http://www.stopstreetharassment.org/2013/10/redefiningrape2/

Rennison, Callie Marie. "Who Suffers Most From Rape and Sexual
    Assault in America?" http://www.nytimes.com/2014/12/22/
    opinion/who-suffers-most-from-rape-and-sexual-assault-in-
    america.html?hpw&rref = opinion&action = click&pgtype = H
    omepage&module = well-region&region = bottom-well&WT.
    nav = bottom-well&_r = 1

Reynolds, Arlene Foy. "Sexual Harassment and the Law" In Kelly et
    al, 203-204

Robins, Julia. "Aesthetic Activism." *Ms Magazine,* Summer 2015, 12.

"Roe at 40." January 8, 2013. http://www.guttmacher.org/media/
    inthenews/2013/01/08/index.html

Roeder, Oliver. "Just Facts: Actually, Orange Really Is the New
    Black." June 16, 2014. http://www.brennancenter.org/blog/
    actually-orange-really-new-black

Rojas, Rick. " Arizona Orders Doctors to Say Abortions With Drugs
    May Be Reversible" March 31, 2015. http://www.nytimes.

com/2015/04/01/us/politics/arizona-doctors-must-say-that-abortions-with-drugs-may-be-reversed.html?hp&action = click&pg type = Homepage&module = second-column-region&region = top-news&WT.nav = top-news&_r = 1

Ronan, Alex. "It's Time to Talk About the Female Victims of Police Brutality." April 29, 2015. http://nymag.com/thecut/2015/04/black-women-and-girls-face-police-brutality-too.html#

"Rose Schneiderman." https://en.wikipedia.org/wiki/Rose_Schneiderman

Ross, Loretta J. "African-American Women and Abortion: 1800-1970." In James et al, 141-159.

Ross, Loretta. "Understanding Reproductive Justice." March 2011. http://www.trustblackwomen.org/our-work/what-is-reproductive-justice/9-what-is-reproductive-justice

Rottenberg, Catherine. "Hijacking Feminism." http://www.aljazeera.com/indepth/opinion/2013/03/201332510121757700.html

Rubin, Gayle. "The Traffic in Women: Notes on the 'Political Economy' of Sex." In Nicholson, Linda, Ed. *The Second Wave: A Reader in Feminist Theory*, New York and London: Routledge, 1997: 26-62.

"The Russian Revolution and the Emancipation of Women." http://www.icl-fi.org/english/esp/59/emancipation.html

Saint Louis, Catherine. "Stubborn Pay Gap Is Found in Nursing" March 24, 2015. http://well.blogs.nytimes.com/2015/03/24/stubborn-pay-gap-is-found-in-nursing/ .

Sanders, Katie. " Steinem: More women killed by partners since 9/11 than deaths from attacks, ensuing wars." October 7, 2014. http://www.politifact.com/punditfact/statements/2014/oct/07/gloria-steinem/steinem-more-women-killed-partners-911-deaths-atta/.

Santos, Fernanda. "Albuquerque Voters Defeat Anti-Abortion Measure." Nov. 20, 2013. http://www.nytimes.com/2013/11/20/us/albuquerque-voters-defeat-anti-abortion-referendum.html.

Sarachild, Kathie. "Consciousness Raising: A Radical Weapon." 1973. In Kelly et al, Ed. *Women: Images and Realities*, 566-568.

"Say Her Name: Families Seek Justice in Overlooked Police Killings of African-American Women." http://www.democracynow.org/2015/5/20/say_her_name_families_seek_justice .

Scarbrough, Kathy. "Women's Liberation is Based on Sex Not Gender." April 6, 2014. http://meetinggroundonline.org/wp-content/uploads/2014/04/KSc-WL-Based-on-Sex-not-Gender.pdf .

Schofield, Ann. "Rebel Girls and Union Maids: the woman question in the journals of the AFL and IWW, 1905-1920." 1983. http://libcom.org/history/rebel-girls-union-maids-woman-question-journals-afl-iww-1905-1920 .

Schenwar, Maya. "Women's Prisons as Sites of Resistance: An Interview with Victoria Law." June 28, 2015. http://www.truth-out.org/progressivepicks/item/31461-women-s-prisons-as-sites-of-resistance-an-interview-with-victoria-law .

"Seattle Strike Enters Fifth Day as Teachers Protest Testing Policies, Racial Inequity & Low Wages." http://www.democracynow.org/2015/9/15/seattle_strike_enters_fifth_day_as .

"Secretary General, Hailing Cuba's Role" http://www.un.org/press/en/2014/sgsm15617.doc.htm.

"Seneca Falls Convention." http://www.historynet.com/seneca-falls-convention .

"Sex and HIV Education." March 1, 2015. http://www.guttmacher.org/statecenter/spibs/spib_SE.pdf.

Sheppard, Barry. "United States: Attacks on abortion rights accelerate." June 1, 2015. https://www.greenleft.org.au/node/59160 .

"Sisters in the Brotherhoods." http://www.talkinghistory.org/sisters/index.html

"Sisters of '77." http://www.pbs.org/independentlens/sistersof77/conference.html .

SNCC Legacy Project. http://www.sncclegacyproject.org/legacy.html

"Sojourner Truth." http://en.wikipedia.org/wiki/Sojourner_Truth

"Southern Strategy." http://en.wikipedia.org/wiki/Women's_suffrage_in_the_United_States#Southern_strategy

Stan, Adele. "How the Koch Brothers Helped Bring About the Law That Shut Texas Abortion Clinics." October 3, 2014. http://prospect.org/article/how-koch-brothers-helped-bring-about-law-shut-texas-abortion-clinics.

"State Attacks on Women's Health." http://www.plannedparenthoodaction.org/issues/state-attacks-womens-health/ .

"State Minimum Wages/2015 Minimum Wage by State." 6/1/15. http://www.ncsl.org/research/labor-and-employment/state-minimum-wage-chart.aspx

"State Policies in Brief: An Overview of Abortion Laws as of December 1 2014". http://www.guttmacher.org/statecenter/spibs/spib_OAL.pdf .

"State Policies in Brief: An Overview of Abortion Laws" June 1, 2015. http://www.guttmacher.org/statecenter/spibs/spib_OAL.pdf .

"State Policies in Brief, as of April 1, 2015: Medication Abortion." http://www.guttmacher.org/statecenter/spibs/spib_MA.pdf

"Status of Women in the States." http://statusofwomendata.org/women-of-color/spotlight-on-women-of-color-employment-and-earnings-data/

"Sterilization Abuse: A Task for the Women's Movement by the Chicago Committee to End Sterilization Abuse (CESA)". January 1977. https://www.uic.edu/orgs/cwluherstory/CWLUArchive/cesa.html

"Stop Street Harassment." http://www.stopstreetharassment.org/2013/10/redefiningrape2/.

"Susan B. Anthony Quotes." http://www.brainyquote.com/quotes/authors/s/susan_b_anthony.htm

"Susan B. Anthony Quotes" http://womenshistory.about.com/cs/quotes/a/qu_s_b_anthony.htm

Thompson, Kirsten M.J. "A Brief History of Birth Control in the U.S." http://www.ourbodiesourselves.org/health-info/a-brief-history-of-birth-control/#at_pco = smlwn-1.0&at_si = 547c8645317288d6&at_ab = per-3&at_pos = 0&at_tot = 1 December 14, 2013.

Toney, Mark. "Revisiting the National Welfare Rights Organization." November 29, 2000. http://www.colorlines.com/articles/revisiting-national-welfare-rights-organization

"Timeline of Feminism in the United States." https://en.wikipedia.org/wiki/Timeline_of_feminism_in_the_United_States

"Trends in the States: First Quarter 2015."http://www.guttmacher.org/media/inthenews/2015/04/02/ .

"Triangle Shirtwaist Fire." http://www.aflcio.org/Issues/Civil-and-Workplace-Rights/Working-Women/Working-Women-in-Union-History/Triangle-Shirtwaist-Fire .

Tuerkheimer, Deborah. "How Not to Protect Pregnant Women."
April 13, 2015. http://www.nytimes.com/2015/04/13/
opinion/the-error-of-fetal-homicide-laws.html?hp&actio
n = click&pgtype = Homepage&module = c-column-top-
span-region&region = c-column-top-span-region&WT.
nav = c-column-top-span-region&_r = 0

Turkewitz, Julie and Jack Healy. "3 Are Dead in Colorado Springs
Shootout at Planned Parenthood Center." Nov. 27, 2015. http://
www.nytimes.com/2015/11/28/us/colorado-planned-parenthood-
shooting.html?_r = 2 .

"Underpaid and Overloaded." 2014. National Women's Law Center.
http://www.nwlc.org/sites/default/files/pdfs/executivesummary_
nwlc_lowwagereport2014.pdf

"U.S. Abortion Rates & Related Information." March
22, 2014. http://www.ourbodiesourselves.org/
health-info/u-s-abortion-rates/

Usova, Georgeanne M. " Native American Women Still Getting
Short Shrift on Emergency Contraception." 3/16/15. https://
www.aclu.org/blog/reproductive-freedom/native-american-
women-still-getting-short-shrift-emergency-contraception.

Valenti, Jessica. "Gamergate is loud, dangerous and a last grasp
at cultural dominance by angry white men." October 21, 2014.
http://www.theguardian.com/commentisfree/2014/oct/21/
gamergate-angry-men-harassing-women

Valenti, Jessica. "If we truly valued motherhood, we would
actually do something to help pregnant women." December
3, 2014. http://www.theguardian.com/commentisfree/2014/
dec/03/-sp-motherhood-pregnant-women-court-case

Van Deven, Mandy. "Demanding the Right to Reproduce: Voluntary
and Forced Sterilization in America." http://rhrealitycheck.org/
article/2009/08/05/demanding-right-reproduce-voluntary-and-
forced-sterilization-america/. August 5, 2009.

Vasquez, Tina. "It's Time to End the Long History
of Feminism Failing Transgender Women."
February 17, 2014. https://bitchmedia.org/post/
the-long-history-of-transgender-exclusion-from-feminism

Villacorta, Natalie. "House votes to block federal funding of
abortion." 1/22/15. http://www.politico.com/story/2015/01/
house-abortion-ban-federal-funding-114497.html

Voices of Feminism Oral History Project. http://www.smith.edu/
   libraries/libs/ssc/vof/vof-intro.html

Volscho, Thomas. "Sterilization and Women of Color." http://www.
   racismreview.com/blog/2007/09/22/sterilization-and-women-of-
   color/ September 22, 2007.

Wade, Lisa. "Sterilization of Women of Color: Does 'Unforced' Mean
   'Freely Chosen'?" http://msmagazine.com/blog/2011/07/21/
   sterilization-of-women-of-color-does-unforced-mean-freely-
   chosen/ July 21, 2011.

"Wage Gap Is Stagnant for Nearly a Decade." http://www.nwlc.org/
   resource/wage-gap-stagnant-nearly-decade

"The Wage Gap, State by State." National Women's Law Center.
   http://www.nwlc.org/wage-gap-state-state

Walker, Rebecca. "Becoming the Third Wave."
   http://www.msmagazine.com/spring2002/
   BecomingThirdWaveRebeccaWalker.pdf .

Wang, Wendy, Kim Parker and Paul Taylor. "Breadwinner Moms."
   May 29, 2013. http://www.pewsocialtrends.org/2013/05/29/
   breadwinner-moms/ .

"War's Overlooked Victims." January 13, 2011. http://www.
   economist.com/node/17900482 .

"We Need to Talk about Gender on Earth Day."
   http://feminist.org/blog/index.php/2015/04/22/
   we-need-to-talk-about-gender-on-earth-day/.

"We Raise Our Voices." http://www.lib.neu.edu/archives/voices/w-
   intro.htm

"WHO Multi-country Study on Women's Health and Domestic
   Violence against Women." http://www.who.int/gender/violence/
   who_multicountry_study/en/

"Why We Can't Wait: Women of Color Urge Inclusion in 'My
   Brother's Keeper.'" June 17, 2014. http://www.aapf.org/
   recent/2014/06/woc-letter-mbk .

Wilcox, Joyce. "The Face of Women's Health: Helen Rodriguez-Trias."
   http://www.ncbi.nlm.nih.gov/pmc/articles/PMC1447119/ .

Williams, Timothy. "History of Abuse Seen in Many Girls in Juvenile
   System." July 9, 2015. http://www.nytimes.com/2015/07/09/
   us/girls-in-juvenile-facilities-often-abused-report-says.html?h

p&action = click&pgtype = Homepage&module = first-column-region&region = top-news&WT.nav = top-news .

Williamson, Alicia. "The Working-Class Origins and Legacy of International Women's Day." http://www.ueunion.org/ue-news/2014/the-working-class-origins-and-legacy-of-international-women's-day.

Wilson, Ara. "1970s Lesbian Feminism." http://www.feministezine.com/feminist/lesbian/1970s-Lesbian-Feminism.html.

"Women and the Peace Movement." https://www.nwhm.org/online-exhibits/progressiveera/peace.html.

"Women and the Russian Revolution. " http://www.bolshevik.org/1917/no7/no07wmru.html.

"Women and Unions." http://womenshistory.about.com/od/worklaborunions/a/late_19th_cent.htm.

"Women in the Chinese Revolution, 1921-1950." http://www.bannedthought.net/India/PeoplesMarch/PM1999-2006/publications/women/china-1.htm .

"Women in the United States House of Representatives." https://en.wikipedia.org/wiki/Women_in_the_United_States_House_of_Representatives

"Women of Color and the Minimum Wage." http://civilrightsdocs.info/pdf/minimumwage/womenofcolor-minimum-wage.pdf.

Women's club movement: https://www.google.com/search?client = safari&rls = en&q = women's + club + movement&ie = UTF-8&oe = UTF-8&gws_rd = ssl

"Women's Employment During the Recovery." 2011. http://www.dol.gov/_sec/media/reports/femalelaborforce/

"Women's Rights Movement in the U.S." http://www.infoplease.com/spot/womenstimeline1.html

"Women's Strike for Equality." http://en.wikipedia.org/wiki/Women's_Strike_for_Equality

"Women's Suffrage in the United States." https://en.wikipedia.org/wiki/Women%27s_suffrage_in_the_United_States

"Working Women in Union History." http://www.aflcio.org/Issues/Civil-and-Workplace-Rights/Working-Women/Working-Women-in-Union-History .

"World Conferences on Women." http://www.unwomen. org/en/how-we-work/intergovernmental-support/ world-conferences-on-women.

"The World Factbook" https://www.cia.gov/library/publications/ the-world-factbook/rankorder/2091rank.html .

"World's Abortion Laws Map 2013 Update." http://www. reproductiverights.org/sites/crr.civicactions.net/files/documents/ AbortionMap_Factsheet_2013.pdf.

Wormser, Richard. "The Rise and Fall of Jim Crow." http://www. pbs.org/wnet/jimcrow/stories_people_wells.html .

"Writings of the Third Wave." http://www.library.spscc.ctc.edu/ electronicreserve/soc101/russell/WritingsoftheThirdWaveGilley. pdf

Zabel, Diane, Ed. "Writings of the Third Wave: Young Feminists in Conversation." Spring 2005. http://www.library.spscc.ctc.edu/ electronicreserve/soc101/russell/WritingsoftheThirdWaveGilley. pdf .

Zahniser, J.D. "Why Doesn't Everybody Know Who Alice Paul Was and What She Did?" http://historynewsnetwork.org/ article/156345

Ziegeweid, Joy. "Justice for Russian Women? Russia Begins to Face Its Domestic Violence Problem." November 2, 2014. http:// hrbrief.org/2014/11/justice-for-russian-women-russia-begins-to- face-its-domestic-violence-problem/#_ftn38

Zirin, Dave. "Jock Culture and Rape Culture" http://www.thenation. com/blog/173387/verdict-steubenville-shows-bond-between-jock- culture-and-rape-culture.

WEBSITES

http://en.wikipedia.org/wiki/National_Woman_Suffrage_ Association#cite_ref-suffrage_11-0 (NWSA)

http://en.wikipedia.org/wiki/ Nineteenth_Amendment_to_the_United_States_Constitution

http://now.org/about/history/highlights/

http://now.org/about/history/history-of-marches-and-mass-actions/

http://thefeministwire.com

http://worldabortionlaws.com/about.html#_ednref8

http://www.aapf.org/sayhernamereport

http://www.advocatesforpregr

http://www.damayanmigrar

http://www.dol.gov/wb/info_c
    Bureau)

http://www.eeoc.gov/eeoc/history,
    eeoc.gov/eeoc/index.cfm (EEOC)

http://www.feminist.com/resources/an

http://www.lorettaross.com/Biography.ht

http://www.ncadv.org (National Coalition A
    Violence)

http://www.pslweb.org (Party for Socialism and

http://www.raisetheminimumwage.com/pages/
    minimum-wage-laws-and-proposals-for-major-u.s.

http://www.uic.edu/orgs/cwluherstory/CWLUArchive/

http://www.un.org/womenwatch/daw/cedaw/cedaw.htm

http://www.unicef.org/infobycountry/cuba_statistics.html

http://www1.cuny.edu/portal_ur/content/womens_leadership/
    feminism.html

https://www.nwhm.org/online-exhibits/progressiveera/
    workingwomen.html (Women's National History Museum):

https://www.uic.edu/orgs/cwluherstory/index.html

Index

international, 325
union, 91, 151, 153, 175
woman's, 71
Mott, Lucretia, 53, 55, 58, 70,
  282
Murphy, Paige, 326
Muslims, 177, 245–47, 249–51,
  256

N

Nailevu, Maria, 330
National American Woman
  Suffrage Association. *See*
  NAWSA
National Association of Colored
  Women, 53, 271, 287
National Association of Colored
  Women's Clubs, 71, 76, 289
National Black Feminist
  Organization (NBFO),
  134–35, 275
National Conference for New
  Politics, 123–24
National Domestic Workers
  Alliance. *See* NDWA
National Organization for
  Women, xiii, xvi, 117, 274,
  277
National Welfare Rights
  Organization. *See* NWRO
National Woman's Party (NWP),
  78–79, 97-98, 272
National Women's Conference,
  276, 323–24
National Women's Liberation
  (NWL), 222
National Women's Suffrage
  Association. *See* NWSA

NAWSA (National American
  Woman Suffrage
  Association), 60–61, 75–76,
  270–72, 287–88
NBFO (National Black Feminist
  Organization), 134–35, 275
NDWA (National Domestic
  Workers Alliance), 7, 226,
  229, 232
New York City, vii, 12, 74, 85,
  87, 144, 146, 197, 271–72,
  274, 308
New York State, 56, 191, 220,
  229, 232, 274, 313
NWL (National Women's
  Liberation), 222
NWP (National Woman's Party),
  78–79
NWRO (National Welfare Rights
  Organization), 157–58,
  307–8
NWSA (National Women's
  Suffrage Association), 57–60
Nyambura, Ruth, 331

O

O'Neill, Terry, 217
oppression of women, 25,
  27–30, 32, 34, 48, 108,
  126–29, 261

P

Paltrow, Lynn, 191
Pankhurst, Emmeline, 73, 74
Parsons, Lucy, 86
Parton, Dolly, 153
Party for Socialism and
  Liberation. *See* PSL

Thomas, Clarence, 168, 204-5,
    277, 303
Tiller, George, 313
Tillmon, Johnnie, 157
Title VII, 8, 118, 152, 156
Tometi, Opal, 226
Tomlin, Lily, 153
trans movements, 235, 240–41
TRAP laws, 183–84, 316
Tubman, Harriet, 54
TWWA (Third World Women's
    Alliance), 134

U
UAW (United Auto Workers),
    104, 119, 140, 159
unions, 12, 14, 62–65, 83–84,
    113, 116, 137, 140, 151, 153,
    218, 221, 229, 231–32, 293
United Auto Workers. *See* UAW

V
Violence against Women Act
    (VAWA), 193, 278

W
wages, 4, 6–7, 55–56, 62, 67,
    83–84, 86, 88–89, 91, 165,
    175, 229, 231–32, 245, 247
Walker, Rebecca, 205, 211-12, 236
war, 78–79, 89, 92, 95, 99–106,
    108, 112, 115, 190, 193–94,
    197, 203, 257, 262, 326–27
wealth, xii, 3, 5, 26, 175, 243,
    248, 285, 288, 330
Weigand, Kate, 108
welfare, 17–18, 134, 157, 166,
    308, 310

Wells, Ida B., 71, 76–77, 287
white women, xx, 4, 6–7, 16,
    51, 53–54, 56, 67–68, 70–71,
    76–77, 95–96, 133–34, 176,
    196, 246–47
Wiley, George, 307
Willard, Frances, 70
Williams, Patricia, 250
WILPF (Women's International
    League for Peace and
    Freedom), 93, 300
Wilson, Dagmar, 112
Wilson, Woodrow, 75, 78–79,
    81, 92
Wollstonecraft, Mary, 52-53, 131
woman president, xvi, 243,
    251–52, 263
woman suffrage, 57–59, 78, 92,
    96, 287
women
    advancement of, 44–45,
        319–20
    incarcerated, 196–97, 227
    low-income, 82, 147, 212,
        311–12
    union, 140, 152
    war on, xix, 223, 232, 238
Women Environmental Program,
    329–30
women leaders, 229, 273
women of color, xx, 29, 82, 94,
    125, 134, 145, 152, 175,
    189, 191, 197–98, 207,
    229–30, 247
women prisoners, 196, 227
Women's Army Corps, 103–4
Women's Equality Day, 159, 203

Made in the USA
San Bernardino, CA
17 January 2018